Lynn Picknett and Clive Prince are writers, researchers and lecturers on the paranormal, the occult and historical and religious mysteries. Since 1989 they have worked together on the research which produced *Turin Shroud: In Whose Image?*, *The Templar Revelation: Secret Guardians of the True Identity of Christ* and this latest book. They both live in London.

THE
STARGATE
CONSPIRACY

Revealing the truth behind extraterrestrial
contact, military intelligence and the
mysteries of ancient Egypt

Lynn Picknett
and
Clive Prince

A *Time Warner* Paperback

First published in Great Britain in 1999
by Little, Brown and Company
This edition published in 2000 by Warner Books
Reprinted 2001
Reprinted by Time Warner Paperbacks in 2003

A CIP catalogue record for this book is
available from the British Library

ISBN 0 7515 2996 6

Typeset in Bodoni by M Rules
Printed and bound in Great Britain by
Clays Ltd, St Ives plc

Time Warner Paperbacks
An imprint of
Time Warner Books UK
Brettenham House
Lancaster Place
London WC2E 7EN

www.TimeWarnerBooks.co.uk

To Philip Coppens

Contents

Acknowledgements

This book would never have been possible without the contributions – in one form or another – of a great many people. We are indebted to all of them for sharing their expertise and research with us, and in some cases simply for taking the time to talk our ideas through. However, we are entirely responsible for the end result: we must stress that the conclusions of this book are not necessarily shared by the people named here.

We are especially grateful to Philip Coppens, Editor of *Frontier* magazine, for the extraordinary degree of support he has given us. Not only did he undertake research on our behalf, but he also put us in touch with some of the – often very elusive – key players in this story, and shared with us his own incisive and brilliant connections, which we would otherwise have missed.

Keith Prince, as usual, helped us enormously with his research, insights and unique view of life.

Craig Oakley was his customary supportive and intuitive self: thanks to him for many in-depth discussions and for help with the diagrams.

Simon Cox was generous in sharing his expertise on Egypt, especially in supplying us with invaluable research material on this and other subjects. He was also a delightful travelling companion who kept us out of trouble in Cairo.

We are, as always, grateful to our agent, Lavinia Trevor, for all her hard work on this project and for unflaggingly pursuing our best interests.

Thanks to Alan Samson at Little, Brown, and his colleagues Caroline North, Andrew Wille and Linda Silverman for their enthusiastic support of, and belief in, this book.

We are indebted to the following people for helping us with the material about Egypt in Chapters 1 and 2: Chris Ogilvie-Herald, whose knowledge of current events in Egypt and whose *Egyptnews* Internet list helped guide us through this often bewildering subject; Jacqueline Pegg of Quest Research, for providing us with invaluable material; Niklas Rasche, for many long discussions about the complex issues in this book; Andrew Collins, especially for the information about Edgar Cayce and Bimini; Rudolf Gantenbrink for his revelations; Ralph Ellis; David Elkington; Ian Lawton; Thomas Danley; Yuri Stoyanov and David Ritchie.

For the material on the Mars enigma in Chapter 3, we are grateful to Ananda Sirisena, Mark J. Carlotto and Stanley V. McDaniel for answering our queries. And thanks also to Nick Pope for supplying us with material on Mars and the extraterrestrial question in general, besides keeping an eye open for unusual titbits of useful information.

For helping to settle questions about astronomy, we are grateful to: Dr Martin Barstow, reader in Astrophysics at Leicester University; Dr Michael Perryman, of the European Space Agency; Dr Malcolm J. Coe of Southampton University. Thanks also to the Library of the Royal Astronomical Society.

For assistance with our research into the Council of Nine in Chapters 4 and 5 we would like to thank Dick Farley, for generously sharing his thoughts and experiences with us; Terry L. Milner, for allowing us to use his research into the strange career of Andrija Puharich; Ira Einhorn, for his insights into the key events of the 1970s; and Jack Sarfatti, for his very useful information. Also Palden Jenkins, David S. Percy and Kim Farmer of the Academy For Future Sciences for taking the time to answer our queries.

We would like to thank Rob Irving for his information about the Barbary Castle crop circle.

Georgina Bruni has given us much useful information in discussions stretching long into the night, and is unfailingly a delightful hostess.

For the material on the esoteric connections we are indebted to: Theo Paijmans, for the astonishing breadth of his knowledge and for being such charming company; Steve Wilson and Caroline Wise, for their knowledge, insight, wisdom and support – not to mention their friendship and much revelry; Mark Bennett, for varied information, particularly in directing us to Christina Stoddard's work; Dawn Zeffert; Gareth Medway.

We would like to thank Uri Geller for sparing the time to tell us about his work with SRI. Thanks too to Shipi Shtrang.

Dr Vanessa Hill helped us with some of the mathematical concepts, for which we are very grateful.

Jane Lyle, as always, was a fountain of knowledge – especially about astrology – and a joy to be with. Thanks, Jane.

For assistance with the breakthrough shamanic material in the Epilogue, we are indebted to: Jeremy Narby, for discussing his ground-breaking hypothesis with us; Michael Carmichael, for the discussion about shamanism and the acquisition of knowledge; Dr Benny Shanon of Jerusalem University.

We would also like to thank the following people for their help in various ways, including support and encouragement, and just being there for us: Vida Adamoli; Marcus Allen; David Bell; Robert and Lindsey Brydon; Jim Cochrane; Nic Davis; Susan Davies; Christy Fearn; Geoff Gilbertson; Moira Hardcastle; Herman Hegge; Robin Crookshank Hilton; Mick and Loraine Jones; Michèle Kaczynski; Gopi Krishnadas; Sarah Litvinoff; Karine Esparseil López and Samuel López; Kevin McClure; Loren McLaughlin; John and Joy Millar; Jack Miller; Hugh Montgomery; Francesca Norton; Catherine Ormston; Steve Pear;

Trevor Poots; Lily and David Prince; Stephen Prior; Magdy Radwan; Mary Saxe-Falstein; Paul Sieveking and Bob Rickard of *Fortean Times*; Gemma Smith; Nikki Stockley; Sheila and Eric Taylor; Greg Taylor; Richard Taylor; Salah El Din Mohamed Tawfik.

Finally, thanks to the staff of the British Library, the Science Reference and Information Service and the Newspaper Library.

Introduction

Strange though it may seem, this is not the book we originally set out to write. In a sense, we are very surprised – and not a little shaken – to have found ourselves on the rock-strewn path that led, ultimately, to *The Stargate Conspiracy*.

We had intended to write a follow-up to our 1997 book *The Templar Revelation*, which argued that Christianity was essentially an offshoot of the ancient Egyptian religion of Isis and Osiris – meaning that our culture is not *Judaeo*-Christian at all, but *Egypto*-Christian. The implications were astonishingly far-reaching, but we also disclosed the most carefully hidden of all the secrets of the heretical Knights Templar in the most controversial revelation of the book – namely, that they believed that John the Baptist was the true Messiah, and that Jesus was, to say the very least, his usurper.

Wanting to learn more about our civilisation's Egyptian roots, we researched further into the ancient religion, and found ourselves examining the Pyramid Texts and the origin of the Hermetic writings. The more we progressed, the more we realised the ancient Egyptians possessed astonishing knowledge, far beyond that generally accepted by modern academics. We discovered that those far-off people had an understanding of cosmology unequalled until our own century, and even now

perhaps they still have something to teach us. But in the end even
the largely unknown and unacknowledged genius of the ancient
Egyptians was not to be the subject of this book.

As non-academics researching ancient Egypt we could not
remain unaware of the upsurge of interest in the 'alternative
Egypt' of Andrew Collins, Colin Wilson and others, whose books
challenge the often rather complacent 'certainties' of mainstream
Egyptology. Above all three authors have become associated in
the public mind with radical new ideas about ancient cultures,
particularly Egypt: Robert Temple, author of the seminal *The
Sirius Mystery* (1976); Robert Bauval, co-author with Adrian
Gilbert of *The Orion Mystery* (1994); and Graham Hancock,
whose runaway success was established with *The Sign and the
Seal* (1992). Since then Hancock has gone on to entrance huge
audiences worldwide with *Fingerprints of the Gods* (1995) and,
with his wife Santha Faiia, *Heaven's Mirror* (1998), and also col-
laborating with Robert Bauval to produce *Keeper of Genesis*
(1996) and (together with John Grigsby) *The Mars Mystery* (1998).
These books encompass a vast range of fascinating and radical
new ideas, many of which have now become so entrenched among
their readers as to be accepted as hard fact. And, like most of
their readers, we, too, began as enthralled admirers.

After many months of researching and writing this book, we
still admired those authors' energy and commitment, but as we
stood back from their work, we have perceived a new and considerably larger pattern taking shape. Whether or not those
authors are aware of it, their work forms an intrinsic part of what
amounts to an orchestrated campaign.

And the matter does not end there. The bitter controversy surrounding the idea of a long-dead civilisation on Mars has also
been absorbed into this campaign and – like the mysteries of
Egypt – has been pressed into service to present a carefully
stage-managed message. Essentially, it proposes that the ancient
gods were extraterrestrials – *and they're back*. But the subtext is
very clever: only certain, chosen people hear their words, and
only certain, chosen people will be part of the revelations to

come. We can hazard a guess at the identity of some of the
chosen, but the others may be rather surprising.

This is the well-worn tactic of 'divide and rule', and has worrying, quasireligious overtones. And it is no obscure and tiny
cult, but a massive phenomenon that, in one shape or form, has
infiltrated much of the West's cultural and spiritual life. But who
lies behind it? And what on earth would anyone hope to gain by
it?

We certainly considered the idea that we may have developed
into sad cases of paranoia – the thought was to recur several
times as we plunged deeper into this investigation – but the evidence remains, staring us all in the face, and there is no doubt in
our minds that a huge conspiracy is trying to make us think in
certain ways. And for such a global plot to work, it requires teams
of fellow conspirators, whose participation may be unwitting or
otherwise. These groups, we were to find, not only included,
rather predictably perhaps, intelligence agencies such as the
CIA and MI5, but also less obvious candidates, from New Age
gurus to cutting-edge physicists, top-level scientists and multimillionaires.

Cynically exploiting our *fin de siècle* hunger for signs and wonders, and our ongoing love affair with the mysteries of ancient
Egypt, the conspirators are in the process of creating a massive,
insidious belief system that feeds on millennium fever, though
perhaps not blossoming properly until the first years of the
twenty-first century.

The fact that modern man's craving for contact with the numi-
nous and the ineffable is being cynically exploited on a vast scale
does not mean that there are never genuine paranormal phenomena or mystical experiences. Nor do we suggest that there are no
mysteries about man's ancient past or his place in the universe.
While we are critical of certain beliefs and claims to have solved
some of those mysteries, it is because we find fault with them, not
because we have a 'skeptical' bias. What disturbs us greatly is the
use to which many otherwise innocent or uplifting beliefs and
concepts are being put.

Even the lives of those with no interest in such subjects will inevitably be touched by this campaign to have us believe and be persuaded to think in a certain way. We came to realise, with heavy hearts, that part of this plot is to prepare us to accept certain ideas that we would normally find unacceptable, perhaps even repugnant. Make no mistake, this amounts to cultural and spiritual brainwashing on a lavish scale.

This story is so challenging that we can only ask for a willing suspension of disbelief, and for our readers to follow our detective work step by step, abandoning preconceptions and personal biases along the way. At the end, perhaps the thought might be allowed: what *if* this book is right? What *if* there really is a 'stargate conspiracy' eating away at the heart of democracy, human autonomy and decency itself? What *if* we are being prepared for the acceptance of something that we would normally find, to say the least, disturbing?

This book is not an attempt to rally the masses or create some kind of political backlash against the conspiracy. Perhaps, in any case, those with the vested interests would ensure that such an attempt would be doomed to ignominious – and immediate – failure. Yet we believe that successful opposition *is* possible, beginning with the realisation that, perhaps like the stargate itself, true resistance is in the mind.

Lynn Picknett
Clive Prince
London, June 1999

Prologue:

The Nine Gods

In the beginning were the Nine gods of ancient Egypt, the Great Ennead, in whom all beauty, magic and power were personified. But although many, they were only ever truly One – each an aspect of the great creator god, Atum. The Pyramid Texts, hieroglyphic inscriptions found on the inside walls of seven pyramids of the Fifth and Sixth Dynasties, implore them both as Nine and as One:

> O you, Great Ennead which is at On [Heliopolis] (namely) Atum, Shu, Tefnut, Geb, Nut, Osiris, Isis, Set, and Nepthys; O you children of Atum extend his goodwill to his child . . .[1]

The mysteries of the Great Ennead were celebrated by generations of initiate priests at Heliopolis. Their worship was a central part of the lives of thousands of ordinary men and women, to whom their discrete identities made them as accessible as the saints are to modern Catholics, while their mysterious Oneness kept in place the divine veil of ineffability.

The Nine – in one form or another – reigned for many centuries, until the Egyptian world changed forever with the influx of conquering races including the Greeks and, later, the Romans. The change seemed complete with the coming of the new religion of the sacrificial man-god, Yeshua (Jesus). But even then it was believed that the Nine merely withdrew to a heavenly realm – or, as many would have it today, to another dimension. The Ennead had departed, perhaps one day to return in glory.

However, the Nine are no longer a mere curiosity of some long past religion, nor are the works of their priests as ephemeral as sand blowing across the face of time. Their sacred city of Heliopolis hid many jealously guarded secrets, incredible knowledge that is only now being rediscovered. From the wisdom of antiquity, these high initiates built the pyramids, feats of construction that are still unparalleled and whose mysteries continue to challenge and enthral. The Nine taught their priests well – and their strange and secret knowledge is coming back to haunt us.

Buried beneath a suburb of Cairo – the most populous city in Africa, with 16 million inhabitants and their mad cacophony of traffic – the wonders of ancient Heliopolis are now marked only by a single obelisk. Once it was one of the unofficial wonders of the ancient world, glorying in its name – derived from the Greek for 'city of the sun god' because it was the centre of worship of Ra, whose daily journey blazed across the heavens. Its Egyptian name of Ounu, which appears in the Old Testament as On, may mean 'the pillared city', although no one knows for certain. Sometimes it was known as the 'House of Ra', while the Arabs called it Ain-Shams, meaning 'Sun eye' or 'Sun spring'.[2]

It is unknown how long the centre at Heliopolis had been established before its first mention in the records, but it was certainly already the supreme religious centre of Egypt 'when records begin' – at least the beginning of the Old Kingdom (c. 2700 BCE).[3] Although several other rival cult centres later rose in power and political influence, Heliopolis always retained its status and due reverence was paid to its antiquity throughout the history of Egypt.

Heliopolis was the principal religious centre of the Pyramid Age, and its theology – the first organised system of religion and cosmology known in Egypt – inspired and motivated the building of the great monuments at Giza. To people of that time and place, theology represented the sum total of all knowledge. All that existed was God: everything was a manifestation of Him/Her, and everything was imbued with the divine spark. Therefore the study of anything was in itself a glorious religious act. To learn was to worship and at the same time to progress along one's own path to godhood. Heliopolis is indelibly linked with Giza, which lies some 12 miles to its south-west. Indeed, the three pyramids are arranged so they point to Heliopolis.[4]

As 'the chosen seats of the gods' and 'the birthplace of the gods', Heliopolis was the most sacred site of Egypt. It contained temples to the creator god Atum, to Ra – the sun god himself – and to Horus, as well as to Isis, Thoth and the Nile god Hapi. One of the city's most renowned buildings was the *hwt-psdt*, the Mansion of the Great Ennead. Another structure was the House of the Phoenix, which may have contained the sacred ben-ben stone, Egypt's most holy 'relic', which was possibly meteoritic in origin.

The priesthood of Heliopolis was famed for its learning and wisdom. Two of its greatest achievements were in the fields of medicine and astronomy – its high priests held the title 'Greatest of Seers', generally understood to mean 'Chief Astronomer'.[5] Its priests were still regarded as the wisest and most learned in Egypt at the time of Herodotus (fifth century BCE) and even remembered in Strabo's day, as late as the first century CE. The priesthood was even famed among the Greeks, and it is said that, among others, Pythagoras, Plato, Eudoxus and Thales went to Heliopolis to study. And although we know few of the names of the great Egyptians who were its graduates, we do know that Imhotep, the genius who designed the first pyramid – the Step Pyramid of Djoser at Saqqara – and was venerated as a god for his medical knowledge, was a High Priest there.[6]

Significantly, the priesthood probably included women. An inscription of the Fourth Dynasty, roughly contemporary with the Giza pyramids, refers to a woman in the Temple of Thoth holding the title 'Mistress of the House of Books'.[7]

It is possible to piece together the main elements of the Heliopolitan religious beliefs from the Pyramid Texts. The earliest text, in the pyramid of Unas, dates from around 2350 BCE, some 200 years after the Great Pyramid of Khufu at Giza is believed to have been built. In fact most Egyptologists agree that the Pyramid Texts are much older than the earliest surviving inscriptions, and that they – and the religious and cosmological ideas – existed at the beginning of the First Dynasty, the 'official' birth of Egyptian civilisation, around 3100 BCE.[8] The Pyramid Texts are the oldest surviving religious writings in the world.[9]

Customarily divided into short 'chapters' called 'utterances' by Egyptologists, these ancient texts form descriptions of the funeral rites and afterlife journey of the king (strictly speaking, 'pharaoh' is a much later term). There is every reason to believe that the Pyramid Texts are not, in fact, merely funeral texts, nor is the wisdom embedded in them relevant solely to the kings of a long-dead civilisation.

The central theme of the texts is the afterlife, or astral, journey in which the king, identified with Osiris, ascends to the heavens where he is transformed into a star. He also encounters various gods and other entities, and is finally accepted into their ranks. He is then reincarnated as his own successor, in the form of Osiris's son, Horus, thus ensuring the literal divinity of the royal line and maintaining the continuity of Egyptian culture.

The Pyramid Texts are undoubtedly the product of the Heliopolitan priesthood,[10] and represent the only surviving unadulterated expression of their religion, and probably the only writings of the religion ever inscribed outside of Heliopolis itself at that time. The same ideas underpin later funeral inscriptions, such as the Coffin Texts (written inside sarcophagi of the Middle Kingdom, 2055–1650 BCE) and the so-called *Book of the Dead*, though these were also influenced by other, rival religious systems. The Pyramid Texts hold the key to reconstructing the beliefs of ancient Heliopolis.

A further problem arises as the Pyramid Texts were intended for a specific purpose, not as a general dissertation on theology. One analogy is with a Christian funeral service today. Obviously it would feature references to Christian beliefs, such as Jesus dying on the cross to save us, which Christians understand, while anyone unfamiliar with the religion would feel completely lost. The Pyramid Texts, in much the same way, are not the equivalent of a Heliopolitan Bible, but more like a prayer book.

A study of the underlying beliefs of the Pyramid Texts reveals an extraordinarily sophisticated yet economical theology and cosmology that can be read on many levels. Several complex concepts are expressed simultaneously in its imagery. There are many academic reconstructions of Heliopolitan thought, but the one we believe to make most sense of the data is that of the American professor of religious history, Karl W. Luckert, as described in his seminal book *Egyptian Light and Hebrew Fire* (1991). According to this, the system is one of deceptive simplicity, hiding a rich and awesome complexity. We came to realise that Heliopolitan beliefs concerning the nature of the universe, consciousness, life and what happens after death are both mystical and practical, yet also incorporate knowledge that rivals that of the most cutting-edge modern science.

It has long been recognised that the Pyramid Texts contain astronomical material. Recent books have argued that these ideas are neither primitive nor superstitious – as many academics still believe – but reveal a detailed and sophisticated understanding of the movement of heavenly bodies. They even take into account the phenomenon known as the precession of the equinoxes, a heavenly cycle of nearly 26,000 years that was deemed to have been discovered as late as the second century BCE by the Greeks (who even then got it wrong).[11] This civilisation existed at least five millennia ago. On such a timeline our own superstitious Dark Ages, when the world was believed to be flat, seem like yesterday.

The most fundamental revelation of the Pyramid Texts is that, despite our preconceptions, the Heliopolitan religion was essentially monotheistic. Its many gods, often animal-headed, were understood to represent the manifold aspects of the one creator god, Atum.

The Heliopolitan religion incorporated the concept of a mystical union with the 'higher' god forms, and even with the source of all creation, Atum himself. This union was the true objective of the process described in the Pyramid Texts, the destination of the soul's ultimate journey. According to the standard view, this was relevant only to the king in his afterlife state, but we believe it was not a journey reserved only for royalty – nor even for the dead. The Pyramid Texts in fact describe a secret technique for enabling a man or woman to encounter God and – dead or merely out of the body – to discover some of his knowledge for themselves.

Atum stood at the apex of the Great Ennead, or the nine primary gods of Egypt. However, exemplifying the concept of 'one god, many god forms', the nine themselves were considered as One, the other eight representing different aspects of Atum.[12] This is a similar idea to that of the Christian Trinity. As Professor Luckert says: 'The entire theological system can be visualised as a flow of creative vitality, emanating outward from the godhead, thinning out as it flows further from its source.'[13]

Before Atum's act of creation, the universe was a formless, watery void, called Nun. Out of this void emerged a phallic-shaped hill, the sacred Hill of Atum. Although a metaphor, it was also believed that this landmark was a physical place, the real site of the beginning of all things. Atum's temple in Heliopolis was probably built on this hill, although some Egyptologists have recently argued it was actually the rising ground of the Giza plateau. Others suggest that the pyramids themselves were intended to represent the Primeval Mound.[14]

The writings of Victorian – and even more recent – Egyptologists have been notably coy or tight-lipped about the story of Atum's act of creation. In fact, he ejaculated the universe as a result of masturbating himself to an explosive orgasm. Though this inevitably invites jokes about the 'Big Bang', it is actually rather an accurate image. Atum's life-giving burst of energy seeded the void of Nun, pushing back its boundaries to give way to the expansion of material creation. In the original story, Atum was considered to be androgynous: his phallus represented the male principle, while his hand represented the female principle. This defines one of the fundamental tenets of the Heliopolitan system and all Egyptian thinking, namely that of the eternal and quintessential balance of male and female, the yin-yang polarity without which, they believed, chaos would rule.

From Atum's arching semen the universe proceeded to unfold, gradually becoming manifest in the physical, material world that we inhabit, but only after passing through several other stages. From the creative act, two beings, Shu and Tefnut, emerged in the dividing of the first principle. Shu is male, representing the creative power, and Tefnut is female, representing a principle of order that limits, controls and shapes Shu's power. Tefnut is also represented as the goddess Ma'at, ruler of eternal justice.[15] Together, Shu and Tefnut are sometimes jointly called the Ruti, represented in physical form as two lions (or rather, a lion and a lioness).

From the union of Shu and Tefnut were born Geb (the earth god) and Nut (the sky goddess), representing the elements of the visible cosmos, more manifest forms of their 'parents'. Geb and Nut, in turn, gave birth to two pairs of brother-sister twins: the famous quartet of Isis and Osiris and Nepthys and her brother-consort, Set. They express the principle of duality in two ways: male and female, and positive-negative/light-dark. Nepthys is the 'dark sister' of the beneficent Isis, while Set is the destructive, obstructive force opposing Osiris's civilising and creative character. These four deities were considered to be closer to us and the material world, than their forebears, although still inhabiting the world of spirit beings 'behind the veil'. Luckert says that they 'exist low enough to participate more intimately in the human experience of life and death' and that they operate 'on a smaller and more visible scale than their parent(s)'.[16]

Collectively, these nine gods make up the Great Ennead, but

they remain only expressions of Atum, reaching through the levels of creation from the first emergence from the void to the world of matter we inhabit. In a sense, Osiris is Geb and Shu and Atum, just as Isis is Nut and Tefnut/Ma'at and Atum. Even Set was perceived as more complex than a simple embodied, archetypal evil, such as the Devil of Christianity.

The system continues. The Great Ennead itself leads on to another series of gods, the Lesser Ennead. The link – or 'go-between' – is Horus, the magical child of Isis and Osiris. He is regarded as the god of the material world, his role here echoing that of Atum in the universe. The foremost of the Lesser Ennead, who are believed to exert a direct influence over humankind, are the wisdom god Thoth – scribe to the Great Ennead – and Anubis, the jackal-headed god who guards the gateway between the worlds of the living and the dead.

This level is the province of many other deities, each dealing with a specific aspect of human life. It is probable that it incorporated local gods and goddesses worshipped in Egypt before the Heliopolitan religion was established. Luckert calls this the 'Turnaround Realm', the meeting point of the world of matter and the 'other dimensions' of the gods, where the reverse process can be experienced by an individual – either at death, or by mystical experiences in life – as an 'inner journey', back to union with the creator. This is the process that is the main theme of the Pyramid Texts, which – far from being 'primitive' – exceeds newer religions in both authority and sublimity, besides being strikingly similar to the traditions of shamanism.

Further significance can be derived from this elegant system. In an association of imagery, the emergence of Atum's Primeval Mound from Nun was equated with the rising of the sun, the source of all life in the material world. This is why Atum is associated with Ra, the sun god, sometimes referred to as Ra-Atum. This is also why Horus, as lord of this world, is also associated with, and sometimes personified as, the sun. The daily 'birth' of the sun is a 'microcosm' of the original creative explosion that gave birth to the universe, so it can be associated with both Atum and Horus. Like so much of the Pyramid Texts, the imagery works on several levels at once.

An objective reading of the Pyramid Texts involves much more than poetic symbolism. For example, its system of creation is a remarkable parallel to modern physicists' conception of the creation and evolution of the Universe. It literally describes the 'Big Bang', in which all matter explodes from a point of singularity and then expands and unfolds, becoming more complex as fundamental forces come into being and interact, finally reaching the level of elemental matter. (Significantly, the leading American Egyptologist Mark Lehner, in his 1997 book *The Complete Pyramids*, uses the term 'singularity' when referring to Atum's place in the myth.[17]) The system also includes the concept of a multidimensional universe, represented by the different levels of creation as embodied in the god forms. In the Pyramid Texts, the higher gods, such as Shu and Tefnut, still exist, but remain essentially unreachable by humankind without going through the intermediaries of the lower gods.

Yet another level of imagery lies within the creation story. While discussing the sophistication of the ideas in the Pyramid Texts with our friend, the Belgian writer-researcher Philip Coppens, he pointed out that certain very new discoveries of modern science are an implicit part of the story. As we have seen, Atum emerged from a formless void, imaged in the form of the primordial watery chaos called Nun. This is often regarded as being based on the way land emerges from the Nile flood as the annual inundation recedes, but this is not really the concept expressed in the Heliopolitan image. As Egyptologist R.T. Rundle Clark says:

> It was not like a sea, for that has a surface, whereas the original waters extended above as well as below . . . The present cosmos is a vast cavity, rather like an air-bubble, amid the limitless expanse.[18]

This is an elegantly clever way of expressing the complex concept of a sea that represents, on the one hand, the void – nothing – yet at the same time stands for unlimited potential – infinity. There may be another reason for choosing this image, though. Scientists have only recently announced the discovery that water can be found in interstellar space in far greater quantities than has ever been expected. Atum represents not just the 'Big Bang' of creation, but also the sun: and scientists are only now realising that the enormous clouds of water throughout the universe play a vital role in the creation of stars such as our sun. In fact, they are now beginning to believe that stars are actually created from such clouds of water . . .[19] It has also been pointed out that, on a terrestrial level, the myth expresses the idea that life originated in the seas.[20] All this suggests the possession of exceptionally sophisticated knowledge by the Heliopolitans.

Significantly, on 12 September 1998, the leading British scientific magazine *New Scientist* published the ground-breaking research of a NASA team led by Lou Allamandola into the origins – and requirements – of life in the universe. Previously scientists had found it impossible to assemble the right 'ingredients' out of which to create even the most basic form of life, but this team had succeeded in creating some of the complex molecules necessary by recreating in the laboratory conditions similar to those found inside clouds of gas in interstellar space. They discovered that creating those complex molecules in those circumstances is extremely easy – in fact, virtually inevitable – whereas trying to do so in strictly terrestrial circumstances is impossible. The most striking example is that of molecules called lipids which make up the walls of individual cells, without which the cell, the basic building block of living things, could not exist. Now that scientists know that this can be done so easily in these conditions, the implications are enormous. It looks increasingly as if life originated in deep space and was then 'seeded' on to planets, probably by comets, and that, even in its most primitive form, it is probably found everywhere throughout the universe. As Lou Allamandola says, 'I begin to really believe that life is a cosmic imperative.'

This, however, is only part of the story, as Philip Coppens pointed out to us. It may be that Allamandola's team are by no means the first to comprehend the requirements for the creation of life. He cites the ancient Egyptian myth of Atum's explosive orgasm that created the universe: his ejaculation can be seen to symbolise, with astonishing accuracy, the idea that all the basic ingredients for life existed from the very first and that the universe, as it continues to expand, carries them within it. The imagery of the Atum myth also encompasses perfectly the concept of 'seeding' the universe with life. Did the Heliopolitan priests really know how life originates and spreads throughout the universe?[20]

This, then, was the 'primitive' religion of ancient Egypt, which was governed by the Great Ennead, the Nine who represented all life and all wisdom. The ancient Egyptian civilisation, so often underestimated even by our most learned scholars, continues to fascinate with mysteries that call to us from antiquity. But we were to discover that something new is afoot, a sudden, unexplained interest in the lost secrets of the Egyptians and a flurry of mysterious activity among their most venerable ruins. Something intriguing is going on at Giza, something that is intimately connected with the preparation for the Millennium and the start of the twenty-first century. People and organisations are searching for the lost knowledge of the worshippers of the Nine for their own purposes. They are about to undertake a momentous, perhaps even a catastrophic venture: to hijack the mysteries for their own ends, even daring to attempt the unthinkable – to exploit the ancient gods themselves.

1

Egypt:
New Myths For Old

Nothing succeeds like Egypt. Although its fabled magic and mystery have by now become something of a well-worn cliché, it is, largely, only academic historians who lament the fact. Something about the land of Tutankhamun, the Sphinx and the Great Pyramid instantly dwarfs all other cultures in our imaginations, although many of them – such as the pre-Columbian peoples of South America – also built pyramids that continue to perplex us with their mystery and sheer technical perfection.

A recent spate of highly successful books has not only asserted that ancient Egypt was considerably more sophisticated than academics will admit, but also promised that mind-bending revelations connected with that venerable civilisation will soon shake the world. These secrets will somehow emanate from ancient Egyptian sources and affect us all in one way or another. And, of course, they will be timed to coincide with the Millennium.

A mystery does surround the ancient Egyptians and their culture. Immensely impressive data does reveal that the ancient Egyptians were far more sophisticated than Egyptologists admit.

Indeed, mainstream Egyptologists seem curiously blind to the achievements and beliefs of the very people they have chosen to study. However, there is a backlash against this academic arrogance – and like all extreme reactions, it presents problems of its own, not least because this particular backlash has been carefully orchestrated.

The last decade has seen the rapid rise of an Egyptological counterculture. It began as a challenge to the rigid views of the academics, but has now effectively become a new orthodoxy with an equally unyielding 'doctrine' of its own.

There is a strong case for challenging much of the standard Egyptological view. Many recent bestsellers – such as *Keeper of Genesis* by Robert Bauval and Graham Hancock (1996), *From Atlantis to the Sphinx* (1996) by Colin Wilson and *Gods of Eden* (1998) by Andrew Collins – have daringly tackled the academics, rightly criticising their stubbornness and blindness and presenting an alternative view of the subject. In our view, much of this was long overdue. Historians and Egyptologists have had it all their own way for too long. Many of them have been far too ready to dismiss the ancient Egyptians as 'primitive', while the evidence of our own eyes, in the shape of the Great Pyramid and the Sphinx, tells us otherwise. And, of course, their incredible knowledge – teased out of the ancient Pyramid Texts – is also routinely ignored or even roundly rubbished.

However, many – but not all – exponents of the New Orthodoxy who dare to 'publish and be damned' appear to be motivated by something more than a sense of solidarity with a culture that is rarely given its due. This wave of new books is not just a timely recognition of ancient Egyptian genius (although of course there is an element of that, which must be applauded). As we discovered, something else is involved here, something deeply unsettling.

Among certain of the so-called 'pyramidiots' (the academics' term for the alternative Egyptologists, which no doubt includes ourselves) we have discerned a very interesting but disturbing tendency. As we will see, some members of the New Orthodoxy –

but by no means all – hide another agenda behind their apparently laudable and open-minded attack on the arrogance of academia. Through the mass media, these writer-researchers have promoted what is essentially a belief system that is not only just as rigidly dogmatic as the academics', but which seems, worryingly, to have quite another agenda. The promotion of certain ideas and the fact that the same ideas occur in several of the most high-profile books about 'alternative Egypt' led us to believe that there was a pre-arranged, orchestrated move to create a new belief system.

As this investigation proceeds and we carefully strip away the layers of false extrapolation and strange affiliations, a much wider conspiracy is revealed. This extends well beyond the confines of Egyptology – Old or New – and involves several intelligence agencies, including the CIA and Britain's MI5, occult groups and even some of the world's top scientists. This extraordinary conspiracy centres upon the creation of the expectation of imminent, quasireligious revelations connected with ancient Egypt, cynically exploiting the spiritual hunger and craving for miracles of the Western world. This is not some minor social experiment, but in effect a large-scale campaign that takes many forms and uses many different religious, spiritual, New Age – and even political – masks. Honed by decades of intensive, and often less than ethical, intelligence experience, this conspiracy is, in our view, the most insidious yet dangerous assault on the collective free will of the West. Those at the heart of this plot care little for either the Egyptian mysteries or the spiritually bereft: all they care about is power and control.

Testament of the pyramids

No first visit to Paris is complete without a trip to the top of the Eiffel Tower, where, windblown but triumphant, one can enjoy a seemingly limitless view over one of the most beautiful cities on Earth. This experience is useful when putting another – even more famous – landmark into context: the Great Pyramid of Giza. Until the Eiffel Tower was built in the last years of the nineteenth century, the ancient Egyptian wonder of the world was the tallest building humanity had ever known. But while every nut and bolt of the iron giant of Paris can be traced to its origins, and all its parts could be easily reassembled today, the same is not true of the Great Pyramid. No one knows how it was built, although many claim they do. While everyone knows the reason why the Eiffel Tower was built, no one knows the true purpose of the pyramids.

Reams of paper and seas of ink have been used in attempts to convey the sheer scale of the Great Pyramid, but nothing can prepare the individual for the moment he or she sees it for the first time. Other famous monuments may disappoint: Stonehenge, perhaps, does not quite justify the tour-guide hype. The Great Pyramid of Giza always exceeds expectations.

One illusion, however, is very quickly shattered. Somehow a romantic notion prevails that the Giza complex – the three most famous pyramids and the Sphinx, along with their attendant temples and causeways – lies in the middle of the desert and that one has to be a cross between Indiana Jones and Lawrence of Arabia in order to get there. The monuments of Giza are in fact ten minutes' walk from the populous suburb of Cairo of the same name. It can come as a shock to find the Great Pyramid towering over a hotel swimming pool. There are few more dramatic, and somehow unsettling, backdrops to poolside relaxation.

The Great Pyramid is profoundly unsettling in many ways, not least because of its sheer scale. Made of 2.5 million limestone blocks, each with an average weight of 2.5 tons, this immense structure covers an area of over 53,000 square yards at its base, with a perimeter of over half a mile. It is 481 feet high, a great height, as those who ill advisedly (and illegally) climb up it can testify. Although its roughly stepped sides now appear to invite an arduous scramble to the summit, originally this was impossible, as the whole pyramid was covered in a smooth, polished limestone cladding.

The Great Pyramid is aligned to the cardinal points of the

compass with an amazing – and aesthetically unnecessary – degree of accuracy. (There is an error of only about 5 inches in the north–south alignment, and one of just over 2 inches from east to west.) The same incredible accuracy applies to the monument as a whole: the length of the sides at its base differ by less than 8 inches (20.5 cm) between the shortest and longest sides, and the accuracy of the right-angled corners is near-perfect.[1] There are many other famous examples of awesome sophistication in the construction and location of the Great Pyramid. These include the fact that it is situated almost exactly on the geodetically significant latitude of 30 degrees, as well as the use in its design of advanced geometric concepts such as *pi* and *phi* (which are, officially, supposed to have been unknown to the ancient Egyptians). For orthodox Egyptologists these facts, while undeniable, can only be put down to coincidence.[2]

Elsewhere in the Giza complex, other, less famous, examples of the builders' art equally give one pause. Most tourists only ever use the curious, now roofless, building known as the Valley Temple, which lies on the southern side of the Sphinx enclosure, as a route to the Sphinx. This is a pity, as it is well worth serious examination itself. Limestone blocks dwarf even those used in the construction of the Great Pyramid, some weighing as much as 200 tons and measuring up to 9 metres in length. (These blocks were taken from the Sphinx enclosure when it was originally hollowed out.) The inner walls and upright square pillars of the interior of the temple are made of granite – again, some weighing over 200 tons. But not until the 1970s were cranes built that could lift a weight of even just 100 tons – half the weight of the largest blocks in the Valley Temple.[3] How did the ancient Egyptians lift them over three millennia ago?

There is something other than sheer scale involved in the workmanship of the Valley Temple. There are, by modern standards, other virtually 'impossible' flourishes in the setting of one stone next to another. For example, at its corners, instead of having two separate stones fitting together to form the right angles, just one massive block has been cut to turn the corner, sometimes by the ludicrously tiny amount of just a couple of inches, with the next stone specifically trimmed to fit the remaining space, and so on. This is all the more incredible when you realise that the stones were all cut to fit when actually in place. It follows the same principle as that of dry-stone walling, used by many rural peoples over the centuries and generally thought to require a fair degree of eye-to-hand skill. But such wall building always used small stones, because they usually had to fit relatively easily into the wall-maker's hand. By contrast, the stones of the Valley Temple, as we have seen, would still defy the lifting powers of the greatest cranes of the modern world, let alone be easily trimmed to go round corners when in place. So *how* did the ancient Egyptians manipulate such massive stones? And *why* did they choose what has to be the most complicated and unnecessarily difficult method they could possibly find? As we toured the Valley Temple, the thought that came irresistibly to mind was that these builders were showing off . . .

The granite blocks themselves present a mystery. Not only is the interior of the Valley Temple made of granite, but so is part of the inside of the Great Pyramid. The King's Chamber is lined with it. The local stone was limestone, so the giant granite blocks had to be transferred from Aswan, about 600 miles to the south of Cairo, then hoisted into place, sometimes being positioned as lintels across the top of upright granite blocks.

There are other examples of unnecessary, even apparently absurd, difficulties encountered by the early builders. At the position of Khafra's (the 'Second') Pyramid, a level base had to be created on a slightly sloping section of the plateau. This entailed the cutting of a 'step' into the rock of the rise and building up the lower part of the slope with limestone blocks to make a level platform. Had the pyramid been built just a few hundred metres to the west, it would have been on level ground to begin with.[4] Clearly the ancient Egyptians either liked to make things as difficult as possible for themselves, or there was a very important reason why the Second Pyramid should occupy exactly that position in relation to the first.

The mysteries of the external structure of the Giza monuments leap to the visitor's startled eye, but the inside of the Great Pyramid is even more baffling. What strikes the first-time visitor immediately is how strangely cramped the passages and entrances to the chambers are, and how difficult it is for even relatively small adults to scrape through. You have to duck down for long stretches of the Ascending Passage to reach the awe-inspiring Grand Gallery, which leads to the King's Chamber, and then you must bend double to get through the immediate entrance, the antechamber. And, before wooden slats were incorporated into the Grand Gallery in the modern era to enable visitors to achieve a foothold, originally there was only a massive smooth stone surface stretching upwards and out of sight. The Great Pyramid is hardly visitor-friendly now; the gods alone know what kind of superhuman agility was required to move around inside it millennia ago.

We are told that the Great Pyramid, like its companions at Giza – and every other Egyptian pyramid – was built as a tomb for a pharaoh: this is, according to mainstream Egyptologists, 'fact'. Unfortunately, as all pyramidiots gleefully point out, no evidence of any human burial has ever been found in any pyramid. One can cite the depredations of grave robbers as much as one likes, but in the 'unfinished' step pyramid attributed to Sekhemket at Saqqara the sarcophagus was found not only intact but also sealed – and when opened was revealed to be empty.[5] And most famously, no signs of human burial have ever been found in the Great Pyramid nor in its two companion pyramids at Giza. Remains were found in the sarcophagus in Khafra's – the Second Pyramid – but they turned out to belong to a bull.[6] The Bent Pyramid at Dahshur contained a dismembered owl and the skeletons of five bats in a box, but nothing of human origin.[7] Clearly, the pyramids were not tombs, but the fact remains that – although many theories have been put forward – no one knows why the pyramids were built, nor even how they were built. (Bizarre though it may seem, the mysteries of the pyramids are not favourites with academic Egyptologists. As Vivian Davies of the British Museum has said: 'I must confess I've never been somebody fascinated with the pyramids.'[8] A similar position is adopted by many of his colleagues.)

The old idea that the pharaohs used thousands of slaves to haul the vast slabs of rock through the desert and manoeuvre them into place through sheer brute force has been shown to be extremely unlikely. Recent archaeological evidence has indicated that the workers were free men who willingly gave up some of their time to assist in the building and were housed in huge camps. The logistics of feeding and watering this army of volunteer workers must have been a nightmare, especially as they were technically, at least, free to leave if they wanted to. There is also the problem of how any number of even the strongest and most willing of men could have manoeuvred those massive stone slabs into place with such finesse.

The Great Pyramid slopes inwards towards the apex at an angle of about 52 degrees and its summit is nearly 500 feet from the ground. The imagination baulks at the problem of how these 'primitive' people did it. They must have had scaffolding that was not only extraordinarily strong, but also adjustable. After all, it would have had to allow for the intricate and physically tough work needed to manoeuvre each mighty stone in place, course by course, higher and higher, all the while sloping inwards to accommodate the gradient. Such scaffolding would also have had to be almost supernaturally strong to sustain the weight of at least one 2.5-ton block of stone, as well as workers and their tools. Academics favour the theory that the pyramids were erected through the construction of giant ramps – made of clay bricks, perhaps – so that the blocks could be dragged into position, after which the ramps were demolished. Once again, however, there is the problem of the inwardly sloping walls and the tiny apex – how would you build adjustable ramps to allow for the gradient? After all, a fixed ramp might work for the first few stone courses, but very soon the gradient would create a widening gap between the ramp and the pyramid wall, hardly the best, or safest, way to manipulate huge blocks of stone. If you had somehow managed to build any part of the side of a pyramid in this way, by the time you came close to the apex there would be a gap of several feet between your fixed ramp and the stonework. What did they do – throw the stones across? Academics have suggested that, in order to overcome this problem, the Egyptians built serial ramps, each inclining further inwards to accommodate the gradient, but such ramps would need to have started many miles away in order to have gentle enough inclines for men to be able to drag stones up them.

Recently, American Egyptologist Mark Lehner built a scale model of a true pyramid on the Giza plateau for a television series called *Secrets of Lost Empires*, a BBC/NOVA/WGBH-Boston co-production that required teams of experts to reproduce the achievements of ancient cultures – at least, in miniature. Given just three weeks, different teams had to build a pyramid, erect a Stonehenge monolith or repair a remote Incan wall. If we were to believe their own publicity, they very largely succeeded, although, certainly in the case of Mark Lehner's team, their 'success' was extremely limited. For a start, they were not required to quarry and move the stone blocks using the soft copper tools that (allegedly) were all that the Egyptians had. If the team could not have used modern methods to cut and move the stones to the building site at Giza, no doubt the Millennium would have come and gone before they hacked out a single stone.

Once they had their stones on site, they had to resort to the putative 'primitive' methods of the original builders. Lehner's team, which included local Egyptian labourers, cut 186 limestone blocks, each weighing up to 6,000 lbs – not, note, 2.5 tons – then manoeuvred them into position, swearing and sweating, using brute force, levers, ropes and water as a lubricant. The resulting pyramid, with its perfect gradient of 52 degrees, was clad with shaped facing blocks, then topped with a limestone pyramidion. Lehner, bursting with pride, announced that 'this limited experience made it abundantly clear that the pyramids are very human monuments, created through long experience and tremendous skill, but without any kind of secret sophistication'.

That is all well and good, until it is realised that Lehner's Pyramid was very much a miniature version of the real thing – not much higher than a tall man with upraised arms. In fact, this stone Wendy House would perch comfortably on the very top of the Great Pyramid. Building a structure where you can easily manoeuvre large stones, if necessary by dragging them out on to the ground and starting again, is wildly different from constructing what was – until recently – the tallest building in the world, where there would have been no room for manoeuvre beyond the first few stone courses.

If the largest single artefact of ancient Egypt has the power to challenge our own sophisticated technology, spare a thought or two for some of the smallest. The Cairo Museum contains many of the sort of artefacts frequently overlooked by visitors, but they are almost, in their own way, as mysterious as the pyramids. For example, many small stone jars and bottles on closer examination prove to be extremely difficult to explain using mainstream academic arguments. We are asked to believe that the ancient Egyptians had only copper tools, yet what we have here are tiny vessels, some just 3 inches high, made of incredibly hard material such as granite. These bottles and vases have elegant, thin-rimmed, perfectly round openings, narrow necks and wider bodies, which have been hollowed out and shaped by a drill that entered through the narrow neck. But how? What diamond-tipped drill could create such extraordinary craftmanship even now? But why go to such lengths just to make a vase in the first place?

Other examples of precision drilling on the Giza plateau are found right under the noses of visitors and Egyptologists. In several places fallen masonry has exposed perfectly round bore holes in granite pillars, sometimes up to 10–12 inches deep, and they are perfectly round and precisely the same size all the way down. Archaeologists and Egyptologists vehemently deny that the ancients had tools such as lathes and drills on the apparently reasonable grounds that no remains of any such tool have ever been found. That may be unfortunate, but we have the evidence of our own eyes – and also that of an expert, the American tool designer and manufacturer Christopher Dunn. His analysis of certain Old Kingdom artefacts has convinced him that not only did the ancient Egyptians have drills, but that the drillholes in granite blocks could only have been achieved by a drill spinning 500 times faster than a modern, diamond-tipped drill.[9]

Dunn has proposed that the Egyptians used an ultrasonic drill, which uses sound to make the bit vibrate at an enormously high rate. Andrew Collins, in *Gods of Eden*, has developed the idea of sound technology used by the Egyptians and other ancient cultures and it does seem likely that they used what magi call the 'Word' – sound – to create many of the achievements that perplex us today.

Such theories go some way towards resolving the question of how the Egyptians were able to cut through solid granite as if it were butter, achieving precision work that would be extremely difficult – and in some cases, literally impossible – for us today, even with our computer-guided laser technology. But the question remains as to how they learned or developed their techniques. Clearly, since the pyramids and other enigmatic examples of their skill exist, they must have had such a technique, even though – bafflingly – no remnants of a drill or a lathe have ever been found. So we have another 'impossible' scenario: evidence of the results of this advanced technology, but no direct evidence of the technology itself. Therefore, say the academics, it's back to those primitive copper tools, despite the fact that no known copper tool could drill perfectly round holes in granite . . .

The implications of this mystery take us into a whole new realm. What we appear to have, in both the pyramids and the expertly drilled artefacts, is evidence of a people who seem to have emerged from an essentially Neolithic Stone Age culture into an advanced, organised civilisation capable of heroic building feats in, at most, just 500 years. As far as we can tell, the great monuments simply came into being without any real process of development.

Faced with this paradox, there seem to be only two ways to

resolve it: by denying that the ancient Egyptians built the monuments, redating them so that they fit into a much earlier epoch and assigning them to an otherwise lost civilisation; or by positing the intrusion into Egyptian society of some other, more advanced culture that came from elsewhere and either taught the ancient Egyptians the necessary skills or built the monuments themselves.

Redating the most enigmatic monuments of Egypt would serve to explain why the archaeological record of the transition from Neolithic to sophisticated culture is incomplete. For example, the assumption that the Sphinx and the Giza pyramids were built by a lost civilisation in the remote past and that they already existed when the peoples of the Nile Valley were still in a Neolithic phase neatly explains the paradox. This idea was developed, for example, by Graham Hancock in his *Fingerprints of the Gods*, arguing that an advanced civilisation once existed, probably before the last Ice Age, but that it was struck down by some natural catastrophe. This reduced the survivors to a primitive level once more, so that the gradual climb up to a higher level of civilisation began again.

Naturally, the scenario of a civilisation that essentially began at its peak and then declined invites speculation. It is as if the first skyscraper was built within 500 years of woad-covered ancient Britons. For the analogy to be more precise, it would have to be impossible for all future generations to replicate that skyscraper, and for its means of construction to lie beyond their understanding, even when civilisation had progressed to space travel and computer wizardry.

Of course, for historians and Egyptologists, the idea of some hypothetical lost civilisation is beneath contempt. They claim that no evidence has ever been found to support this contention and so refuse even to consider it. Yet there is plenty of circumstantial evidence for the existence of this mysterious, lost 'elder culture'. For example, many ancient maps – most famously the Piri Re'is map – appear to show that the globe was surveyed and very accurately mapped by an advanced culture in the distant past.[10] Innumerable anomalous artefacts and monuments across the globe support the idea of a lost civilisation.

Where Egypt is concerned, the situation is not quite so clear-cut. If the standard dating of the Old Kingdom pyramids is correct – that is, they are at the most 5,000 years old – there is a problem. Five thousand years is by no means a long enough period in which to 'lose' an advanced civilisation, though there have been many recent attempts to assign much greater antiquity to some of the monuments at Giza, which have the advantage of allowing a longer time for most traces of this elder culture to have been lost.

On the other hand, some of the standard dates are undoubtedly correct. On the evidence as it now stands, it does appear that the Giza pyramids are 'only' as old as the history books say. This means that proponents of the 'lost civilisation' hypothesis also have to assume some form of continued contact between the ancient lost civilisation and the Egypt of the relatively recent era of the Old Kingdom, effectively putting them back where they started, because there is no archaeological evidence of such a continuity.

This confused logic can be a minefield for enthusiasts of the 'lost civilisation' theory. Robert Bauval and Graham Hancock argue that in 10,500 BCE (as we will see, a highly significant date to them), an advanced culture in Egypt decided upon the ground plan of the Giza complex.[11] For those authors, and many others, this mysterious elder culture consisted of the survivors of the great catastrophe that destroyed Atlantis. These Atlanteans were, it is asserted, incredibly sophisticated. It was their input that created the anomalous technological wonders of the ancient world.

But much of Bauval and Hancock's own evidence also supports the standard dating of the pyramids, so we have to assume that this civilisation of 10,500 BCE continued in some way so that it could build the Great Pyramid around 2500 BCE, as is generally agreed. This is a gap of 8,000 years: it is frankly incredible that there should be no remaining traces of such a culture. If it did survive until 2500 BCE, what became of it then?

Andrew Collins, in *From the Ashes of Angels*, has proposed that the elder culture that existed in Egypt in remote antiquity took refuge, because of some catastrophe, in the mountains of Kurdistan, in such sites as the fabulous underground city of Çatal Hüyük, to re-emerge centuries later to pass some of their knowledge on to the peoples of Egypt and Sumer. This would account for the sudden eruption of civilisation in those two centres at about the same time. Even so, we are still left with the same central problem: why come out of hiding, build some anomalously impressive structures at Giza that still defy explanation, and then vanish again?

The other theory to account for the paradoxes of the pyramids proposes that the knowledge did not come from a lost, human civilisation, but that it was brought to Earth by extraterrestrials. The 'ancient astronaut' school of thought first came to the notice of a wide audience in the 1960s and 1970s, thanks to the phenomenally successful books of Erich von Däniken. Although now largely dismissed as sadly lacking in persuasive evidence, there is no doubting the incredible influence of *Chariots of the Gods?* and its sequels, nor the way that the whole concept of the gods as spacemen was enthusiastically accepted by millions for the first time, entering irreversibly into our collective consciousness. Since von Däniken seized the popular imagination, others – notably Zecharia Sitchin and, more recently, Alan F. Alford – have promoted similar ideas. This school interprets the myths of the ancient world as romanticised memories of encounters with extraterrestrial beings and their technology. The 'gods' are simply biological entities who have developed an advanced, spacefaring civilisation. It also attempts to explain the anomalies of ancient technologies, such as the pyramids, as the result of such contact.

It is possible that there are many other inhabited planets in the universe, some of which may have developed to a point where interstellar travel is routine. However, the evidence put forward by the proponents of the ancient astronaut theory is far from conclusive, and by its very nature it is largely speculative. Besides, their rather mechanical and materialist interpretation of ancient myths – that the gods were physical space travellers – only too often seems contrived, and completely ignores the elements of mysticism and ineffability in the history of human religion.

While we have no overwhelming personal or logical objections to Atlantis, the elder culture or the extraterrestrial hypotheses, we are concerned with another aspect of the 'New Orthodoxy'. This is the insistence that new discoveries about our past have a significance that goes well beyond merely rewriting history. This is the claim that, in some way, the ancient Egyptian civilisation has a direct relevance to us today, that it has left some kind of 'message' that will bring about real changes in our immediate future . . .

Sirius revisited

One of the most influential books ever written about the mysteries of Egypt is Robert Temple's *The Sirius Mystery*, originally published in 1976, and with an extensively revised edition in 1998. As the inspiration for writers who wished to reconsider the ancient past, this book actually spawned much of the current New Orthodoxy.

Temple began by considering a puzzle posed by the Dogon people, who live in the West African country of Mali. The Dogon have an elaborate system of belief that centres on the importance of the star Sirius, which is, in galactic terms, a near neighbour. At 8.7 light years away it is the second closest star to our own solar system. Two French anthropologists, Marcel Griaule and Germaine Dieterlen, who lived with and studied the Dogon for many years before and after the Second World War, had noted one very curious feature: the Dogon believed that Sirius was accompanied by another star, of incredible heaviness, which was invisible. They called it *po tolo* – the *po* star. (*Po* is a tiny seed of a type of cereal known as fonio, aptly encapsulating the smallness of the star.) In fact, it is now known that Sirius is a binary (or perhaps even trinary) star system, and that the bright star we can see from Earth has a companion invisible to the naked eye – or, indeed, to any but the most powerful telescopes. The existence of Sirius B, as the companion star is known, was only suspected by astronomers in the first decades of the nineteenth century, when anomalies in Sirius's movements suggested the gravitational pull of a massive celestial body nearby. It was not conclusively observed until 1842, and not photographed until 1970.

It is now known that Sirius B is a white dwarf star, one that is composed of extremely dense matter so that, although relatively small, it still exerts a huge gravitational pull. Amazingly, the Dogon even appear to know the period that Sirius B takes – about fifty years – to orbit around its larger companion. They commemorate this with a special ceremony that takes place every hundred years, but it counts as fifty, because of their peculiar 'double-year' calendar system.

The Dogon also claim that Sirius is, in fact, a trinary system – a third star, which they call the 'Star of Women' (*emme ya tolo*) is also in orbit around Sirius A. When Temple wrote the original version of *The Sirius Mystery*, the existence of Sirius C had, in fact, been proposed, but not conclusively proven by astronomers. Temple claims that, since then, the existence of Sirius C has been proven and accepted by astronomers, further evidence of the extraordinary knowledge of the Dogon.

The Dogon's knowledge about the existence of Sirius B still mystifies. They, in fact, have an even more extensive knowledge of the cosmos than Temple describes in his book.[12] In addition to knowing about the existence of the rings of Saturn and the major moons of Jupiter, they know that the Milky Way really moves in the form of a spiral, that our moon is lifeless and that Earth spins on its axis. They know that the stars are really suns – for example, their alternative name for the Star of Women (Sirius C) is *yau nay dagi*, which means the 'Little Sun of Women'.

Some sceptics have attempted to explain away the Dogon's knowledge of Sirius by ascribing it to itinerant Christian missionaries who felt the urge to pass this piece of somewhat anachronistic and highly specialist knowledge on to the Dogon. In turn, the Dogon felt compelled to add it to their religion. In fact, the first Christian mission in Mali was not established by American Protestants until 1936, when the Sirius-based religion was already deeply embedded in Dogon culture.[13] Some, such as Robert Bauval,[14] have suggested that perhaps, in the recent past, Sirius B was brighter and therefore visible from the Earth. But astrophysicists have established that this ceased to be possible tens of millions of years ago. Even if that were the case, the two stars are so close together that at this distance they would have appeared as one.[15]

The Dogon also believe that their ancestors were taught the arts of civilisation by gods called the Nommo – or rather demi-gods, because the Nommo were believed to have been emissaries of the one god, Amma – who descended to Earth in an 'ark' in the remote past. The Nommo were described as water spirits, who inhabited all bodies of water, from the seas to the smallest ponds. Dogon depictions of the Nommo show them to be fishlike.

Temple argues that the myths of the Dogon actually preserved the memories of the visit of an amphibious, extraterrestrial race, who came from a planet in the Sirius system, thus explaining both the legend and the Dogon's otherwise inexplicable knowledge about that star. And it was the Nommo, he suggests, who were behind the development of human civilisation. Temple also tries to show that the knowledge of the Dogon originated in the ancient civilisations of Egypt and Sumer, and that this once wide-spread knowledge about the civilising aliens from Sirius had somehow been passed on to the Dogon alone. In an immensely detailed, closely argued and apparently scholarly book, Temple produced evidence from the myths and legends of ancient Egypt – besides those of Sumeria, Babylonia and Greece – to support his case. Because of his sober and academic-sounding tone, Temple's work was taken much more seriously than the work of Erich von Däniken of a few years before.

However, problems remain with *The Sirius Mystery*, which became the grandfather of almost all recent books of the New Egyptology. For a start, the Dogon themselves do not specifically link the Nommo with Sirius. This is Temple's interpretation. It could be, for example, that the Nommo came from some other star system, and simply told our ancestors about the true nature of the Sirius system, perhaps because they were particularly interested in it as the brightest star in the night sky. The Dogon, in fact, claim to have knowledge of fourteen solar systems with planets, and also say that there are many other 'Earths' that are inhabited.[16] In fact, astrophysicists consider it very unlikely that the Sirius system could support planets of any kind, let alone one capable of supporting life, given the complexities of coping with light, heat and gravitational pulls from at least two, and possibly three, suns.[17]

As far as Temple is concerned, Sirius C is an established, scientific fact. He cites a paper by two French astronomers, D. Benest and J.L. Duvent, published in the journal *Astronomy and Astrophysics* in July 1995, entitled 'Is Sirius a Triple Star?' But as the question mark suggests, the two authors are less certain than Temple implies. Benest and Duvent review the previous claims for Sirius C – almost entirely based on observations available in 1976, when the first edition of *The Sirius Mystery* was published – and try to calculate whether or not such observations are compatible with the presence of a third star, and then speculate on its likely properties. They conclude that measurements of anomalies in the movements of Sirius A and B could be explained by the presence of a third star of about one-twentieth of the mass of our sun, making it about as small as a star could be, orbiting Sirius A every 6.3 years. They do not claim, though, that this proves the existence of Sirius C, pointing out that this can only be determined conclusively by observing the star itself. These properties of Sirius C – the only ones possible according to the laws of celestial mechanics – are completely different from those accorded it by the Dogon and by Temple. And there are other problems: the measurements of the movements used by Benest and Duvent are all ground-based, so obviously there is great potential for error – the new observations from the Hipparchos satellite should prove more accurate.[18] We checked with the

European Space Agency, but it appears that the new data about Sirius has not yet been examined for signs of Sirius C by astrophysicists. However, we did talk to Martin Barstow, an astrophysicist at Leicester University, who has made a special study of the Sirius system (particularly Sirius B, as he is a specialist in white dwarf stars). He told us that, although the idea of Sirius C was intriguing and could not be ruled out, there was insufficent evidence for its existence as yet.

So, although it is impossible to say categorically that Sirius C does not exist, neither is it true to claim emphatically that 'the existence of Sirius C has now been confirmed', as Robert Temple does.[19] And even if its existence is eventually proven, its characteristics could not be remotely similar to those ascribed to Dogon belief by Temple.

Undeniably, Sirius was deemed to be a very important star by the ancient Egyptians, for reasons that are not entirely clear, despite the confident assertions of Egyptologists. The usual explanation is that, because the heliacal (dawn) rising of the star occurred just before the annual, life-giving inundation of the Nile, the Egyptians made a simplistic connection between the two events, and believed that Sirius somehow caused the flood. This explanation is easily revealed to be nonsense. While it is true that the heliacal rising of Sirius marked the beginning of the ancient Egyptian year, the onset of the flood was not a regular event, and it could happen at any time within a period of over two months.[20] In some years the flood would have started before Sirius's heliacal rising. As the yearly rising and setting of the stars fell out of step with the seasons, the two events ceased to have any correlation early in Egypt's recorded history. It is assumed by Egyptologists that the calendar was fixed at a period when Sirius's dawn rising coincided with the inundation, but there is no proof of this. There is no way of knowing for sure why Sirius was so important to the ancient Egyptians but there could be a very mundane explanation: it is, after all, the brightest star in the sky.

Temple may claim that the ancient Egyptians hailed Sirius as important because beings from that solar system bestowed the art of civilisation upon them, but his theory depends entirely on establishing that the Egyptians, like the Dogon, knew of the existence of Sirius B. In our view, the case he presents is by no means conclusive.

Much of Temple's case for the ancient Egyptians knowing the 'Sirius secret' is based on the alleged relationships between words in various languages and the interpretation of myths, but these often prove to be unsatisfactory. His information about ancient Egyptian myths relies too heavily on classical writers, rather than the ancient Egyptian sources themselves, which leads to several errors. Perhaps his greatest mistake is in making too much of the fact that Sirius was known to the Greeks as the 'Dog Star'. This name arose because it was found in the constellation of Canis Major (the Great Dog), which follows behind Orion as the constellations rise each night. To the Greeks, Orion was the hunter, so the small constellation at its heels was taken to represent his hunting dog, hence the name given to the main star of the constellation.[21] This is entirely a classical Greek concept, and emphatically not one that was shared by the ancient Egyptians, for whom Sirius/Sothis was firmly the star of the goddess Isis, as well as sometimes also being associated with Horus, her son.[22] However, the Dog Star epithet leads Temple to link this with Anubis, the dog- or jackal-headed god of the underworld, and to draw conclusions concerning Sirius based on the myths connected with him, as well as with dogs in Greek and other mythologies. Here we have a whole series of connections made by Temple to support his hypothesis, but they are, in fact, based on a faulty premise.

Such is the influence of Robert Temple that his ideas, even if they are, as we have shown above, sometimes based on flawed reasoning, often surface in the work of others. For example, Robert Bauval and Adrian Gilbert, in their *The Orion Mystery* (1994), also state that Anubis was connected with Sirius, giving as their source Robert Temple's *The Sirius Mystery*![23] No other source makes this claim for the simple reason that the ancient Egyptians themselves never made any such connection.

Temple's desire to incorporate all things doggy into his argument extends to his claim that the Great Sphinx of Giza was not intended to represent a lion, but a recumbent dog – Anubis once more.[24] That indisputably canine god is indeed frequently depicted lying down, but the ancient Egyptians were very specific and conservative about their iconography, and took pains always to represent them in a strictly standard way. One of the main features of representations of Anubis was his long, bushy tail, resembling a fox's brush. Try as we might, we cannot distinguish the Sphinx's tail as anything other than that of a lion.

Temple makes one particular assertion that we are surprised has gone unchallenged for many years. He brings into his argument certain connections with the Greek god Hermes and sections of the Hermetic literature, the highly prized books of arcane wisdom that emerged from Greek-dominated Egypt in the late centuries BCE or the first centuries CE. Temple's justification for making connections with the Hermetica is the supposed 'fact' – repeated several times in his book – that Hermes was the Greek equivalent of Anubis.[25] This is completely wrong. Hermes was unequivocally identified with Thoth, the ibis-headed ancient Egyptian god of wisdom and learning.[26] And to make a connection with Sumerian mythology, Temple states that 'Anubis was not entirely a jackal or dog, he was merely jackal or dog-*headed*'[27] (having apparently forgotten the connection he had made between Anubis and the Sphinx!). Again, this is simply inaccurate. Anubis was often depicted as a complete dog, lying down with a watchful expression, most famously as found in Tutankhamun's tomb.

Such mistakes and flawed logic, of which there are many examples in *The Sirius Mystery*, seriously weaken Temple's overall thesis that the true nature of the Sirius system was known to the ancient Egyptians and somehow transmitted to the ancestors of the Dogon. Temple argues that the 'secret knowledge' of Sirius B and of contact with its inhabitants reached the Dogon through the Garamantes, a North African people who were in contact with the Greek-speaking world and passed on the Sirius secret, having themselves learned it from the Egyptians, when they migrated through the area that is now occupied by the Dogon in the 11th century CE.[28] However, anthropologists consider it likely that the Dogon did not arrive in their new homeland until the fourteenth or fifteenth centuries CE, coming from further to the south-west, across the Niger.[29]

Temple makes another error, which in itself may appear to be minor and excusable, but which is of major importance to this investigation. He analyses the origins of the word 'ark', which he connects with the Egyptian *arq*, meaning 'end' or 'completion', and states that *arq ur* was the ancient Egyptian name for the Sphinx,[30] a meaning that has been taken up by many of those with another agenda. But *arq ur* does not mean 'Sphinx'. The idea that it does is a mistake, which originally came from Temple's misreading of Sir E.A. Wallis Budge's *An Egyptian Hieroglyphic Dictionary*. It is true that, against the entry for *arq ur*,[31] it says 'Sphinx, 2, 8', but this is not the definition of the word, but a reference to Budge's own source – a French Egyptological journal called *Sphinx: Revue critique embrassant le domaine entier de l'Egyptologie*. So 'Sphinx, 2, 8' really refers to page 8 of volume 2 of this publication. *Arq ur* actually means 'silver', and in any case, as Budge's source shows, the word entered into the Egyptian language very late, being borrowed from the Greek *argyros* (and not, as Temple claims, the other way round).[32] This slip, which seems so trivial, has serious repercussions for the beliefs of many thousands of people today.

One very curious aspect of Temple's *The Sirius Mystery* is that it attracted the attention of not only both the American and British security services, but also the Freemasons. In the 1998 edition, Temple describes how the Dogon mystery was first brought to his attention by his tutor and friend, the American philosopher Arthur M. Young, in 1965.[33] In 1968, when Temple decided that he wanted to study the mystery further, Young provided him with a privately made translation of Griaule and Dieterlen's *Le renard pâle*, their main work on the Dogon. Temple tells how this copy was stolen from him in London by someone whom he later learned worked for the CIA, presumably in an attempt to interfere with his research.[34] (Temple is an American, but he has lived in Britain since the late 1960s.)

This is puzzling. Why should the CIA have wanted to stop Temple researching the Dogon enigma? Or did they simply want to acquire a rare English translation of the French work because they somehow perceived the Sirius mystery to be a matter of national security? Surely the CIA are not short of reliable translators.

Even more baffling is the fact that Temple found himself the victim of a campaign of harassment by the CIA when *The Sirius Mystery* was published in 1976.[35] For example, they put pressure on a business associate of his to make him break up their partnership. Temple claims that this harassment continued for fifteen years. Why? If, like the theft of his copy of *Le renard pâle*, it was intended to prevent his researches, it was remarkably inept and unsuccessful; after all, it was far too late to harass him when the book was already being sold. Neither did the input of the CIA prevent him from reissuing the book – so what was the point? (This CIA harassment is all the more baffling because, as we will see in Chapter 5, Temple himself is a staunch defender of that organisation.) The plot thickens when it is realised that not only American intelligence agencies were taking an interest in the book. Temple discovered that one of the British security services had actually commissioned a report on it – and that MI5 had carried out security checks on him.[36]

Temple also relates how he was approached by a prominent American Freemason, Charles E. Webber – an old friend of his family (who have been high-ranking Freemasons for generations) – who asked him to become a Mason. According to Temple, Webber was not just any rank-and-file Freemason, however, but a 33rd degree Mason, the highest rank in the Ancient and Accepted Scottish Rite, the dominant form in the United States. And he wanted Temple to join specifically so that they could discuss his book as equals and without the risk of his revealing Masonic secrets to an outsider. Webber told him:

We are very interested in your book *The Sirius Mystery*. We realise you have written this without any knowledge of the traditions of Masonry, and you may not be aware of this, but you have made some discoveries which relate to the most central traditions at a high level, including some things that none of us ever knew.[37]

Why were the CIA, MI5 and the Freemasons so interested in Temple's *The Sirius Mystery*? Indeed, their interest by no means stopped there: these shadowy agencies lurked behind every corner as our investigation proceeded, and their role in an insidious but very powerful conspiracy was to become disturbingly clear.

The New Egyptology

Central to the New Orthodoxy of Egyptology is its redating of the Sphinx of Giza, that enigmatic stone hybrid that lies downhill from the three pyramids, in its own hollowed-out enclosure. It was originally carved out of an outcrop that protruded above the limestone bedrock, after which the builders dug out the enclosure to fashion the body.

Its ancient name was Sheshep-ankh Atum – 'Living Image of Atum', the creator god – it is thought that 'Sphinx' is a corruption of Sheshep-ankh.[38] Among its other names were Ra-Horakhti, from Horakhti meaning 'Horus of the Horizon' (Horus the hawk-headed god in his guise as the sun god Ra) and Hor-em-Akhet, 'Horus in the Horizon', rendered in Greek as Harmarchis.[39] There are many similar combinations of the god names of Horus and Atum, representing the ancient Egyptian concept of their gods as fluid, and dynamic, principles.

The standard theory about the Sphinx is that it was built by Khafra, who also constructed the Second Pyramid, and carved in his likeness. This is based on the supposed resemblance between the Sphinx's mutilated face and a statue of Khafra in the Cairo

Museum. However, analysis by forensic experts has confirmed what is obvious to anyone with eyes – namely that the two look nothing like each other.[40] In fact, the only evidence linking it to Khafra is the Sphinx Stela, an inscribed stone plaque set up between its paws. This describes how Thutmoses III (1479–1425 BCE), while sleeping beside the Sphinx when out on a hunting trip, had a dream that instructed him to clear the sand away from it. At the bottom of the stela, in hieroglyphs that have since flaked off completely, were the words: 'Khaf . . . the statue made for Atum-Harmakhis'. Egyptologists have read 'Khaf' as 'Khafra', and extrapolated that the sentence originally told how Khafra made the Sphinx. This is certainly wrong. From copies made of the stela it is known that the word was not enclosed in a cartouche,[41] the standard oval-shape that – as any student of hieroglyphs learns in their first lesson – always indicates the name of a king.

It has been suggested that the head of the Sphinx was originally that of a lion – which makes perfect sense – but was later recarved in the likeness of a reigning king or pharaoh. This theory is based on the fact that the present head is too small for the body, though it is worth noting that, for much of its history, the Sphinx was buried up to its neck in sand, so later Egyptians could have recarved the head without necessarily knowing that the likeness of a lion's body lay beneath. Significantly, the head and face of the Sphinx are noticeably less eroded than the body, even though it has been standing up to its neck in sand for a substantial number of years, suggesting that the head has been recarved in more recent times.

The erosion of the Sphinx triggered off a major controversy in recent years, leading to a number of new books that reached a massive international audience. Study of the erosion on the Sphinx's body and the sides of the Sphinx enclosure was initiated by maverick American researcher John Anthony West, based on observations originally made by R.A. Schwaller de Lubicz in the mid 20th century.

Usually described as a 'philosopher', Schwaller de Lubicz (1887–1961) was in fact an occult scholar who lived in Egypt between 1938 and 1952, studying the symbolism of the temples, particularly at Luxor. As a practising alchemist he was already steeped in Hermeticism and other esoteric lore and saw the same principles embodied in the temples of pharaonic Egypt. He was particularly interested in the numerology, mathematics and geometry of the temples, which he believed conformed to certain principles he already understood from his occult studies. He wrote a number of books about his interpretation of the Egyptian culture, the most comprehensive being his three-volume *Le temple de l'homme* (*The Temple of Man*), published in 1957. In particular he espoused a Pythagorean system in which the number nine was the most important, and this led to his fascination with the Great Ennead of the Heliopolitan religion. He believed that the Heliopolitan system was an expression in mythological terms of certain fundamental principles, and translated the Egyptian *neter*, meaning 'god', as 'principle'.[42] Schwaller de Lubicz often spoke of the 'Nine Principles', which develops greater significance as our investigation proceeds.

John Anthony West first discovered the works of Schwaller de Lubicz while working on his book *The Case for Astrology* (1970). After studying the works at length, West decided to write a more easily accessible account of Schwaller de Lubicz's theories, previously only available in rare, weighty French tomes. West's version was entitled *Serpent in the Sky* (1979).

West had noticed in Schwaller de Lubicz's book an observation that the heavy erosion on the body of the Sphinx was not caused by wind-blown sand, but by water. As he comments in *Serpent in the Sky*:

In principle, there can be no objection to the water erosion of the Sphinx, since it is agreed that in the past, Egypt suffered radical climatic changes and periodic inundations – by the sea and (in the not so remote past) by tremendous Nile floods. The latter are thought to correspond to the melting of the ice from the last ice age. Current thinking puts this date around 15,000 BC, but periodic great Nile floods are believed to have taken place subsequent to this date. The last of these floods is dated to around 10,000 BC.[43]

West realised that not only could this be tested, but also that it may have other, more momentous, implications. He wrote in 1979: 'In other words, it is now possible to prove "Atlantis", and simultaneously, the historical reality of the Biblical Flood.'[44] (Note that both Schwaller de Lubicz and West believed that a flood – or series of floods – had been responsible for the Sphinx's erosion.)

After trying for some time to find a geologist to analyse the erosion, West eventually attracted the interest of Dr Robert Schoch of Boston University. After analysing the pattern of erosion, Schoch concluded that it had indeed been created by water – rain water.[45] His work has since been confirmed by other geologists. When the BBC made a *Timewatch* television programme about the Sphinx in 1994, for example, they commissioned their own independent geologist to check Schoch's results, and he arrived at the same conclusion. In fact geologists generally have been happy to agree with Schoch. Egyptologists, on the other hand, refuse to be convinced, whatever the quality of the evidence. For example, Dr Zahi Hawass, then Director-General of the Giza Plateau, said: 'If geologists prove what Schoch is saying, still in my opinion, as an Egyptologist, the date of the Sphinx is still clear to us.'[46]

As climatologists can pinpoint fairly accurately periods of rainfall in the past, this would help to date – even to redate – the Sphinx. Schoch concluded, working back from the level of erosion, that the rock forming the body of the Sphinx and the enclosure wall had been exposed to the elements between 7000 and 5000 BCE. This, of course, makes the Sphinx considerably older than mainstream Egyptologists claim.

Schoch's work was taken by Graham Hancock and John Anthony West to support an even earlier date for the Sphinx. They say that Schoch, as an academic with a reputation to lose, was simply being conservative by assigning the Sphinx's erosion to the most recent wet period before the accepted dating of the

Sphinx.[47] In fact, Schoch had concluded that the erosion was *perfectly consistent* with the rainfall in that period, writing in 1995 that his analysis led him to the conclusion that 'the earliest portions of the statue date back to between 7,000 and 5,000 BC'.[48]

West believed that a flood had been responsible for the erosion of the Sphinx. Schoch had, in fact, proved him just as wrong as he had the orthodox Egyptologists. This did nothing to prevent Schoch's findings being transmuted into 'evidence' for .the Sphinx's far greater antiquity. As West says: 'You really have to go back before 10,000 BC to find a wet enough climate in Egypt to account for the weathering on this type and scale. It therefore follows that the Sphinx must have been built before 10,000 BC.'[49]

Schoch, however, disagrees, writing: 'I think that his [West's] estimation of the age of the Sphinx . . . is an exaggeration.'[50]

Graham Hancock, also picking up on Schoch's work, writes in *Fingerprints of the Gods*: 'Indeed, for two or three thousand years before and about a thousand years after 10,500 BC it rained and rained and rained.'[51] This assertion has become as enshrined as fact for the New Egyptology as much as Khafra building the Sphinx is fact for academic Egyptologists, which makes it all the more intriguing to discover that *there was no eleventh-millennium BCE wet period*. Significantly, Hancock gives no source and no evidence for his assertion, while on the other hand there is abundant evidence that there was no such wet period.[52] Dr Sarah O'Mara of Drylands Research at Sheffield University – the world authority on the climate of deserts, past and present – states that up to 8000 BCE: 'we have no evidence that any humans were living in this area [Egypt]. This was an area that was very dry, very cold. It was the time of the last Ice Age.'[53] That Ice Age, which had begun around 20,000 BCE, ended in 8000 BCE, ushering in a period that fluctuated between wetter and drier periods. And Michael Rice, in his book *Egypt's Making*, writes: 'It is probable that the Valley floor could not really have supported a substantial human civilization until about 10,000 years ago [i.e. around 8000 BCE].'[54]

The climate at the time of the Old Kingdom, when the

pyramids were built, was considerably wetter than it is today. In fact, as late as 2500 BCE, when the Great Pyramid was probably built, the annual rainfall in Egypt was the same as parts of England today.[55] Between 7000 and 5000 BCE, the climate of Egypt was very wet. Then, after 5000 BCE, the annual rainfall began to decline steadily until shortly after 2500 BCE, when the climate stabilised into its current pattern. The height of the Nile floods declined dramatically between 3100 and 2700 BCE, and this may have been the very reason for the emergence of Egyptian civilisation, as before that time the floods had been too high to sustain a large population on the Valley floor. As Michael Hoffman, the authority on pre-dynastic Egypt says: 'For a time between 7000 and 2500 BC the deserts bloomed.'[56]

It has also been suggested – by Robert Temple among others[57] – that the water erosion could have been caused by the Sphinx enclosure being filled with water up to the Sphinx's neck to make a sacred pool. However, Schoch was perfectly specific: the erosion results from running water – rain, not a static body of water.

Schoch's work demonstrates convincingly that the Sphinx really is older than mainstream Egyptologists claim, perhaps dating back as far as 7000 BCE. But even that seems to fall short for West and Hancock, who appear to want to push it back further – specifically to 10,500 BCE. This is certainly something of a date with destiny for those researchers, and one that they, and their colleagues, seem to us to be doing their utmost to make us believe in. But why?

As above, so below?

Another recent theory to catch the public imagination is that of Robert Bauval, who was born in Alexandria in Egypt of Belgian parents. He has been interested in ancient Egyptian culture – and specifically the pyramids – for most of his life.

In 1994 he and Adrian Gilbert produced *The Orion Mystery*.

Its main feature was Bauval's theory that the three pyramids of Giza were designed and built to represent the three stars of the Belt of Orion. The fact that the three structures mimic the position of the stars of Orion's Belt, once pointed out by Bauval and Gilbert, is indeed evident – but is that really what the builders intended? Those authors dedicate most of *The Orion Mystery* to establishing the case that it was.

The match between the pyramids and stars is not perfect, though. If the stars are superimposed on the ground plan of the pyramids, it can be seen immediately that the correlation is only approximate. If the two brightest stars are positioned over the Great Pyramid and Khafra's Pyramid, then the third star fails to align with the smallest, Menkaura's Pyramid. (In fact, the only time that all three pyramids line up perfectly with the stars is in graphics used in Hancock/Bauval television programmes.) Whether you accept the Orion/Giza correlation depends on the level of accuracy you expect from the pyramid builders.

When Bauval tries to make other pyramids fit his theory, he has even less success. For example, in *The Orion Mystery* he brings in the pyramids at Abu Roash, to the south of Giza, and Zawiyet-el-Aryan, to the north (neither, incidentally, were ever completed). He maintains that they correspond with other stars in Orion.[58] However, they do not match up very persuasively. This is not, admittedly, a major problem. We cannot be certain that the architects of this grand design intended to map out the whole of Orion on the ground, or even that they recognised the constellation in the way we do today; it may have been just the three stars of the Belt that they mirrored at Giza.

Apparent confirmation of Bauval's theory of the Giza/Orion's Belt correlation comes from the alignments of the four small shafts running from the two main chambers – the so-called King's and Queen's Chambers – within the Great Pyramid, two from each, one to the north and one to the south in each case. These shafts run straight into the walls, before angling upwards through the main body of the pyramid. They are very small, only a little more than 8 inches (20 cm) square. Those in the King's

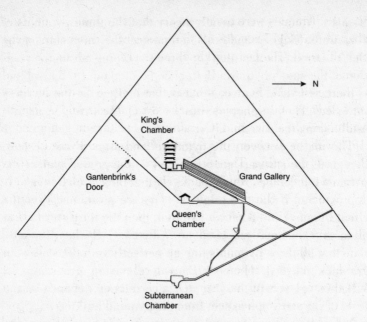

King's
Chamber

Gantenbrink's
Door

Grand Gallery

Queen's
Chamber

Subterranean
Chamber

N

A cross-section of the Great Pyramid showing the main passages and features.

Chamber (the upper one) run diagonally up through the massive blocks of stone, right through the walls to the outside, which has given rise to their official designation as air shafts. Those running from the Queen's Chamber are rather stranger, since they neither exit into the open air on the outside, nor open into the chamber itself. They were discovered behind the walls of the chamber in 1872.

It has been recognised since the early 1960s that these shafts may have been designed to point towards certain stars significant to the ancient Egyptians.[59] The shaft going north from the King's Chamber, for example, appears to have been 'targeted' on the star Thuban, in the constellation of Draconis, the northern pole star in the Pyramid Age. It has also been suggested that the southern shaft that runs from the King's Chamber was targeted on the stars of Orion's Belt. If so, this would add support to the idea that the pyramids were built to represent them. Bauval calculated that, around 2475 BCE, the southern King's Chamber shaft would have aligned with the lowest and brightest star of Orion's Belt, Al Nitak.[60]

In recent years huge controversy has centred on discoveries – and rumours of discoveries – on the Giza plateau, and especially within the Great Pyramid. Certainly the excitement generated in 1993 with the discovery of a tiny door in the Great Pyramid shows no signs of abating. The Internet rumour machine is still very busy spinning tales, which may or may not be founded in fact. In March 1993 a German engineer, Rudolf Gantenbrink, sent a robot fitted with a video camera from the Queen's Chamber into both shafts. Then, now famously, the robot – called Upuaut 2 (after the ancient Egyptian god who was 'Opener of the Way') – encountered what appeared to be a very small door blocking the shaft, complete with handles and an intriguing gap beneath. A door of any size implies that something lies behind it. What could it be? Imaginations have been fevered ever since, but the general consensus is that some kind of chamber lies behind 'Gantenbrink's Door'. At the time of writing – nearly six years after Gantenbrink's discovery – we are still waiting to find out where that door leads.

Gantenbrink's data had another use: it was seized upon by Robert Bauval, who saw it as a vindication of his theory, developed in the late 1980s, that the southern shaft from the Queen's Chamber was designed to align with Sirius. From the angle of the shaft he could now calculate where it had been pointing when the pyramid was built. From these new alignments, Bauval estimated that it had been constructed around 2450 BCE.[61] Ironically, this would make it about a century younger than mainstream Egyptologists think, erring in the wrong direction for the New Orthodoxy. (Recent carbon dating results tend to indicate that the Great Pyramid is even older, perhaps by as much as four centuries.[62]) Bauval was so enthusiastic about Gantenbrink's discovery that he took it upon himself to make the announcement to the world's media in early April 1993.[63]

However, some of Bauval's assumptions are open to question. For example, he presents a very circular argument that uses the stellar alignments of the shafts to prove the date of the Great Pyramid, but also relies on this date to prove that the shafts have stellar alignments. There is also an anomaly concerning the dates indicated by the two shafts: the Queen's Chamber shaft would (according to Bauval's calculations) have been perfectly aligned with Sirius around 2400 BCE, whereas the higher King's Chamber shaft was perfectly aligned with Al Nitak some seventy-five years earlier. It was therefore impossible for both shafts to have been pointing to 'their' stars at the same time. But then perhaps we – and Robert Bauval – are expecting the ancient Egyptians to have been overprecise. After all, seventy-five years would have meant a mere fraction of a degree difference in alignment. All in all, Bauval's ideas are certainly bold and challenging, though we have serious reservations about their wider implications.

Bauval's theory has become one of the standard lines of the New Egyptology. Rarely is it questioned among readers or researchers in this field. However, one outspoken critic is none other than Rudolf Gantenbrink himself, who attacks Bauval for using his data to support his theory of alignments with Sirius, a theory that, in any case, Gantenbrink rejects. In August 1998 he told us:

His theories are pure nonsense, and they are largely disproved. He uses the wrong data for the angle of the shafts . . . and the astronomical data are even more hazardous. There is no solid academic base for his theories whatsoever.[64]

Gantenbrink points out that the concept that the shafts were intended to align with any star depends on them being straight, but they only appear to be so when the Great Pyramid is shown in a north–south cross-section. In fact, all the shafts have bends from left to right – that is, from east to west. In the case of the two shafts running from the King's Chamber, neither end (in the chamber and outside) is in line with the other. (The shafts from the Queen's Chamber do not reach the exterior of the pyramid.)

Bauval's theory requires the shafts to be as straight as rulers, directed at a specific point in the sky. If, as is the case, the shafts have kinks in them, it seems unlikely that they would have been intended to point at any particular heavenly body. As Gantenbrink told us: 'So any star alignment . . . could only work on the side view, but never in three-dimensional reality.' Gantenbrink's somewhat dramatic conclusion based on his review of the flaws in Bauval's data is that 'The star alignment is simply a HOAX!'

Bauval's announcement to the world's media of the discovery of the door also attracts comment from Gantenbrink. Certainly, Bauval completely sidestepped the usual protocol. The news should never have been released without the permission of the people for whom Gantenbrink was working at the time, the German Archaeological Institute in Cairo and the Egyptian Supreme Council of Antiquities. Bauval gives as his reason for such unilateral action his great frustration with the dilatoriness of the Egyptian and German authorities in announcing the discovery. In his view, they were dragging their feet, and he felt that people should know – yet his first approach to the media was just fourteen days after Gantenbrink made his discovery! What was the real reason for Bauval's haste in making the announcement to the world?

Gantenbrink has no doubts about Bauval's motivation. He told us: 'This was a clever PR campaign. Without my discovery, we simply would not know a guy called Robert Bauval.' Gantenbrink goes further: he even blames Bauval's premature and unauthorised release of his news to the press for the Egyptian authorities' refusal to allow him to continue his work in the Great Pyramid.

We had been intrigued to discover that the idea that the southern shaft from the Queen's Chamber aligned with Sirius appeared in Masonic literature dating from at least the late nineteenth century.[65] At the time we were impressed. Was Bauval's work confirmation that Freemasons have long possessed secret information about the pyramids? We put the idea that Bauval's work would demonstrate this unexpected knowledge to Gantenbrink, who responded: 'It would, but it doesn't! It only indicates where Bauval got his idea from.'

The alleged alignments are only part of Bauval's attempt to link his theory with a much more remote period of Egypt's history. Bauval accepts that the Giza pyramids were built around 2450 BCE, more or less the time proposed by Egyptologists (who in fact say they are a century older). But he notes that the three pyramids were not a perfect match for the stars at that time: the pyramids are oriented at 45 degrees to a north–south meridian running through Giza, so for the three stars of Orion's Belt to properly match the groundplan of Giza they should also be positioned at an angle of 45 degrees to the celestial meridian.[66] This crossing of the celestial meridian occurs when the stars are exactly due south – when they are at their highest point in the sky ('culminating' in astronomical terminology). But Bauval noted that Orion's Belt was not aligned at 45 degrees to the celestial meridian at the time that he believes the pyramids were built.

However, because of the precession of the equinoxes the constellations change in orientation over the course of centuries. Bauval, assuming that the builders deliberately mismatched the pyramids with the stars, decided to find out when they actually did align. He concluded that:

> It is not until 10,500 BC . . . – 8000 years *before* the 'Pyramid Age' – that the perfect correlation is finally achieved with the Nile mirroring the Milky Way and with the three Pyramids and the belt stars identically disposed in relation to the meridian.[67]

He therefore hypothesised that either the groundplan of the pyramids had been laid out at that time – even if they were not actually constructed for another 8000 years – or that the builders were trying to tell us something about the epoch of 10,500 BCE.

There are problems with this. Even Robin J. Cook, who worked with Bauval and provided the diagrams for *The Orion Mystery*, takes issue with his conclusions. In his *The Horizon of Khufu* (1996), Cook examined the same question and stated emphatically: '. . . this was not the case in 10,450 BC.'[68] In fact, Cook found a correlation that did fit Orion's Belt in the 'Giza position' in 2450 BCE.[69] Cook disagrees that the Giza complex was intended to pinpoint the year 10,500 BCE, and it must be said unequivocally that his evidence is much more persuasive than Bauval's. But even so, do we have to take Cook's word for this? Unfortunately for Bauval's tidy theory, this is very easy to double-check – when we did so, we discovered that Cook is right. Using the same astronomical computer simulation as Bauval – SkyGlobe 3.6 – we discovered that the stars of Orion's Belt were emphatically not in the 'Giza' position at the spring equinox in 10,500 BCE (nor at any other time when it culminated in that epoch).[70] In fact, it is very easy to tell when Orion's Belt is at a 45 degree angle to the meridian, as at this moment Saiph – the 'left leg' star of Orion – is directly below Al Nitak, the most easterly (left) of the three stars of Orion's Belt.[71] In fact, for it to culminate in the 'Giza position' you have to go back to about 12,000 BCE – and even then, it does not culminate at the significant moment of dawn on the spring equinox.

Does this mean that Bauval merely slipped up in his calculations by 1,500 or so years? Anyone can make a mistake. And does this just mean that Bauval's putative advanced civilisation laid out the pyramids in 12,000 BCE rather than 10,500 BCE? Tempting though it is to ascribe this 'slip' to human error, there is in fact much more at stake here. Once again – as with Hancock's non-existent eleventh-millennium BCE 'wet period' – we find a high-profile New Egyptologist desperately trying to prove that 10,500 BCE was in some way highly significant, even when the facts indicate otherwise.

While we appear to have two – apparently persuasive – independent lines of evidence, both astronomical and geological, converging on the date 10,500 BCE, both can easily be seen to be based on a distortion of the facts. Bauval reveals his enthusiastic

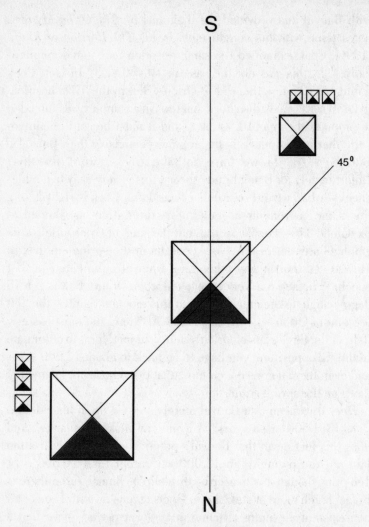

A ground plan of the Giza pyramids. They lie at approximately 45 degrees to the north–south meridian.

Opposite: Above – *The culmination of the constellation of Orion in 10,500 BCE. Note that the stars of Orion's Belt are not in the 'Giza position'. Below – Orion as it should appear in the 'Giza position'. This has not happened since approximately 12,000 BCE.*

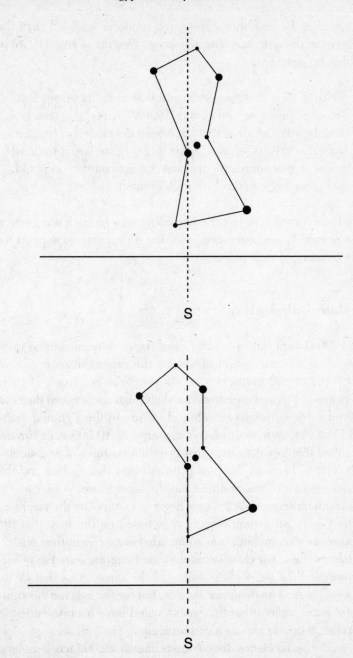

S

S

belief that the two lines of research reinforce each other in the
television documentary *The Mysterious Origins of Man* (1996) in
which he states:

> We're finding that the astronomy is leading us to conclude
> that the Sphinx was erected in 10,500 BC, and this matches
> exactly with the ideas that have been developed in the geo-
> logical analysis of the Sphinx. So there are two hard
> sciences now indicating that the Sphinx could be very old,
> and going back to the 11th millennium BC.

We have seen that in fact the astronomy does no such thing where
the pyramids are concerned, and that it provides no support for
the redating of the Sphinx.

A date with destiny

In 1996 Robert Bauval and Graham Hancock teamed up to write
Keeper of Genesis, which develops the argument in favour of
10,500 BCE and elaborates on its significance. Much of their
hypothesis is based on astronomical correlations between the Giza
complex, descriptions of celestial events in the Pyramid Texts
and the sky as it would have appeared in 10,500 BCE. Having
reached that key date from just two dubious lines of argument –
the 'match' between the Giza pyramids and Orion's Belt and the
water erosion of the Sphinx from the alleged wet period of the
eleventh millennium BCE – they begin to extrapolate the meaning.

A key point of their argument is based on the idea that the
Sphinx as a recumbent lion is intended to represent the constellation of Leo, which also implies that the ancient Egyptians
recognised the signs of the zodiac in the same terms that we do
today. There is no evidence for this, but for the sake of the argument let us accept that the Sphinx could have been intended to
represent Leo. It carries a certain logic.

As the Sphinx faces directly east, Bauval and Hancock assume that it was intended to look towards its heavenly counterpart on the day that it rose with the sun exactly east, which only happened on the two annual equinoxes, at spring and autumn. Traditional astrology counts the spring equinox as the more important of the two. The astronomical Ages – of Pisces, Aquarius, and so on – are defined by the section of the sky (or astrological house) identified with the constellation against which the sun rises on the spring equinox at a given period. Because of the precession of the equinoxes, this constellation changes about every 2,160 years. For most of the last 2,000 years the sun has risen in Pisces, so we are said to be in the Age of Pisces. Next will come the Age of Aquarius. In 10,500 BCE the world was in the Age of Leo, which is why Hancock and Bauval believe the Sphinx was carved in the shape of a lion.

Such steps in their argument are only assumptions, which may or may not be valid. None constitutes proof, and there is no independent evidence to support any of them. We can accept each of them individually 'for the sake of argument', but remain cautious about any conclusions drawn from them, since we can by no means be sure of the basic premise.

Hancock and Bauval argue that 10,500 BCE represents the fabled First Time (*tep zepi*) when the ancient Egyptians believe their civilisation began. On the Sphinx Stela the Sphinx of Giza is described as, among other things, 'presider over . . . the splendid place of the First Time',[72] showing that Giza was associated in some way with *tep zepi*. Bauval and Hancock bolster their argument with computer simulations of the sky as it appeared in 10,500 BCE, finding other significant correlations that happened in or around that year. In fact several of these correlations actually happened not at one moment but on a whole range of dates, often several centuries on either side of 10,500 BCE. So why are they still homing in on that particular point in time?

Bauval and Hancock's method was to find significant correlations between the stars and constellations in which they are interested – Orion, Leo, Sirius and the Sun – and to use them as added proof that the Giza complex was laid out specifically to 'encode' the importance of the year 10,500 BCE. But again, this is circular reasoning: they are only looking for correlations that happened in that year. Their logic for choosing that year in the first place is manifestly wrong.

To demonstrate this, we used SkyGlobe 3.6, the same computer sky map program they used, to find correlations in the year 8700 BCE that, by Bauval and Hancock's reasoning, could be just as significant. For example, on the spring equinox of that year the sun rises at exactly the same moment as Regulus, the brightest star in Leo, which Bauval and Hancock call its 'heart'. The sun, in fact, covers Regulus at the moment of sunrise. And, at exactly the same moment in the south, Orion's Belt is in the 'Giza position' (as given by Robin J. Cook). If that had happened in 10,500 BCE, it could have been used as evidence that the year was especially significant.

It is curious that Hancock and Bauval should construct such a complicated (and contrived) argument to explain the astronomical significance of the Sphinx and its relationship with Leo, since there is a much simpler explanation – one that was originally suggested by none other than R.A. Schwaller de Lubicz.

He pointed out that, throughout most of Egypt's early history, on the day of the first heliacal rising of Sirius – their New Year's Day, the most sacred day of their calendar – the sun rose in Leo.[73] Checking Schwaller de Lubicz's idea using SkyGlobe, we found it to be correct. Between about 6000 BCE and 2500 BCE the sun did rise in Leo on the day of Sirius's first heliacal rising. Therefore, if the Sphinx was intended to represent Leo, and was made to look eastwards towards the dawn and its heavenly counterpart, this would provide a much more logical – and considerably less convoluted – reason for its construction than the idea that its purpose was to pinpoint the year 10,500 BCE. This explanation also has the advantage of fitting Robert Schoch's water erosion theory, which dates the Sphinx to between 7000 and 5000 BCE.

There is a major puzzle here. It was Schwaller de Lubicz – that great hero of Hancock, Bauval and West – who made these observations, so clearly they must know about them. Yet none of these authors so much as mentions this alternative explanation, clearly preferring to promote their own 10,500 BCE agenda.

The crucial point of *Keeper of Genesis*, however, was the 'discovery' of the existence of a secret chamber beneath the hindquarters of the Sphinx, as 'revealed' by astronomical correlations.[74] Although meant to be the great revelation of the book, this is in fact its weakest point. At the spring equinox in 10,500 BCE, Leo rose directly east of the Sphinx, and therefore lay immediately under its gaze. At this moment the sun lies below the horizon, 12 degrees below Leo's hind quarters. Bauval and Hancock assume that this is what the ancient Egyptians were trying to draw our attention to. Their so-called 'Genesis Chamber' can be found in an analogous position, a hundred feet under the Sphinx. What secrets would it hold!

Even if their arguments about the importance of 10,500 BCE were correct – and we have already seen that they lack firm foundations – why do they assume that this is connected with some coded message, sent across time to reveal the location of a completely hypothetical chamber? (On a more logical basis one could argue that the Sphinx might be *looking* at something of great significance. Follow its gaze today, however, and you find a Pizza Hut/Kentucky Fried Chicken outlet.)

There have been many criticisms of Bauval and Hancock's astronomical hypothesis. During a 1998 lecture cruise around the coast of Alaska, Hancock found himself in the unusual position of being criticised by a fellow speaker, the leading archaeo-astronomer Dr E.C. Krupp of the Griffith Observatory in California. He pointed out the flaws in the central argument of *Keeper of Genesis*, specifically that the Sphinx should be on the other side of the Nile for their claimed identification of Horakhti (another name for the Sphinx) with the constellation of Leo to work. Afterwards, Krupp reported his frustration that Hancock countered such challenges by evoking 'artistic licence' on the part of the ancient builders.[75]

Hancock's major hypothesis is that there was an advanced

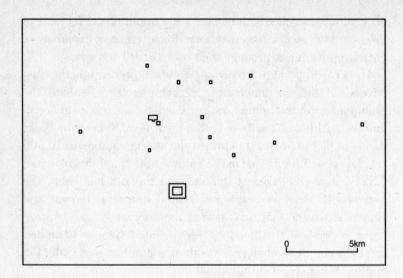

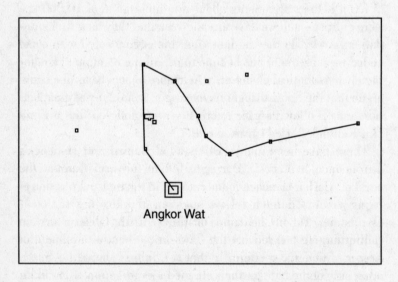

Angkor Wat

Above: Top – *A ground plan of the temples of Angkor.*
Below – *The correlation between the constellation of Draco
and Angkor, according to Graham Hancock.*

Opposite: *The closest match possible between Draco and Angkor.*

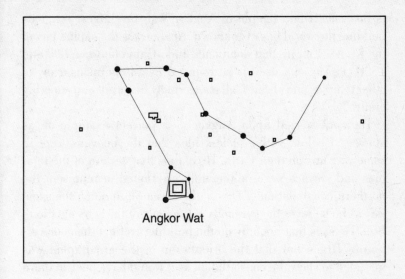

Angkor Wat

civilisation before the last Ice Age, which came to an end around 10,500 BCE as the result of some global cataclysm that brought about the melting of the ice and the rising of sea levels. He claims that knowledge from that civilisation survived, filtering through to later cultures and resulting, for example, in the building of the pyramids some 8,000 years afterwards.

Hancock has continued to expound this theory and the alleged significance of 10,500 BCE in his book (co-written with his wife, Santha Faiia) *Heaven's Mirror* (1998) and the Channel 4/Discovery Channel television series *Quest for the Lost Civilization*. In both, he demonstrates the ubiquity of the significance of the date throughout the ancient world by examining the most colourful and mysterious sites in Europe, Central and South America, Egypt and the Far East. At all of these places he finds astronomical alignments that fit his theory, although when we double-checked they appeared to us to be highly contrived, very debatable – or often simply wrong.

A prime example of this questionable theorising concerns the magnificent Cambodian city of Angkor, the centrepiece of which is the vast Hindu temple of Angkor Wat, the largest religious building the world has ever known. Angkor was the capital city of the Khmer Empire that dominated Indo-China between 800 and 1500 CE. The city itself is surrounded by an enormous array of other temples and shrines, all staggeringly beautiful and superbly crafted.

Hancock seized upon Angkor as a perfect example of 'as above, so below' – the ancient idea that the heavens were in some way mirrored on Earth. He claims that certain of the temples and shrines were deliberately positioned to represent the northern constellation of Draco (the Dragon), in much the same way as he believes the pyramids at Giza mirror the stars of Orion's Belt. He says that not only do the buildings reflect the composition of Draco but that the orientation of the groundplan was intended to show the constellation as it would have been at dawn on the spring equinox in – not too surprisingly – 10,500 BCE.[76]

A pause for thought reveals that Hancock's Angkor scenario is surely the least credible of all of his examples supporting the 10,500 BCE theory. For a start, Angkor was a brand new city, created by the Khmers after their rise to power in the ninth century CE. Most of its temples date from after the year 1000 CE; Angkor Wat, for example, was built as late as the twelfth century. Hancock has claimed that the pyramids had been laid out according to a grand design that had been created 8000 years before. This stretches credulity to breaking point. Surely even the most robust mystery school tradition, in which secret plans were handed down to initiates from generation to generation, would have had major problems in keeping such an agenda alive over such a huge number of years. Now we are asked to believe that the same master plan was put into effect at Angkor, 3,500 years after the pyramids were built and 11,500 years after the plan was first created.

The so-called alignment between Angkor and Draco does not in fact exist. Hancock has been very selective, taking only certain of the temples to use in his groundplan and leaving all those that fail to fit his scheme out of the picture entirely – but even so the resulting shape only roughly corresponds to Draco. Individual temples and individual stars simply do not match up, yet Hancock is claiming that the builders somehow created precise matches between them.

The ease with which, in our view, Hancock's theories can be discredited does a great disservice to the very subject that he is ostensibly trying to promote: serious debate about the undoubtedly real mysteries of mankind's ancient past. In the very act of dismissing them there is a danger of throwing out the baby with the bath water, of rejecting any daring new hypothesis about our past, and of condemning the original evidence – the anomalies that intrigued Hancock in the first place. It would be a terrible shame to let dubious theorising bring the whole field into disrepute: there are real mysteries and challenges to the accepted historical paradigm. Academia does not have all the answers.

The work of both Bauval and Hancock is riddled with subjectivity, with an insistence on the importance of the year 10,500 BCE, although almost all of the arguments in its favour simply cannot be supported. Despite the flaws in their arguments, they appear to be convinced that something of great historic significance happened then, something that has a relevance to us today.

Selling Cayce

A clue may lie in the prophecies of America's 'Sleeping Prophet', the psychic Edgar Cayce (1877–1945). Both Bauval and Hancock make apparently casual allusions to him without actually endorsing his psychic information.

According to the standard story – which, as we will see, only approximates to the whole truth – Cayce was an ordinary, God-fearing Kentucky-born citizen who wanted to be a minister but failed to show the required aptitude for book learning. He became a stationery salesman, but his public reputation grew from his talent for falling into trances – 'sleeping' – and while in that altered state, diagnosing illnesses and advising on treatment.

This later expanded into him giving 'life readings', either for individuals or to a circle of followers, in which he predicted the future and gave information about the past. Interestingly, while in normal consciousness his views were those of a mainstream Christian, but while entranced he frequently told of past lives – reincarnation – and claimed to have once been a high-ranking priest of ancient Egypt himself, one Ra Ta.

According to Cayce, the civilisation of Atlantis flourished for some 200,000 years, and finally came to an end around 10,500 BCE. He claimed that some of the survivors travelled to Egypt, where they built the Sphinx and the Great Pyramid between 10,490 and 10,390 BCE. This was also linked to an exodus from the Caucasian Mountains to Egypt, led by Cayce's previous incarnation Ra Ta, displacing the original, yellow-skinned natives of that country. The Atlanteans arrived in Egypt shortly afterwards.[77]

Cayce's influence on the New Egyptologists extends well beyond sketchy details of a putative past life. He was responsible for the introduction of the single most emotive theme to run through many of the most recent high-profile books about Egypt: the idea of the Hall of Records, a hidden chamber somewhere in Egypt, containing ancient records of mankind, perhaps including the secrets of Atlantis. According to Cayce the refugee Atlanteans arrived in Egypt after the sinking of the island in 10,700 BCE, bringing with them the records of their civilisation. In 10,500 BCE these were deposited in the 'Hall of Records', also called the 'Pyramid of Records' – an underground pyramid. These contain 'the records of the people of One God from the beginning of man's entrance into the earth'.[78] The Hall of Records, enclosed in its underground pyramid, lies between the Sphinx and the Nile, connected by a passage running from the right forepaw of the Sphinx – according to Cayce.

In our present *fin de siècle* era, a rising Hall of Records hysteria is carefully being whipped up by books, videos and the instant whispering machine of the Internet. Where is this fabled place located? What does it contain? Who will find it – and what will happen when they do? Already this has become, in every possible sense, the modern quest for the Holy Grail: the ancient, elusive object of the heart's desire is somewhere waiting to be found by the select few, like the mythical Grail knights, who will suffer and fight in order to find it and unlock its secrets. Some will no doubt die in the attempt, but the Chosen will eventually win through, and when the Grail Hall is uncovered, somehow magically the whole of our civilisation will be transformed. We shall understand our past and even our future. We shall suddenly see humankind for what it is, and know the truth about the gods. Oh how we shall be glad, and be grateful to the Grail Hall knights who bring these secrets to us! And because they are chosen, and we are not, we shall see them in the new light of the gods themselves.

The basis of this comes from Cayce. He linked the finding of the Hall of Records to the triggering of global changes: 'After the end of the cycle [in 1998], there is to be another change in the earth's position, with the return of the Great Initiate for the culmination of the prophecies.'[79] He also said that 1998 marks the beginning of the 'time of preparation for the coming of the Master of the World'.[80] Many have associated this statement with the Second Coming of Jesus, although perhaps it is strange that Cayce, of all people, did not explicitly do so himself. In fact, he also believed it referred to the emergence of a new race of human beings.[81] According to the Sleeping Prophet the end result will be:

> With the changes that will be wrought, true Americanism, the universal thought that is expressed and manifested in the brotherhood of man, as in the Masonic order, will be the eventual rule in the settlement of affairs in the world.[82]

Cayce may have been right, and any person who bravely throws himself behind the prophecies may have the right idea. Certainly, neither of us has any objection in principle to the idea of accurate psychic prediction or the miraculous, nor to the idea that information from our very remote past may impinge in some real and even apocalyptic way on our own times. If Cayce was right then all eyes should be turned to the various expeditions that, overtly and covertly, are now seeking to locate the Hall of Records. But that depends on whether Cayce was right . . .

Of all his 'readings', collected from 1909 onwards, 14,249 have been preserved for posterity, but despite claims by his followers that his predictions are almost entirely accurate – 'close to one hundred per cent'[83] – it is actually hard to find one that is! Edgar Cayce must have one of the most dismal track records of any alleged prophet.

For example, in February 1932 he was asked to give predictions of the most significant events over the next fifty years. Cayce predicted the 'breaking up of many powers' in 1936.[84] When asked to be more specific about which powers, he named Russia, the United States, Japan and the United Kingdom. Astonishingly, Cayce's supporters regard this as a success, claiming that it accurately foretells the beginning of the events that would lead to the Second World War. In *Edgar Cayce on Prophecy*, produced by the Association for Research and Enlightenment (ARE), the organisation of Cayce followers, Mary Ellen Carter points out that the following events happened in 1936: the abdication crisis in Britain; the start of the Spanish Civil War; the first of Stalin's great purges in Russia; and the formation of the German–Italian fascist alliance.[85] Only two of these events happened in countries singled out by Cayce, and it is certainly debatable whether the British abdication crisis constitutes 'the breaking up' of the nation. The most significant events concerning the imminent global conflict were those in Spain and the German–Italian alliance – but Cayce had mentioned none of these countries. Even then, none of this constitutes a great 'breaking up of powers' in 1936. And what happened to the Second World War? Cayce simply did not predict the coming global conflict.

If 'readings' highlighted by the followers of Edgar Cayce for their amazing accuracy look doubtful when placed under scrutiny, on other occasions, he could be even vaguer. When asked in 1932 about the outcome of Gandhi's campaign for Indian independence, he replied that it 'depends on individuals'.[86] And during the Second World War, someone asked him 'What is

Hitler's destiny?' to which the great prophet answered 'Death!'[87] At least here he had every chance of being 'close to one hundred per cent' accurate. But astonishingly, it was regarded as another of his successes. In 1943, Cayce predicted that within twenty-five years – i.e. by 1968 – China would not only become more democratic, but also Christian. Astoundingly, this was published in an ARE book in 1968, which implicitly argues that what Cayce really meant was that China would be purged by Maoism and civil war so that democracy and Christianity would be able to take root.[88] Perhaps it is time to cross that prophecy off the list as well.

Another much-vaunted prediction concerns the re-emergence of the sunken Atlantis. On 28 June 1940, Cayce made one of his most famous pronouncements: 'Poseidia [one of his terms for Atlantis] to rise again. Expect it in '68 or '69. Not so far away!'[89] This prediction, it was claimed, was fulfilled when an enigmatic roadlike stone feature, which could have been manmade, was discovered under the water off the coast of Bimini Island in the Bahamas in 1969. Had the discovery of the 'Bimini Road' made Cayce's prediction come true? Perhaps. But according to Andrew Collins and Simon Cox, several of the key figures who discovered the Bimini Road were hardly disinterested, as they were members of ARE, specifically looking for some form of confirmation of Cayce's readings about Atlantis and the Bahamas.[90] Moreover, the Bimini Islanders had known about the road for years and had actually offered to show it to the 'discoverers'. In any case, the discovery of some – admittedly tantalising – anomalous features off the Bimini coast hardly constitutes the 'rising' of Atlantis.

Cayce also predicted that the secret of how the Great Pyramid was built would be revealed – in 1958.[91] If it was disclosed, it must be the best-kept secret of all time. Most of us are still waiting.

Over the centuries many prophecies from people of all beliefs and walks of life have come true. To receive due honour and recognition prophets need evidence of some accuracy. Where Cayce was concerned, apart from some impressive medical 'readings', this evidence is sadly lacking. The fact that someone is highly successful with one psychic skill does not automatically mean that they have an equal talent in other psychic areas.

In 1931 Edgar Cayce founded the Association for Research and Enlightenment (ARE) to promote his life's work, with its headquarters at Virginia Beach, Virginia. This remained a fairly small and underfunded organisation until well after his death in 1945. In the early 1970s there seems to have been a sudden influx of wealthy members. ARE is now a rich and powerful body, which has funded archaeological work in Egypt and elsewhere to try to substantiate Cayce's claims. In fact, ARE has had a major role in shaping modern Egyptology of both mainstream and new varieties. We have seen how Cayce's insistence on the significance of 10,500 BCE has crept into major works of the New Orthodoxy camp, and their highly flawed evidence for this is now trotted out as fact by most other writers of the genre. But Cayce and ARE also stand behind at least two major figures from the – apparently – opposite camp.

Mark Lehner – who built the mini pyramid for *Secrets of Lost Empires* – is the most prominent American Egyptologist stationed in Egypt today. He is highly respected internationally. His 1997 book *The Complete Pyramids* was hailed as a masterly overview of an only too often thorny subject, and was promoted by many major museums, including the British Museum. It is less well known that in 1974 he wrote a book for ARE entitled *The Egyptian Heritage, based on the Edgar Cayce Readings*, which attempted to reconcile Cayce's pronouncements with the findings of modern Egyptology. According to Lehner in his early days, the Great Pyramid was built as a repository of knowledge, and a 'Temple of Initiation for the White Brotherhood'.[92]

In 1973 Edgar Cayce's son, Hugh Lynn Cayce, selected the promising young student Lehner to be ARE's 'insider' within the ranks of academic Egyptology, and it was ARE that paid for his training.[93] They also funded his recent carbon-dating tests of material taken from the Great Pyramid[94] (which seems to indicate that it is about 300 or 400 years older than was thought – but not the 8,000 hoped for by ARE). Today he no longer advocates Cayceism, and appears not to espouse any 'alternative' views, now being very much a mainstream Egyptologist. Perhaps it was as a sly dig at his own past associations with ARE that he recently criticised what he calls 'New Age archaeology, inspired by revealed information'.[95]

But Mark Lehner is not the only person on the Giza Plateau to have reason to be grateful to ARE. Amazingly, that arch-enemy of all pyramidiots, Dr Zahi Hawass – who since 1987 has been in the powerful position of Director of the Giza Plateau and who was recently promoted to Undersecretary of State for the Giza Monuments – was also put through his training as an Egyptologist by ARE. Through fellow ARE members, Hugh Lynn Cayce arranged a scholarship for Hawass at the University of Pennsylvania between 1980 and 1987, where he gained his Ph.D. in Egyptology.[96] Hawass has maintained his association with ARE ever since, and is a regular lecturer at their conferences at their Virginia Beach headquarters.

It is, to say the least, interesting that the two most prominent and influential representatives of Egyptological orthodoxy at Giza are linked to Edgar Cayce's organisation.

First and last times

Robert Bauval and Graham Hancock seem to be particularly keen for us to believe that there was something special about the year 10,500 BCE, perhaps because of the prophecies of Edgar Cayce. Cayce also predicted major events for the future, especially beginning in 1998. Bauval and Hancock also attach great importance to the year 2000 – although, once again, their reasons for doing so appear, on the evidence, to be distinctly questionable.

Like many others, those authors believe that the year 2000 will mark the end of the Age of Pisces and the beginning of the Age of Aquarius, with corresponding influences over world events. The dominant religion of the current Age of Pisces – represented by two fish – has been Christianity, which has a fish as one of its symbols. Back in the Age of Taurus, we are told, bull cults – such as that of Apis in Egypt – were in the ascendant, as was the worship of ram gods during the Age of Aries.

This is a very Western-centred viewpoint. Christianity has dominated Europe for most of the Age of Pisces, but it can hardly be said to have ruled the world for much of that time. It did not reach the Americas, for instance, until the sixteenth century, nor did Christian missionaries start spreading the word in Asia until much before the seventeenth century, and its expansion in Africa came even later. On the other hand, although this period also saw the rise of another major religion – Islam – its emergence in the seventh century corresponded to no change in astrological Ages.

There is a great deal of debate among astrologers about exactly when one Age gives way to the next, because the constellations are of different sizes and the sun takes a varied number of years to pass through them. And when the sun is midway between two constellations, exactly when is it deemed to pass from one 'house' to the next? In fact, astrologers do not think at all in terms of an abrupt, immediate switch from one Age to another, but rather of periods of transition, or overlap, in which the influence of one Age gradually fades away while the new one gains in strength. It is therefore nonsensical to talk about any one year as *the* year of change: we will not emerge from our collective mother-of-all hangovers on 1 January 2000 and find ourselves abruptly plummeted into the Age of Aquarius. Few astrologers would even place its advent around the year 2000, although many have suggested that its influence is already beginning to be felt. Most estimate that we will be unequivocally in the Age of Aquarius about three centuries from now, around 2300. Some would even put it as far off as 2700.[97]

Bauval and Hancock seem particularly keen to convince us of the astrological significance of the year 2000, although their data produce some odd results when calculated back to previous Ages. The dates they provide in *Keeper of Genesis*[98] are:

Pisces	160 BCE–2000 CE
Aries	2320 BCE–160 BCE
Taurus	4480 BCE–2320 BCE
Gemini	6640 BCE–4480 BCE
Cancer	8800 BCE–6640 BCE
Leo	10,960 BCE–8800 BCE

They arrived at this table by working 2,160 years back to the start of each previous Age, beginning with the year 2000, but this produces some very bizarre results. For example, in 8800 BCE – which they say is the end of the Age of Leo – the sun was resolutely rising within Leo at the spring equinox, and did not pass out of that constellation until 300 years later. This can easily be verified.

There is more. Extraordinarily, Bauval and Hancock seriously contradict themselves in the very same book. They argue that the correlations between pyramids, Sphinx and the heavens in 10,500 BCE, which they believe marks the date of the First Time, was also the beginning of the Age of Leo.[99] If that is true, then – by their own reasoning – the Age of Aquarius will not begin until 2460! They seem so obsessed with attaching significance to both dates – 10,500 BCE and the year 2000 – that, as far as any objective reader is concerned, they actually create a curiously irrational double-think. When they are arguing for the significance of 10,500 BCE they use one argument, but when they argue for 2000 CE they use quite another, without apparently realising that both arguments are mutually exclusive. But why bother? Why should they go to such lengths to argue for these particular dates? Could it have anything to do with the prophecies of Edgar Cayce, in which both dates are very significant?

Another reason why Bauval and Hancock attach importance to 10,500 BCE is its astronomical associations. That date is roughly half a precessional cycle (a little under 13,000 years) away from our own era. This means that the constellations at the spring equinox are now the mirror image of what they were at 'the First Time', although this will not be completed for another four or five centuries. However, Bauval and Hancock take this as a sign that the world is moving into what they call 'the Last Time'.[100] Although we are unclear about the precise meaning of their term, the connotations appear to be obvious enough. But it should be said that this term was not used by the ancient Egyptians themselves, being an invention of Bauval and Hancock.

Many people are now obsessed with the year 2000, but it obviously has a greater import for Bauval and Hancock as the year, they believe, in which great changes are going to happen on Earth. In *Keeper of Genesis*, Bauval and Hancock actually suggest that, in some way, the Great Pyramid will 'trigger' the Age of Aquarius in the year 2000. (Of course, this prophecy may well be fulfilled, just as Cayce's followers went looking for, and believed they found, Atlantis in 1968, to ensure the fulfilment of his prophecy.) They say:

> We wonder whether it is possible that the sages of Heliopolis, working at the dawn of history, could somehow have created an archetypal 'device', a device designed to trigger off messianic events across the 'Ages' – the Pyramid Age when the vernal point was in Taurus, for example, the Christic Age in Pisces, and perhaps even a 'New Age' in Aquarius?[101]

Anything is possible. We are eclipsed by no one in our admiration for the 'sages of Heliopolis', but the phrasing of the above paragraph seems to suggest to us either prior knowledge of the existence of such a 'device' or that Bauval and Hancock see themselves as guardians of some secret knowledge, who deign to spoonfeed us information as they so desire and are determined to create an expectancy in our minds for some imminent revelations.

Chambers of the underworld

The by now fabled Hall of Records – whether or not it actually exists – is an intrinsic part of this plot to enliven the Millennium. If it does, then there is every reason to suspect that its existence is already being manipulated in the mass perception well before its grand opening to the world's media by the select few with their own well-honed private agenda. Although it will undoubtedly be the biggest archaeological find in history, this will be merely a drop in the ocean of revelations planned for us.

Does the Hall of Records exist? Certainly, the idea of records from an earlier time can be found throughout Egypt's history. Among the most important of the many such sources is the famous Westcar Papyrus, which contains a legend concerning the great Khufu himself.[102] This tells how Khufu, builder of the Great Pyramid, wanted to gain access to certain secrets found within the sanctuary of Thoth in Heliopolis in order to use them in the building of his pyramid. Khufu's son, Hardadaf, told him a story of a great magus named Ded'e, who knew where 'the secret things of the house of Thoth were hidden'. Khufu sent for Ded'e, who told him that the things he sought were hidden in Heliopolis. Some Egyptologists believe that this refers to records that were the originals from which the Pyramid Texts were derived.[103] (Note that this original version of the Hall of Records is located at Heliopolis.)

In later times, particularly during the period of Arab rule, there were plentiful legends of hidden secret writings in Egypt,[104] which is only to be expected, given the reverence in which that ancient civilisation was held by those who came later. Several similar legends also refer to inscriptions on pillars set up in Egypt. These have passed into Masonic lore.[105]

Herodotus, the Greek historian who visited Egypt in the fifth century BCE, wrote of 'the subterranean apartments on the hill on which the pyramids stand, which he [Khufu] had made as a burial vault for himself, in an island, formed by draining a canal from the Nile.'[106] This is often taken to mean that Herodotus was told that Khufu was buried beneath the Great Pyramid. A strict interpretation suggests that he is saying that a complex of vaults was built beneath the Giza plateau, though not necessarily directly under the Great Pyramid.

In *Gods of Eden* Andrew Collins develops the idea of a complex of tunnels and chambers within the plateau, pointing out that it is limestone, which is characteristically riddled with caves.

There are many legends concerning a secret repository of ancient Egyptian knowledge. The Greeks, Arabs and, latterly, the Freemasons all have stories about coded inscriptions or caches of scrolls secreted somewhere in Egypt, so Edgar Cayce's prophecies were nothing new. But he was not the only influential psychic to promote such an idea.

In the 1920s a British psychic, H.C. Randall-Stevens, came up with psychically derived information about the Great Pyramid and the Sphinx. It very closely parallels Cayce's. As with the Sleeping Prophet, this knowledge was alleged to be derived directly from the survivors from Atlantis who escaped to Egypt, this time led by an astronomer called Mizrahiml. Randall-Stevens said:

At the present time papyri and relics are still hidden below the Sphinx in numerous passages. These will shortly be found and given to the world in general to read.[107]

The Osiran Scripts tell me that this huge and imposing colossus is the ornament surmounting a hall, which communicates with the Pyramids by radiating underground passages.[108]

Opposite: *Different views of what lies beneath the Sphinx.* Above: *British psychic H.C. Randall-Stevens's 1927 plan.* Centre: *The Rosicrucian H. Spencer Lewis's 1936 version. Except for the addition of a chamber at the rear of the Sphinx, this is virtually identical to Randall-Stevens's.* Below: *Bauval and Hancock's 'Genesis Chamber'.*

HALF SECTIONAL ELEVATION OF SPHINX, SUBTERRANEAN TEMPLE, CAUSEWAY AND PASSAGES. NOT TO SCALE

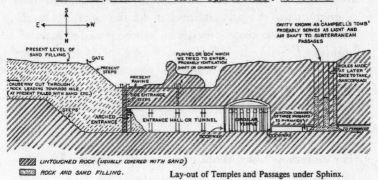

UNTOUCHED ROCK (USUALLY COVERED WITH SAND)
ROCK AND SAND FILLING.

Lay-out of Temples and Passages under Sphinx.

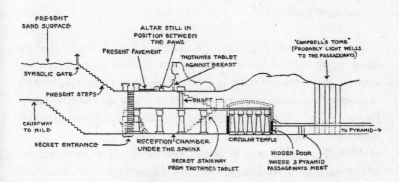

Eventually a temple will be discovered underground in the rear of the Sphinx, which connects with other chambers and a great temple or grand chamber under the Great Pyramid. There the divine cosmic mysteries will be revealed to those appointed.[109]

Randall-Stevens gives a diagram of the chambers and tunnels under the Sphinx and the Giza plateau, and also adds this telling paragraph:

The emigrants from Atlantis were people governed by the laws of Cosmic Masonry and those who landed in Egypt built centres of Masonic Initiation from which the country was administered.[110]

But did Randall-Stevens – like Edgar Cayce – really find his ideas in the spirit world, or did they have a more terrestrial source? Investigation reveals a very interesting tradition of which both men may have been aware – the Ancient and Mystic Order Rosae Crucis, the prominent American Rosicrucian society commonly known as AMORC.

AMORC, which has become well known for its extensive advertising and well-organised correspondence courses, was founded in the early 1920s by Harvey Spencer Lewis, who died in 1939. He had been initiated into the Rosicrucian Order in the great occult centre of Toulouse, in southern France, and founded AMORC in order to study (according to one of its brochures) 'the mysteries of time and space; the human consciousness; the nature of matter; perfecting the physical body . . . development of will; important discoveries in Rosicrucian chemistry and physics'. More significantly, the order claimed a pedigree that went directly back to the Mystery Schools of ancient Egypt.

Spencer Lewis claimed to have inside knowledge of the Giza Plateau: indeed, the idea of a complex of tunnels and chambers beneath Giza – linking the Sphinx to the three pyramids – is a major part of AMORC's beliefs. Lewis said this information was taken from the 'Rosicrucian archives', although he offered no evidence to support this claim.[111] Interestingly, the diagrams of these tunnels and chambers in AMORC documents are virtually identical to those of Randall-Stevens, and are too similar to be merely coincidental. And the latter's account of the arrival of the Atlanteans in Egypt also resembles Cayce's (although Cayce's description of the Hall of Records is different from those of Randall-Stevens and Lewis).

Bauval and Hancock's diagram showing the secret 'Genesis Chamber' locates it in more or less the same place as in the AMORC documents. On the face of it, this appears to be exciting confirmation that Bauval and Hancock have proved independently, using astronomical data, the claims of psychics and occult brotherhoods over the last eighty years. But have those two authors really presented a much wider public with great esoteric secrets for the first time, enabling us all to participate in the ancient mysteries? Unfortunately the answer must be probably not. In our opinion Bauval and Hancock want to give the impression of providing independent corroboration: after all, we have seen that their argument about the location of the Genesis Chamber was highly contrived.

Is the New Orthodoxy not so new after all, but merely older, occult ideas repackaged? Obviously there is nothing wrong with presenting an eager public with old, mystical concepts, be they from AMORC or Freemasonry. But if this is the case, why do they seem to be unwilling to acknowledge it?

Hancock and Bauval's driven attempts to forge a link between the ancient Egyptian First Time – *tep zepi* – and the Age of Aquarius creates a sense of expectancy in their readers. Everything they have written so far appears to us to be geared to making that connection, with the distinct impression that soon a great secret will be revealed, and that they are its guardians. In other words, Hancock and Bauval seem to be a part, wittingly or unwittingly, of a programme designed to climax at the time of the Millennium and the first years of the twenty-first century.

Hints about the nature of that agenda may be gleaned from the

increasingly messianic tone of their recent postings on the
Internet, as in that from Robert Bauval on 29 July 1998:

> The millennium is rushing in. There is much work to do for
> all who feel part of the same quest, namely to bring about a
> new and much needed spiritual and intellectual change for
> this planet. Giza, without a doubt, has a major role to
> play.[112]

And from Hancock on 14 August 1998:

> Poised on the edge of the millennium, at the end of a century
> of unparalleled wickedness and bloodshed in which greed
> has flourished, humanity faces a stark choice between matter
> and spirit – *the darkness and the light* [our emphasis].[113]

In our view, this messianic fervour is no accident: Hancock and
Bauval, like other individuals and groups, appear to be working
to a private programme fuelled by a very real missionary zeal.

Millennium magic

In October 1998, Bauval announced the·creation of his 'Project
Equinox 2000', based around a group of twelve authors (plus
himself) whom he refers to as the 'Magic 12'. The membership of
this group was not fixed at the time of writing, but it originally
included Graham Hancock, John Anthony West, Andrew Collins
and, of course, Robert Temple. Other names mentioned by
Bauval in this context are Colin Wilson, Michael Baigent,
Christopher Knight and Robert Lomas.

The idea is that the Magic 12 are to hold a series of conferences in different locations around the world on the key
astronomical days of the year 1999 – the equinoxes and solstices.
The locations have been selected as the major Hermetic sites of
the world, including Giza, Alexandria, Stonehenge and San Jose

(headquarters of AMORC). Bauval states that the 'principal objective is to perform a global ritual' symbolising the return of the magical Hermetic tradition to Egypt.[114] The year's events will culminate at midnight on 31 December 1999, when, from a specially erected platform in front of the Sphinx, Bauval and his 12 companions will deliver a 'message to the planet'. He also says that this event will mark the 'return of the gods' to Egypt.[115]

Whether or not the Great Ennead comply with Bauval's stage directions and time their return to coincide with the climax of his announcement, one can only reel in amazement that Dr Zahi Hawass has actually granted permission for this event to take place in front of the Sphinx. The likes of Coca-Cola or IBM would have been happy to pay millions to have secured what must essentially be the prime advertising spot of the big Millennium party. So why has Bauval been given it?

An intrinsic part of the planned spectacular is a twelve-hour concert, complete with state-of-the-art laser displays, designed and presented by Jean-Michel Jarre. It is scheduled to begin at sunset on 31 December 1999 and end at sunrise on 1 January 2000, encompassing Bauval's midnight 'Message to the Planet'. Industry rumour has it that Jarre's current recording, ready for release in late 1999, is a follow-up to his 1980s album *Equinox*, and, like Bauval's project, it will be called *Equinox 2000*. The common name suggests some degree of co-ordination between the two.

Bauval's Project Equinox 2000 is funded by Concordium, a non-profit foundation based in New York that sponsors research into alternative technology and philosophies that may, in Bauval's words, 'bring enlightenment and spirituality to the world'.[115] He has also established the 'Phoenix Experiment Base' in the Sphinx village, Nazlet-al-Samman, in order to monitor all activity at Giza until the Millennium.

There is no harm in providing the best Millennium show of all against such a stupendous backdrop, nor in wishing the planet love and peace. But let us not forget that an intrinsic part of the Millennium show is the announcement of the return of the ancient

Egyptian gods. This may be merely some poetic turn of phrase or a kind of metaphor, but – as we shall see – part of the plan we have uncovered demands that the gods are real, and that they are returning.

The belief that the second coming of certain ancient gods – and the accompanying global transformation – is imminent is by no means confined to Robert Bauval and Graham Hancock. In the new edition of *The Sirius Mystery* Robert Temple suggests that the ancient amphibious gods, the Nommo, who are now in suspended animation somewhere in orbit around Saturn, are about to return to Earth. He says darkly that 'these matters . . . may affect us all sooner than we think.'[117]

In the minds of this new breed of Aquarian missionaries, the imminent momentous events will either take place at, or focus on, the Giza plateau.

2

High Strangeness at Giza

Everything about Giza today is a mass of contradictions. At any given moment there are dozens of rumours and counterrumours about clandestine excavations, all manner of cover-ups and – by far the most exciting – secret discoveries that will somehow transform the world. Activity and rumour have escalated according to some kind of programme designed to culminate at the Millennium. But who lies behind this campaign? And can we successfully sort out the truth from the rumours about Giza?

Officially, nothing much is happening on the Giza plateau except that the Great Pyramid was closed on 1 April 1998 for 'cleaning', which seems reasonable, because the many thousands of tourists leave an incredible amount of grime and condensation on the venerable stone of the interior. A build-up of breath and sweat could cause a dangerous deterioration of the pyramid; besides, some renovation work was clearly needed – to improve the temperamental lighting system, for example. But in addition to cleaning and electrical work it was suggested, from many sources – some considerably more reliable than others – that other activities were going on at Giza: secret tunnelling, inside the Great Pyramid and elsewhere on the plateau; clandestine searches by shadowy groups for fabled hidden chambers and ancient secrets; conspiracies galore. With some cynicism, we turned our attention towards Giza, although we were in for something of a shock.

There is a certain hypocrisy in the official Egyptian attitudes to visitors to the Great Pyramid. Many tourists are frequently derided – with good reason, for American and European New Agers seem to regard the pyramids as their own and show a marked reluctance to allow the Egyptian authorities, or anyone else, to try to limit their enthusiasm for meditating inside, outside or even on top of the pyramids at any time of the day or night. They arrive in Egypt with the firm intention of planting their flag and seizing the country as their own, the jewel in the crown of New Age colonialism. They clamber and chant everywhere regardless of local feeling: a decade ago a party of 350 trooped into the Great Pyramid for a group meditation for the so-called 'Harmonic Convergence' – a huge number, considering the small and cramped King's Chamber, and the oppressively 'close' atmosphere within that massive stone bulk, particularly when it hosts such a massive influx of people.

It is freely acknowledged that 'metaphysical' groups are in fact allowed into the Great Pyramid after the Giza plateau has been closed to the public each night – for a fee. In fact, in December 1997, when Dr Zahi Hawass announced the forthcoming closure of the pyramid, he specifically said that this arrangement would continue.[1]

But not all visitors to the Great Pyramid keep their eyes either shut in meditation or glued to a guidebook. Several seasoned and knowledgeable travellers have reported evidence of ongoing work in the 'relieving chambers', a series of low vaulted chambers, about 3 feet high, above the King's Chamber. (They are generally taken to have been built specifically to relieve the pressure of the thousands of tons of rock that would otherwise have pressed down far too dangerously on the roof of the King's Chamber, although recently some doubts have been expressed about this being the purpose of these chambers.[2]) Such rumours of this and other clandestine work in the pyramid proved too tantalising, so we, together with writer-researcher Simon Cox, hastened off to Egypt, arriving there the day before the Great Pyramid was closed for what was then described as an eight-month 'cleaning and restoration' programme. However, the Great Pyramid did not re-open on 1 January 1999, and the Egyptian Cultural Centre in London have since told us that it may never be reopened to the public.

Tunnel vision

One unexplored chamber in Giza is known: assuming Gantenbrink's door really is an entrance, then it must open on to something. But what? As with everything else at Giza these days, there is a political background to the story.

The German robotics engineer made the discovery on 22 March 1993, the day after Zahi Hawass had been dismissed because of a scandal over a stolen Fourth Dynasty statue (although Graham Hancock has suggested that his dismissal was in fact somehow connected with Gantenbrink's work).[3] The man who dismissed Hawass, Dr Muhammed Bakr, President of the Supreme Council of Antiquities, was himself sacked three months later. He claimed that a 'mafia' – which had controlled everything at the pyramids for the last twenty years – was responsible.[4]

Hawass himself was only out of office for about a month, and was reinstated in April 1994. He had spent that time in California, which may be significant, for – as British writer-researcher Chris Ogilvie-Herald wrote in *Quest for Knowledge* magazine, of which he was then editor – Hawass's reinstatement 'was said to have been brought about by American intervention'.[5]

After Robert Bauval had released the news of Gantenbrink's discovery to the media on 16 April 1993, the German Archaeological Institute in Cairo officially reacted to Gantenbrink's discovery by dismissing it as unimportant (perhaps a case of sour grapes?). Dr Bakr went considerably further; at first he even dismissed it as a hoax.[6]

Gantenbrink was refused permission to continue with his work, because of the breach of protocol in the way the news of his discovery was released to the press. As described in the previous chapter, Gantenbrink places the blame for this fairly and squarely on Robert Bauval, but this has not prevented Graham Hancock from portraying Gantenbrink as a martyr to the cause and a victim of the Egyptological establishment – nor from hinting that this was part of some conspiracy. He wrote in *Nexus* magazine in late 1996: 'The official reason given by the Egyptian Antiquities Organization . . . was that Gantenbrink leaked the news of the discovery to the British press and thus, apparently, broke a "rule" of archaeology.'[7]

After the publicity surrounding the story of the discovery, nothing happened about the shaft or chamber until 1996, when a new – Egyptian – team was established to take the investigation further. This was to be led by a close friend of Zahi Hawass, a specialist in remote sensing (the use of satellite- or aircraft-borne technology to scan the Earth's surface, or beneath it), an Egyptian geophysicist who worked for NASA on the Apollo moon landings named Dr Farouk El Baz. A Canadian company called Amtex became involved and equipment worth $1 million was flown to Giza. The intention at the time was to open Gantenbrink's Door on live television, but nothing came of it.[8] In January 1998 Hawass promised that Gantenbrink's Door would be opened by May of that year.[9] Not only did this historic moment fail to materialise, but no explanation has ever been given for the non-event.

A particularly persuasive and persistent rumour has circulated that a tunnel was secretly being dug in order to reach 'Gantenbrink's Chamber' from the lowest of the relieving chambers above the King's Chamber, which is named 'Davison's Chamber' after the British diplomat Nathaniel Davison, who officially discovered it in 1765, although there is some evidence that its existence was already known.[10] (The other relieving chambers were discovered by Colonel Howard Vyse in 1837, who named them after prominent figures in contemporary British society, such as Wellington and Nelson.) Entry to Davison's Chamber is difficult: a somewhat inadequate wooden ladder is propped up against the 27-foot (8.7-metre) wall of the upper end of the Grand Gallery, but it stops short of the top. The last few feet have to be climbed using a rope, followed by an uncomfortable wriggle through the tunnel into the chamber itself. Davison's, like all the relieving chambers, is only about 3 feet high and is obviously impossible to stand up in, with a rough and very uneven floor made of the granite roofing slabs of the King's Chamber. Never intended to be seen, the builders took no trouble to make them smooth.

Was a tunnel really being dug southwards from Davison's to Gantenbrink's Chamber, as we had heard? Dozens of rumours concerning Egypt are circulating at any given time. Many of them emanate from people with only the slightest familiarity with concrete facts about Giza. The source of this particular rumour, though, was Thomas Danley, an acoustics engineer and NASA consultant for two space shuttle missions, who specialises in 'acoustic levitation' (raising objects through the use of sound and vibration). In October and November 1996, he participated in a project of the somewhat controversial Joseph M. Schor Foundation, together with a film crew led by American documentary producer Boris Said. They were going to perform acoustic experiments in the Great Pyramid on camera and had official permission to spend four nights there.

Given this golden opportunity, Danley and his team went up into Davison's Chamber, where he noticed that a tunnel originally dug in the early nineteenth century seemed to have been reopened. The excavation was first made by Giovanni Battista Caviglia (1770–1845), one of the most unusual characters of nineteenth-century Egyptology. A ship's captain from Genoa, he was also a Hermeticist and occultist. He became convinced that the pyramids contained great arcane secrets. He carried out major excavations all around Giza between 1816 and 1820, the first large-scale digs ever undertaken in that area.

Interestingly, Caviglia wanted to dig a tunnel from Davison's Chamber to intersect the southern air shaft from the Queen's Chamber because he thought that a hidden room would be found at that point.[11] Astoundingly, Gantenbrink's discovery in 1993 seems to have proved him right. Caviglia's excavation was abandoned after they had tunnelled for only about 10 feet, probably because of the appalling conditions in which they had to work. The tunnel was subsequently refilled with rubble and largely forgotten. However, in November 1996 Danley crawled into it and found that it had recently been extended some 30 feet beyond the end of the original Caviglia tunnel – work that was obviously still in progress. He also found bags of rubble being stored in the upper relieving chambers. Danley showed this find to the Egyptian inspector assigned to accompany the team, and was disconcerted to discover that he knew nothing of any such tunnelling, though he agreed to report it to his superior – Zahi Hawass. Danley also reported what he had seen on the Internet and on American radio on his return from Giza.[12]

On a subsequent visit in February 1997, Danley saw that a new power cable now ran up the wall of the Grand Gallery and into the tunnel leading up to Davison's Chamber, indicating that work was continuing up there out of sight. When we visited the Great Pyramid with Simon Cox in the spring of 1998, we saw for ourselves that a video camera had been installed at the top of the Grand Gallery, not pointing back down, as it would if intended merely to check on the upcoming tourists, but angled so that it would record anyone climbing up the ladder into Davison's Chamber.

In July 1997, an American 'independent Egyptologist' named Larry Dean Hunter visited the pyramid to check Danley's story. He was sent there by Richard Hoagland (most famous for his championing of the Face on Mars, and a major player in the unfolding story of our investigation).[13] Hunter did not actually climb up into Davison's Chamber, but photographed the cable, video camera and some canvas bags full of rubble at the top of the Grand Gallery. Strangely, all he came back with were photographs of those bags and a stray limestone chip, which could have come from anywhere. What he, and Hoagland, hoped to achieve by this is unclear, yet because of the publicity Hoagland generated for this non-story, it has actually eclipsed Thomas Danley's first-hand account of ongoing work in Davison's Chamber. (Curiously, Hoagland's website posting makes no mention of Danley at all.)

Hunter also involved Mohammed Sherdy, assistant editor of the *El Wafd* newspaper. As Zahi Hawass denied that anything was going on in the relieving chambers apart from some 'cleaning' work, Hunter surmised that something was seriously amiss. Either work was going on that the authorities knew nothing about, or the authorities did know and were covering it up. But, in a meeting with Hunter and Sherdy in his office in July 1997, Hawass produced a faxed letter from film-maker Boris Said – who had been in charge of Danley's team – denying any knowledge of the situation.[14] Sherdy later said that he had been allowed access to Davison's Chamber – but reported that he saw no tunnel.

Nothing at Giza is simple. In an interview in January 1998, Said confirmed that a 'new tunnel' was being dug from Davison's Chamber, but added – somewhat confusingly – that he saw nothing sinister in that, although he stopped short of offering any explanation of its purpose. He also said: 'They [the Egyptians] are tunnelling all over the plateau.'[15]

Many would ask why the Egyptians should not be digging – secretly or openly – at Giza? It is their land and their heritage, not a colony of the West. Few foreigners would object if they excavated beneath other Egyptian landmarks, such as the great Citadel, built by Saladin, which overlooks Cairo. The problem is that the monuments of ancient Egypt are acknowledged as belonging to the whole world: even President Hosni Mubarak said as much in print in 1998.[16] Anything that happens at any of the ancient sites – Karnak, Luxor or Giza – must be made known internationally as soon as possible according to an unwritten agreement. Ancient Egypt belongs to everyone, and every time anyone seriously stirs its dust, we should all know about it: this is the general understanding that underpins all excavations and major discoveries. Where notable finds are concerned, Egyptology is a common currency that transcends politics, so evidence of secret tunnelling, not just in any ancient site, but in the Great Pyramid itself is of colossal significance.

In March 1997 – several months after Danley's report – Hawass stated categorically: 'There is no secret work at Giza!'.[17] The only conclusion was, in our view, that someone was, to say the least, being economical with the truth about a major archaeological irregularity.

In February 1998 our colleague Simon Cox had seen unambiguous evidence of the existence of an unofficial tunnel. In fact, Simon, using the well-known Egyptian lubricant of *baksheesh* to grease relevant palms, had actually managed to enter Davison's Chamber itself. There he saw – and photographed – final confirmation that there is indeed a tunnel being dug into the southern wall of the chamber. From Simon's account it appears that Caviglia's tunnel has been reopened and extended further into the heart of the pyramid. Excitingly, if it continues in a straight line and on the same level, it will intersect the southern shaft from the Queen's Chamber. In other words it will strike approximately at the level of Gantenbrink's Door. Is this what 'they' are up to – covertly investigating the mysterious door and what lies behind it? It is very suggestive, considering that the Egyptian authorities have officially dismissed Gantenbrink's Door as unworthy of examination, pointing out that it is very small – about the size of an A4 piece of paper – and even, curiously, suggesting that nothing lies behind it. But do they, in fact, protest too much?

Secrets in the sand

While we were at Giza we found out for ourselves the difficulty of making public any exciting discoveries. We heard – from particularly reputable sources – that three new chambers had already been discovered in the Great Pyramid, around the King's Chamber.[18] Yet because for various reasons we could not reveal those sources, the news was technically worthless. And in any case, there is always a need for caution when dealing with activity at Giza. Wild rumours spring up like mushrooms overnight, describing exotic secret finds by the authorities that will – by now a standard implication of all such tales – somehow trigger miraculous changes in the world.

It seems that a search for hidden chambers in the Giza complex has been continuing for at least twenty-five years. One of the first twentieth-century attempts to find undiscovered chambers took place in Khafra's Pyramid in 1968, with a project led by Nobel prizewinning physicist Luis Alvarez, who tried to locate chambers by measuring the passage of cosmic waves through the stone structure. (Alvarez was also the originator of the 'deep impact' theory of dinosaur extinction, and in the early 1950s, part of a CIA-backed study into Unidentified Flying Objects.[19]) The 1968 Giza project involved twelve US and Egyptian agencies, including the US Atomic Energy Commission, the Smithsonian Institute and Cairo's Ain Shams University. Initial computer analysis of the resulting data at Ain Shams led their project leader, Dr Amr Goneid, to state (as reported in *The Times*) that the results 'defy all known laws of physics' and that 'there is some force that defies the laws of science at work in the pyramid'.[20] But once again the confusion machine seems to have gone into overdrive: Alvarez subsequently announced from America that nothing untoward had happened, and that no new chambers had been detected.

The next phase of this project concerned the Sphinx. The idea that something highly significant is under the Sphinx has been around for centuries. During Napoleon's expedition to Egypt – which included scholars as well as soldiers – it is said that they actually found a doorway in the Sphinx's chest in 1801, but, because of the imminent arrival of the enemy, had to beat a hasty retreat before it could be explored. We know about the story of the French finding the door in the Sphinx because Arabs who were present described it to the nineteenth-century French Egyptologist Auguste Mariette. It has been argued that this door was actually the Sphinx Stela, but this is unlikely as the stone plaque is not flush with the surface of the Sphinx like a door.[21]

Many of the most noted Egyptologists of the nineteenth century firmly believed in the existence of chambers underneath the Sphinx. Mariette himself believed that a tomb lay beneath it. This was largely based on the observation that every time the ancient Egyptians depicted the Sphinx in stone carvings or on papyrus, they showed it lying on a plinth above what appears to be a tomblike chamber.[22]

Interest in the possibility of the existence of such a chamber revived in the early twentieth century. In 1926 the French archaeologist Emile Baraize undertook excavations in both the body of the Sphinx and the surrounding enclosure. The rough-and-ready haste of his excavations suggests that he may have been specifically looking for something, not merely excavating for its own sake in the normal cautious manner. Indeed, he appears to have succeeded at least partly in his aim, finding a tunnel accessed by a hole in the Sphinx's rump. He explored it, then sealed it up, but, incredibly, kept the news of this amazing discovery to himself. This particular location, as we have seen, interested both psychic H.C. Randall-Stevens and AMORC. They – and, later, Robert Bauval and Graham Hancock – pinpointed the area immediately beneath the Sphinx's hindquarters as the location of one of the putative secret chambers. What is peculiar about Baraize's work is that, although he excavated that site extensively for eleven years, not one of his many detailed reports or papers has ever been published.[23]

Following Baraize, there was a long gap until 1973 when the lead was taken by an intriguing organisation called SRI International (formerly the Stanford Research Institute) from California. One of the world's largest scientific research organisations, SRI has always enjoyed close links with the US Department of Defense and the intelligence community. It made three expeditions to Giza in the 1970s, two led by a physicist, the wonderfully named Dr Lambert Dolphin Jr, primarily to search for hidden chambers beneath the Sphinx. Why this idea suddenly resurfaced after fifty years of inactivity is unknown. According to Dolphin, the first SRI expedition in 1973 was, in fact, a continuation of Luis Alvarez's project of five years before.[24]

Dolphin himself is a particularly interesting character. A graduate of San Diego State University and Stanford University, he joined SRI in 1956, becoming one of their most senior physicists. But there is more to Dolphin and his interest in ancient sites than meets the eye. He is a devout Christian with a decidedly fundamentalist leaning, who left SRI in 1987 to, in his own words, 'devote the bulk of my time to Bible teaching, writing and Christian counseling'.[25] However, Dolphin's website perhaps reveals another dimension to his religious beliefs; its links include material by pro-Life, anti-gay and zealously anti-Muslim groups and individuals. He has written that he believes both Old and New Testaments to be 'historically accurate, divinely inspired and fully authoritative in all areas of faith and life'.[26]

Like most Christian fundamentalists, Dolphin seems to have, paradoxically, a greater fascination with the Old than with the New, Testament because – apart from the Book of Revelation – it contains all the truly apocalyptic material. Christian fundamentalists love the excitement of hellfire and damnation, one of many traits they share, surprisingly perhaps, with Jewish extremists, creating once again an apparently paradoxical alliance. At the same time that Dolphin was leading the SRI team in Giza, he was also using identical remote-sensing techniques in controversial investigations beneath the Temple Mount in Jerusalem.[27]

Working with a right-wing Jewish organisation, the Jerusalem Temple Foundation led by Stanley Goldfoot, which believes that now is the time for the Third Temple to be built in Jerusalem, Dolphin used his expertise in a search for the foundations of the original building. This is an extremely sensitive area – literally and figuratively – as the Temple Mount is now under Muslim control, so they worked at night. Even so, Israeli authorities stopped their activities because of the risk of riots. The *Jerusalem Post* described the event:

There are significant and to some minds worrisome links between a handful of American Evangelical leaders and right-wing Israelis like Goldfoot. Some of the personalities on his board are important men. Lambert Dolphin heads a key section of the world's most massive research conglomerate, the Stanford Research Institute, a $200 million-a-year concern whose main clients are the US government and corporations like Bechtel.[28]

In 1976, according to Dolphin, SRI undertook remote-sensing investigations at Saqqara, looking for the tomb of the great scribe Imhotep; Alexandria, where they tried to locate the lost Library; and Giza, where seismographic tests indicated the possible presence of chambers beneath Khafra's Pyramid.[29] In 1977 Dolphin and SRI were back at Giza, initially funded by the US National Science Foundation.[30] Then in 1978 Edgar Cayce's followers – ARE – popped up, contributing funds to SRI's project whose official name was the Sphinx Exploration Project.[31]

Someone who will emerge as the single most influential – but largely unknown – individual in this book's investigation now enters the frame. This is Dr James J. Hurtak, the American polymath and mystical philosopher, and founder of a California-based organisation called the Academy for Future Sciences (AFFS), at whose feet many of the movers and shakers in this story are happy to sit. Hurtak holds degrees in Oriental Studies and History, Social Sciences, Linguistics, Patristics and Greek Texts and speaks and writes seven languages, being currently described as a 'Silicon Valley-based consultant in higher technology'.[32] In 1986 he presented a paper on the use of air- and satellite-borne radar to detect archaeological features to a conference on remote sensing in Brazil.[33]

Hurtak carried out work at Giza in the late 1970s, which seems to be have been in some way connected with SRI's presence there at that time. While he has never been officially employed by them, he has always maintained close contact with its senior figures.[34] In particular, he has a close friendship with Lambert

Dolphin Jr, who – according to Hurtak – 'shared private insights' about Giza with him in 1976.[35] (Hurtak also knows Mark Lehner.[36]) In 1977 and 1978 Hurtak and some unnamed colleagues undertook a private expedition to Giza. They were there primarily to use lasers to measure the angles of the shafts from the King's and Queen's Chambers, specifically to test their hypothesis that the shafts aligned with certain stars and constellations, namely Orion and Draco – and the star Sirius.[37] The results of this investigation have never been made public.

What is interesting about this work is that the possibility of correlations with Orion and Draco had been proposed as early as the 1960s. But – outside of the Masonic literature, as we have already seen – the idea of an alignment with Sirius did not apparently surface until Bauval and Gilbert's *The Orion Mystery* in 1994. Interestingly, Hurtak was exploring a possible correlation between the Giza pyramids and Orion's Belt in 1973.[38] We found that this was not the only time he has been ahead of the game.

SRI International also plays a major part in the official history of investigations at Giza in the 1970s. Its team used various techniques, including aerial photography, thermal imaging and measurements of the electrical resistance and fluctuations in the magnetic field around the Sphinx and its enclosure, to remote sense any underground anomalies. Some were found, although they mostly proved to be natural cavities in the bedrock (as would be expected in limestone). A few suggested the presence of a tunnel running north-west to south-west behind the rear of the Sphinx, as well as some kind of cavity in front of its paws.[39]

In 1978, a company called Recovery Systems International joined the project to undertake drilling work to examine these anomalies. According to Mark Lehner, this company had 'probably' been formed specifically in order to take part in this project.[40]

Recovery Systems International began to sink a drill in the Giza plateau close to the Sphinx. At a depth of 60 feet they drilled up fragments of granite, which, as we have established, is not naturally found in that area. It is even rumoured that the Egyptian Army then stepped in and stopped the project. In 1980 pieces of granite were also raised from 50 feet beneath the plateau by an Egyptian team surveying the depth of the watertable in the area.[41] Clearly granite is, in that limestone country, anomalous – unless the drills had hit underground chambers lined with it. (If such chambers do exist, it would make sense for them to be lined with granite, because the watertable in that area is quite close to the surface, and porous limestone chambers would have become completely waterlogged. Granite, on the other hand, is made of sterner stuff, and is an excellent water repellent.) Then in 1980 Zahi Hawass reopened the Baraize tunnel at the back of the Sphinx, which had been forgotten by all except those with access to his unpublished field notes and reports. This band included Mark Lehner and an Egyptian named Mohammed Adb al-Mawgud Fayed, who was the son of a man who assisted Baraize in the 1920s and had actually worked on the clearing of the Sphinx enclosure as a boy. Hawass relates that, after fifty-four years, Fayed could still point successfully to the small stone at the back of the Sphinx that concealed the entrance to the tunnel.[42] Fayed's son subsequently became ARE's representative in Cairo.

SRI and ARE, with Mark Lehner, also collaborated on another remote-sensing project at the Sphinx in 1982, called the Sphinx Mapping Project, this time using acoustic techniques to look for hidden cavities. This appeared to negate the existence of any chambers beneath the paws, though it did find possible indications of some beneath the enclosure floor.[43]

In 1990, Hawass granted a licence to the now famous project of John Anthony West and Robert Schoch: the Sphinx Project, which was backed by Boston University, where Schoch was a professor. (The Egyptian authorities have an eminently sensible rule that any project must have the support or involvement of a recognised academic institution.) The project director – and the man who applied for the licence, possibly because of West's own reputation as a maverick – was the American film producer Boris

Said, whose Emmy award-winning documentary on the work, *Mystery of the Sphinx*, was broadcast on NBC in 1993. Investors in the project included two leading ARE members, Dr Joseph Jahoda and Dr Joseph M. Schor, who was also present as ARE's official observer.[44]

Dr Jahoda who, as a senior member of ARE, has played an important role in their involvement at Giza, is also president of the Astron Corporation, a major contractor of the US Department of Defense and NASA that specialises in producing radio communication systems.

We now know that the project's main find was the telling water erosion of the Sphinx, but it also undertook seismographic work to try to detect chambers underneath the Sphinx, conducted by seismographer Dr Thomas Dobecki. He detected what appeared to be a large rectangular cavity (9 metres by 12 metres), about 5 metres beneath the paws. Once again promising work came to an abrupt end: Hawass (then the director-general of the Giza Pyramids) suddenly terminated the Sphinx Project's licence, accusing the team of being 'unscientific'.

In 1995 a new project arrived at Giza to explore the area using seismography and ground-penetrating radar. Officially the purpose of this project was to locate underground faults that might cause subsidence around the monuments and thus endanger the public,[45] but a side effect of such 'remote-sensing' work would have been the discovery of subterranean anomalies, such as chambers. This was a joint mission by Florida State University and the Schor Foundation, founded by Dr Joseph Schor, who had attended the 1990 project. He is the (now retired) director and vice-president of Forest Laboratories Inc., a pharmaceutical company that produces vitamins. In Robert Bauval's words, the Schor Foundation is 'a non-profit organization dedicated to finding evidence of the lost "Atlantean" civilization and "Hall of Records" predicted by the sleeping prophet, Edgar Cayce.'[46] Multimillionaire Schor is a life member of ARE and one of its principal donors. By teaming up with Florida State University, the Schor Foundation ensured that the Giza project would have the necessary academic credentials in order to be licensed by the Egyptian authorities.

This team included Thomas Dobecki and, again, Joseph Jahoda (who was also a member of the Schor Foundation), with Boris Said filming the events. While the official purpose of the project was to locate potentially dangerous pockets of subsidence, this was apparently not its real aim. Said has since claimed that he had been recruited specifically to film the search for the lost Atlantean Hall of Records, which had been the real intention of Schor's team from the first.

Said now claims that the whole expedition was deliberately cloaked in secrecy by Schor, saying:

> Now, finally, I'm convinced that Dr Schor never wanted to go public with this information at all. I believe that it was always his intention to keep news of the secret chamber and its contents from the public. I believe he used me. I believe he used my ability to get a permit, my ability to get things done in Egypt, to further his own private purposes. I think he intended to keep this from the world from the very beginning.[47]

This project's licence would be abruptly terminated in December 1996 through the intervention of Robert Bauval and Graham Hancock (see pages 96–7).[48]

Schor's team also carried out work inside the Great Pyramid, which seemed to indicate the presence of a narrow corridor behind the west wall of the King's Chamber. This was confirmed by Zahi Hawass at an ARE conference in August 1997.[49]

After this, leaked information claimed that the team had detected not one but nine chambers beneath the Sphinx, some of which contained metal objects. This story originated with none other than Graham Hancock, who, speaking on Art Bell's radio show in the United States in July 1996, quite specifically claimed that his information had come, off the record, from members of Joseph Schor's team. Hancock stated categorically that they had found nine chambers, and that this momentous discovery was being kept secret. He also added that he was confident about the reliability of his source, implying strongly that it was true. Around the time Robert Bauval was saying the same in lectures – for example, at 'The Incident' conference in London in October 1996. Incredibly, Hancock and Bauval are now indignantly repudiating such rumours, saying that there are no hidden finds at Giza. And they reinforce their breathtaking volte-face by pouring scorn on those who, in their view, spread such irresponsible rumours.

In another twist to this story, NBC planned live television coverage of the opening of the chambers under the Sphinx for some time in late 1996 or early 1997. This programme was to be based specifically on the work of the Schor Foundation/Florida State University. Among the invitees to this historic event was Richard Hoagland.[50] After the big build-up, it never happened, presumably thanks to Hancock and Bauval's success in getting the Schor Foundation/FSU's licence revoked. If the highly respected NBC was committed to this broadcast, is it too naive to suspect that there must have been something worth revealing? If these chambers exist, why were they never filmed as promised, and why are we still waiting even for confirmation of their existence?

Since then the focus of attention has shifted. Boris Said, who has since ended his association with Schor, claims that the expedition was also interested in a tunnel at the bottom of a 120-foot shaft – known as the water shaft – beneath the causeway leading from the Sphinx to Khafra's Pyramid. This is reached by an underpass that cuts into the causeway about halfway between the Sphinx and the Pyramid. When we visited Giza, we saw that a shaft descends at that point to a depth of some 20 feet, with a tunnel running off to the north. The top of the shaft is behind an iron cage, which is locked – a sensible precaution to avoid losing tourists. But there were definite signs of work continuing further below: a very modern pickaxe and other tools were lying at the bottom of the visible shaft, beside the usual mess of water bottles and chocolate wrappers.

This shaft is remarkably interesting, in fact. It descends in three stages to an incredible depth of 120 feet underneath the plateau, as Boris Said discovered when he took Thomas Dobecki down there in 1996. Dobecki took echo-sounding readings, particularly to discover what lay beneath a gigantic black basalt sarcophagus lid. They claim to have found about 10 feet of empty space and what appears to be a tunnel, 8 feet wide, running in the direction of the Sphinx, 300 yards to the east.[51] Hawass, too, is highly excited by this discovery, suggesting that it is nothing less than the – symbolic – tomb of Osiris.[52]

It is puzzling that so much interest has recently been focused on this shaft – and where it leads – because this is not a new discovery. Bizarrely, the current situation appears to be a rerun of events that took place as long ago as the 1930s. That shaft appears in the works of H. Spencer Lewis of AMORC, where it forms the entrance to an underground complex of tunnels and chambers that link the pyramids and the chamber under the Sphinx.[53] And significantly, H.C. Randall-Stevens's psychic communications told him exactly the same. This coincided with, possibly because it was prompted by, the discovery of the subway and the shaft by the great Egyptian Egyptologist Selim Hassan in the 1930s.

Randall-Stevens claims that Hassan also found a network of underground 'rooms and chambers, none of which bear any relationship to tombs or funerary chambers. They are colonnaded sanctuaries and hallways – temples and ritual chambers.'[54] This is amazing. If Hassan had made one of the greatest archaeological discoveries of all time, why does no one know about it? What Randall-Stevens seems to have been describing was nothing less than a massive underground complex that had never even been suspected. Hassan's work would have been interrupted by the onset of the Second World War, but this hardly explains the complete silence on the subject up until our own day. What are they waiting for? Why is this amazing ancient Egyptian treasure trove being kept under wraps?

On investigation this putative archaeological treasure trove disappointingly dwindles to almost nothing. Randall-Stevens's description of the underground complex is ridiculously – and possibly deliberately – exaggerated to a huge degree. There are chambers and sarcophagi down there dating from no further back than the Saite period (sixth–seventh centuries BCE), but – according to the testimony of independent researchers such as Chris Ogilvie-Herald and Ian Lawton, who managed to gain access in September 1998[55] – they are not especially impressive, nor is there any network of tunnels and halls such as Randall-Stevens described. The very newspaper reports of Hassan's discovery cited by Randall-Stevens say nothing about the existence of such a complex.[56] So why are Said and Schor now focusing attention on that particular location? Perhaps it is simply another piece of mystery-making; after all, few others have access to the place to check it out for themselves. Then again, that same spot has recently attracted the attention of Zahi Hawass, who believes it to be a major archaeological discovery – nothing less than the symbolic 'tomb of Osiris'.

Unfortunately, nothing connected with Giza is ever simple or straightforward. Film footage of the water shaft taken by Boris Said in 1996 has become the subject of intense legal wrangling which has, at least, succeeded in adding to its fascination for the New Egyptology community. According to Said, he and Schor approached Fox Television with the footage, hoping to clinch a documentary deal with them. Then Schor and Said disputed the terms of the film deal, which means that, until the dispute is resolved, the footage in question cannot be shown commercially. However, Robert Bauval – presumably with both Schor and Said's blessing – did present it at a conference in London in October 1998.[57]

Admittedly, this particular sequence is certainly worth viewing, though perhaps for reasons the film-makers did not intend. It certainly out-Indianas Dr Jones: four-wheel-drive vehicles screech to a halt, throwing up sprays of dust on a remarkably tourist-free Giza plateau, and a team of 'archaeologists' leap out and abseil down a huge shaft. Squeezing through a sand-clogged tunnel, they break through into a dark chamber, apparently the first people to do so for many centuries (other than the film crew waiting to film their entrance). Then they find a sarcophagus lid embedded in the floor, and excitedly pour the contents of their water bottles over it to wash away the centuries-old dirt.

In our view, the whole event was stage-managed for optimum dramatic effect. The shaft they abseil into bears no resemblance to the one where they find the sarcophagus. The latter does appear to be the water shaft, but it cannot be accessed by abseiling; its three tiers are reached by means of a metal ladder. In other words, they were filmed going into one place and coming out of quite another to make it look more dramatic. In any case, the sarcophagus they 'discovered' so excitedly on camera had already been known about for some time.

Why is this particular place being so determinedly turned into a legendary location when all the evidence is that, although it has archaeological interest, it is not particularly remarkable? Could it be simply because such a thing is easily achieved – and lo and behold, another myth is attached to Giza!

Confusion certainly reigns on the plateau – more, we suggest, by design than accident. But because of the actions and statements of key people, it is impossible to know with any certainty exactly what is rumour and what is genuine information.

Moves and countermoves

Confusion itself seems somehow to be stage-managed. A few years ago matters were neatly clear-cut where Egypt was concerned. Two camps stood in opposition to standard Egyptologists: the New Egyptology, fronted by Hancock and Bauval; and the esotericists, such as Joseph Schor and ARE. The picture is considerably muddier now because all the main players have been plotting with almost Machiavellian vigour, jostling for position and making alliances with those who will serve their interests best, producing some very odd bedfellows.

In May 1998 Graham Hancock and John Anthony West issued a joint statement on the Internet. Superficially it seemed very magnanimous, a nobly proffered olive branch. After years of acrimonious scrapping with Dr Zahi Hawass, they were suddenly giving him this unqualified endorsement:

> We are now absolutely convinced that the precious monuments of Giza could not be in better hands than those of Dr Hawass. We have seen him at work. We have seen his passion and genuine love for the pyramids and the Sphinx. And we have seen that above all else he is determined to ensure the preservation of these monuments for the future. There are no conspiracies. There are no hidden finds. There is no skullduggery.[58]

Robert Bauval also issued a statement shortly afterwards, saying: 'Graham Hancock, John West and myself are now satisfied that no "behind the scene" activities, secret explorations and/or secret agendas are being implemented at Giza.'[59]

A similar volte-face concerned Mark Lehner: after *Keeper of Genesis* had suggested strongly that he was part of an ARE plot, Bauval and Hancock recently went on record giving him their seal of approval.[60]

Having portrayed Lehner and Hawass as the villains of the piece in books, articles and lectures for years – as well as being the most high-profile instigators of claims of 'hidden finds' and 'secret agendas' – it came as something of a surprise to find Hancock and Bauval suddenly defending them and denouncing rumourmongers. It is no less surprising to find Hawass reciprocating; back in May 1997 he had called a conference at the Foreign Press Association in Cairo to complain about the 'fringe element' distracting him from his real work, and specifically condemned Bauval and Hancock for their influence over the public.

It has now been announced that Zahi Hawass will be the next Head of the Supreme Council of Antiquities (SCA) – the official all-powerful Egyptian committee that decides on all excavations – on the retirement of the present incumbent in 1999.[61] That means that Hawass will be in power at the time of the Millennium, which makes him most attractive as a friend and colleague. We have already seen that Hawass has agreed to give Bauval, Hancock and the rest of the Magic 12 – the authors who have received their seal of approval – a platform in front of the Sphinx for their 'message to the planet' on Millennium night.

This was not the only change of heart of those authors in recent years. According to *Hieroglyph: The Hancock and Bauval Newsletter*, the two authors considered that the project being undertaken at the Sphinx by the Schor Foundation and Florida State University, and which had been licensed by the SCA, 'had many aspects about it that were unsatisfactory'.[62] The exact grounds for their complaint is unclear, or rather appears contradictory. Initially, they were upset by the Schor Foundation's withholding of its alleged discovery of nine chambers beneath the Sphinx, which Bauval and Hancock had revealed to the public in lectures, articles and radio appearances. However, the announcement that there were plans to open these chambers on live television seems to have intensified their opposition. This is very curious: first Bauval and Hancock protested because they believed a major discovery was being covered up; then they complained because it was being made public . . .

They subsequently mounted a campaign to get the Schor Foundation/Florida State University's licence revoked, exploiting their own high profile among their reading public.[63] For example, Zahi Hawass received 'literally thousands'[64] of letters from around the world protesting about the project, written mainly because of Bauval and Hancock's campaign. The licence was duly cancelled, and the project stopped.

Two years later, though, Bauval and Hancock wrote that they now 'feel that a reconsideration by the SCA of the Schor Foundation to carry on with their work is in order'.[65] It should come as no surprise to discover that the Schor Foundation/Florida State University had their licence returned and in October 1998 they were granted permission to undertake drilling work near the

Great Pyramid (where underground tunnels are believed to exist) in order to test the reliability of the remote-sensing techniques employed at the Sphinx. If this is ultimately successful, Hawass may allow Schor's team to return to the Sphinx enclosure. Joseph Jahoda was present on site in October 1998.[66]

This is an extraordinary situation. Although the SCA – the official licensing authority – may have granted the Schor Foundation/Florida State University team a licence, Hancock and Bauval were saying that they considered the SCA to be wrong, and launched a successful campaign to have it revoked. When they deemed that it was time for the team to be given their licence back, that is what happened. It is incredible that those two authors consider themselves to be a higher authority than the SCA – and that the SCA itself seems to agree with their self-image. Why do the Egyptians fall in with their plans so readily?

An air of glasnost now pervades Giza, though, as Bauval is now lobbying Hawass to allow Rudolf Gantenbrink back there.

Then there is the remarkable case of Nigel Appleby and his 'Operation Hermes'. Appleby claimed to have worked out the location of the Hall of Records, beneath the outskirts of Cairo, based on certain geometrical alignments and astronomical computations – indeed, he claims to have recognised the Orion/Giza correlation several years before Robert Bauval. Appleby planned a major expedition to find the Hall of Records, amid escalating publicity: his Operation Hermes was, we were led to believe, backed by the British Army (he is a Territorial soldier), who were to provide extraordinary services, including the supply of four-wheel-drive vehicles and the use of Hercules transport aircraft to ship the expedition and its equipment to Egypt.

However, disaster lay in wait for Appleby. Although his *Hall of the Gods* went straight into the Top 10 hardback bestseller list in the United Kingdom in June 1998, it would not remain there for long. It was withdrawn from sale within a week due to allegations of plagiarism by a number of authors.[67] Initially it was Ralph Ellis, author of *Thoth: Architect of the Universe*, who made the allegations, but then he was joined by Robert Temple, Andrew

Collins, and Christopher Knight and Robert Lomas (co-authors of *The Hiram Key* and *The Second Messiah*). But the organisers of this campaign – who persuaded most of the other authors to make their complaints and co-ordinated the issuing of public statements, mainly on the Internet – were none other than Graham Hancock and Robert Bauval. According to Appleby himself, they even offered to pay the legal fees incurred by some of this group.

The fact that *Hall of the Gods* was withdrawn within a week of being published was surely no accident. It ensured maximum publicity (and humiliation for Appleby) and threw Operation Hermes into chaos. Hancock and Bauval followed this up with a posting on the Internet about the affair, signed jointly with the other authors (except Ellis), declaring that they had no affiliations with Appleby or Hermes, 'nor [do we] intend to have in the future'.[68] Then, oddly, within a few weeks the announcement was made of a joint Robert Bauval/Nigel Appleby lecture cruise on the Nile, advertised for November 1998. Bauval has also publicly called for the other authors to forgive and forget.[69] For his part, Appleby has recently gone on record praising Bauval's fairness.

Superficially this sounds like an admirable state of affairs, with Bauval emerging as a decent, magnanimous gentleman trying to calm troubled waters. Once again, though, the situation is much more complex than it may first appear. When Nigel Appleby's work first received publicity in 1997, Hancock and Bauval commissioned Simon Cox, who is a professional researcher, to prepare a report about Appleby and his theories, which they included in the joint statement posted on the Internet. Now that peace has broken out all round, however, Appleby has written an article for *Quest* magazine defending himself against his detractors, particularly singling out Cox's report as an example of the campaign against him.[70] Ironically he ends his piece by thanking Robert Bauval for resolving the matter, and for brokering a deal between him and the other authors – despite the fact that Cox's report was initially commissioned, and then made public, by Bauval and Hancock themselves. (The two authors in fact hold the copyright.)

The story then becomes even more complicated. After making a major issue of the importance of keeping the public aware of every new development, Hancock, Bauval and the other authors signed an agreement with Appleby that somehow brought an end to the affair. The terms of this agreement have never been made public, so once again we are dependent upon Bauval and Hancock's reassurances that everything was on an even keel. And the only person who refused to sign this mysterious agreement, Ralph Ellis, has now become the focus of their antipathy. There is another almost incredible volte-face in which Bauval, having supported Ellis in his complaints against Appleby, switched his support to Appleby against Ellis. This appears to be a 'divide and rule' policy.

By now Bauval and Hancock have succeeded in establishing themselves as the major power brokers in all matters concerning unorthodox explorations at Giza, as well as reinforcing their position as the leaders of the alternative Egypt field. We are not alone in our concern about Hancock and Bauval's bid to monopolise the New Orthodoxy of Egyptology. Several other authors, such as Alan F. Alford and Ralph Ellis, have also expressed disquiet about their high-handed actions.

For their part, Bauval and Hancock have even backtracked about the conspiracies central to *Keeper of Genesis* and which they promoted widely at conferences and in the media. In many ways this is a pity. They had made strong cases and left some intriguing loose ends. They themselves raised questions that they then, after their change of heart, left unanswered, abruptly offering bland assurances that, essentially, their own suspicions and allegations were unfounded, usually on the rather unsatisfactory grounds that the people they were criticising turned out to be really nice guys once you got to know them.

What is perhaps most disturbing is the reaction of their audiences. Only a year or two before, Hancock and Bauval were happily applauded when they denounced Zahi Hawass for suppressing the truth about secret finds at Giza and also condemned ARE and the Schor Foundation for pursuing their own private agendas. But now the same readers and followers are – largely without question – accepting Bauval and Hancock's about-turn endorsements of Hawass *et al*, as well as the new assurances that all is in order at Giza.

With all these astonishing back-trackings and changes of heart, it is difficult to know who belongs to which camp, or even what the various groups stand for. While Bauval and Hancock may simply be exercising their right to change their minds, certain provocative underlying affiliations may be discerned. For example, Alan Alford has referred to Graham Hancock 'wittingly or unwittingly, following a masonic agenda . . .'[71]

The words and actions of the representative of orthodox Egyptology, Zahi Hawass, only add to the problem. It seems that his many, often quite glaring, contradictions, appear to be part of some elaborate game. We have already noted his connection with ARE, who helped arrange his training as an Egyptologist. Although, in his official capacity, he maintained a dismissive attitude to the 'fringe element', it was not surprising to find him appearing in a short promotional video about the search for the Hall of Records made by Boris Said and the Schor Foundation in late 1995.[72] In this, Hawass appears in the tunnel beneath the rear of the Sphinx, declaring: 'This tunnel has never been opened before. No one really knows what is inside this tunnel. But we are going to open it for the first time.' (When the existence of this sequence was leaked to the public in 1996 it caused much excitement among followers of the Giza drama, who wondered what the rest of the film might reveal. However, it appears that it was made as a 'screen test' for a future film if the chambers were ever found.)

It is hard to know the nature of anyone's true affiliation in this story, but we have already seen that Zahi Hawass is closely associated with ARE. He also has connections with another esoteric organisation that sets great store by the existence of hidden chambers at Giza, having been in the 1980s a consultant to and frequent lecturer at AMORC's Museum of Egyptology in San José, California.[73]

Such confusion encourages the spread of some of the wilder rumours, of which there are many. One particularly lurid story was recently posted on the Internet by the independent American researcher Larry Dean Hunter who, as we have seen, investigated claims of tunnelling in Davison's Chamber on behalf of Richard Hoagland, together with Amargi Hillier, who lives in Nazlet-al-Samman, the village in front of the Sphinx. (Hunter is a former officer with US Navy Intelligence.) It claimed that a massive, 250-foot high chamber had been found inside the Great Pyramid. This they call the Hall of Osiris, which they claim leads to another chamber in which lies the body of the god Osiris himself. This is astonishing, not least because of the idea of a god having a physical reality outside of myth and legend. This is typical of Hunter and Hillier's overheated apocalyptic output:

For the first time in many thousands of years, the mass world population will start to receive an inside glimpse concerning something truly powerful, hidden from humankind by God, regarding the Great Pyramid. We are sure these revelations will accelerate the 'quickening' into high gear. God is quietly whispering to everyone, letting them know they are getting close to the fulfilment of the words of Isaiah 19.19: 'In that day there shall be an altar to the Lord in the midst of the land of Egypt, and a pillar at the border thereof to the Lord.'[74]

This quotation is a notable favourite among those who blend a fervent Christian fundamentalism with a passion for ancient Egypt. Superficially, this seems to offer an almost haphazard mix of the Old Testament (the Lord) and ancient Egyptian myths (the god Osiris) – a strange blend indeed. Believers in the God of the Old Testament – Yahweh – do not, as a rule, attach any significance to pagan deities. One would be very hard pressed, for example, to find a rabbi – a supreme example of a Yahweh-worshipper – eagerly awaiting the discovery of the body of Osiris or taking seriously the idea that his God planned global changes involving the deity of the nation that, according to the Bible, enslaved his own race. Furthermore, Hunter and Hillier link all this to Cayce's prophecy of the opening of the Hall of Records in 1998. Ironically, they are attempting to evoke Cayce's prophecies to support the idea of secret chambers within the Great Pyramid, though Cayce himself categorically stated that there are no such chambers to be found.[75]

Given the accessibility provided by the Internet, it is hardly surprising that incredible rumours spread like wildfire these days. But there are also signs that some are circulated deliberately to accord with specific agendas, and that they originate from official circles.

Late in 1997, our friend Georgina Bruni, a columnist for *Sightings* magazine, was introduced to a leading Egyptian political journalist at a reception in London. During their conversation, Georgina brought up the subject of the rumoured secret search for the Hall of Records. To her surprise, the journalist told her that the chambers beneath the Sphinx had already been opened a few months before by a team from the Schor Foundation, but that the Egyptian government had placed an official embargo on the story, going so far as to call in journalists to impress upon them the seriousness of the official ban on publishing the story.[76] This Egyptian journalist went much further. He claimed that the chamber under the Sphinx contained the body and treasure of an Egyptian queen, perhaps Akhenaten's wife, Nefertiti, as well as a statue of the lioness-headed goddess Sekhmet. He also said there were many other finds, including another chamber containing ancient texts, written or inscribed in both hieroglyphics and another language that was described, significantly, as 'Altean'. Some of these writings have, he claimed, already been deciphered, and tell how Atum descended from the sky, and describe how an earlier civilisation came to Egypt and built the pyramids.

There seems little doubt that this story was told in good faith, by a London-based correspondent who specialised in political, rather than archaeological, stories. He was simply telling

Georgina Bruni what he had heard in political circles in Cairo. The story may well have originated from within Egyptian governmental circles, but much of it is, frankly, incredible. For example, how could records in an *unknown* language be translated at all, let alone so soon after they were discovered?

So what is going on at Giza? It seems as if a game is being played out, though only the players themselves know the rules and the goal. The rest of us can only watch and wonder. Some of the evidence certainly suggests that clandestine searches are being made at Giza, as suggested by the testimony of Thomas Danley and Simon Cox about secret tunnelling in the Great Pyramid. On the other hand, highly publicised ventures, such as the filming of the water shaft, turn out to be insubstantial and hardly worth our attention. Where Giza is concerned there is a strange tendency to mix persuasive, academic evidence with rumour and inflated claims with downright nonsense. So how can the objective researcher make sense of it all?

One starting point is to ask what various people have to gain from focusing their attention so avidly on Giza? Clearly they perceive some benefit from all their digging and skulduggery. The most obvious possibility is that they really believe there is something to be found that is of value or use, anything from treasure to religious artefacts or some kind of ancient technology. Most theories about Giza incline to take that line, but much less attention has been paid to another aspect that could be turned to advantage – the potency of Giza as a symbol for disparate creeds. This in itself is something of inestimable value, especially for those whose business it is to exploit the power of belief systems. Is Giza itself, rather than something found there, the goal?

Of all the players in the Giza game, most can be seen to have definite and easily discernible motivations; for example, Hawass wants to be the world's leading Egyptologist, Joseph Schor and ARE want to find the Hall of Records, and so on. The motivations of certain individuals and organisations who have played key roles are not so easy to define, such as the enigmatic Dr James J. Hurtak and SRI International, who seem to be have been working together at Giza in the 1970s. Far from fading from the picture, Hurtak has recently gone into partnership with Boris Said in his Magical Eye production company, being listed as their scientific adviser.

Inside the seer's circle

As we have seen, one name frequently cited in connection with Giza is that of the American 'prophet' Edgar Cayce. His prediction of the discovery of the Hall of Records in 1998 explains why his organisation, ARE, repeatedly appear in this story. They are obviously looking for the Hall of Records, although why they need to pour money into the search when presumably they believe it will be found eventually anyway is a mystery.

Edgar Cayce, we discovered, warrants closer scrutiny. What emerges is a very different image from the well-worn, accepted picture. We see him as a simple Joe, relatively uneducated but eager to learn, who remained in humble circumstances for most of his life. The very first headline mentioning him – in the *New York Times* in 1910 – emphasised this image, reading: 'Illiterate Man Becomes Doctor When Hypnotized'.[77] This is very strange; not only was he not illiterate, but he also had a long-standing job as a sales assistant in a bookstore. In fact, he spent most of the first seven years of his working life in bookshops.[78] He was also famed for his prodigious memory: over thirty years later he was proud of the fact that he could still quote from the publishers' catalogues he had to study in his job.[79]

There was another more secret side to Edgar Cayce, which we have never seen mentioned in any of the mainstream books that currently feature him, although some of the writers must certainly be aware of it simply because they share the same private affiliations as him. His entranced alter ego predicted that Masonic ideals would become the governing principles of the future American Golden Age. This is a concept of which the conscious Edgar Cayce would have approved. He left his job in the book trade at the age of twenty-two to join his father, Leslie B. Cayce (known locally as 'the Squire'), in his job as a travelling insurance salesman for the Fraternal Insurance Company.[80] As its name suggests, this company sold insurance to Freemasons, so all its employees would have also been members of the Brotherhood. Presumably the reason Edgar only joined his father in this work at the age of twenty-two was the fact that young men must reach twenty-one to enter a lodge. We have not identified the Masonic rank of either father or son, but we know that Cayce Senior was authorised to found new lodges and Edgar used to help him do so, implying no insignificant status on their part.[81] (In fact, Cayce only worked with his father for a few months, being struck down with the first of his attacks of aphasia – psychosomatic loss of voice. It was the treatment for this – hypnosis – that seemingly unlocked Cayce's famous psychic powers.)

As his psychic career developed, Edgar Cayce became known in the very highest echelons of American society. In a memoir written in 1932 (though not published until 1997), he wrote that, in 1918 or 1919: 'I was called to Washington to give information for one high in authority. This, I am sure, must have been at least interesting, as I was called a year or so later.'[82] Although Cayce is being discreet here, it is not difficult to work out to whom he was referring – almost certainly President Woodrow Wilson himself, possibly because he had a stroke in 1919, and Cayce could have been brought in for his healing talents.[83] (According to two Cayce biographers, he was summoned to give advice about the formation of the League of Nations.[84])

A link with Woodrow Wilson is entirely plausible: one of Cayce's friends, and earliest promoters of his powers, was David E. Kahn, who had served with one of Wilson's cousins in the First World War.[85] Afterwards, Cayce, Kahn and Major Wilson went into business together to form the Cayce Petroleum Company to locate oil in Texas using Cayce's psychic abilities. In its short four-year life, the company was a disaster. As Cayce wrote: 'Nothing came of our efforts to produce oil except a financial loss to many people.'[86] Even without Cayce's vaunted psychic powers, surely they must be among the few prospectors *not* to have found oil in Texas! Hardly a good advertisement for his abilities.

It was Kahn who propelled Cayce into the limelight, fixing up contacts with the great and the good. He had first met Cayce in Alabama in 1912 and was deeply interested in his diagnostic readings. When he went into the US Army in 1917, Kahn sang Cayce's praises to his superior officers, with the result that a request for a reading was sent by an unidentified member of the Italian royal family.[87] This was hardly the humble milieu in which we have been led to believe Cayce moved. Indeed, he said of Kahn: 'Through him I made the acquaintance of some most prominent people – bankers, businessmen, lawyers, journalists, people in almost every walk of life.'[88] In 1924 Kahn also introduced him to a circle of businessmen headed by New York stockbroker Morton Blumenthal, who agreed to finance a hospital and research institute at Virginia Beach in return for Cayce's advice on their investments. This was the prototype ARE, although it only lasted for at most two years, when funding was withdrawn after a disagreement with Cayce. Blumenthal and his circle then transferred their allegiance to another psychic.[89]

In the mid-1920s three members of this group had acquired property on Bimini, and for some reason they had an idea that some treasure was buried there, so they flew Cayce and his family over to find it for them.[90] Unsurprisingly, he failed to do so, but the sequel is perhaps more significant: only after his return from that trip did Bimini and Atlantis begin to feature in his readings.

Cayce's influence had reached the Army, Italian royalty and the President, but he also had contacts in the world of intelligence. According to David Kahn, interviewed in 1965, the meeting between Cayce and President Wilson was arranged by Colonel Edmond Starling, head of the Secret Service.[91] Kahn also described Starling as 'a lifelong friend' of Cayce, although the former's name never appears in Cayce's memoirs; the prophet was characteristically very discreet. Like Cayce, Starling came from Hopkinsville in Kentucky, which is perhaps why they were lifelong friends, although the latter belonged to an older generation and so it is more likely that they met through Cayce's father. It is tempting to speculate that Starling and Cayce Senior were fellow members of the Hopkinsville lodge.

These associations can be seen as a microcosm of a much wider picture. As our investigation proceeded, an initially unlikely pattern began to form: strange alliances that surface time and time again among psychics, politicians, Freemasons, the world of big business and the intelligence agencies. Whether or not Cayce's predictions were accurate is largely irrelevant. What really matters is that many highly influential people *believed* he possessed genuine powers. If they followed him then, do the same categories of people also believe in him now? Is this a motivating force behind what is currently going on at Giza, especially around the crucial last years of the twentieth century, when the Hall of Records will, according to Cayce, finally be found?

Although it may seem far-fetched that modern political movers and shakers may be influenced by the prophecies of Edgar Cayce, it is known that leading members of the Egyptian government – and members of the presidential family – firmly believe in the reality of the Hall of Records.[92] Cayce himself drew together a chain of associations that included the Masons, intelligence agencies, politicians and other influential personages, but others besides Cayce – individuals and organisations – embrace a similar chain of associations.

The mind's eye

The connections between psychic phenomena, technology and the world of intelligence and defence are embodied in another organisation with a key role in events at Giza, especially in the 1970s – SRI International. As Mark Lehner said: 'SRI was in the business of looking for hidden chambers at Giza well before I or the Edgar Cayce Foundation met up with them'.[93] Perhaps this is a little odd: ARE's involvement with Giza is perfectly under-standable, given Cayce's prophecies, but why was SRI searching for hidden chambers?

Founded by Stanford University in California as the Stanford Research Institute in 1946, SRI was originally planned as a means of attracting commercial business research to bring extra revenue to the university. This was not a success, and the parent body had to subsidise it for several years.[94] SRI's fortunes changed dramatically when it began to take on military and intel-ligence contracts, much of it classified. This included weapons testing for the Atomic Energy Commission and research into chemical warfare. It also developed other, considerably weirder, weaponry for both the Pentagon and the CIA. (Stanford University's own metamorphosis from regional to national aca-demic centre resulted from its acceptance of Department of Defense contracts, although the majority of this work was actually carried out by SRI.)

By 1968, SRI rivalled the university itself in size, and even employed more staff. But by then Stanford's students had discov-ered the extent of the university's involvement with defence and intelligence agencies, and over the next three years the adminis-trators were forced to reveal that many departments – but particularly the Research Institute – were heavily involved in classified projects, including work on electronic surveillance for the CIA. Predictably, this horrified the students. As Stuart W. Leslie says in *The Cold War and American Science* (1993): 'The extent of Stanford's classified research program, although common knowledge among the engineers, shocked an academic community still coming to terms with the Vietnam War.'[95] The students, appalled, started a campaign against the university's links with the military, with a series of demonstrations and sit-ins specifically targeting the Research Institute. As a result, the uni-versity stopped taking on research on behalf of classified projects, and divested itself of the embarrassment of the main recipient of such favours. Stanford Research Institute became a private company, changing its name to SRI International.

Now on its own, SRI came to rely on defence contracts even more, the revenue enabling it to become one of the largest independent research institutes in the world. In 1993, approximately 75 per cent of SRI's income came from the Department of Defense.[96] It now has offices in ten countries outside the United States – including the United Kingdom – and operates an Artificial Intelligence Laboratory at Cambridge University. It has a National Security Advisory Council, made up of former Department of Defense 'decision-makers', and carries out research for NASA.

In its work at Giza, SRI used 'remote sensing' – a hi-tech but resolutely mainstream scientific technique – which is entirely different from another of their specialities, the similarly named 'remote viewing' that was the focus of work on which they concentrated on behalf of the CIA during the 1970s. Masterminded by researchers Russell Targ and Harold ('Hal') Puthoff, this was pure *X-Files* research. It almost certainly inspired much of the concept of the cult series, not to mention being the catalyst for the Pentagon and CIA's own lengthy remote-viewing programmes.

Remote viewing (RV) is an entirely psychic or paranormal technique, although it was investigated, and then taught, in Pentagon and CIA-funded projects known, for example, as Grill Flame or Sun Streak – and, significantly, Star Gate – over a twenty-year period at a cost estimated at approximately $15 million, although many sources put it much higher.[97] The term 'stargate' has been popularised in recent years because of the successful 1994 movie and later television series of the same name, which presented the idea of an ancient device that, properly operated, could transport human beings to other worlds. Presumably the producers knew that the ancient Egyptian *sba* meant both 'star' and 'gate' or 'door',[98] although the reason why a remote-viewing project was given the name Star Gate remains tantalisingly unclear.

Essentially remote viewing deliberately induces a form of out-of-body experience (OOBE) in order to 'travel' to distant locations – usually across space, but occasionally even across time – and then to report back on what was 'seen'.

In the 1970s SRI's research into RV was well-known among the international parapsychological communities, where it was on the whole received positively as exciting evidence for the existence of a mind, or consciousness, that could act independently of the physical body and brain. (Its implications are enormous, not least because it appears to confirm what religions and mystics have always taught: that there is an individual consciousness – spirit or soul – that can operate beyond the confines of the body, and which therefore could, theoretically, continue to exist after the body dies.)

Targ and Puthoff's research attracted media attention in the 1970s, mostly because it appeared that, with minimal training, almost anyone could learn how to remote view. Their experiments were featured in several television documentaries. In one, the researcher, persuaded to participate, passed with flying colours, correctly describing a 'target' location that she had 'seen' with her invisibly travelling consciousness. But back at SRI it soon became clear that there were remote-viewing 'stars', notably New York artist Ingo Swann and former police chief Pat Price. After being trained as a remote viewer, Price went to work for the CIA. He was later to die in mysterious circumstances.[99] Swann went on to train remote viewers for the Pentagon, and afterwards for a private company. But of all the stars who took part in SRI experiments, none were as famous as the young Israeli psychic who arrived in 1972: the handsomely charismatic Uri Geller, now internationally known as the metal-bender extraordinaire.

Geller had been 'talent-spotted' while entertaining in nightclubs in Israel and was taken to the United States, where his powers were tested by SRI in a controlled scientific environment.[100] The man entrusted with persuading Geller to go to SRI was to become not only his mentor, if only for a short time, but also the key player in an astonishingly complex network of interlinked conspiracies and agendas. His name was Dr Andrija Puharich – truly, as we shall see, a name to conjure with.

The publicity surrounding Targ and Puthoff's RV research at SRI never mentioned one major fact. The research into the RV psychic surveillance technique was funded directly by US intelligence agencies, especially the CIA's Office of Technical Services and Office of Research.[101]

The SRI research was bolstered by an injection of $150,000 from the CIA over a period of two years. There were also, according to Jim Schnabel's *Remote Viewers* (1997): 'two small contracts with the Navy and NASA, plus money left over from private grants for the Geller research'.[102]

In the mid-1990s, SRI's CIA and Pentagon backing was finally made public, partly because of the demands of the Freedom of Information Act, but also as a result of the testimony of ex-RVers themselves, especially David Morehouse, a former US Army officer, who had worked as a 'psi spy' on Operation Sun Streak in the late 1980s and early 1990s. In his book *Psychic Warrior* (1995), Morehouse describes his reaction to reading a file on the background to the RV projects:

> I couldn't believe it. This programme had been in existence since early 1974, for nearly 15 years. It wasn't experimental any longer . . . they knew it worked – they'd proven that at Stanford, and all the evidence was here. There were books written on the stuff by the researchers involved; nobody paid any attention to them. The books didn't mention the intelligence involvement, but evidence of government funding was written all over the place.[103]

Morehouse also stated: 'The government was funding paranormal research in half a dozen private, and as many state and federal research centres across the United States. They were pumping tens of millions of dollars into remote viewing and various related techniques.'[104]

During the 1970s, SRI undertook several different psi-related projects, but it was the remote-viewing research that was their most cherished and important. This was the time that SRI began their work at Giza. Was this just a coincidence, or was more going on behind the scenes?

A clue may lie in the experiences of the remote viewers. Many of them spontaneously reported encountering pyramids during their RV sessions. This, like all information gathered by remote viewing, was routinely taken seriously by the experimenters or 'handlers'. Neither SRI nor the intelligence agencies themselves would have failed to seize upon this information, especially as they were already involved with excavations at Giza, directly or indirectly. However, it is known that when Lambert Dolphin Jr took charge of the SRI expedition to Giza in the 1970s he had information about the plateau gleaned from SRI's remote viewers.[105] Significantly, Dolphin's friend James Hurtak also seems, in his usual elusive fashion, to have been involved in the establishment of SRI's remote-viewing project. When they initially established it they called in a veteran parapsychologist, Harold Sherman, to advise them,[106] and we know that Hurtak was in contact with him at that time. In the words of a spokesperson for Hurtak's Academy for Future Sciences, Hurtak 'shared insights' with Sherman about remote viewing.[107]

However, there is another side to remote viewing, which raises some disturbing questions about the military and intelligence agencies' enthusiasm for experimenting with it. Some commentators, such as Alex Constantine, argue that remote viewing was more concerned with beaming information *into* people's minds than information-gathering from distant locations.[108] Constantine maintains that remote viewing as we know it is merely misinformation, that the whole purpose of the Pentagon's research was experimentation with mind control, and that the 'psychic spying' aspects were merely colour. Although Constantine presents a compelling case that some of the remote viewing projects had this hidden agenda, on the evidence, this rather extreme view seems unlikely. It is perfectly logical to assume that there was at least an element of 'remote influencing' in their research because, if remote viewing is a viable military technique, then some form of counter technique – like radar jamming – must also have been taken into account. Few researchers have even considered this aspect, so we cannot know for certain how far remote influencing has been taken by the authorities, although the mass of parapsychological evidence suggests strongly that all psychic processes are two-way and also occult tradition has always maintained that they can be used for good or evil.

For these reasons, the possibility of remote influencing should be borne in mind in all the following discussions about remote viewing, especially when dealing with some of the more extreme claims made by remote viewers.

Search for the Stargate

Perhaps no one will ever know the full picture of what has been going on at Giza during these last thirty or so years. The presence of apparently disparate groups and organisations such as ARE and SRI – with their often weird mix of hi-tech science and psi – and the Joseph M. Schor Foundation might at first suggest individual, even personal, aims and agendas. When the surface of this activity is scratched a little more deeply, however, the military and intelligence interest becomes increasingly clear.

Some more colourful than others, rumours spread about Giza and the organisations involved, even producing claims that the US government is searching for a physical artefact or ancient device, perhaps even of extraterrestrial origin. Are they looking for a real working stargate, as in the movie, maybe following instructions given by remote viewers? Or, more disturbingly, have they already found it? This stupendous – and very romantic – idea remains speculation. If the Americans are involved with ancient stargate technology, then it would be the most top secret project in history, and the number of people 'needing to know' about it would be minimal. But what can be said with certainty is that virtually all the individuals and groups involved in the present activity at Giza are engaged in exploiting the culture, religion and even the gods of the ancient Egyptians to fulfil various aims and agendas. Essentially they show little respect for the mysterious geniuses who built the pyramids and the Sphinx for their own specific mystical reasons.

If the intelligence agencies are seeking a device – or possibly information – then this implies that they regard the ancient Egyptians as being somehow more advanced, in some way, than our own civilisation. Once again, we return to the idea of a lost, advanced people, or perhaps an extraterrestrial connection, as promulgated most effectively by Robert Temple in *The Sirius Mystery*. Remember that – rather inexplicably – it attracted the attention of not only the Freemasons but also the CIA and MI5.

But what do Hancock and Bauval think about the extraterrestrial question? After writing *Keeper of Genesis* they continued to investigate the mysteries of Giza, and discovered some thought-provoking connections between some of the other people and organisations involved in clandestine activity on the plateau and the newly emerging mysteries about Mars.[109] For a while, it seemed as if the conspiracy that they had uncovered also had a Martian angle. The original intention behind *The Mars Mystery* (co-written with John Grisby, but oddly credited to Hancock alone in the United States) was to reveal it to the world. Its original subtitle was to be *Message at the Edge of the World*.[110] When the book appeared in 1998, although it included material about a possible civilisation on Mars and its connection with ancient Egypt, it had dropped the examination of the link with the modern Giza conspiracy in favour of a study of the dangers of the Earth being hit by a comet or asteroid.

While not explicitly expressing a belief in extraterrestrial intervention in human development, there is every indication that Hancock and Bauval are at least sympathetic to the idea. Bauval frequently acknowledges his own debt to Temple's book, and was responsible for the publication of the new edition in 1998.[111] In recent interviews, Hancock has played down the extraterrestrial angle, saying that it is not necessary for his theories, but it has been stated that a chapter on this subject was removed from *Fingerprints of the Gods*.[112] Moreover, he and

Bauval went on to write *The Mars Mystery*, which not only championed the idea of an ancient Martian civilisation, but also made an explicit connection with Egypt. Also suggestive is Hancock's recent endorsement of the work, and implicitly the claims, of alien abductee Whitley Strieber (see Chapter 7).

Hancock and Bauval's interest in the controversy surrounding Mars marks a significant development in this story. This forms another element that has been introduced into the wider picture over the last few years. The belief that there is some connection between ancient Egypt and a long-dead civilisation on Mars has been steadily growing over the last twenty years, but is it based on anything more substantial than a fantasy? Is there any real evidence for a Martian civilisation, and for a link between it and the ancient Egyptians?

3

Beyond the Mars Mission

In April 1998 the latest US space probe, Mars Global Surveyor, sent back new images of the surface features of the area of the Red Planet known as Cydonia Mensae. These were among the most eagerly awaited images in history, believed to be about to reveal details of the so-called 'Face on Mars', proof to many that Mars once supported a civilisation much like our own. With a resolution ten times better than previous images, these new pictures of the Face were released on the Internet to a largely stunned audience. The long-awaited images did not show new and conclusive detail of a strange face on the surface of Mars. They revealed a very eroded and very shapeless lump of rock, without discernible facelike features. The anticlimax, and in many cases, bleak disappointment, was appalling – analogous only, in our experience, to the results of the carbon-dating in 1988 that revealed the Shroud of Turin to be a fake. And although many believers in the Face are fighting back, the excitement about the anomalies on Mars has largely subsided. If Mars has a message for us, it appears to be keeping quiet about it, at least for the time being.

The pyramids of Mars

Mars is our near neighbour. Only 34 million miles away at its closest, the Red Planet is the fourth from the sun, the second closest to us after Venus. Just half the size of Earth, it has almost the same length of day (a little over 24.5 hours), but its year is 687 days, and its temperature ranges from an inhospitable 'high' of just 20 degrees Celsius to a low of −120 degrees.

Associated in the minds of the ancients with armed conflict – our word 'martial' comes from the Latin *Mars*, the Roman god of war – the Red Planet has long exerted a particularly powerful, often awe-inspiring, influence on mankind. But only in February 1972 did the Mariner 9 probe show us what the planet was really like, sending back the first close-up images of our neighbour: it was rocky, barren – and yes, it was rather red.

However, neither the redness nor the rockiness attracted the most attention, especially in certain quarters. Images of the surface of Mars, taken on 8 February 1972, in the region known as the Elysium Quadrangle (15 degrees north of the Martian equator), appeared to show apparently pyramidal features – two large and two small three-sided pyramids. A second picture of the region, taken six months later on 7 August, showed the same features. These apparent structures were seized upon as evidence of an ancient Martian civilisation by, among others, Dr James J. Hurtak, then Professor of Oriental Studies at the California Institute of the Arts, who a few years later, as we saw in the last chapter, would carry out secretive work in the Great Pyramid.

In the 1970s Hurtak was described – by British author Stuart Holroyd – in these terms:

Hurtak . . . was not so much a teacher as an experience, a guru-figure whose teaching was not an explanation of objective reality but a spontaneous creation of ideas and experiences that made his students explore new areas for themselves and in themselves. Dressed always in a crumpled suit and wearing a black beret perched on the back of his head, Hurtak held classes which sometimes ran as long as eight hours, during which he would alternate between reading long passages of scripture and delivering rambling commentaries on them.[1]

Outside classes, Hurtak would lead groups of students on night-time and weekend outings to 'power spots' in the Californian desert, revealing – if nothing else – a sympathy with the New Age faith in unseen energies and a living Earth.

Few people took the Mariner 9 images of the Elysium pyramids seriously, although they did inspire a *Dr Who* television story[2] and, ironically, intrigue that arch-'Skeptic' Dr Carl Sagan, enough for him to write in *Cosmos* (1981):

The largest [of the pyramids] are 3 kilometers across at the base, and 1 kilometer high – much larger than the pyramids of Sumer, Egypt or Mexico on Earth. They seem eroded and ancient, and are, perhaps, only small mountains, sand-blasted for ages. But they warrant, I think, a careful look.[3]

In 1976, a new American space mission, Viking, photographed the surface of Mars.[4] The two spacecraft involved, Vikings I and II, each consisted of an orbiting vehicle to send back pictures and other data and a lander that touched down on the surface to undertake – among other tasks – a search for life. In this, they apparently failed, although the results are still disputed among some scientists.[5] The journey took the probes nine months, and each spacecraft cost $500 million. Viking I's lander was originally intended to touch down on 4 July 1976 to mark the American Bicentennial, but worries about the viability of the chosen landing site led to a delay to 20 July, thus instead marking the seventh anniversary of the first moon landing. Viking I landed successfully and sent back the first television pictures from the surface of Mars. Viking II landed on 3 September 1976 and the landers continued to transmit data on the Martian weather conditions back to Earth for six years afterwards.

On 25 July 1976, from an altitude of 1,162 miles, Viking I photographed the region of Mars known as Cydonia Mensae, about 40 degrees north of the Martian equator, on the other side of the planet to Elysium. The image that was returned to Earth showed what looked like a human face staring outwards into space. This feature, about a mile long, was noticeable enough to be pointed out at a NASA press conference the next day, but, as it could reasonably be supposed to be merely a trick of the light, this, too, was deemed of no special interest. The image was filed away with the 51,538 other pictures taken during the mission. (Incredibly, only 25 per cent of these images have ever been scientifically analysed, as the budget ran out before the task could be completed.) This particular frame was given the official identification code of 35A72 – that is, the thirty-fifth image taken by Spacecraft A, Viking I, on its seventy-second orbit.

This time the story was rekindled when the image was 'rediscovered' some time later, although, even among those familiar with the Face on Mars controversy, few know the full story. In effect, the image was rediscovered twice, but only the second of these events has received widespread publicity. The little known story of the first rediscovery begins with H. Guard Hall, the chief of operations at the Jet Propulsion Laboratory, the facility in Pasadena in California that controls space probes such as Viking. He was at that time the boyfriend (later the husband), of one of James Hurtak's leading 'disciples', a Dutch woman named Marijke Posthuma (an artist, illustrator and set designer who once worked for The Beatles). Hurtak had told Posthuma about the image of the Face in December 1976, so she and Hall searched through the archived images until they found it.[6] Hurtak then used the image in lectures as early as April 1977.[7]

Intriguingly, Hurtak was already referring to the Face as 'Sphinx-like', making an immediate and emotive connection with Egypt. Even more intriguing is the fact that Hurtak had predicted the existence of a Sphinx image on Mars in 1975, the year before the Viking pictures had been taken.[8] But it was his extraordinary extrapolations from this image that have far-reaching implications. Hancock and Bauval said that Hurtak: 'predicted that further finds of similar structures, including a Sphinx-like monument, would be made on Mars, and that these structures would be linked to the Giza monuments in a great cosmic blueprint.'[9] Astonishingly, in some ways this was to be proved right: Hurtak's ideas about Mars were to become the lynchpin of a new system of belief.

The story only really gathered steam in 1979 – the second rediscovery of the image – when Vincent DiPietro, an electrical engineer specialising in digital image processing at NASA's Goddard Spaceflight Center in Maryland, came across the image apparently by chance. DiPietro became intrigued, as did a friend, Gregory Molenaar, a computer scientist also under contract to NASA from the Lockheed Corporation. They wondered if it was possible to enhance the image to show more detail and determine whether it really was a face or something that only coincidentally looked like one. Their immediate problem was that the standard techniques for computer-enhancing the image available at that time were unsatisfactory, so they had to write their own software to do it, which they called the Starburst Pixel Interleaving Technique, or SPIT for short.

After searching through the Viking archives, DiPietro and Molenaar found a second image (70A13) of the Cydonia region also showing the Face. This had been taken thirty-five days after the first picture, from 1,080 miles above the surface of Mars, with the feature lit from a different angle by the sun. It showed the same apparent facelike structure as the first, apparently proving that, whatever else it might be, it could not be an illusion created by a simple trick of light and shadow.

DiPietro and Molenaar discovered another seemingly significant feature on frame 70A13: what appeared to be a five-sided pyramidal structure, about 10 miles south of the Face and approximately 1.6 miles long by 1 mile wide. This has become known as the D & M Pyramid, after the two researchers. DiPietro and Molenaar were convinced that these two features, located so closely together, were not accidents of erosion or tricks of the camera, but were artificial structures, presumably erected by some long-gone Martian civilisation. They made their conclusions known to the public on 1 May 1980.

The lead in promoting DiPietro and Molenaar's discoveries and the issue of the Face on Mars was taken up enthusiastically – not to say fanatically – by science writer Richard C. Hoagland, who, in 1997, sent 'independent Egyptologist' Larry Dean Hunter off to check Thomas Danley's discovery of secret digging in the Great Pyramid.

Born in 1946, Richard Hoagland had worked for several science museums, such as the Hayden Planetarium in New York, and was advisor or consultant on space science for several television stations, including NBC and CBS, where he worked with legendary newsman Walter Cronkite. He is also the former editor of *Star & Sky* magazine, and a presenter for CNN. In 1971 Hoagland, with one Eric Burgess, came up with the historic idea of decorating the side of Pioneer 10 – the first space probe to leave the solar system – with a plaque bearing representational and symbolic information about the human race, including an upraised hand of peace and a diagram showing that man comes from the third planet from the sun. Hoagland and Burgess passed on the suggestion to Carl Sagan, and after that it became history.[10]

Between 1975 and 1980 Hoagland was a consultant to NASA's Goddard Spaceflight Center in Maryland, organising media events, which is where his much-repeated 'NASA consultant' title originated. And he was also a prime mover behind the campaign to name the first Space Shuttle *Enterprise*, something clearly of personal significance: as we will see, he also changed the name of his Mars Mission to the Enterprise Mission as a tribute to his friend Gene Roddenberry, creator of *Star Trek*.[11]

Since first becoming involved in the Mars debate in 1983, Hoagland has become the main advocate for the presence of artificial structures on the Red Planet. He fulfils the role of self-appointed oracle of all things Martian so successfully that, to the vast majority of the public, he is now the main source of information about the Face.

When he first became interested in DiPietro & Molenaar's work in the summer of 1983, Hoagland was working on a project concerning the rings of Saturn at SRI International at their headquarters in Menlo Park in California.[12] In July 1983 he was studying DiPietro and Molenaar's enhanced images of the Cydonia region and noticed a series of other artificial-looking features to the west of the Face. To Hoagland's eye there seemed to be a whole complex of pyramidal and other structures, covering an area of about 12 square miles. He excitedly termed it the 'City'. This appeared to be made up of several massive, and some smaller, pyramids, plus some much smaller conical 'buildings' grouped around an open space that he called the 'City Square'. In the north-east corner of the City was an enormous structure that appears to be made up of three huge walls, which Hoagland dubbed the 'Fortress'.

Perhaps the most significant assumption Hoagland made – and surely the one with the least justification on such slight knowledge – was his association of these features with Egypt. As soon as he discovered the City, Hoagland wrote: 'I was reminded overwhelmingly of Egypt.'[13] He then went on to identify various other features in Cydonia: the 'Cliff', a 2-mile-long wall-like feature near a crater 14 miles directly east of the Face; and several small (250–400-foot) objects dotted about the Cydonia plain that he called 'mounds'.

The relationship between the City and the Cliff presents a significant example of Hoagland's characteristically circular reasoning. He surmises that the Face, which lies east of the City Square, was built so that the City's inhabitants, standing in the Square, would see the sun rise out of the Face's mouth on the Martian summer solstice. Although the sun does not rise there on the solstice today, because of changes in the angle of Mars's axis over time, it did so in the past – the last time being about half a million years ago. Hoagland concludes that the Cydonia Complex was built at least 500,000 years ago because the alignment with the sun on the summer solstice proves the dating – but the dating also proves the summer solstice alignment, and so on, round and round.[14]

Hoagland decided to set up a project to study these features further. He approached SRI and in October 1993 met its vice-president for corporate affairs, former intelligence officer Paul Shay, at the Institute for the Study of Consciousness in Berkeley, California (founded by Arthur M. Young). This was to prove a significant meeting. Shay recommended that he collaborate with Lambert Dolphin Jr, the physicist who had led SRI teams in Giza between 1973 and 1982.[15]

In December 1983, Hoagland and Dolphin formed the Independent Mars Mission, with $50,000 from SRI's 'President's Fund', an internal funding source under the discretion of SRI's President, Dr William Miller. Other key people involved in the Independent Mars Mission were Randolpho Pozos (anthropologist), Ren Breck (manager of InfoMedia, the computer conference company run by the thinking person's ufologist, Dr Jacques Vallée), Merton Davies (a specialist in the cartography of Mars and other planets) and Gene Cordell (a computer-imaging specialist). One of the first to join the new project was physicist John Brandenburg of Sandia Research Laboratories (which specialises in nuclear weapons research). He was a leading scientist in Ronald Reagan's Strategic Defense Initiative ('Star Wars') programme, and had previously worked with DiPietro and Molenaar on their analysis of Cydonia.

The first lecture given by Hoagland and Pozos on the work of the Independent Mars Mission took place at the Institute for the Study of Consciousness in early 1984. One of those present was social scientist Tom Rautenberg, who later joined the project. His initial reaction to Hoagland's revelation about the Face is highly significant:

At first I thought it was some kind of a joke, or maybe a complex social experiment being conducted by the CIA – to study psychological reactions to such a hypothetical discovery. I mean – SRI involvement, 'Faces' on Mars . . . ? What would *you* think? . . . Was this an elaborate psychological experiment, sponsored by the defense community?[16]

The involvement of SRI in anything seems enough to ring alarm bells, at least among social scientists such as Tom Rautenberg. SRI's connections with the CIA and Defense Department experiments – such as remote viewing – are too well known to be dismissed, and their reputation obviously precedes them. And now they were funding Hoagland's Mars Mission, after having sent Dolphin to Giza in the 1970s . . .

Another early recruit to the cause was a designer and illustrator named Jim Channon, a former lieutenant colonel with the US Army, who had been stationed at the Pentagon. Channon was the creator of the 'First Earth Battalion', which was, in Hoagland's words, 'a pragmatic proposal to combine the "spiritual warrior" goals of "the New Age" with the pragmatic grounded methodology of the military services'.[17]

Prior to this, Channon had been a member of an Army War College project called Task Force Delta, whose purpose was, in Jim Schnabel's words, to 'investigate alternative philosophic realms for anything militarily useful'.[18]

The Independent Mars Mission – with its SRI funding and resources – lasted for seven months, until July 1984, when it presented its findings at a conference at the University of Colorado in Boulder. Their conclusions were that the anomalous features of Cydonia were suggestive of artificial construction, and that efforts should be made to return to Mars to study them further.[19]

If the features on Mars are artificial, who built them? There are three possible answers:

(1) They were built by an ancient, long-dead Martian civilisation, who were perhaps wiped out by some cataclysm, such as a comet or meteor impact, as suggested by Graham Hancock, Robert Bauval and John Grigsby in *The Mars Mystery*, although apparently there were enough skilled Martians left to build the mile-long Face as a warning to us.

(2) They are the product of an extraterrestrial civilisation from

somewhere else in the universe, one that perhaps also visited Earth.

(3) The least likely solution, given our current understanding of Earth's prehistory, is that they are the work of an advanced civilisation that originated on Earth and travelled to Mars.

Hoagland, at least, was in no doubt about which one of these options he espoused.

The message of Cydonia

It is important to distinguish between the two main phases of Hoagland-led research into Mars. The first, seven-month-long, SRI-backed project – the Independent Mars Mission – took place in 1983–4, and concluded simply that at the very least there was a good case for believing that the features were artificial. Then came Phase Two, the Mars Mission (later called the Enterprise Mission), beginning in 1988, which was more concerned with actively promoting the alleged meaning of the structures at Cydonia, and their connection with the ancient civilisations of Earth, particularly Egypt. Underlying all of Phase Two is one, over-riding message, which is that the builders of Cydonia are back . . .

Between July 1984 and late 1988, nothing much seems to have happened. Then came a revival of the project, with an influx of new personnel, and, it seems, a very different agenda . . . There was a notably close connection between the new Mars Mission and the US intelligence community.

The new project received support and encouragement from Representative (Congressman) Robert A. Roe, who was chairman of the House of Representatives Committee on Science, Space and Technology. Roe agreed to support Hoagland and his team in their lobbying of NASA to rephotograph Cydonia in any subsequent Mars missions. (The official line from NASA was that it would not be making a special point of photographing the Face or other alleged structures again as it did not deem them worthy of notice.) Roe took the Mission's side in its battle with NASA, even speaking to Hoagland quite explicitly about what he believed to be NASA's 'agenda' in opposing the idea of a civilisation on Mars.[20] Roe was clearly on Hoagland's side and not NASA's – which was very strange, considering that the Congressional Committee of which he was chairman had direct responsibility for NASA's budget, and 'oversight' responsibility – and therefore major influence – over its policies and plans.[21] Roe, it should be noted, was also a member of the Congressional Permanent Committee on Intelligence.[22]

In January 1991, nearly two years after his key meeting with Hoagland and other members of the Mission, Roe abruptly resigned from the Science, Space and Technology Committee, causing Hoagland to suggest that this was part of some conspiracy. Was Roe being 'leaned on' by some group whose interests he was failing to serve? Perhaps significantly, however, he remained on the Intelligence Committee.

The key members of the new project were David M. Myers, Erol Torun and Mark J. Carlotto. This trio introduced several new elements into the story, carrying the original 'Message of Cydonia' – that the ancient Martian civilisation has something to teach us now – into something much bigger and more far-reaching.

Dr Mark J. Carlotto is the manager of the intelligence section of The Analytical Science Corporation (TASC) in Massachusetts, and had been working on the Cydonia images since 1985, enhancing the interpretation of satellite photographs for defence and intelligence agencies, skills that were obviously of great use to the Mars Mission. Carlotto used a variety of image-enhancement techniques and processes on the Face to produce clearer images than those of DiPietro and Molenaar. He highlighted new – highly controversial – details, such as teeth in the mouth and the presence of a second eye socket on the shadowed side, thus apparently confirming the symmetry of the Face. His work also revealed what appeared to be distinct bands and lines on the forehead that some have taken to be a headdress, similar to those of the Egyptian pharaohs – which certainly seems to be running ahead of the available scientific data by miles.

Carlotto also enhanced other Cydonian features, most significantly the D & M Pyramid. It was his version of this, which had a much greater clarity of detail than DiPietro and Molenaar's original, that enabled Erol Torun – a systems analyst with the Defense Mapping Agency in Washington, DC, whom Hoagland described as being 'on loan' to his private Mars Mission[23] – to make calculations based on the angles between the different faces of the pyramids. His contribution to the Mars Mission was his study of the geometrical relationships in and between the various Cydonian 'structures', particularly the D & M Pyramid. He concluded that not only did the geometry show that they were artificial but that they also encoded certain sophisticated mathematical concepts that appeared to be trying to 'tell us something'.[24]

David Myers, who joined the team in 1989 and became full-time director of operations and editor of its journal, *Martian Horizons*, made further contributions to the discoveries about the significance of the geometry of Cydonia. (Together with his British colleague David S. Percy, he would add a whole new dimension to this work.)

The main features of the post-1988 Mars/Enterprise Mission have been these:

* The promotion of the idea that the Cydonia Complex incorporates sophisticated geometrical and mathematical relationships that were never meant to be merely aesthetically pleasing but were actually intended to express certain important mathematical concepts in a way that could be 'decoded' by others, for example, ourselves. Cydonia is, in effect, a message left for us by an ancient civilisation.

* These mathematical concepts largely relate to hyperdimensional physics, and, when properly decoded, will give us access

to new technologies, such as sources of energy and anti-gravity propulsion devices. As Hoagland wrote in almost messianic vein:

> For it is now clear . . . that, if appropriately researched and then applied to many current global problems, the potential 'radical technologies' that might be developed from the 'Message of Cydonia' could significantly assist the world in a dramatic transition to a real 'new world order' . . . if not a literal New World.[25]

* There is a direct relationship between the monuments of Cydonia and those of ancient human civilisations, particularly that of the ancient Egyptians. For example, the Face is constantly described as a 'Sphinx', which, with its proximity to 'pyramids', obviously relates it to Giza. This is what is called the 'terrestrial connection'.

* By linking the message of Cydonia with even more controversial modern mysteries such as crop circles, the same consistent message can be discerned, which suggests that the builders of Cydonia are still around.

Hoagland is now firmly of the opinion that the Cydonia monuments were built by a civilisation from elsewhere in the galaxy, who visited Earth in the remote past, having revised his estimate of the Face's age from half a million to several million – perhaps even a billion – years:

> For, if 'the Martians' hadn't come from Earth . . . or Mars . . . then there was just one place left they could have come from . . .
> From beyond the solar system . . . and bearing a humanoid image either in their 'genes' or minds.[26]

In other words, Hoagland is implying that these putative extra-terrestrials actually created the human race, and this idea, odd though it may appear, is rapidly gaining currency throughout the world. Hoagland and his colleagues have been invited several times to present their findings to NASA itself, which is rather odd, because over the years Hoagland has become increasingly strident in his accusations that NASA – or rather, a highly placed cabal within it – is part of a conspiracy to prevent the truth about Cydonia reaching the public. For example, he has taken the lead in promoting the theory that the Mars Observer, which was officially lost in space in August 1993, was actually continuing to send data back to Earth in secret. He has also suggested that NASA are either deliberately 'fudging' the facts by withholding data from the latest Mars Global Surveyor images, making the publicly issued pictures look less like a face. It is therefore very strange to find Hoagland being actively courted by NASA in 1988 and 1990, with several invitations to address in-house audiences on the subject of Cydonia. Clearly, in some way it suits NASA – or certain people within that organisation – to have Hoagland at the centre of attention.

The first address was at NASA's headquarters, NASA-Goddard Space Flight Center, in August 1988. According to Hoagland, at a presentation at NASA-Lewis Research Center in Cleveland, Ohio in March 1990, the director, Dr John Klineberg, introduced him with these portentous words: '[This is] the man who managed to convince the President to state that a return to Mars is one of our major goals.'[27] Perhaps significantly, Hoagland claims that Klineberg's introduction disappeared from the video that NASA distributed after the event, because of 'simultaneous equipment failure' in two cameras – which hardly inspires confidence in NASA's technical competence – though the opening words were captured on audio tape by Hoagland's team.

Hoagland also gave a lecture to a meeting at the United Nations in New York in February 1992, which was enthusiastically received by a capacity audience.[28] Apparently they had no problem with his – admittedly well-presented and authoritative – theory that by then almost automatically linked Mars with ancient Egypt. Presented as it was with wonders and mysteries by a man who seemed to know, they lapped it up. Hoagland's conviction and enthusiasm were contagious; almost certainly as a result of his influence, two countries – Sierra Leone and Grenada – featured the Face on Mars on their official postage stamps.

Hoagland is also one of the most regular guests on Art Bell's nightly radio show, which is devoted to weird and wonderful paranormal, psychic and New Age topics and has an audience of 15 million listeners. By any standard, that is a huge number of people, who are presumably sympathetic to what has been described as Art Bell's 'blend of conservative political views and New Age credulity'.[29]

Through the Enterprise Mission website, a series of videos, and Hoagland's book *The Monuments of Mars* (first published in 1987, and already in its fourth, revised, edition), as well as regular media appearances and lecture tours, Hoagland has become the main source for the dissemination of information about the Martian enigmas, eclipsing much more solid, but unappealingly cautious, work by other researchers. A sign of this phenomenon is the title of the video series: *Hoagland's Mars*.

Facing facts

One of the main objectives of Hoagland's Mars Mission was to lobby NASA for a commitment to rephotographing Cydonia. For much of that time NASA either refused point-blank or issued contradictory statements. Then, in April 1998, they effectively wrong-footed the pro-Cydonia lobby by announcing that the Mars Global Surveyor, which had just begun to orbit the Red Planet, *would* be photographing Cydonia, achieving far better resolutions than the Viking mission. The results would be disseminated on the Internet almost immediately, as soon as the Jet Propulsion Laboratory (JPL) had completed the necessary processing of the digital information.

When these images – of the Face and the City – were finally issued by NASA to huge disappointment and even incredulity,

there was considerably less to suggest a Face. The many erst-
while enthusiastic proponents of the buildings on Mars theory
who had second thoughts included Stanley V. McDaniel –
another leading advocate of the Cydonia structures, although he
parted company with Hoagland on many points – and even
Mark Carlotto. McDaniel now says that the City's apparent pyramids and other structures 'appear consistent with a natural
geological interpretation'.[30] In particular the four mounds
making up the City Square, which plays an important part in
Hoagland's line of reasoning, are not symmetrically placed or
uniform in size and shape. The City Pyramid, McDaniel admits,
now looks more like a mountain than a building. And Mark
Carlotto, while not dropping all claims of artificiality, said: 'In
the 1976 Viking images, the impression of a face was unmis-
takable. But illuminated from below, the Face looks less
remarkable.'[31]

Hoagland, however, is as adamant as ever that the Face exists,
and – characteristically blunt – dismisses the new images as
'crap'.[32] He insists that the Mars Global Surveyor pictures show
more, not less, evidence of artificiality, even claiming that 'room-
sized cells' can be distinguished within the main City Pyramid.
Just as there were claims that the Turin Shroud's carbon-dating
tests were tampered with, many still sympathise with this view,
claiming that NASA deliberately fudged the data by extracting
some portions of it before issuing the new images, so that, for
example, certain parts of the contrast were missing.

Hoagland's Enterprise Mission website proclaimed that the
new images showed that 'It *is* a Face!'. Within days it had produced its own 'rectified' version of the new NASA pictures, this
time looking more like the original Viking ones, which was only
to be expected because they had filled in the 'gaps' in the new
data with the relevant parts of the original images.[33]

Hoagland clearly believed NASA was lying, and was furious. If
there were no Face on Mars, then there was nothing on which to
hang a 'Message'. But, for Hoagland and those who share his
views, there *had* to be a Face and a Message: it is all part of a

much wider and more insidious agenda, which includes the 'Message' – and legacy – of ancient Egypt.

NASA's marked lack of interest in pursuing the Cydonia enigma might, as many have suggested, conceal the fact that the US government is fully aware that the Face and the pyramids are artificial and want to withhold this information from the public.

Given the way that politics works, it is virtually certain that, should the US government even suspect that there is any truth in the claims of artificial features on Mars, it would want to make its own evaluation before deciding whether to disclose or conceal this knowledge.

There remain features on Mars – in Cydonia and elsewhere – difficult to reconcile with the natural processes of erosion and geology. For example, there is the so-called 'Crater Pyramid' in the Deuteronilus Mensae region, about 500 miles north-east of Cydonia.[34] Viking images of this area had shown an object, close to the rim of the crater, that cast a long, thin spirelike shadow. The object itself is hard to make out, as the camera was directly above it, but based on the shadow and angle of sunlight, it is calculated to be around 600 metres tall – hardly the pyramid Hoagland was swift to dub it, once again apparently seeking above all else to link Mars with Egypt, no matter how inconvenient the facts.

Such features continue to raise questions, although in the future they may be explained in some prosaic way. The only truly valid conclusion at the moment is that – as far as most people are concerned – there simply is not enough data to go on. We do not know enough to state categorically that there was not a civilisation on Mars in the distant past. On the other hand, much more investigation of the anomalies on Mars is needed before they can be positively identified as being man- (or rather, Martian-) made. Every drop of data has been wrung from the available images, and it still isn't enough to tell us definitively one way or another.

Our own view is that the Martian anomalies are very much a subject for investigation. Although so far we have concentrated on Hoagland and his team, other independent researchers have conducted a great deal of excellent work that, even within the frustrating confines of available data, has raised important questions.

For example, in 1993 Stanley V. McDaniel published an analysis of the Mars situation in *The McDaniel Report* (as it is known for short).[35] Initially intended as a critique of NASA's close-minded attitude to further investigation of Cydonia, McDaniel reviewed the evidence for the artificiality of the features and concluded that, at the very least, there is a case for further investigation. More recently, McDaniel and Monica Rix Paxson edited *The Case for the Face* (unfortunately published in 1998, just weeks after the new NASA images were released), which presents a series of much more soberly scientific papers on the enigma. Another independent group was the Mars Anomalies Research Society, founded in 1986 by former NASA astronaut Dr Brian O'Leary, whose members include Vincent DiPietro and John Brandenberg.

Many independent researchers reject the attempts of Hoagland's Enterprise Mission to construct additional wonders on the shaky foundation of the data so far available, in particular questioning the claims of geometric alignments and sophisticated mathematical 'codes' so crucial to their interpretation. McDaniel organised the Society for Planetary SETI* Research (SPSR) in 1994, which is in effect a rival to the Enterprise Mission. DiPietro and Molenaar, whose original work inspired the whole field, have themselves criticised attempts to go beyond the known facts:

> For the record, we do NOT support the work of those who have intertwined inventions of their own fantasy with excerpts of our work with the Mars data. . . . conjecture about alignments, which some writers have added are their own inventions, have nothing to do with the data as we have interpreted it.[36]

*SETI: Search for Extraterrestrial Intelligence.

Mark Carlotto is careful to be fair in his assessment of Hoagland's 'geometric code', saying: 'It's hard to disprove, but it's also hard to prove. I try to stick to the things I can prove. I approach the matter as a scientist while Hoagland approaches it as a writer.'[37] But Carlotto does admit that 'Hoagland tends to process images until he gets what he wants.'[38]

The question is open. Some of the data may be intriguing, but it is too limited for any conclusions to be drawn as yet. Although Mark Carlotto sensibly points out that there is no rush to find the meaning of the Face – after all, it is going nowhere – there are others who seem to be in an unseemly haste to come to a hard-and-fast conclusion, those who want to build the Mars mystery into their own agenda, centred on the year 2000.

Worlds apart

What particularly interests us is why Hoagland and others in his project have tried to promote the Message of Cydonia idea, its connection with Earth's ancient past and its importance for our immediate future. Hoagland has effectively hijacked the mystery of Cydonia, making it very much his own, or at least the 'property' of his Mission. But what drives him and his colleagues to seek to convert us all to these ideas?

Central to Hoagland's own 'mission' is his emphasis on the (alleged) connection between Cydonia and ancient Egypt. But is there a connection other than the – arguable – observation that they both have pyramids?

The Cydonia enigma has recently been given a very significant boost in the form of an endorsement by Hancock, Bauval and Grigsby in *The Mars Mystery*. Although mainly concerned with the possibility of the Earth being hit by an asteroid or comet, the authors accept not just the reality of Cydonia and other Martian anomalies, but also its encoded mathematical Message and connection with the ancient civilisations of Earth, particularly ancient Egypt. Once these alleged connections are scrutinised, though, great flaws appear in their logic. The basic argument is that, because there are pyramids and a Sphinx in both Giza and Cydonia, the two are connected. But of course that depends on the Face on Mars being a Sphinx. The Cydonia clique describe it as being Sphinx-like; indeed, James Hurtak was using such emotive language even before it was officially discovered.

This eagerness to call the Face a Sphinx is very odd. Even if the Face were genuinely artificial, the fact remains that it is just a face, not a lion's body with a man's head. Besides, the Face only 'works' because it stares out into space – the only angle from which we could recognise it – whereas, of course, the Sphinx can only be perceived from a position on Earth. This is no good for the Hoagland camp. They have to devise increasingly unlikely scenarios to fit their Face/Sphinx correlation, requiring some extremely tortuous reasoning. Hoagland states that, if the Face on Mars is divided down the middle, and each half is mirror-imaged on to the other, we achieve two, distinctly different new images. One, he claims, is 'simian' in appearance, the other 'leonine' – an anthropoid and a lion. The Great Sphinx at Giza is a man's head on a lion's body. Conclusion: we have two Sphinxes – in close proximity with pyramids – on both worlds![39]

Serious problems are raised by this interpretation of the Face, and not merely the fact that the 'simian' looks, to us at least, much more like a cartoon dog, and the lion is similarly hard to see. One of the main problems with analysing the Face is that one half of it lies in deep shadow. Some of the image-enhancement techniques have been claimed to bring out certain details on the shadowed side, such as a second eye socket, but such claims are themselves controversial. There is no way in which the shadowed side can be reconstructed to show any fine detail, and certainly not half a lion's face!

The argument about the Face may be extremely shaky, but the situation worsens when the clique tries to use linguistics to reinforce their case. Hoagland, and others such as Graham Hancock and Robert Bauval, make much of the fact that the name Cairo, in Arabic *Al Qahira*, means 'Mars'.[40] Hancock, Bauval and Grigsby go so far as to describe the naming as 'inexplicable'.[41] But in fact it is very easily explained. Al Qahira literally means 'the Conqueror', which was the Arab name for Mars.[42] Cairo/Al Qahira was founded in 969 CE by the Fatimid general Jawhar al-Siqilli, following his conquest of Egypt. When the site of the new city was established it was noted that Mars was at an astrologically propitious point in the sky – and this, together with the fact that it was built to honour a conqueror, explains the choice of the name.[43] It has no connection with any putative relationship between features on Mars and those on the Giza Plateau. In any case, Cairo was not always the capital of Egypt: until the time of the Crusades it was merely a satellite town of the more important city of Al Fustat.[44] The populous suburbs of Cairo have only begun to nudge up to the Sphinx in the last fifty years. Before that, Giza was completely separate from Cairo, 6.5 miles (10 kilometres) out in the desert, effectively undermining the theory that connects Giza and Cairo/Mars.

Hancock, Bauval and Grigsby also point out that 'Horakhti', meaning 'Horus of the Horizon' – a name of the Sphinx – was also a term used by the ancient Egyptians for Mars. Their central argument in *Keeper of Genesis* was that Horakhti was a representation of the constellation of Leo, though. Which one is it to be?

Another linguistic 'fact' cited by Hoagland, Hancock and Bauval is that the original Egyptian name for Horus, *Heru*, also meant 'face', so Horakhti can, according to those authors, be translated as 'Face of the Horizon'.[45] Hoagland claims that, from the City of Cydonia, the Face would be seen on the horizon, so here we have a remarkable parallel. Two faces on the horizon, on two worlds . . . But this is a highly contrived game: according to Wallis Budge's *An Egyptian Hieroglyphic Dictionary* the two words, meaning 'Horus' and 'face', may sound the same phonetically (although as ancient Egyptian vowel sounds have to be guessed at, no one knows for certain), but that is as far as it goes.[46] They are two entirely different words. It is like claiming that the English word 'knight' is interchangeable with the identical-sounding 'night'. And in hieroglyphs the two words are 'spelled' entirely differently and represent totally different concepts. Besides, *heru* is plural, meaning 'faces', which significantly alters the hypothesis of Hoagland et al.

The advocates of the Mars–Egypt connection seem to be enthusiastically incestuous in their adoption of each other's ideas and theories to prove their points and convey their message. Hoagland has eagerly taken up the New Egyptology, including that of John Anthony West, in support of his claims of a Mars–Egypt link. For example, he reports Robert Schoch's redating of the Sphinx from water erosion, claiming that, like Hancock and Bauval, it is evidence for a much older date of construction than 7000 BCE.[47]

Hancock and Bauval based most of their arguments on Hoagland's work and interpretation of the Mars material, which they seem to accept as if scientifically proven. Hoagland is given an especially warm acknowledgement in *Keeper of Genesis*, and it can therefore be assumed that the three had a close working relationship even at that relatively early stage in the development of Bauval and Hancock's hypothesis.

Hoagland, too, had his much-admired source: Robert Temple's *The Sirius Mystery*, which he has absorbed into his own belief system, lock, stock – and errors. For example, he often quotes the 'fact' that *arq ur* means 'Sphinx'.[48] This mistake – arising from that incorrect reading of Wallis Budge's *An Egyptian Hieroglyphic Dictionary* – finds its way into the work of many of the Mars–Egypt proponents.

Suspicions about Cydonia

During his lecture at the United Nations in New York in February 1992 Hoagland stressed the significance of 'radical new technologies' that could be derived from the decoded Message of Cydonia. These claims rely on the challenging concept of hyperdimensionality.

Physicists today believe that the universe encompasses far more dimensions than just the four (three of space, one of time) we know about and perceive with our senses. The only way we can begin to visualise the concept of a multidimensional universe is by analogy. One of the best is that of an imaginary world called Flatland, a two-dimensional place inhabited by two-dimensional beings, where there is only length and breadth, no up or down – something like a sheet of paper.[49] Imagine how Flatlanders would perceive a three-dimensional object that interacted with their world. For example, if a sphere passed through, the Flatlanders would only see it in cross-section; first a dot would appear, which would then become a circle that grows until the middle of the sphere passes through, and then it would decrease in size to become a dot again, and vanish. (No doubt such a 'paranormal' phenomenon would cause much consternation among Flatlanders and probably be hotly debated by learned Flatland societies as well as dismissed as a delusion by their 'Skeptics'.) This analogy with the hypothetical Flatland enables us to understand that events taking place in the higher dimensions now acknowledged by theoretical physicists would have visible effects in our three-dimensional world, although the cause would remain beyond both our senses and even our most sophisticated instruments.

Physicists deal in such 'extra' dimensions because of certain phenomena associated with nuclear physics, although there is some debate about how many dimensions make up the universe. These hyperdimensions cannot be observed directly, since we and all our measuring devices are stuck in the three-dimensional universe, but they can be understood mathematically. Hoagland's contention is that certain geometrical relationships in the Cydonia Complex are references to such hyperdimensional mathematics. The geometrical key is the repeated use of the angle of 19.5 degrees. For example, two sides of the D & M Pyramid are found at 19.5 degrees to Mars's lines of latitude, and this angle recurs in the position of the small mounds in the same region.[50]

According to Hoagland – and others of like mind – 19.5 (more precisely, 19.47) degrees is significant because it is the tetrahedral constant, which means that it relates to the tetrahedron, the simplest of the regular solids, with four sides of equilateral triangles, including a triangular base. If this shape were put inside a sphere, for example a planet, with one point touching one of the poles, the other three points will each touch the surface at a latitude of 19.5 degrees on the opposite hemisphere. This is a fact.

It has been observed that on all the planets in the solar system where it is possible to see the surface – Venus, for example, is always covered with clouds – there is invariably some great disturbance caused by an upwelling of energy at either 19.5 degrees north or 19.5 degrees south of the equator. The great Red Spot of Jupiter is located at this position. On Mars, Olympus Mons, the largest known volcano in the solar system (350 miles across), lies at 19.5 degrees north. On Earth, it is the location of the heavily volcanic islands of Hawaii, and the largest volcano on the planet, Mauna Loa.

The phenomenon of 19.5 degrees is thought to result from the rotation of the planets, being in effect a 'shadow' of highly potent forces of higher dimensions. In other words, the site of 19.5 degrees is a point where the other dimensions break through, becoming manifest in the three-dimensional world as a revelation of hyperdimensional forces.

This, claims Hoagland, is why the 19.5-degree angle recurs so often in Cydonia. It is a clue intended to lead us to an understanding of the hyperdimensional cause of the planetary upwellings of energy responsible for Jupiter's Red Spot and Mars's Olympus Mons. This in turn enables us to appreciate hyperdimensional physics. Hoagland argues that if the energy generated by higher dimensions can be tapped, we will have an unlimited source of power as well as the ability to develop such technologies as antigravity propulsion devices and interstellar space travel. These technologies, he believes, will solve many of the world's problems and bring about, in his words, a 'new world order'.

There are problems with this. Even in Hoagland's lecture to the

United Nations, where he talks at length about the importance of 19.5 degrees and tetrahedral geometry, he admits that the upwelling of planetary energies at these points had already been worked out years before by mathematicians dealing in hyperdimensions. The Message of Cydonia, in fact, merely repeats what very terrestrial scientists have known for years.

More importantly, Hoagland and Erol Torun drew a number of significant conclusions from Cydonia's latitude. One of their key claims is that the latitude of the D & M Pyramid – 40.868 degrees north – was not only chosen because it embodied important mathematical concepts (being the tangent of the exponential constant *e* divided by *pi*), but also because the same concepts appear in the geometry of other features of Cydonia. The complex is therefore, they concluded, 'self-referencing', which means that the mathematics in the 'buildings' relate to the Complex's position on the planet, proving that none of it is a mere coincidence.[51]

A difficulty arises as the co-ordinates for surface features based on the Viking survey have a marked margin of error. They are certainly not precise enough to fix a feature's latitude to three decimal places of a degree. New, and more accurate data from Mars Global Surveyor suggests that all the previous figures should be revised so that the features are in fact slightly closer to the Martian equator, meaning that the D & M Pyramid stands at 40.7 degrees north.[52] This is not particularly significant in itself (it represents an error of approximately 17 kilometres on the ground), but it is enough to invalidate the precise mathematical relationships of Hoagland's theory.

In addition, other researchers, such as Tom Van Flandern of the US Naval Observatory, have pointed out that it is accepted that the Martian poles have shifted significantly over millions of years, so Cydonia has not always been located at that latitude.[53] (Interestingly, Van Flandern has calculated that, before the pole shift, Cydonia would have been on Mars's equator.) There is also evidence that Mars's crust has 'slipped' several times because of 'crustal displacement', again changing the position of the Cydonia region.[54]

Even the theoretical harnessing of the energy generated by hyperdimensional forces – as hypothesised by Hoagland – is nothing new, although there are no known ways to actually do so – and the Message of Cydonia does nothing to enlighten us about this. Neither does it even hint how workable technologies might be developed from harnessing this energy. The 'amazing' geometry of Cydonia has added nothing to our understanding – of Mars, Martians or of mankind.

The Hoagland camp's confident theorising does not stop there. When Hoagland's colleague David Myers claims that a line running from a particular mark on the D & M Pyramid to a 'teardrop' on the Face measures exactly 1/360th of the diameter of Mars[55] (thus 'proving', incidentally, that the builders must have used the same system of measuring angles as ourselves), he is truly on a slippery slope. There is no justification for choosing to join these two insignificant points up except that they are, for Myers, the required distance apart. One would eventually find two points that would oblige somewhere in Cydonia.

The angles Erol Torun claimed to have found in the D & M Pyramid provide most of the basis for the decoding of the Message of Cydonia. What he claims to have found is in itself highly debatable: a five-sided pyramid that he managed to discern from an enhanced image of a partly eroded feature half in shadow. All the measurements have to be treated with caution, so any conclusions based on them must, at the very outside, be highly speculative. (The Mars Global Surveyor has not, unfortunately, re-imaged the D & M Pyramid yet.) In fact, Torun himself admits that there is an unknown margin of error in the Viking images – which makes his whole case for precise geometric relationships completely redundant.[56]

Another prime mover in the Mars Mission is the British award-winning film photographer David S. Percy, who was appointed European director of operations by Hoagland (although they have since had a disagreement and no longer work together). In this capacity Percy enthusiastically promoted the Message of Cydonia in the United Kingdom and other European countries. He also produced the video of Hoagland's address at the United Nations. Percy has lectured widely in Britain on the Cydonia–Mars connection, using state-of-the-art computer graphics to illustrate his points. Like Hoagland, whose media background enables him to present his ideas in a relaxed and professional manner, Percy uses his skills as a film producer to excellent effect. His images of Cydonia surpass even the earlier enhancements for clarity and sharpness. In particular, the all important D & M Pyramid – so crucial for the 'decoding' of the alleged geometrical and mathematical message – appears as a clearly defined feature, with the original blurred edges now in such sharp focus that they almost seem to be etched into the Martian landscape. In his lectures, Percy describes these images as being Mark Carlotto's – but he adds vaguely that they have undergone 'further enhancement and rectification in London recently'.[57] He gives no details of this process, but when we asked what he had meant, he admitted that he had done it himself.[58] Although professionals who have worked with the images of Cydonia – such as DiPietro, Molenaar and Mark Carlotto – have published detailed technical descriptions of the process they used, Percy has not obliged.

Percy added a new connection to the enigma. Hoagland had already noted the similarity between Silbury Hill – the largest manmade mound in Europe, which lies just south-west of Avebury in Wiltshire in England – and one of the Cydonian features called the 'Tholus', or Spiral Mound. In the library of his luxurious London flat, while looking at an aerial photograph of Avebury, Percy then experienced a great revelation, which he describes (somewhat mysteriously) as 'far memory'.[59] His newly inspired eye suddenly noted that the great circle of ditch and earthen rampart that encloses its standing stones was a representation of nothing less than the large crater in Cydonia! He went on to demonstrate that the Avebury circle and Silbury Hill lie in the same relative positions as the Cydonia crater and Martian Spiral Mound – if the latter is scaled down by a factor of 14:1.

Percy and David Myers (the Mars Mission's director of operations, and later co-author with Percy of a book called *Two-Thirds*), worked on this correlation and concluded that the Avebury complex had been deliberately laid out, some 5,000 years ago, as an 'analogue' of Cydonia. Percy claims that maps of the two areas, appropriately scaled up or down, can be superimposed over each other to reveal a perfect match.

Perhaps not unexpectedly, problems arise with this hypothesis. The only real correlation between Avebury and Cydonia is the relative position and size of two features, the crater/Avebury circle and the Spiral Mound/Silbury Hill. Even then the match is not perfect. When scaled down and superimposed, the crater is smaller than, and not the same shape as, the Avebury circle. Percy also claims correlations between other features that are even less persuasive. For example, the D & M Pyramid's Avebury analogue is a certain tumulus surrounded by a grove of trees. In fact it fails totally to match its alleged Martian counterpart, not corresponding in size, shape or relative position with the D & M Pyramid. In any case there are many similar tumuli in the area. No other Cydonian features are 'analogued' at Avebury, although Percy makes much of odd indentations, lumps and bumps in the ground that he finds at the approximate position of the City on Mars. None of these are at all convincing. But there is one spectacular omission: there is no analogue of the Face at Avebury. Could it be that nothing could be found at Avebury – even by forcing the data to fit – to even vaguely remind us of the location and features of the Face, so it has been quietly forgotten?

In fact, only two features of Avebury correspond to any at Cydonia: the earthwork circle and Silbury Hill. It seems odd that an analogue of Cydonia, built on Earth, should centre on reproducing a natural feature of Cydonia – the crater – while not including the many supposedly artificial features. Finally, many landmarks of the Avebury complex have no analogue in Cydonia, the most obvious being West Kennet Long Barrow. Yet despite all these discrepancies and convoluted hypothesising, Hoagland incorporated Percy's 'discovery' of the Cydonia–Avebury connection into his United Nations lecture.

Another area that greatly excites Hoagland, Percy, Myers and their colleagues is the vexed subject of crop circles. They maintain that these 'transtime crop glyphs', as they prefer to call them, contain geometrical and mathematical 'codes' that duplicate, and reinforce, the Message of Cydonia. By linking the builders of Cydonia with this very visible, yet enigmatic, modern phenomenon, Hoagland is effectively saying that the Martian builders are still around, and are active on Earth now. He describes 'the fact that someone – *demonstrably not from Earth* – is now attempting to drive home the "Message of Cydonia" as a "message in the crops", before our very eyes right here on Earth!'[60]

One particular crop formation is given pride of place in the work of Hoagland and Percy because it incorporates tetrahedral geometry: the Barbary Castle formation, which appeared in a Wiltshire field in 1991. This 'crop glyph' was even featured in Hoagland's UN lecture because, he claimed, it includes geometrical features that match some of the code of Cydonia. If this were true, it would confirm not only the terrestrial connection, but also the return of the builders of Cydonia. Hoagland in particular invests great personal belief in the 'They're Back' interpretation of this formation, in which he and his team claim to have identified some of the same key angles they detected in the plan of Cydonia. David Percy goes even further, managing to overlay the Barbary Castle pattern on Avebury, to demonstrate how its geometry was used as the plan for the layout of the roads!

Whatever the truth about crop circles in general, there seems little doubt that this one is a hoax or – as many of the circlemakers themselves tend to think of it – a work of art. The inspiration for the design is actually known. It is not a specially constructed design to encode some of the secrets of hyperdimensional physics, but is based on a design in a sixteenth-century alchemical treatise by Steffan Michelspacher, *Cabala, speculum artis et naturae in alchymia*.[61]

The identity of the makers is well known among the confraternity of circlemakers, and the *modus operandi* has already been described by Rob Irving, a writer, photographer and occasional circlemaker. Irving told us:

> There's really no mystery about it . . . In the context of 1991, this was the most complex of its time. But compared to what's being done now – fractal patterns five times bigger, which have been filmed being made – it's very primitive . . . It would be sniffed at now.[62]

With just a few simple implements and the application of some basic geometrical rules, such a formation could be made 'within a couple of hours', he said.

The formation wasn't even executed with any finesse: there are kinks in some of the lines and mistakes in the geometry. Significantly, Hoagland and Percy actually use the errors in their reconstruction of the grand design of this pattern![63]

So what is the Message of Cydonia, according to Hoagland? He says:

> Cydonia turns out to be: nothing less than an architectural affirmation of the fundamental *physics* of the Universe – the ultimate embodiment of a grand, 'Universal Architecture' . . . at the most archetypal level . . . This message is *identically* 'coded' elsewhere in the solar system . . . including, *here on Earth*![64]

The emerging picture

It seems, certainly in Hoagland's case, that data – itself by no means conclusive – has been forced to fit his preconceived ideas that somehow involves both Martian anomalies and the monuments of ancient Egypt. The most significant part of this scenario is the idea that there is a 'Message' somehow essential to mankind's present and immediate future. But why? Where does this belief originate?

There are only two possible reasons for these ideas: entirely spurious notions have been superimposed on a genuine mystery in order to give them an apparent feasibility; or the proponents of these ideas somehow knew, or thought they knew, in advance that these connections exist.

Perhaps the release of this information is an exercise in deception, or in 'softening up' the public to accept certain ideas, even to the point of promoting those ideas when the facts (as currently known) do not support them. There seems to us to be an air of desperation to make us believe, whether we want to or not and whether the evidence fits or not. And that is worrying.

With all of its monumental implications for our understanding of Man's recent past *and* our immediate future – the 'radical new technologies' it promises and the implicit suggestion that the builders of Cydonia are about to return, if they have not already – the Message of Cydonia promoted primarily by Hoagland is not supported by the evidence. Clearly, it has been deliberately grafted on to what is, admittedly, a very intriguing enigma, in much the same way that Hancock and Bauval have grafted the date of 10,500 BCE on to the genuine ancient Egyptian mysteries.

The way that the Martian enigmas are being promoted by the likes of Hoagland presents a striking parallel to certain investigations of ancient Egypt. The common features of both are:

(1) At the core lies a genuine mystery. The achievements of the ancient Egyptians in, for example, building the Great Pyramid, and the unmistakably advanced knowledge of the Pyramid Texts, do not conform to the accepted view of history. Likewise – even given the most recent crop of images – with currently available information it is not possible to dismiss the notion that there might well be artificial structures on Mars.

(2) On to the genuine mystery has been grafted a series of 'solutions' and explanations that simply do not stand up to objective scrutiny – for example, Hancock and Bauval's case for a

10,500 BCE date, and Hoagland *et al*'s extrapolation of the Message of Cydonia.

(3) These superimposed views are not just proposed to make us believe that these mysteries will prove that the history books are wrong, but to impress upon us the idea that they will have a direct impact on us today, pointing to some earth-shattering (perhaps literally) change in the near future. Examples include the belief that the Great Pyramid will somehow trigger the dawn of the new Age of Aquarius in the year 2000 and the imminent return of the builders of Cydonia.

(4) There is a degree of 'official' involvement behind the scenes. We have seen that, for whatever reasons, it appears that a search for something at Giza is under way. It is also clear that Hoagland's research projects have received encouragement and assistance from individuals and organisations closely connected with the intelligence community, from the original help of Paul Shay in setting up the initial Mars Mission, to the support of Congressman Roe. (Obviously, the involvement of some of the individuals with intelligence agents may well have a 'non-conspiratorial' explanation. For example, Mark Carlotto's expertise in analysing satellite data for military and intelligence purposes is something that could naturally lead to his participation in the Cydonia investigation, but the sheer number of the people who are connected with intelligence personnel and organisations and also support and encourage Hoagland's work is, in our view, somewhat suspicious.)

We have noted that Hoagland's work appears to fall into two distinct phases: the first, backed by SRI in 1983–4, was concerned with promoting the idea of the existence of a very ancient civilisation on Mars. But, since 1989, the second phase has been about the 'Message', the connection with humanity's own ancient history and our present and future.

Was Phase One, as social scientist Tom Rautenberg thought at first, in fact a sociological experiment to determine public reaction to the concept of life on Mars? And then did someone realise that the Mars material could be used more effectively to put across another message, part of a separate but interlinking agenda?

Another motive may have lain behind the 1983–4 SRI-backed project. The Iron Curtain was still in place and the attendant suspicions of Soviet plotting was very strong: the Eastern Bloc countries were perceived to be keeping many secrets very close to their chests. Perhaps Hoagland/SRI's Phase One was an attempt to draw out of the Soviets their knowledge or suspicions about Mars. It is certainly a curious coincidence that, within a month of the Boulder conference at which Hoagland announced his initial findings, the Russian English-language propaganda newspaper, *Soviet Weekly*, carried an article by Vladimir Avinsky on his research into what he termed 'the Martian Sphinx' and 'pyramids'.[65]

Hoagland and his team then tried to establish a line of communication with the Soviet Academy of Sciences to exchange data on the subject. Significantly, their intermediary in this was Jim Hickman of the Soviet Exchange Program of the Esalen Institute in California (of which more later).[66]

Not only do marked parallels lie between the way that the stories of Egypt and of Mars are being presented, but the stories themselves are also being deliberately fused to make one big, dramatic picture. These days there are few non-academic interested parties who fail to associate the features of Cydonia with Egypt. Those with their own agendas have been very successful: we have seen the attempts by Cydonia researchers such as Hoagland to link the Message with ancient Egypt (and other cultures, such as megalithic Britain). On the other hand, Hancock and Bauval have made the journey the other way round, beginning with the mysteries of Egypt, and then linking them back to Mars. This is one story, not two, as is demonstrated by the overlap of people and groups involved.

For example, it is reported that, in 1996, on their return to the United States from the Giza project, members of the Joseph Schor

Foundation consulted both Richard Hoagland and James Hurtak, the two main proponents of the pyramids of Mars and of a Mars–Giza connection.[67] And Boris Said, the film-maker who has been chronicling events at Giza since 1990, recently enrolled James Hurtak as part of his team. Hurtak had talked about the Mars–Egypt connection as being part of a 'great cosmic blueprint' as far back as 1975.

There are other curious crossovers of personnel between the pyramids of Mars and the Mars–Giza camps. Dr Farouk El Baz was appointed head of the team that continued Rudolf Gantenbrink's work to explore the 'Sirius shaft' in the Great Pyramid. El Baz's past association with NASA may be coincidental, but SRI – as we have seen – certainly does not lack contacts within defence and intelligence agencies. (Since leaving NASA, El Baz founded and is now director of the Center for Remote Sensing at Boston University. One of the Starship *Enterprise*'s shuttle craft in *Star Trek: The Next Generation* is named after him – true fame.)

By far the most prominent of all crossover individuals is Lambert Dolphin Jr, the SRI teamleader at Giza between 1973 and 1982, who was also the co-founder with Hoagland of the Independent Mars Mission in 1983, a project funded and resourced by SRI.

This is a strangely thought-provoking scenario, but it becomes even stranger, particularly when considered in the context of the knowledge we have gathered so far and the conclusions we can extrapolate from it.

(1) Intelligence agencies in both the United States and Britain have shown interest in the idea of extraterrestrial contact at the dawn of civilisation; for example, in their reaction to Robert Temple's research.

(2) Clandestine explorations, backed by the US government, are being carried out in Egypt. Clearly, they believe there is something worth looking for, which will presumably be of some

practical use to them, either by their ownership of it or by preventing anyone else from having it.

(3) Certain writers and researchers are promoting 'messianic' messages based very much on their own interpretation of legitimate questions about the origins of Egyptian civilisation and the anomalous features on Mars. These two strands have been gradually, but concertedly, drawn together. The 'consensus' story emerging from these influential authors – whose readership worldwide totals many millions – is that of extraterrestrial influence on the evolving human civilisation. (Interestingly, in the 1998 edition of *The Sirius Mystery*, Robert Temple discusses the Face on Mars in positive terms, writing: 'I would not be surprised at a Martian connection with the Sirius Mystery.'[68])

(4) There appears to be a great deal of behind-the-scenes encouragement of the work of Hoagland's research team, which makes the most extreme claims. Examples include the involvement of intelligence-connected individuals and groups, including SRI, right from the beginning, and NASA's 'courting' of Hoagland and his team in the late 1980s and early 1990s.

A glaring paradox is found in the above points. On the one hand, the involvement of official bodies may simply mean that they have come to the same conclusions as Hancock, Bauval, Hoagland and Temple – and are, like them, excited by the idea of imminent revelations about Egypt and Mars. Perhaps they even have prior knowledge . . . Do the 'powers that be' already know about the influence on humanity of an extraterrestrial race – either from Mars or elsewhere? Are they secretly trying to recover some knowledge of that race?

Superficially, this may seem likely. On the other hand, as we have seen, the 'messianic' messages claimed for both the Egyptian and Martian scenarios do not bear scrutiny. They use faulty reasoning, misread source material or are manifestly massaged to accord with some personal – or group – hidden agenda.

So why should official bodies such as SRI and NASA, who have reputations – and funding – to lose, take this all so seriously?

We can suggest two main hypotheses that may account for the mounting official interest in such apparently off-the-wall scenarios: one is a conspiracy about something real, and the other is a conspiracy to make us believe something that is unreal.

Hypothesis One: The messages for mankind extrapolated from both terrestrial and Martian mysteries are basically false. At the very least they are wishful thinking or delusions or, more disturbingly, the data have been forced to fit into a preconceived set of beliefs. The proponents of these ideas want to use the mysteries to further their own agendas, perhaps in order to promote their religious, quasi-religious – or Masonic – ideologies. They could even form an exercise in the manipulation of mass psychology – as suspected by Tom Rautenberg when he first heard of SRI's involvement with the Cydonia enigma – but on a much grander and more worrying scale.

This hypothesis would account for much of the data, though not some of the official activities. We are convinced, for example, of clandestine activity at Giza, which is obviously expected to produce some kind of tangible results. Another example involves the curious circumstances surrounding NASA's photographing of the Crater Pyramid. In our opinion, this 600-foot spire perched on the edge of a crater is the most compelling of the anomalous Martian features, and very difficult to explain in terms of natural processes. What is curious is that, back in 1976, Viking took four pictures of that area in rapid succession, the only time during the entire mission that this happened.[69] As Mark Carlotto has pointed out, this must have been preprogrammed into the orbiter, as the time delay on radio instructions would not permit mission control to react so quickly. It seems too much of a coincidence that the only instance of such rapid-fire photography should occur at that one particular spot – but how did NASA know in advance that there was something interesting to photograph in that area?

Hypothesis Two: Those promoting the message for mankind – both publicly and behind the scenes – somehow know it to be true, yet realise it is important to proceed with caution where the public is concerned. Information is gradually being fed to the masses to 'acclimatise' us all to such ideas. Perhaps the idea behind the 'mass psychology' experiment is to gauge public reactions to some forthcoming genuine announcement(s) about extraterrestrial influences on our past – and even on our present and future.

In this scenario, false evidence is being proposed to support a genuine phenomenon. This is a bold and apparently bizarre proposition, but the whole history of intelligence operations is one of absurdity and contradiction, albeit with a steely underpinning of single-minded agendas. This hypothesis deserves to be taken seriously, if only to see where it leads. Its advantage is that it explains why, on the one hand, official bodies appear to be searching seriously for something, while on the other the reasons for doing so simply do not sustain closer examination.

Our two hypotheses will be tested as this investigation continues: as we have seen, in the first, the so-called messages for mankind are simply fabricated or delusory. But is there any other information that might support the second hypothesis?

Could the 'powers that be' know that extraterrestrial influence on human civilisation and the connection with Mars are genuine, even if they have to create false evidence to persuade the public that this is so? If they really have such inside information, how did they acquire it? Evidence that convinced hard-headed industrialists, scientists and intelligence operatives about the reality of alien intervention in human affairs must have been so persuasive as to be virtually incontestable, but at the same time impossible to entrust to the public domain. But what kind of evidence could possibly be so watertight?

A clue may lie in the fact that a favoured target of the Pentagon's remote-viewing experiments was Mars. The original SRI experiments, between 1973 and 1976, included sessions by Ingo Swann and physical researcher Harold Sherman in which they remote viewed the surface of Mars (and indeed, other planets).[70] The results of these experiments have never been made public,[71] although it is known that the Face on Mars was detected by RVers some years before the Viking mission.

In a conversation with Uri Geller in January 1998 about his time at SRI, he told us that the Face on Mars had, in fact, been discovered by remote viewing in the early 1970s, long before the Viking mission. For various reasons he could not reveal the identity of the remote viewer in question, but in October 1998 we asked James Hurtak's Academy For Future Sciences about his supposed 'prediction' about a facelike feature on Mars that – according to Hancock and Bauval – he had made in 1975. The reply was: 'Dr Hurtak shared his insights of "remote viewing" with Mr Harold Sherman'.[72] This was rather puzzling, as we had not actually mentioned remote viewing; in our view, this was tantamount to an admission that the Face had been discovered by remote viewing. The AFFS's reply went on: 'However, the principle [sic] artifact that Dr Hurtak saw was the pyramidal formations [sic] which has always been his uniqueness and not the Face itself.' So although Hurtak himself may not have remote viewed the Face, the implication is that Harold Sherman did. This is interesting, because we do know that Sherman remote viewed Mars for SRI.

Sherman began as a sports writer before becoming interested in the paranormal and UFOs in the 1940s. He coined the phrase 'Little Green Men' to describe aliens. Sherman was by 1975 a veteran psychical researcher, in his seventies, who had been brought in by SRI specifically to help set up the first remote-viewing project.[73]

The issue of remote viewing may seem like something from *The X-Files*, a ripping yarn about invisible spies and mind control, not based on hard fact. No matter how it may challenge our mundane certainties about the ways things are, though, remote viewing works, which is why so much time and taxpayers' money was invested in it by several governments, and particularly the US government. When the cream of the crop of US RVers repeatedly –

and consistently – described the surface of Mars, individuals within the government and associated agencies took note.

The US Army's highly talented remote viewer Joe McMoneagle 'visited' Mars several times, always sketching the scenes that met his disembodied gaze. There, unmistakably, were pyramids and, he claimed, tunnels under the Cydonia complex in which the remnants of an ancient civilisation continued to exist.

In his 1996 book *Psychic Warrior*, David Morehouse tells of his own remote-viewing missions to Mars eight years before. He had been given Mars as a blind target, without knowing that this location had been set for him. He saw nothing significant, just a barren reddish landscape that had been deserted for thousands of years. After this 'mission', Morehouse was shown a folder enclosing details of the target location: pictures of Mars, taken from orbit and the ground. He writes of the other material in the folder:

> There was a chemical analysis of the atmosphere, and some high-altitude photographs of the surface with captions indicating which spots had led several scientists to believe Mars was once inhabited.[74]

Morehouse, who also sketched a dream in which 'the sky tears and another dimension is revealed', had a tendency to remote view particularly significant scenes, even if he only realised it in retrospect. In *Psychic Warrior* he describes being set a blind target and homing in on a boxlike object hidden in a cavern that appeared to be protected by an aura of extreme danger. He told his 'monitor' that it was 'something very powerful and sacred' and said it would 'vaporise' anyone who got too close, adding: 'I felt very uncomfortable and vulnerable in that cavern'.[75] An hour or so after this 'mission', Morehouse was shown an artist's impression of the target – the fabled Old Testament Ark of the Covenant, whose mysterious power could fell whole armies. It seems that he had successfully used one paranormal ability to get the target right – perhaps a form of telepathic contact with the mind of the experimenter – but had he really tuned in to the Ark itself?

No one knows for certain how remote viewing works, only what it can produce. Seated in a mundane office with a monitor asking questions, the RVer's invisible consciousness takes flight and visits elsewhere, sometimes even else*when*, for time is no barrier to the remote viewer who can 'scroll' up or down through past, present and future by the force of will alone. Sometimes, of course, they fail to describe the targets, and come up with either a 'displacement' description, an accurate description of a place that was not the target, or something that might just be fantasy. Sometimes the remote viewers can describe frankly outlandish scenarios.

Despite the many successes of remote viewing, the problem has always been the accurate interpretation of what is seen. Even everyday perception involves the brain making decisions about the meaning of the shapes of objects and people seen. In this process, context is everything, and the more obvious and detailed the context, the more accurate the brain's interpretation of the shapes seen. The same applies to remote viewing, particularly when the target was Mars prior to 1976 – before the first good photographs of its surface reached us on Earth. The mind of the remote viewer would automatically try to make sense of unfamiliar landmarks, perhaps reacting as if to an inkblot test and turning a rocky outcrop into a recognisable Face.

We ourselves know that remote viewing can, and often does, work, but it is by no means 100 per cent accurate. One cautionary tale involves Courtney Brown, professor of political science at Emory University in Atlanta. Trained in remote viewing in 1992 by a former member of the Pentagon RV unit (he refuses to name him, but it was, in fact, Pentagon remote-viewing star, Major Ed Dames), he hit upon the idea of using remote viewing as a scientific research tool, specifically to investigate the question of extraterrestrial visitors on Earth.

Brown made several 'research trips', via remote viewing, to Mars in 1993 and 1994. The first was part of his training, when it was a blind target (clearly a favourite destination for RV trainers). He described a pyramid, and nearby a volcano erupting, devastating the area and causing the inhabitants to flee for their lives. Afterwards, his trainer showed him the target picture: it was Cydonia.[76]

Brown maintains, thanks to the evidence of his remote-viewing 'eyes', that there are not only survivors of the Martian race living underground on Cydonia, but also on Earth – beneath the mountains of New Mexico and in villages in Latin America. According to Brown, Martian civilisation at the time of its great catastrophe had achieved approximately the level of development of ancient Egypt, although we do not know whether that is the level understood by mainstream academics or that of the technologically advanced Egyptians of the New Orthodoxy. All but wiped out, the Martians were rescued by the arrival of the – by now familiar – Grey aliens, who took the survivors forward in time to our present and altered them genetically so they can live on Earth.

Things went badly wrong for Courtney Brown, though. He also claimed, based on the remote viewing evidence of his team, that a spaceship was following in the tail of the comet Hale-Bopp, a claim that he promoted widely, especially on the Art Bell show. Subsequently, the Heaven's Gate cult committed mass suicide specifically so that their souls would be 'beamed up' to the Hale-Bopp spaceship. Someone else who believed that there was something suspicious about Hale-Bopp, to the point of accusing the US government of a cover-up, was none other than Richard Hoagland, who promoted the theory with his usual zeal.[77]

However, all this may well assume quite another interpretation when the possibility of remote influencing is taken into account . . .

'The day we opened the door'

One may smile at the apparently fantastical beliefs of a remote-viewing professor of political science, and dismiss the wilder claims for a Mars–Egypt connection, but the fact remains that there *are* reasons to take seriously the idea of life on Mars, even if it died out millions of years ago. The breakthrough appeared to come when NASA announced, on 7 August 1996, that evidence of micro-organisms on Mars – life, if a very primitive sort – had been found in a meteorite in Antarctica that had originated on Mars. Designated as ALH84001 (ALH = Allen Hills, where it was found; 84 was the year; 001 means it was the first collected in that year), its age is estimated at 4.5 billion years, and the microfossils in it at 3.6 billion years. It is believed to have been blown into orbit by an impact on Mars about 15 million years ago, and to have drifted around in space until it landed on Earth 13,000 years ago. The microfossils are of minute bacterialike organisms, the largest being 200 nanometers (billionths of a metre) in length. The meteorite is just under 2 kg in weight, and 'about the size of a small potato'.

Although thousands of meteorites rain down on the Earth's surface every day, clearly this one was perceived to be different – but why? And what was the reason for the veritable circus of hype that erupted so abruptly over it? The sheer scale of the publicity surrounding the announcement and the way in which the whole business was stage-managed seemed odd at the time, but in retrospect it seems even more unusual.

A major press conference at NASA's Johnson Space Center in Houston was attended by the international media, ensuring that the news made headlines all around the world. The conference was hosted by NASA administrator Daniel Goldin, who hailed the event as 'a day that may well go down in history for American science, for the American people, and indeed humanity' – obviously he is not one to think small. He also called it, somewhat portentously, 'the day we opened the door'. Later that day, President Clinton made a public statement hailing the event as historic and pledging that NASA would 'search for answers and for knowledge that is as old as humanity itself but essential to our people's future': strange words, which appear to convey a subtext to those with inside knowledge, but only succeeding in mystifying the rest of us. What could there possibly be about micro-organisms in a piece of rock from Mars that is 'essential to our people's future'?

For a normally conservative organisation with a scientific reputation to maintain, NASA's orchestrated media splash was unprecedented. This is particularly odd, because the evidence presented at that conference was by no means conclusive enough to justify such a major event. Many scientists, particularly in Europe, have since expressed reservations about NASA's interpretation of the facts. The question of whether the 'fossils' really are biological in origin is still being hotly debated in the scientific community. They may well be, as claimed, evidence of primitive life on Mars, but it was NASA's *certainty* about it, not to mention the almost evangelical fervour and the sheer hype with which they promoted it, that is so surprising as to suggest another agenda.

Bewilderment only increases when it is realised that such claims had been made before, though never with as much publicity as ALH84001. It is intriguing that this evidence had been brought to the attention of NASA Administrator Daniel Goldin just weeks before the announcement – by two of the original 'discoverers' of the Face on Mars, John Brandenburg and Vincent DiPietro.[78] Brandenburg had been researching the history of Mars in order to establish whether it had ever had conditions suitable for sustaining life, when he came across scientific papers written in 1989 by a British team reporting the discovery of organic carbon in a meteorite known to have originated on Mars.

Even further back, Dr Bartholomew Nagy of the University of Arizona had reported the discovery of bacterial microfossils in meteorites in the mid-1960s, although he did not discuss their origins. Nagy's findings – particularly the question of the biological nature of the material – were published in the 1960s and early 1970s and had been disputed by other scientists at the time. Nagy had found what he believed to be microfossils in a specific type of meteorite known as carbonaceous chrondites. Later, Brandenburg tried to establish where these meteorites came from. He could do this relatively easily, as individual 'signatures' are found in the composition of different types of rocks, based on the proportions of certain isotopes, that associate them with Earth, Mars or elsewhere. (This is how we know that ALH84001 is Martian, for example.) Brandenburg found that the carbonaceous chrondites studied by Nagy had the characteristic signature of Mars. (Since this technique is well established, it is a mystery why nobody had, apparently, used it before. Perhaps they had.) Nagy died in December 1995, just a few months before NASA's announcement vindicated his earlier work, notching the subject up into that almost hysterical publicity circus. It may well have shocked and saddened him.

Brandenburg published a paper on his research in May 1996, and lectured on his discoveries in Germany in July. A month before his paper was published he had personally approached Daniel Goldin with the results. Four months later came the big announcement.

ALH84001 had been discovered in Antarctica in 1984, but was only recognised as Martian in 1993. It had been analysed in secret at the Johnson Space Center in Houston – specifically to look for indications of biological constituents, which begs a question or two about the protocol of the scientific method. Brandenburg (who was present at the Houston press conference) speculates that pressure had been put on the NASA team to release their announcement before his work stole their thunder, although there was an ethical problem in this rivalry because his May 1996 paper had been peer-reviewed for publication by the very scientists at the Johnson Space Center who were secretly studying ALH84001! Others have speculated that Brandenburg's work may simply have inspired NASA, who needed a good excuse for their suddenly renewed interest in Mars.

In a further twist to this story, shortly after the press conference a Washington call girl confessed to the press that a client, Dick Morris – one of President Clinton's advisors – had told her some time before the announcement that evidence of life on Mars had been discovered but was classified as a 'military secret'.[79]

It has also been pointed out that Daniel Goldin, who hosted the press conference so exuberantly, is known to be a political appointee with a former career in top-secret defence-related industrial work. He had been appointed by President Bush – himself a former head of the CIA – and has overseen a marked increase in the amount of defence work conducted by NASA, as well as an influx of ex-Defense Department personnel into key posts within the space agency.[80]

The whole subject of the Martian microfossils and the press conference that announced them has provoked a flurry of conspiracy theories, which divide into two camps: one centred on the suspicion that this is part of a 'softening up' process that will eventually lead to the revelation of *intelligent* life on Mars, while the other argues that the story was a stunt to create a new climate of excitement about Mars, leading to more government funds being allocated to NASA in order to explore the planet further. These theories are not mutually exclusive, although one school maintains darkly that NASA wants to explore Mars for other, clandestine reasons of its own. Such theories are stimulated by the obsessive secrecy that surrounded the work of the NASA team at Houston, and the over-the-top manner in which the discovery was announced, sidestepping the usual stages of peer-reviewed scientific papers, going instead straight to a live worldwide press conference.

There has certainly been a marked scramble to explore Mars recently: funding for Mars Global Surveyor – currently sending back images – was rushed through after the loss of Mars Observer in August 1993. It was launched in 1996. Since the August 1996 announcement, a series of new Mars probes are being planned to continue the search for life on the Red Planet, including the bringing back of samples from the surface, and plans for a manned mission are now being seriously considered for the first time in decades. Russia and Japan are also working on their own Mars missions.

With or without persuasive evidence from those vexed microfossils, excitement about Mars is building, especially in US governmental circles. Officials within the Clinton administration and in NASA seem to have a strong belief in life on Mars, perhaps even in intelligent life, and we have seen the eagerness of certain influential individuals and organisations – such as the Pentagon's remote viewers, SRI and the Hoagland camp – to promote a widespread sense of belief and expectancy about Mars. Are 'they' looking for a stargate, either a physical or hyper-dimensional portal through which they could more easily reach Mars, and perhaps even make contact with Martians? More importantly, do 'they' really believe that such a thing exists?

Or is this multi-pronged attack on public awareness simply an insidious exercise in mass manipulation, perhaps testing how we would react to the idea that there were, and possibly still are, Martians? This could be a dummy-run for a real announcement in the near future, likely to be timed to coincide with the Millennium and the first few years of the twenty-first century, when people in the West have come to expect momentous public revelations.

The plot thickens considerably, however, with the discovery that some prime movers in the West are utterly convinced that the stargate has already been opened – and that contact with extra-terrestrials is already well established.

4

Contact?

Few of the enthusiastic followers of the Face on Mars story realise that the ideas of both Richard Hoagland and James Hurtak – the main advocates of the Mars/Giza connection – are largely shaped by a highly influential cultish group who claim direct, telepathic communication with extraterrestrial intelligences. These alleged non-human entities have, we were to discover, adopted many different aliases over the course of several decades, but today are most often known as the Council of Nine, or simply 'the Nine'. This may seem odd, perhaps even bizarre, but – one might think – hardly relevant. Who cares what peculiar ideas these people may hold privately?

As we progressed in our investigation, however, we were astonished, not to say disturbed, by the influence exerted by the people who believe in the Nine – and, ultimately, the Nine themselves. We gradually uncovered evidence of the extraordinary hold that these alleged non-human intelligences have over top industrialists, cutting-edge scientists, popular entertainers, radical parapsychologists and key figures in military and intelligence circles. We were to find that the Nine's influence even extends to the threshold of the White House itself.

Behind the scenes

Richard Hoagland's influential Enterprise Mission had two directors of operations, for the United States and Europe respectively,
David P. Myers and David S. Percy. Both had significant roles in
the promotion of the Message of Cydonia. American writer and
former US Navy officer Myers joined the team in 1989, and
London-based film producer Percy went on board shortly afterwards. Both left the Mission together in 1992.

It was Myers who 'discovered' many of the key measurements
and angular relationships of the Cydonia monuments on which
Hoagland bases his decoding of the Message. And it was Percy
who surveyed the stone circle of Avebury in order to establish its
relationship with Cydonia, as well as with other English sites
such as Stonehenge and Glastonbury Tor. However, the source of
Myers's 'unique insights' (as Hoagland calls them in his acknowledgement in *The Monuments of Mars*) is neither mathematical
skill nor deductive reasoning: he and Percy are part of a network
of people who believe they are in direct contact with a group of
advanced godlike extraterrestrials.

Myers and Percy are co-authors of a highly idiosyncratic, 600-
page tome with the enigmatic title of *Two-Thirds* (1993). It relates,
in novel form, the history of the galaxy according to these beings.
It tells how colonists from a distant planet – Altea – arrived in our
solar system some 1.6 million years ago. They first colonised
Mars (which they made habitable with their advanced technology)
and built the Cydonia complex. Many generations later they came
to Earth, where they genetically modified the indigenous beings,
eventually creating hybrids who became the human race. Acting
under instructions from their own higher intelligences, the
Alteans built Avebury as an analogue of the Cydonia complex, as
well as the pyramids and the Sphinx of Giza. Although told in the
form of fiction, Myers and Percy claim on the cover of their book:
'*Two-Thirds* is *the key* to the understanding of our history and is,
in fact, non-fiction.'

The book includes an extensive section of photographs and

graphics illustrating the Message of Cydonia and its 'terrestrial connections', as well as 'transtime crop glyphs'. Other key elements in Myers and Percy's philosophy is the concept of hyperdimensionality and the technology that could be inspired by the Message of Cydonia. It is no coincidence that these are precisely the main points of Hoagland's crusade: he acquired them from Myers and Percy in the late 1980s.

Although Hoagland is undoubtedly fully aware of the source of Myers and Percy's 'insights', he is (perhaps understandably) reluctant to mention it in his books and lectures. David Percy, in his lectures on the same subject in Britain, never mentions the source of his wisdom, although he was once forced to do so in public. After his lecture to the British UFO Research Association (BUFORA) in 1995, at which we were present, he was challenged by UFO researcher John Rimmer to reveal the origins of his information, and admitted that it was, in fact, partly derived from telepathic contact with the Nine. Recently, Percy has admitted being a member of the main circle of 'contactees'.[1]

James Hurtak also claims to have been in touch with the same extraterrestrial source of wisdom since 1973, shortly before championing the connection between the Elysium pyramids and those of Egypt. He is less reticent about acknowledging the Nine, even writing a book called *The Keys of Enoch* (also known as *The Book of Knowledge*, first published in 1977) which embodies the spiritual teachings he claims he was chosen to receive. Hurtak has told two different versions of this: in *The Keys of Enoch* he tells how the Old Testament prophet Enoch appeared in his room on the night of 2–3 January 1973.[2] But in 1977 he told one of the world's most respected UFO researchers, Jacques Vallée, that, driving through the Californian desert on the same night, a bright light hovered over his car and a beam of light 'programmed' him with the 'Keys' that form the basis of his teaching.[3]

Hurtak's work, like that of Myers and Percy, describes a system based on a hierarchy of intelligences that rule the universe, and explains how they have intervened throughout the history of the Earth. Atlantis and the 'message' of ancient Egypt also play a major role in Hurtak's philosophy. *The Keys of Enoch* is a much more self-consciously religious work than *Two-Thirds*. Subtitled *A Teaching Given on Seven Levels To Be Read and Visualized In Preparation for the Brotherhood of Light To be Delivered for the Quickening of the "People of Light"*, it even looks like a Bible, with the Hebrew for Yahweh – YHWH – embossed in gold on its white-and-gold cover, and its text displayed in two columns and divided into short numbered verses. This book evidently believes itself to be very holy, very sacred, taking itself extremely seriously indeed. The sixty-four 'Keys' of spiritual wisdom, covering all aspects of ethics and history, are presented in resounding quasi-Biblical language, although it is virtually impenetrable. For example:

> The key to the end of our consciousness time zone is the vio-
> lation of the spectra of color codes and in the geometry of
> radiations which will explode gel forming capacities. For
> this reason, the Host of the Living Light comes to deliver
> those who are living under and within the Light of
> Righteousness.[4]

Despite the fact that Hurtak has been promoting these beliefs since 1973, becoming a New Age guru par excellence, he has managed with astounding success to keep this side of his life completely separate even from the promotion of his other unconventional ideas, such as his belief in the Face on Mars. For example, when Hancock, Bauval and Grigsby quote from his book *The Face on Mars* (co-written with Brian Crowley), they make no mention of his status as a New Age mystic and leader.[5] In fact, elsewhere Hancock and Bauval describe him as a specialist in remote sensing.[6] Boris Said, who is now making films about Egypt and other ancient civilisations based on Hurtak's ideas, describes him as his film company's 'scientific consultant.'[7]

What these admirers omit is the fact that Hurtak has been actively – and successfully – promoting what is effectively a new religion over the last quarter of a century. (This omission is odd, since we know that Bauval at least is familiar with *The Keys of Enoch*.[8]) Not only has Hurtak established a particularly firm grip on the New Age, but his revelatory teachings have attracted a highly influential body of followers that includes multimillionaires and senior politicians. One of his disciples described him to us as 'almost the Messiah'.

It is also curious that – as the two main proponents of the Mars–Earth connection – Hurtak and Hoagland should completely ignore one another, even when discussing each other's work. For example, Hoagland manages to elaborate on the Elysium pyramids in *The Monuments of Mars* without mentioning Hurtak even once, despite the fact that he was the first person ever to talk about them publicly. The compliment is returned: in Hurtak's *The Face on Mars*, Hoagland's name is completely absent, even when discussing the City and the Fortress, features that he discovered and named. And the two men have other connections, most significantly perhaps being their links with SRI International, both having worked closely with Lambert Dolphin Jr.

Surely it is too much of a coincidence that the two major proponents of the Mars–Earth theory in the last twenty-five years should be involved with the same group of alleged extraterrestrial intelligences – the Council of Nine? This is a somewhat disturbing scenario: between them, these men have great influence, a wide variety of contacts, and many disciples, culled from New Age, intellectual, scientific and political circles, even the intelligence community. Yet they and their many followers clearly believe that they are in contact with the Nine, either directly or indirectly. So who or what are the Council of Nine?

Enter the Nine

The Council of Nine are not some recent channelling fad. The story began almost 50 years ago thanks entirely to the work of one man whose name has already appeared in this investigation. He was Dr Andrija Puharich, Uri Geller's mentor and the ultimate *eminence gris*, whose disturbing talent for creating belief systems has – we were to discover – helped to shape events in the last years of the twentieth century, and may well even mould the way we think after the Millennium.

This American doctor, born in Chicago of Yugoslavian parents in 1918, was a reasonably successful inventor of medical gadgets such as improved deaf aids. But that was only part of his life, his more public face. He was also known as a brave pioneer in the 'Cinderella science' of parapsychology, or – as many have come to view it – the study of the hitherto unplumbed powers of the human mind.

From 1948 until 1958 Puharich ran a private paranormal research centre called the Round Table Foundation in Glen Cove, Maine, carrying out experiments with several famous psychics such as the Irish medium Eileen Garrett and the Dutch clairvoyant Peter Hurkos (Pieter van der Hirk). In 1952 he took an Indian mystic, Dr D.G. Vinod, to the laboratory, although apparently not so much to test his abilities as to listen to his teachings, which came by what is now known as 'channelling': more or less identical to old-fashioned trance mediumship, in which the medium becomes a conduit for various discarnate spirits.

The first of these sessions took place on 31 December 1952. Vinod entered the trance state and at exactly 9pm, spoke. His first words were, portentously: 'We are Nine Principles and Forces.' One of the 'Nine', who identified himself only as 'M' (a second communicator, 'R', also appeared over the next few months), furnished some extremely detailed scientific information concerning a variant of the Lorentz-Einstein Transformation equation (relating to energy, mass and the speed of light).[9]

Puharich worked with Vinod for a month, then had to return to service with the US Army, which kept him away from the Round Table Foundation for several months, returning later in 1953. A final seminal session with Vinod occurred on 27 June that year, when a circle of nine people, led by Puharich, gathered to listen to the disembodied nonhuman intelligences known as the Nine. Two of the 'sitters' on that momentous occasion were the philosopher and inventor Arthur M. Young and his wife Ruth, who also have key roles in this curious scenario. Another sitter was Alice Bouverie (née Astor), daughter of the founder of the Astoria Hotel in New York. Already the message was percolating through to the upper echelons of American society.[10]

The Nine presented themselves as a kind of collective intelligence or gestalt, consisting of nine entities or aspects that together made up a whole. Puharich said that the Nine are 'directly related to Man's concept of God', and that 'the controllers of the Universe operate under the direction of the Nine. Between the controllers and the untold numbers of planetary civilizations are the messengers.'[11] The Nine themselves – speaking through Dr Vinod – said: 'God is nobody else than we together, the Nine Principles of God. There is no God other than what we are together.'[12] The group disbanded when Vinod returned to India. That, however, was by no means the end of the Nine.

As far as outsiders can ascertain, the Nine – when speaking through Vinod – never identified themselves as extraterrestrials, but that was to change. Three years later Puharich and Arthur Young went to Mexico with Peter Hurkos to use the Dutch psychic's powers to locate certain artefacts at the ancient site of Acámbaro.[13] In the Hôtel de Paris they met an American couple, Dr Charles Laughead and his wife Lillian, who were working with a young man who claimed to be in telepathic contact with various alien races. Shortly after his return to the United States, Puharich received a letter from Laughead – a copy of which they sent to Young – giving communications from the extraterrestrials. And this referred to the Nine, giving the correct date for their first contact via Dr Vinod as well as the same information about the Lorentz-Einstein Transformation.[14] This appeared to be exciting independent corroboration of the Nine's existence, and confirmation of their ability to make contact with people other than Dr Vinod. (Perhaps significantly, Laughead's letter was signed 'yours fraternally'.)

Over the next twenty years, Puharich devoted himself to more general parapsychological and medical research. He set up a company, the Intelectron Corporation, to market his many patented medical inventions. On the parapsychological side, apart from testing various psychics, he made a special, in-depth study of shamanism. He was particularly interested in shamanic techniques for altering states of consciousness, including the use of various hallucinogenic plants and 'sacred' mushrooms. Never one to stand on the sidelines, Puharich threw himself into these studies, even being initiated into the mysteries of Hawaiian shamanism, emerging as a fully fledged kahuna. At least as significant – in the light of what was to come – was his personal training in hypnosis to the level of master hypnotist, at which stage are revealed such mysteries as the 'instant command technique' so often used, and arguably abused, by stage hypnotists. Out of this admirably 'hands-on' research he wrote two books, *The Sacred Mushroom* (1959) and *Beyond Telepathy* (1962).

Throughout the 1960s, Puharich investigated the extraordinary 'psychic surgeon' of Brazil known as Arigó (José Pedro de Freitas), whose trance states led to some highly unorthodox treatments of the sick, who flocked to his door by the thousand and, in many cases, were inexplicably cured. Puharich found Arigó's work and psychic abilities genuine, though this was to be overshadowed by his discovery of a new, excitingly paranormal, talent from another part of the world.

In 1970 a stage act by the young Israeli Uri Geller was causing a stir in the nightclubs of Israel and had already attracted the interest of the Israeli authorities. Through an Israeli Army officer, Itzhak Bentov, Geller came to the attention of Puharich,[15] who had spent some time in Tel Aviv earlier in 1970, training Israelis in the workings of his medical devices, especially one for the 'electrostimulation' of hearing for the deaf. Puharich returned to Israel to meet Geller to evaluate him as a potential subject for further testing. The rest is history – although some of it was, until now, secret history.

In November, Puharich carried out a more detailed study of

Geller – this time with Itzhak Bentov, who was present when Puharich hypnotised the young Israeli in an attempt to discover the source of his powers. Writer Stuart Holroyd later (rather worryingly) described hypnosis as 'a routine procedure in Puharich's investigation of psychics',[16] which raises some ethical questions about his methods. The altered state of consciousness known as hypnosis is by no means fully understood, but it is well known that entranced subjects are notoriously eager to please their hypnotists by creating fantasies that comply with his or her own predilections or agendas. Hypnotist and subject can soon become partners in a strange and wild dance in which sometimes one person leads and sometimes the other, although it is usually the hypnotist who calls the tune.

In deep trance, Uri described being three years old, seeing a light in the sky and encountering a shining being. Then a voice spoke through him (in English), telling the researchers that Geller had been 'programmed' on that occasion, and that Puharich was to take care of him. The voice also warned of a serious threat of war between Israel and Egypt, which – if it took place – would escalate and ultimately lead to a Third World War.[17] Further hypnosis sessions followed. The entities explained that Geller had been programmed for a special mission to Earth – 'He is the only one for the next fifty years to come'[18] and announced that they were a form of conscious computer, living aboard a spacecraft called Spectra. After a few sessions, Puharich asked: 'Are you of the Nine Principles that once spoke through Dr Vinod?' The reply was: 'Yes.'[19]

Puharich had another subject in mind, one that would assume a much wider appeal – virtually becoming a new religion – as the twentieth century draws towards its close. He asked the communicating entities: 'Are you behind the UFO sightings that started in the United States when Kenneth Arnold saw nine flying saucers on June 24, 1947?'[20] Again, the answer was affirmative.

Puharich wrote: 'Now I was totally convinced that Uri and I had been contacted by such a local cosmic being; by this I mean some representative or extension of the Nine Principles.'[21]

On his second trip, Puharich stayed in Israel for almost three months, in daily contact with Geller and bombarded with demonstrations of paranormal phenomena nearly every day. Messages from Spectra/the Nine continued, either channelled through the hypnotised Geller or appearing spontaneously on audio tapes, but in every case the tapes either erased themselves or vanished before their eyes. Unfortunately, that means that only Puharich's written transcripts survive as records of the events.

It was undoubtedly a weird time. Puharich and Geller saw several UFOs, and witnessed the teleportation of objects from one place to another, often through solid walls, besides experiencing a series of bizarre synchronicities. This, however, was merely window-dressing. Their mission was to pray and meditate to prevent the predicted Israel–Egypt war, as tension between the two countries increased over Christmas 1971. Eventually, President Sadat of Egypt made an astonishing climbdown, and the war was averted in the nick of time. (Two years later an Israeli–Egyptian conflict occurred with the Yom Kippur War of October 1973, but when Puharich queried this with the Nine he was told this was fine; there was no risk of the conflict escalating and 'the war will be fought just like an ordinary war'.[22])

When Puharich returned to the United States in February 1972, determined to have Geller's wild talents evaluated scientifically, he contacted SRI International. Significantly, although SRI supremos Targ and Puthoff were in charge of the testing, the key figure in this scenario was former lunar astronaut Edgar Mitchell, the 'funding and contracting agent'.[23] Significantly, the Geller experiments at SRI coincided exactly with the first CIA involvement with psychic experiments there, specifically their sponsorship of research into Ingo Swann's extraordinary talent for remote viewing. And in Uri Geller they had the golden child of the Israeli secret service, Mossad.[24] Is it too unlikely that Geller, also, was being investigated by the CIA? Geller has gone on record as admitting he worked for them.[25] And, as we shall see, Puharich himself was on their payroll, at least from time to time. And a further connection with intelligence agencies lay in Hal Puthoff's former employment by the National Security Agency (NSA), an even more secretive organisation than the CIA, and with powers at least as great.[26] In an interview in 1996, Geller made the telling comment: 'And probably, I believe, the whole thing with Andrija was financed by the American Defense Department.'[27]

When Geller arrived in the United States in August 1972, the Nine recommenced their antics with more messages on instantly wiped tapes and teleportations. Significantly, Geller himself was not a convert to the Nine, even at this stage. He found their pranks childish and ultimately unimpressive. He was to say of them in August 1972: 'I think somebody is playing games with us. Perhaps they are a civilization of clowns.'[28]

At the time that Geller began his SRI tests, in November 1972, the Nine – through their representative Spectra in those early days – started to describe their plans for an imminent mass landing of spaceships, claiming that Puharich and Geller's roles were to prepare mankind for this momentous event. The Nine described the 'Knowledge Book' that they had left hidden in Egypt some 6,000 years ago, during one of their previous visits to Earth. They then began to talk about another extraterrestrial race, called – somewhat unfortunately – Hoova, who had come to Earth 20,000 years ago, specifically to the area now called Israel, where they had encountered Abraham, claiming that this meeting was the origin of the Biblical story of the ladder joining Heaven and Earth.

On 27 February 1973, Puharich took Geller to meet Arthur M. Young at his house in Philadelphia, thus completing a circle that had begun twenty years before with the channelling of Dr Vinod. Sadly there are no accessible records of what happened at this meeting.

Unfortunately for the Nine, their carefully laid plans for Geller never came to fruition. In October 1973 he appeared on *The David Dimbleby Show* on British television and was launched into overnight psychic superstardom. Geller and Puharich went their separate ways soon afterwards, and the former has distanced himself from the Nine ever since. Although he admits that extraterrestrial intelligences might be responsible for his powers, he – very sensibly – points out that he cannot vouch for what the Nine said through him, as he was always in a hypnotic trance at the time.[29] He thinks that his own subconscious fantasising may have played a large part in the communications – which is often the case during hypnosis – although he does corroborate some of the other events related by Puharich, such as their shared UFO sightings in Israel and Sinai.

The Nine, it transpired, did not really need Geller, despite having told him that he was to be 'the only one for the next fifty years to come'. They continued seamlessly after Geller's departure, with other channellers and a new group of devotees. The key people who now entered the story were Sir John Whitmore and Phyllis Schlemmer. The new group formed an organisation called Lab Nine, based at Puharich's estate at Ossining in New York State.

Puharich and Lab Nine had many wealthy and influential backers, including members of Canada's richest family, the Bronfmans (the owners of the Seagram liquor business) and an Italian nobleman called Baron DiPauli. It is portrayed as an almost hippy-style commune – with a loose band of hangers-on moving around the central nucleus of Puharich, Whitmore and Schlemmer – but what hippy commune attracts quite so many rich people or such a sprinkling of members of the intelligence agencies? And what other community could boast a fully qualified kahuna shaman and master hypnotist like Puharich – with none other than James Hurtak as his de facto second-in-command?

It was at this time that Puharich also carried out a series of experiments with the so-called 'Geller Kids' or 'Space Kids', children with pronounced psychic gifts. Ostensibly, this was to investigate the extent of their powers – such as metalbending – but significantly, Puharich soon had them remote viewing and hypnotised them to tell him where their powers originated.[30]

One of the most useful and colourful characters with whom Puharich surrounded himself at Ossining was Phyllis Schlemmer (née Virtue). Born of Italian and Irish ancestry in Pennsylvania, from an early age she was aware of her gifts as a medium. At her Catholic college the priests often asked her to accompany them on exorcisms, as she could 'see' possessing spirits leaving the victims. As she grew older, she regularly channelled a number of spirit guides. After the break-up of her first marriage, she moved to Florida where she developed her career as a psychic, working for the police and mining companies, and even broadcasting her own television show. She founded the Psychic Center of Florida in Orlando, a school for developing psychics, in 1969. Her main spirit guide was an entity called 'Dr Fiske', but in 1970 a new control simply named 'Tom' 'came through'. She assumed it must be her grandfather Thomas, who died when she was just five.

Phyllis Schlemmer met Puharich at a conference in the late 1960s, and the two were in regular contact thereafter. In January 1974, a cook from Daytona Beach, who is referred to in Nine-related literature only by the pseudonym 'Bobby Horne', enrolled at Schlemmer's Psychic Center, developing healing talents so remarkable that she recommended him to Puharich as a potential subject for further study. It was not to be a fortuitous recommendation for poor Bobby.

Puharich travelled to Miami to meet Horne in March 1974. On their first meeting – as was Puharich's habit, as we have seen – he hypnotised the young man, who began to channel an extraterrestrial entity called Corean. Puharich was delighted, believing he had found a worthy successor to Geller in his quest to establish regular contact with the Nine. He went on to have several channelled 'interviews' with Corean, but refused to let Horne himself hear the tapes of these sessions, claiming that this specifically followed Corean's own instructions.[31] It was decreed that Horne should be told neither the identity of the entity nor the content of its communications. Puharich behaved in a highly unethical way for a hypnotist, asking obviously leading questions of Corean, such as if he was connected with Hoova, the civilisation supposedly in contact with Uri Geller. In fact Corean had not mentioned Hoova, but afterwards this became a regular subject of discussion for him. Then, amazingly, Puharich compounded his already extraordinarily unethical behaviour by implanting a posthypnotic suggestion in Horne's subconscious mind to enable Schlemmer to continue to put him into trance in his, Puharich's, absence.[32]

Turning her back on her origins as a 'traditional' spiritualist medium communicating with the spirits of the dead, Schlemmer had begun to channel only extraterrestrials since the spring of 1974, when Puharich took her to meet a friend of his, an adventurer and explorer named Count Pino Turolla.[33] At his Florida house Schlemmer went into a trance and again channelled Tom, to be told that he was not, as she had believed, her deceased grandfather, but an extraterrestrial. Tom was to become the main communicator of the Nine later, when Schlemmer assumed Horne's role. (Interestingly, Count Turolla was one of the people involved in the supposed confirmation of Edgar Cayce's prophecies about Atlantis with the discovery of the Bimini Road in 1968.[34])

With Horne replacing Geller as the new 'Chosen One', a circle formed around him, with a nucleus consisting of Puharich, Schlemmer and Sir John Whitmore, the heir to an aristocratic British family. Educated at public school and the élite military academy of Sandhurst, he later became a successful racing driver. At the time of the Lab Nine operation he owned houses in England and the Bahamas. He had first become seriously involved with this bizarre set-up in April 1974; the previous year he had spent some time with James Hurtak in California as one of his inner circle of 'disciples'. As Stuart Holroyd wrote:

> He [Hurtak] often spoke about UFOs and about his personal contacts with extraterrestrials, who, he said, had often intervened in Earth history since prehistoric times, when they had established a civilization in the Tarim Basin to the north of Tibet.[35]

Tom had also identified the Tarim Basin as the site of the first arrival of an extraterrestrial civilisation on Earth, during the same period – 34,000 years ago – identified by Hurtak.

Shortly after first sitting at Hurtak's feet, Whitmore met Puharich in New York to discuss the promotion of Uri Geller's powers shortly before Geller dropped out of the scene and Bobby Horne became the focus of the group's attention. The Nine, speaking as Corean, told the trio that they had been chosen for a special mission to bring the news of the imminent return of extra-terrestrials to Earth. This central message attracted others to the sitter group, and formed the basis of all future Nine communications.

Puharich, Whitmore, Schlemmer and an increasingly reluctant Bobby Horne began to proselytise in both the United States and Britain in the spring and summer of 1974, although they kept the group small and intimate, not intending it to explode into a mass movement, at least in the immediate future. Meanwhile Bobby Horne was suffering from increasing pressure from the Nine, being expected to drop all other activities to follow the group around the world to channel at any time of the day or night and produce phenomena almost constantly. He began to make excuses or fail to show up, and even became suicidal as the demands of the exhausting business spiralled out of control.[36] (Later, Whitmore was to airily dismiss Horne as showing 'signs of instability'.[37]) The Nine eventually decided to let him go – their second failure, after Geller – and announced that from then on Schlemmer would be their 'transceiver', with Tom as their spokesman.

Closely involved with these events then was writer Lyall Watson, who had become the star of the alternative culture after the runaway success of his book *Supernature* (1973). He was a sitter at many of the Nine's channelling sessions, and they announced that they wanted him to be – as it were – their official biographer, as well as become joint channeller with Schlemmer. Watson had grave reservations about what was happening, though, and declined either to write the book or become more involved. Clearly, the Nine were keen to exploit Watson's fame, as they had been with Geller.

A new and intense phase began when Tom started to show a

rather autocratic streak, expelling what he called 'negatives' – such as Watson and a neurosurgeon called Norman Shealey – from the circle. (Shealey, now a well-known holistic therapist, had been trained at ARE.) With anyone who was likely to ask awkward questions out of the way, Puharich was appointed as director of the group and Whitmore was 'advised' to hand over as much of his considerable fortune as was necessary to further the work as a gesture of his 'faith'. They were impressed and supremely motivated with a sense of personal destiny, of being the chosen ones whose purpose was to spread the word to at least 75 per cent of the world of the mass landing of representatives of the Nine due to take place in 1976. That was the task set by the Nine.

The number of people associated with Lab Nine at Ossining grew, but the identities of many of its members were concealed in the literature by pseudonyms. It is known that they included SRI physicists and at least one prominent figure who was a personal friend of President Gerald Ford.[38] One famous name very much part of the Lab Nine scene in the mid-1970s was Gene Roddenberry, creator of *Star Trek*.[39]

It is unclear how much Roddenberry was influenced by the Nine. His involvement began in 1974, several years after the original *Star Trek* TV series finished, but around the time that he was developing ideas for the first of the series of movies. It is said that some of the concepts in the first of these, *Star Trek: The Motion Picture* (1979), came from the Nine, and that they influenced some of the characters, concepts and storylines of the *Star Trek: The Next Generation* and *Deep Space Nine* TV series. (For example, a character named Vinod appeared in an episode of *Deep Space Nine* called 'Paradise'.) It is known that in 1974 Whitmore commissioned Roddenberry to write a film script based on the Lab Nine events, called simply *The Nine*. Although the movie did not materialise during Roddenberry's lifetime, in 1995 the Hollywood industry newspapers reported that Jon Povill – producer of the TV series *Sliders* – was planning to make *The Nine* at last.[40]

Puharich, Whitmore and Schlemmer eagerly undertook

'missions' on behalf of the Nine, mainly travelling around Middle Eastern and other trouble spots meditating for peace, although they were often suspected of being spies. (Perhaps this is not surprising. On one trip, in November to December 1974, they travelled from Helsinki to Warsaw, Poland, where they set up their own radio receiver. This, according to Puharich, was to facilitate experiments in contacting Tom – perhaps something of a slur on Schlemmer's mediumistic talents? Even if the purpose of the radio was as innocent – if rather unusual – as Puharich claimed, its use by American citizens in an Eastern Bloc country during the Cold War seems almost criminally naive. Later in the same trip they attempted to enter Moscow, but were turned away at the airport because they had no visas).[41] While these prime movers were away, the 'second-in-command' back in the United States was James Hurtak, who had been appointed 'spiritual leader' by the Nine,[42] and whose own extraterrestrial channelled material agreed with many of their pronouncements. One particular similarity was the idea that the civilisation of Altea had created Atlantis, and after a great catastrophe the survivors had influenced the emergence of the civilisations of Egypt and Central and South America.

In 1975 Puharich and Whitmore commissioned British writer Stuart Holroyd to write an account of the group, as *Prelude to the Landing on Planet Earth* (1977). The paperback edition was re-titled *Briefings for the Landing on Planet Earth*, which calls to mind Hoagland's insistence on calling his United Nations lecture a briefing. At this time, other people were also channelling the Nine. One particularly influential channeller was Englishwoman Jenny O'Connor, who was introduced by Sir John Whitmore to the influential avant garde Esalen Institute in California, where – incredibly – the Nine actually gave seminars through her.[43]

Another group came from a background of paranormal research. In 1976, after reading Puharich's biography of Geller, *Uri*, former airline pilot Don Elkins and Carla Rueckert went to Ossining to meet him, then accompanied him to Mexico to study the psychic healer Pachita in 1977 and 1978. Elkins and

Rueckert, who ran a Kentucky-based group with James Allen McCarty, were already deeply committed to the concept of alien intervention by the time they met Puharich. Elkins began in the mid-1950s as a UFO investigator, then in 1962 turned his attention to extraterrestrial 'contactees', at which time Carla Rueckert began work with him. They founded a group called L/L Research in 1970, specifically to study such phenomena. After their Mexican trip with Puharich, Rueckert began to channel another emissary from the Nine, a group entity called Ra. Significantly, the third member of the trio, James Allen McCarty, who joined L/L Research in 1980, had already worked closely with a group in Oregon who had claimed to channel the same entity as Edgar Cayce.[44]

Elkins committed suicide in 1984, and the extraterrestrial communications ended, although L/L Research continues to promote the spiritual teachings of Ra, who spoke of a body called the Council of Saturn, based somewhere in its rings, which protects the Earth and keeps it in a kind of quarantine. From a session on 25 January 1981, Ra explained (with very proper godlike disdain for mere earthly grammar and syntax):

> In number, the Council that sits in constant session, though varying in its members of balancing, which takes place, what you would call irregularly, is nine. That is the Session Council. To back up this Council, there are twenty-four entities which offer their services as requested. These entities faithfully watch and have been called Guardians.[45]

Tom also speaks of twenty-four entities who represent the twenty-four civilisations and work with the Nine. Hurtak similarly writes about the Council of Twenty-Four in his *The Keys of Enoch*.

Ra was then asked if this was the same Council of Nine with whom Puharich and another channeller named Mark Probert[46] were in contact and – we do not have to hold our breath here – he replied, yes, that was so.[47] Ra also said that Earth was inhabited by beings from Mars, which is a slightly different version of the

Earth–Mars connection. As usual, Atlantis and Egypt also feature prominently in this scenario, with Ra declaring that he himself had built the Great Pyramid.

In 1978 Puharich's house at Ossining was burned down in a mysterious arson attack, and he disappeared to Mexico for a while to study the 'psychic surgeon' Pachita. When he returned, in 1980, he seemed to have no more contact with the Council of Nine. He died in January 1995 after falling down the stairs in the South Carolina house lent to him by one of his rich patrons, Joshua Reynolds III.

The Council of Nine, through Schlemmer and other 'transceivers', continued to thrive without their one-time mentor. The Schlemmer–Whitmore group, with its wealthy backers and ever-expanding circle of devotees, continues to meet regularly to this day. In 1992, a compilation of the collected wisdom of Tom, *The Only Planet of Choice: Essential Briefings from Deep Space* was published, carrying a front-cover endorsement by James Hurtak. It soon became a runaway New Age bestseller. It was originally edited down by Palden Jenkins from countless hours of transcripts of Schlemmer's channelling since 1974, interspersed with questions from the sitters (who included David Percy[48] and Gene Roddenberry). A second edition was hastily re-edited two years later, this time by Mary Bennett (who also edited Myers and Percy's *Two-Thirds*).

Meanwhile Hurtak's own *The Keys of Enoch* has continued to sell widely. While based on the 'Keys' allegedly programmed into him by Enoch himself in 1973, the book includes material about the Council of Nine, although Hurtak claims that the revelations come from an even higher source to which the Nine are merely subordinate. The Nine in this scheme of things are the intelligences that govern one solar system only – ours. Hurtak's version is even grander in scope and implications than Schlemmer's. In his system the Council of Nine may govern our solar system and 'level of existence', but there are yet higher authorities, the most supreme being the '70 Brotherhoods of the Great White Brotherhood', also called the 'Hierarchy'.

David Myers' and David Percy's novelised form of the same

myth, *Two-Thirds*, was published in 1993. Although it does not mention the Council of Nine by name, it describes the same cosmic system of civilisations and higher, discarnate intelligences who guide them and were responsible for the genetic engineering that created the human race. *Two-Thirds* concentrates on the story of the Altean race and its influence on Earth. The role of the Nine is taken by entities rather curiously called 'Essenes' (usually without the definite article), who communicate with the Alteans by telepathy, explaining how they built the Cydonian monuments, the Great Pyramid and the Sphinx at Giza, and how they implemented the genetic modification of the emerging human species. (Essenes's connection with the first-century Jewish sect of the same name is implicit.) The whole book was channelled from the Nine by David Myers, who clairaudiently hears Tom's voice in his head, rather than channelling in an altered state, like Bobby Horne or Phyllis Schlemmer.

Hearing voices and speaking the words of extraterrestrials is not an activity that most people admire and respect, although channelling is hugely popular in New Age circles, where it is actively encouraged. Most of the outpourings that allegedly come from spirit guides, great names from history or deceased relatives are at best regurgitated thoughts and memories from the unconscious mind of the medium or channeller, and at worst they are simply made up on the spot. The words of the Nine deserve closer scrutiny because they are surprisingly consistent – as if coming from the same source – even when emanating from different channellers with no knowledge of each other. So who exactly are the Nine, or rather, who do they claim to be?

A momentous revelation

Their precise identity was revealed in September 1974 in a channelling session with Schlemmer, in response to the question by Gene Roddenberry: 'To whom am I talking? Do you have a name?' Tom replied:

As you know, I am the spokesman for the Nine. But I also have another position, which I have with you in the project. I will try to give you names so you can then understand in what you work and who we are. I may not pronounce who I am in a manner which you would understand because of the problem in the Being's [his name for Schlemmer] brain, but I will explain so that the Doctor [Puharich] perhaps will understand. I am Tom, but I am also Harmarkus [Harmarchis], I am also Harenkur, I am also known as Tum and I am known as Atum.[49]

The next day, following up the name Harmarchis, Puharich asked: 'How did the Egyptians come to build and name the Sphinx after you?' Tom replied:

You have found the secret. [A pause for 'consultation'.] The true knowledge of that will be related to you another time. But I will say briefly to you concerning the Sphinx: I am the beginning. I am the end. I am the emissary. But the original time that I was on the Planet Earth was 34,000 of your years ago. I am the balance. And when I say 'I' – I mean because I am an emissary for the Nine. It is not I, but it is the group . . . We are nine principles of the Universe, yet together we are one.[50]

'Tom' claims to be Atum, the ancient Egyptian creator god of whom the Sphinx was created as a living image (Sheshep-ankh Atum), the head of the Great Ennead of Nine gods, which the ancient Egyptians regarded as 'Nine that are One'. Tom has also said: 'We are the Universe', which again accurately reflects the old Heliopolitan belief. Interestingly, the entity whom Carla Rueckert channelled claimed to be Ra, the ancient Egyptian sun god, who is another form of Atum. (The major clue was in the Nine's name from the start: the English word Ennead – group of nine – is used as a translation of the ancient Egyptian *psit*, which literally means the number 'nine'. The Egyptians themselves actually referred to the Heliopolitan gods as '*the* Nine'.) The Nine also claim to be the Elohim – the gods – of the Old Testament, and the Aeons of Gnosticism. Another very significant piece of information was added by Jenny O'Connor, when the Nine gave seminars through her at the Esalen Institute in the late 1970s. Although there are few available records about what the Nine taught there, it is known that they divulged that they came from Sirius.[51]

Tom himself – allegedly the god Atum – is emphatic about the importance of the monuments of Giza, in particular the Great Pyramid, but he has refused repeatedly to be drawn on its purpose, saying only that this will be revealed when the landing has happened. However, when asked by Puharich if there were undiscovered chambers in the Great Pyramid, he replied, 'To a degree,' adding, 'The entrance is from the Sphinx'[52] – confirmation of the Council of Nine's own belief in passages under the Sphinx. This is proof, if any were needed, that the Nine share an interest in the events at Giza discussed in Chapter 1.

There is another link between the Nine and conspiracies surrounding Giza. We have noticed the term 'Altea' throughout various strands of this investigation. Wherever it crops up lurks the shadowy influence of the Nine. The rumours that began to circulate in Egypt in 1997 – apparently originating in Egyptian government circles – specified that Joseph Schor's team had found the Hall of Records, housing information that told how Atum had 'descended from the skies' and including records written in 'Altean'. Although this appears to be part of some kind of misinformation programme, the use of the term Altean and the emphasis on Atum – suggesting that he was an extraterrestrial – clearly relate to the teachings of the Council of Nine. Yet this rumour seems to have originated within the Egyptian government. Do the Nine have friends in high places even beyond the confines of the West? And is it a coincidence that one of the names given to Atlantis by Edgar Cayce was Alta?

Another intriguing aspect to this story is the way that the rumour surfaced, passed on to columnist Georgina Bruni by an Egyptian political journalist at a reception in London. Although she has

never been a part of the Nine circle, Georgina has known Sir John
Whitmore since the early 1990s, having contacted him after reading *Briefings for the Landing on Planet Earth* and becoming
fascinated with the story of the Nine. The story, with its Atum and
Altea references, would have a special significance for her – which
makes us wonder if something more than simple coincidence made
her the recipient of the Egyptian story. Was she specially targeted?

An ancient Egyptian priest speaks

The first communications through Dr Vinod were not the only
extraordinary events in which Puharich was a major player. In his
1959 book *The Sacred Mushroom* he describes a series of communications through another remarkable psychic, which took
place between summer 1954 and February 1956, beginning less
than a year after the Vinod sessions ended. The most intriguing
thing, however, is that nowhere in his writings does Puharich
connect these communications with the Vinod sessions –
although it would have been obvious to do so.

In 1954 Puharich, with the rank of Captain, was based at the
US Army Chemical Center in Edgewood, Maryland, having been
redrafted. During this time, the work of the Round Table
Foundation was being continued by Arthur Young and the other
trustees, including Alice Bouverie who was working with a young
Dutch psychic called Harry Stone. On 16 June 1954, to test his
psychometric (object-reading) powers, she gave him a gold pen-
dant that had belonged to Queen Tiye (mother of Akhenaten).
After apparently having a fit, Stone went into a deep trance and
began to utter words in a strange language, then drew a series of
hieroglyphs before talking in English about a drug that would
stimulate psychic abilities. He spoke, among other things, about
entering an underground hall where a statue of a dog-headed
man came to life.

Not surprisingly, Bouverie was very excited by this material.
She immediately contacted Puharich at the Army base for advice

about what to do next, sending him the drawings and a copy of Stone's strange utterances. Puharich took them to another Army doctor on the site – who just happened to be an expert in extremely rare and archaic forms of hieroglyphs – and, to his surprise, verified that Stone's writings were indeed ancient Egyptian. The communicator had identified himself as Rahotep (which Puharich rendered as Ra Ho Tep), naming his wife as Nefert. He also claimed to be speaking with the voice of Tehuti (the wisdom god Thoth), and mentioned the name Khufu.

Puharich was astounded to learn that a man named Rahotep *was* known from ancient Egyptian history, and that he had been married to a woman called Nefert. Their tomb at Meidum was excavated by Auguste Mariette in the nineteenth century, and a statue he found of the couple is now in the Cairo Museum. They had indeed lived in the Fourth Dynasty, possibly in the reign of Khufu, builder of the Great Pyramid. (Egyptologists place Rahotep either in Sneferu's or Khufu's reign.) Moreover – very significantly – the historical Rahotep had been the high priest of Heliopolis![53] In addition, Puharich's anonymous Army colleague also imparted an astounding piece of information:

There is a shaft on the south side of the Great Pyramid which is so arranged that on a certain day of each year, which is the beginning of the Egyptian year, the star Sirius – deified as the god Sept – on rising would shine into the eye of the dead Pharaoh down this long passageway which ended in the interior of the King's Chamber.[54]

This is an amazing – and very precise – piece of information, especially coming from an Army doctor, even if his hobby was Egyptology. Of course, however, it is completely wrong. According to all known ancient Egyptian sources, Sirius was deified as the goddess Sothis (or Isis), and its light could never shine directly into the King's Chamber, since there is a kink in the shaft. But how did he believe that any of the southern shafts are aligned with Sirius? This idea was not prevalent at the time, although it seemed to foreshadow the much later theories of Robert Bauval and James Hurtak. (It was found in Masonic writings, though, which may have been the inspiration of them all.)

During Puharich's leaves of absence, and after the end of his tour of duty in April 1955, he and Alice Bouverie continued to work with Harry Stone, who had several more sessions in which he was 'possessed' by Rahotep, producing more fascinating information. From September 1955 Stone's abilities to contact Rahotep declined, the messages gradually becoming incoherent until they stopped completely in February 1956.

As with the Nine's communications, strange phenomena accompanied the Rahotep channellings. Occasionally Alice Bouverie herself went into trance and, via automatic writing, produced messages that corresponded with those of Harry Stone. But the most important aspect of these communications was that Rahotep's main concern was to impart information about a drug used by the priests of Heliopolis to 'open the door' to the gods: a mushroom that induced hallucinatory experiences, a sort of chemical stargate. From Stone's drawings, Puharich was able to identify the mushroom as *amanita muscaria*, or fly agaric. Bouverie's automatic writing predicted that a specimen would shortly be found near the Round Table Foundation's building in Maine. Shortly afterwards one was indeed found in the nearby woods, a rare, though not unique, occurrence in that area. They used the mushroom with Stone, and later with Peter Hurkos, who reported that the mushroom had no effect on his psychic abilities, except perhaps in the area of precognition.[55] Coincidentally, this dovetailed amazingly neatly with Puharich's major preoccupation of the time, which was the search for a drug that would stimulate or enhance psychic abilities. Puharich had settled on the psychoactive drugs used by shamans as the main focus of his research, and in 1953 had contacted R. Gordon Wasson, the first researcher to study the shamanic mushroom cult of Mexico. The two set up an experiment to see if the Mexican shamans, or curanderos, could, under the influence of the mushroom, 'visit' the Round Table Foundation's laboratory in Maine. The long-distance experiment never happened, but it is interesting that Puharich was already thinking in terms of remote viewing (although he did not use that term then).

Certain themes already familiar from the Nine's communications were also central to those of Rahotep. For example, they both stress the importance of the Sphinx. On one occasion Harry Stone uttered the phrase 'Na na ne Hupe', which, Puharich tells us, was ancient Egyptian for 'We are under the care of Hupe', adding for our benefit, that 'Hupe is one of the names of the great sphinx at Giza near the Great Pyramid'.[56] (We have not been able to verify this fact.)

Sirius is also prevalent, although obliquely. Harry Stone talks about the god Sept, whom Puharich identifies with Sirius. Most significant of all is the fact that the historical Rahotep was high priest of Heliopolis, with its Great Ennead of Nine gods. Stone's communications led Puharich to do further research about the Heliopolitan religion, and he wrote:

> Heliopolis was the center of a religion which had for its pantheon nine great gods called the Ennead, which means the Nine. The Nine of Heliopolis are Atum, Shu and Tefnut, Geb and Nut, Osiris and Isis, and Set and Nepthys.[57]

Puharich referred to the high priest of Heliopolis as the 'chief spokesman' of the Ennead. He was using the term 'the Nine' way back in 1959: the communications themselves took place between his first contact with the 'Nine Principles' in 1952–3 and his renewed acquaintance with them through his meeting with the Laugheads in Mexico in 1956. Surely Puharich must have made the connection, realising that these were not separate stories, but one, centring on contact with the Nine entities who claimed to be nothing less than the ancient gods of Heliopolis?

Although Puharich's methodology can be criticised, his sincerity is rarely open to doubt. At the end of *The Sacred Mushroom* he wrote: 'I do not doubt that discarnate intelligences exist, any more than I doubt that finite carnate intelligences exist.'[58] It is also relevant that all of this channelled information hinged on the shamanic use of certain psychoactive substances, which Puharich was researching at the time on behalf of the US Army. The Rahotep communications make explicit the use of such practices as part of the Heliopolitan religion.

There seem to have been several instances of the Nine – or, at least, sources associated with ancient Egypt – communicating with different groups and individuals of the late twentieth century, including Harry Stone, Phyllis Schlemmer, Uri Geller and many others. They seem to be repeating essentially the same story, stressing the same points, such as the importance of the Sphinx, and by implication if nothing else, signifying the imminence of some momentous event that will somehow involve ancient Egyptian secrets. James Hurtak, arguably their greatest prophet, says in *The Keys of Enoch*: 'Giza was the region of the Council of Nine, represented by nine pyramids keyed into the "Pyramid of Cheops [Khufu]".'[59] Although these are separate and apparently independent contacts with living humans, their similarity suggests that they are part of a greater scheme, perhaps helping and guiding mankind through perilous times ahead.

These communicators are not just any ancient Egyptians. While Harry Stone's guide announced himself as Rahotep, high priest of Heliopolis, those of the Puharich circles went much, much further, claiming to be the Ennead, the gods of ancient Egypt – the Nine. In independent channelling sessions they said much the same, and seemed to be the same. Their words have inspired hugely influential individuals, such as Richard Hoagland, to spread their message with true, even fanatical, missionary zeal. Indeed, the Nine's influence extends well beyond the more predictable outlets of New Age circuits and the hothouse worlds of maverick researchers.

But are the Nine truly the gods of Heliopolis, the ancient Nine who were worshipped thousands of years ago in Egyptian mystery schools and temples?

5

Behind the Mask

The Nine have clearly impressed a huge number of people – through books such as *The Only Planet of Choice* and *The Keys of Enoch*; through lectures, personal contact and word of mouth, especially in New Age and alternative Egypt–Mars circles; and even, arguably, in subliminal form through the most popular television science fiction ever. Belief in the Nine is widespread and self-generating, for each new 'convert' passes on the message, as has always been the way with exciting, strongly held, quasireligious beliefs. The many devotees of the Nine include senior scientists, industrialists, associates of NASA and operatives for the CIA, as well as those whose media professionalism ensures that the Nine are given the best possible image.

The Nine eventually revealed themselves as the Great Ennead, or nine principal gods of ancient Heliopolis, and claim to be returning to Earth to help mankind at a critical stage in its evolution. Suspending disbelief for the moment, the disturbing possibility is that they are simply stating the truth, in which case perhaps we should all immediately become their devotees, awestruck, obsequious, hanging on their every word. After all, we are only flawed humans, and they are gods, our creators. Perhaps it is too easy to dismiss the concept of the Nine. Perhaps we owe it to ourselves and the whole human race to surrender gracefully, and admit that the gods have returned.

At this point, however, we should pause. Evolution has brought us a long way: mankind is not only self-aware but cerebral. We have learned to think, analyse and discern. Not only do we need to take the claims of the Nine seriously – for if they really are the gods their return is the single most significant event in history – but we also have to be aware of anything that may reveal cracks in the carefully constructed edifice with which they surround themselves. Are the Nine for real, or are they some kind of hoax or delusion? And if they are a fabrication, who created them – and why?

The hidden message

Unlikely though it may seem, the Nine have a strong hold on the hearts and minds of key players in this story, even to the extent that their teachings have helped to shape our cultural concepts of space, both through the phenomenally successful science fiction of *Star Trek* and those promoting the alleged science fact of the Mars Mission in more recent years.

The teachings of the Nine emphasise that there are many civilisations throughout the galaxy, some of whom are banded together in a *Star Trek*-like Federation, but all of whom are more or less aware of the existence of the Nine. Some operate closely with them, because the Nine need them to interact with the inhabitants of the physical universe, including Altea and Hoova, the two civilisations that have played a major part in human history. Spectra, the conscious computer with which Uri Geller was alleged to have been in contact, is one of the lower forms of computerised intelligence operated by the higher entities.

The Alteans, who arrived in the solar system some 1.6 million years ago, settled on Mars and were responsible for the building of the Cydonia complex. Earth was then off limits, as it had been earmarked for the development of a new sentient race, intended to be the Alteans' 'partner society'.[1] Later they were allowed to go to Earth to assist in the genetic development of the new Earth races under the guidance of the Nine.

Altea and Hoova helped in the genetic manipulation – or 'seeding' – of the human race. According to the Nine, as reported through their channellers, one indigenous race already existed on Earth – the blacks, the only one actually to evolve here.[2] This implicit racism caused hostility towards *The Only Planet of Choice*, but Tom has since stressed a belief in the equality of all races, and cautions against any racism based on a misunderstanding of their teachings. Some believe this sounds remarkably like damage limitation, and the suspicion of racism has remained in many critical minds.

In fact, the Nine reveal a marked, if sometimes ambiguous, positive discrimination. According to them, the Jewish race was created by Hoova, as was Jesus, whom they call – rather inadvisedly, as it turns out – the 'Nazarene'. The Jews are 'the saviours of the planet' and, directly descended from Hoova, are truly the 'Chosen People', with special powers and a momentous role in Earth's history. They made a grave mistake in not accepting Jesus as their Messiah (who was sent from Hoova), though, so to rectify this and regain their rightful place in the scheme of things, they must first come 'to acceptance' – presumably of Jesus the Nazarene.[3]

According to Tom, Jesus and Jehovah are one and the same, and have a special relationship with the Nine. Jesus was 'the last of us to visit planet Earth'.[4] The Second Coming will take place as part of the mass landing, when Jesus will arrive as the Jewish Messiah. There are, it is claimed, secret records of Jesus, hidden in Egypt and Israel: 'At the proper time there will be a correlation of finding these records within six months of each other.'[5] The seeding of Earth was an experiment by the Nine to see how 'the originals' (the black races) would evolve in comparison with 'those that colonized'. This was hardly a smooth or peaceable process, for mankind's genetic evolution has also been interfered with by the dark forces, usually said to hail from the Pleiades and often described simply as the 'Others', although they are also, more melodramatically, described as the followers of Satan – 'the Beast'.[6]

The Nine claim that the first colonisation from Hoova began in the Tarim Basin in Tibet, in 32,400 BCE. Atlantis was founded by colonists from Altea and existed for some 15,000 years in the region of the Caribbean/Yucatan/southern Mexico, roughly where Edgar Cayce placed the lost continent or island. This story is different, though: it was the Nine who destroyed Atlantis out of rage in 10,850 BCE – very close to the date so favoured by Cayce, Bauval and Hancock.[7] Hurtak gives the end of Atlantis as 12,000 BCE, which disagrees with Tom's date but has its own significance.

After the destruction of Atlantis, the survivors became the founders of the civilisations of Egypt and Central and South America. As in the Cayce version, the Great Pyramid was built by these survivors, starting around 10,700 BCE, although for some reason it was not completed until 5000 BCE.[8] Significantly, many popular theories about the building of the Great Pyramid, such as those of Hancock and Bauval, state the case for a similar two-stage construction.[9] Undoubtedly the Great Pyramid is central to the Nine. They claim it is used to bring to Earth 'energy' from other civilisations, as well as to regenerate the cells in the human body. Tom says it has other uses, but, tantalisingly, refuses to elaborate on them. And as we have seen, he told Puharich that there were 'undiscovered chambers' under the Great Pyramid that could be reached via an 'entrance from the Sphinx'.

Myers and Percy claim the Altean colonists not only built the Great Pyramid, but also the Sphinx, which they call the Ark Hur, from – they claim – two Altean words meaning 'the shining beginning-ending'. And according to Hurtak, the Great Pyramid was built by the Nine as a physical stargate. He says:

Once again, astronomers will understand why the ancients saw the pyramid as the gateway to the stars and the form through which star intelligences came to serve human creation.[10]

And according to Hurtak the pyramids – including those on Mars – are devices for channelling energy that comes from space. In 1973, the Nine explained to him that the shafts in the Great Pyramid aligned with Orion's Belt[11] – which had been theorised by some astronomers – but they failed to take it further and make Bauval's extrapolation of the pyramid–star correlations. The theme of hidden chambers in the Great Pyramid also surfaces in Hurtak's *The Keys of Enoch*, where he describes the 'Chamber of the Son' between the King's and Queen's Chambers.[12]

According to Tom, the Earth was created as a battleground, to enable the Nine to confront the Others (the Pleiadean followers of the Beast) on a physical level. Interestingly, this is reminiscent of the Gnostic battle between light and darkness, which seems to be similar to the imminent conflict now being predicted by Graham Hancock. Every being in the universe has to be incarnated on Earth at some point, in order to experience the delights, responsibilities and drawbacks of free will, which, Tom says, exist nowhere else in the universe – hence the book title *The Only Planet of Choice*. All other civilisations are subject to the government of higher intelligences, such as the Nine. The various races of the Earth were, it seems, created as an experiment in free will, with the black race, apparently, serving as a kind of 'control'. As the Nine claim that the black races are Earth's only indigenous people, they are not – like all other races – essentially part space-god. Tom says that this experiment was 'to see in which manner the originals, that were not seeded, would evolve in comparison with those that colonized'.[13] (But what happens if the experiment is judged a failure . . . ?)

The most complex and thought-provoking connection between the Nine and religion on Earth is found in *The Keys of Enoch*. Between its quasi-Biblical covers, it simmers with a Hellfire-and-damnation Old Testament zeal, besides containing strong messianic and apocalyptic elements. For example:

And I was told by my guides, Enoch and Metatron, that I was not to eat of the false powers of the earth, nor encourage my seed to marry with the fallen spiritual races of the earth.[14]

This is rather worrying. The assumption that there are 'fallen spiritual races' with whom the righteous should not breed is insidious and, in such a seminal book, seems to us to be more than a little disquieting. The very concept of whole races being somehow genetically unworthy and of not measuring up to the standard of the 'righteous' is, surely, the thin end of a wedge with which recent history is only too familiar. The religious scheme of *The Keys of Enoch* is very interesting in that it is calculated to embrace all the major religions of the USA – or rather, of the *white* United States. It is a mixture of Old Testament Judaism and Christianity, and also speaks approvingly of Mormonism (which Hurtak regards as the direct heir of the Heliopolitan priesthood – an exceptionally unlikely scenario). Hurtak says very little directly about Islam, although it is one of the dominant religions among African-Americans. He refers to Muslims obliquely – perhaps not unexpectedly – as 'the Children of Darkness',[15] which perhaps reveals what is, for him, the identity of the villains in the imminent battle for the Earth. (Tom is fairly evasive about the Muslims but conveys a negative attitude based on their treatment of women, and says that Islam has – unfortunately, of course – been influenced by the 'Fallen One'.[16])

Also rather disturbing is the Nine's attitude to the Holocaust. They uphold the Jews as the Chosen People, but remonstrate with them for not accepting Jesus – 'the last one of us' – as Messiah. Tom speaks of the Holocaust, in which 6 million Jews were exterminated by Hitler, with huge sorrow, yet claims it was an act of self-sacrifice and salvation:

The greatest portion of these six million came at that time to sacrifice self, to make your planet earth aware that there were those who would attempt to rule and control humanity.[17]

Tom also explained that the atrocity of the Holocaust was

necessary for the creation of the state of Israel, an important part of the plan for Earth. Essentially the victims chose to be incarnated at this time and place and to be victims of the Holocaust as a selfless act of sacrifice to make us all aware that evil people existed . . . At this point the thought occurs that Tom may represent the gods of our solar system but in this case surely our own morality has the edge? Aren't we already aware of the existence of evil? Did we really need the horrible deaths of 6 million people to bring it home to us? (And Tom shares with many the misconception that the Holocaust only involved Jews. Of course, many thousands of others were killed by the Nazis, including members of specific groups such as gypsies, homosexuals and Jehovah's Witnesses.) In any case, are we alone in finding Tom's sweeping pronouncement about the Holocaust deeply offensive?

The Nine think in sweeping global terms that lend themselves to Hurtak's quasi-Biblical prose and apocalyptic ideas. They have explained in detail their plans for the future of mankind to their faithful, the apostles of the new world order. As Sir John Whitmore wrote in his foreword to *The Only Planet of Choice*:

> This book along with other books on crop circles, the new genre of Sci Fi films, a few global crises, whistle blowers, paranormal events, controlled leaks and not so controlled ones, are all part of the essential awakening of Earth.[18]

The Nine's basic message, and the reason they have made contact with certain humans recently, is that something has gone wrong with mankind's genetic programming. This is causing problems, not only for Earth, but also for other civilisations who have to pass through incarnations here, so the Nine have to step in to put things right.

Unsurprisingly this matches Hurtak's system: he claims that something has gone wrong with humanity's 'programming' and that, over the thirty-year-period that will end in 2003, the intelligences that rule the universe are coming to repair it by upgrading human intelligence. We have failed the program and, through Hurtak and the others, the 'White Brotherhood' (to which the Nine are subordinate) are trying to rectify the situation.[19]

We have seen how the Nine spoke of the imminent mass landings on Earth: that was in the 1970s, and the failure of this momentous event to materialise means that they are now claiming the need for it has diminished. When communicating with the Puharich–Whitmore–Schlemmer group in the mid-1970s, Tom also spoke of the Nine interfering with radio and television transmissions in order to communicate directly with the people of Earth and prepare them for the landings. This did not happen either because, Tom said, the landings were no longer necessary.

In April 1976, James Hurtak told Jacques Vallée that he and Puharich, along with others who had access to 'confidential and secret information', were working to make the public aware that Earth was to be contacted by 'highly evolved beings' within the next eighteen months, that is, by the end of 1978.[20] Right from the start, the Nine pushed the idea of preparing for an imminent global upheaval, a purging or final showdown between the forces of light and darkness, something close to fundamentalists' hearts as the great battle of Armageddon. At first, this was the Nine's mission statement (1974):

It is important that it be stated in the chronicle of the three of you [Schlemmer, Whitmore and Puharich] that there will be physical civilizations that will come to raise the level of this planet Earth, to bring it out of its own contamination, to purify it and prepare the people to keep it in a pure state so that it does not become in a collapsed state for future generations.[21]

As usual, it is Hurtak who uses the most blood-curdling words to describe this future upheaval: there is a 'galactic war and housecleaning that is being completed throughout the universe',[22] a war that will also be manifested on Earth, with the coming apocalypse, followed by a golden age, in which a new form of government will arise. The 'lesser brotherhoods' of light who work with the 'younger spiritual teachers' of Earth are now being 'forced out of their positions of power' so that the 'greater forces of Light will externalize on the earth plane'.[23] (The use of force is interesting here: could these 'younger spiritual teachers' not be persuaded to surrender their positions of power for the greater good rather than having to be forced out of them? This seems a somewhat unspiritual, if not downright totalitarian, approach.) Hurtak goes on to warn that 'materialists who seek to destroy the world . . . will be as desiccated mud when the foundations of the earth are removed'.[24] Hurtak is nothing if not patriotic, declaring that the centre of the new 'Spiritual Administration' will arise in America, the heir to Atlantis, which he refers to as Altea-America.[25] He also often indulges in a serious pun when mentioning the rise of the New JerUSAlem . . .

The scene is set for a final showdown between the forces of good and evil, one that will affect the entire galaxy. (Myers and Percy indicate that the countdown began in October 1991.[26]) No doubt the many thousands of the followers of the Nine are hanging on to every channelled word with bated breath, waiting to play their part in some supremely satisfying drama, in which they are, of course, on the side of the righteous. After all, the West has not really been totally involved in a good war for half a century – how exciting it will be when the great 'housecleaning' finally arrives! The Millennium, the Apocalypse, and Armageddon are all balm to the souls of unhappy, bored and frustrated people who see themselves as knights in shining armour on the side of the righteous in the coming battle. It would, of course, be a terrible thing if none of it ever happened, and life just went on as usual; that would be their truly nightmare scenario.

The more this investigation proceeded, the more the full impact and influence of the Nine began to dawn on us. They have changed the way people think – ordinary people and not-so-ordinary people – including, as we will see, some of the world's most talented and daring scientists and thinkers. But one area in which their power is supreme is that of the New Age, that much derided – and seriously underestimated – international community of semi-mystical self-improvers. While it is easy to dismiss their fads and crazes as harmless, they are in their own way a serious force to be reckoned with.

The New Age movement is not so much a 'subculture' as a rapidly growing alternative society that, despite its size, remains virtually invisible. Nobody knows how many people make up this global community, stretching from California to Glastonbury to the ashrams of India, but it must run into hundreds of thousands, if not millions. Few outside the community itself realise what a vast and thriving economy it has. New Age publishing is big business, as are the workshops that go on tour, attracting large audiences who pay stiff prices for the privilege of sitting at the feet of a big-name guru. However, this happy world of workshops, consultancies and specialist holidays is strangely fragmented, as each healing, meditation or channelling group operates very largely on its own, and often in intense rivalry. However, the economic and political potential of such a vast, untapped community – if it could be brought together and directed – is enormous.

The New Age has already fallen in love with the Nine, largely thanks to their hugely successful *The Only Planet of Choice*, which has sold at least 50,000 copies in Britain alone, and which continues to sell steadily. Our friend Theo Paijmans, who hosts a three-hour weekly radio show from Amsterdam on the subject of UFOs and the unexplained, tells us that every week without fail callers ask questions based on *The Only Planet of Choice*. And in the United States, Carla Rueckert's *The Ra Material*, based on her channelling of the Nine, is extremely influential. According to Palden Jenkins, who edited the first edition of *The Only Planet of Choice*, more and more channelling, meditation and healing groups are beginning to 'realise' that the source of their inspiration is none other than the Nine.[27] There seems to be a covert campaign – on a massive scale – of spiritual takeover and unification.

The Keys of Enoch has been a very influential book for over twenty years, and Hurtak himself tours the world giving courses and workshops on its teachings to eager audiences. Yet once again, amazingly, he cleverly manages to keep this side of his life completely separate from his more academic activities. His latest venture, as scientific consultant to Boris Said's Magical Eye film production company, is to work on a 'monumental series of upcoming documentaries'[28] based on his work.

Hurtak has referred to the opening of a 'gateway' between the world of the gods – or rather, the Nine Principles of God – and this world. Clearly the thousands who follow the Nine believe that this 'stargate' has been open for some time, and that we have been prepared for the return of the old Egyptian gods. This is a truly momentous scenario, and the implications are profoundly disturbing. But the question is: are the Nine who they claim to be?

The cracks appear

Undoubtedly, the Nine have already failed on several major counts. For a start, what happened to the promised 'mass landings' of the late 1970s? As with many other channelling cults, major events failed to materialise as prophesied, but the Nine's glib excuses, hastily given to paper over the cracks, were lapped up by devotees who simply could not bear their belief to be undermined by anything, especially the truth. This is a well-known psychological syndrome among cult followers, whether in the shape of the imminent return of a god or the coming of the Space Brothers. Time and time again the cultists have taken up their required positions, often after having sold all their belongings, and waited for the great event. And waited, and waited and waited . . . And, when nothing happens, tired, cold and virtually destitute, they piece their lives back together by accepting the flimsiest excuse. Although the followers of the Nine were not required to sell up, they did have to chase around the world, and Whitmore was persuaded to part with a large proportion of his wealth. Tom announced that the landings are no longer necessary and that conditions have changed. But why? What, exactly, has changed?

The Nine are also, as we have seen, exceptionally poor at forward planning, having failed with both Uri Geller and Bobby Horne. Why didn't they simply appoint Phyllis Schlemmer as 'transceiver' in the first place? And they enticed Lyall Watson, and others, into the circle, only to see them either flee or ask, unacceptably, too many awkward questions.

The Nine's message of 'peace and love' often seems contradicted by the way in which they treat their human followers, and by the sheer unpleasantness that seems to have surrounded, in particular, the Schlemmer circle. Bobby Horne was pushed to the brink of suicide by the endless pressure to channel the Nine, and Don Elkins, the leader of L/L Research, did commit suicide, while the balance of his mind was disturbed, in 1984. This is nothing, of course, compared to the other great unpleasantness in the Nine's alleged history: their destruction of Atlantis because they were 'angry'.[29] They also claim that certain people have been 'implanted' at birth in order to carry out missions on their behalf, which, if nothing else, goes against their fine words about free will. Tom was challenged on this point by Whitmore, but answered that these people had chosen to be implanted before they were born, so they had no memory of doing such a deal.[30]

The Nine's version of Earth's (and galactic) history, is simply unprovable. Much rests on the credence given to such matters as Atlantis, the monuments of Mars and the vast antiquity of the Sphinx, all of which are arguable, but none of which are facts. The Nine often rely on the notorious, and convenient, impossibility of proving a negative, such as the non-existence of Atlantis. Where they do venture into recorded history – or even the myths and traditions of religion – the Nine often make demonstrable blunders. For example, Tom said that Hoova had descended to Earth and was encountered by Abraham, giving rise to the Biblical tale of the ladder joining Heaven and Earth. In fact this vision was seen by Jacob, not Abraham.[31]

Another term used by the Nine is, commonly – and erroneously – used by millions: 'Jesus the Nazarene', meaning Jesus who came from the town of Nazareth. Unfortunately, this comes from the Bible's mistranslation of the source: the word should be Nasorean, meaning a member of a particular sect.[32] While it is understandable that ordinary people might get such facts wrong – after all, the mistake occurs in the Bible – it is surely less likely that gods would err similarly.

Furthermore, when Puharich seized on the name 'Harmarchis' as one of those used by Tom-Atum, Tom delightedly treated this as a breakthrough, saying: 'You have found the secret.' It may be a historical fact that Harmarchis was one of the names of the Sphinx, and that it was a representation of Atum (although Egyptologists had known this for years), but Tom then goes on to elaborate: 'I will say briefly to you concerning the Sphinx: I am the beginning. I am the end.'[33]

This appears to be related to that by now familiar mistake – the idea that one of the ancient Egyptian names for the Sphinx was *arq ur*. This has become a favourite line among the followers of the Nine, who always quote it as if it were a fact. For example, Richard Hoagland, in his 1992 'briefing' of the United Nations, gave this definition:

In the . . . Egyptian language it [the Sphinx] was called the *arq ur*, and that is really interesting because as we've probed into the etymology, *arq ur* meant: 'the end of the beginning connected to the beginning of the end'. Almost like a cycle, like an end-point, like a constant process, as if it represents the end of something and the beginning of something else.[34]

In fact, *arq* means 'end' or 'completion' and *ur* means 'great'. There is nothing in either *arq* or *ur* to signify 'beginning', though the Nine claim that there is, which is good enough for their followers, including Hoagland. But David Myers, in *Two-Thirds*, goes further and traces the name back to the ancient Altean language: 'Ark Hur', which, according to his information, means 'shining beginning-ending' – again, echoing Tom's words to the Schlemmer group.[35]

A major obstacle lies in the way of these interpretations – of course, *arq ur* does not mean 'Sphinx' at all. As we saw earlier, this error was made by Robert Temple in *The Sirius Mystery*, resulting from a simple misreading of Sir E.A. Wallis Budge's *An Egyptian Hieroglyphic Dictionary*. As we have seen, it is true that the word 'Sphinx' does appear against the definition of *arq ur*, though not as the name of the monument, but as the abbreviation of the title of Budge's *source*, the French journal *Sphinx*. There, in volume 2, on page 8 (as clearly indicated in Budge's book), in an article by Professor Karl Piehl, is Budge's source for the *arq ur* hieroglyphs, which, taken together, in fact mean 'silver'. The word is not even ancient Egyptian, since it was borrowed from the Greeks in a later period; it is an Egyptian phonetic rendering of *argyros* (a fact that renders any attempt to analyse the meaning of the Egyptian syllables completely futile). Temple's mistake had no bearing on his own work, as he mentioned the 'Sphinx' definition only in passing and drew no conclusions from it, but the same error has appeared in communications from the Nine, leading us to speculate about whether or not they have been reading Temple's book. Interestingly, Hoagland claims that Temple is the source for his *arq ur* definition, so it is possible that he was simply passing on the error through sloppy research, though his particular interpretation of *arq ur* – 'beginning and ending' – is not Temple's, but comes directly from the Nine.

So could the Nine be readers of Robert Temple – or, more charitably – could Phyllis Schlemmer or one of the sitters have read it and unconsciously contaminated the incoming communications from the Nine? Tom could then have picked their brains; after all, he claims he is limited to the words and concepts already in place in his transceiver's mind. Unfortunately, the relevant exchange between Tom and Puharich took place two years before Temple's book came out (although it did exist in manuscript at the time,[36] so it is possible that a copy could have been circulating among those connected with Lab Nine – although if Temple did show his manuscript to anybody it was most likely to be his mentor Arthur M. Young). Perhaps Tom, like Temple in his later book, simply misread Budge's dictionary.

So what do we make of the bizarre story of the Nine? Is it some kind of elaborate hoax, or a collective delusion on the part of Puharich, Whitmore, Schlemmer, Hurtak and their associates?

Outside commentators, such as Stuart Holroyd and Colin Wilson, who have observed many of the key events at close hand, agree that this is not a hoax nor a delusion, and that something genuinely paranormal was going on. At the same time these evaluators have expressed serious reservations about whether the source of the communications really was what it claimed to be – the Nine gods of the ancient Egyptian Ennead. Even Holroyd, who Whitmore recruited specifically to write the 'official history' of the Nine, came to this conclusion.[37] A number of inexplicable phenomena took place around the Nine's group, particularly when Uri Geller was involved. Even Holroyd became convinced that the story was worth pursuing, and after initial reservations accepted Whitmore's offer to write the book when poltergeist-type disturbances took place in his house as he listened to sample tapes of Schlemmer's channelling.[38]

Colin Wilson, in his seminal 1978 book *Mysteries*[39] and even in the foreword he wrote for *Prelude to the Landing on Planet Earth* has categorised the Nine along with many similar mediumistic or channelled communications in which it is hard to doubt that the medium is honest, though the source of the messages remains another matter. Wilson speculates that it is some kind of dramatisation by the medium's subconscious mind using their innate psychic powers, or that some mischievous spirit entities – whom he calls 'the crooks and conmen of the spirit world'[40] – have attached themselves to the medium. (Or perhaps it is a combination of the two, where a spirit plays up to the wishes or expectations of the medium and the group surrounding them.)

Certainly, unexplained phenomena are often what finally persuade a ditherer to accept a particular belief system as the only 'true' path or religion. Whether it is the apparently miraculous Shroud of Turin, statues that bleed and weep or visions and a host of 'meaningful coincidences' – synchronicities – the excitement of the paranormal is usually what clinches a conversion. After all, few laymen realise what parapsychologists have known for years – that, strangely enough, belief and expectancy themselves actually create phenomena, rather than the other way around. It is the human mind that almost always creates the miracles, not as hoaxes or figments of the imagination, but actually 'out there' in the real world through the mysterious ability of psychokinesis. This can take many forms, from metalbending to healing the sick, even endowing inanimate objects with a temporary 'consciousness'. The point is that weird phenomena can surround any belief system – Hindu statues ooze milk, while Catholic statues weep or bleed – but they are all taken as 'signs' of contact with a particular deity or saint and as proof that the religion they represent is the true one. The overwhelming evidence is that all this comes from our own, largely unknown abilities, that are normally kept under wraps by sociological, psychological and, paradoxically, religious conditioning. Society as a whole tends only to humour the paranormal as a novelty, and only too often sets out to destroy those who base their lives on it. Except, that is, for magi, shamans and courageous researchers who have long known about the secret 'rules' of paranormal phenomena.

There is another possible explanation for the phenomenon of the Nine: the events of their story were somehow orchestrated and manipulated, quite deliberately, by very human agencies. Colin Wilson had theorised that, because of the consistency of the communications, from Dr Vinod in the early 1950s through to Uri Geller, Bobby Horne and Phyllis Schlemmer in the 1970s, it was Puharich himself who was the psychic, the real magnet for the phenomena, though perhaps only at a subconscious level. Wilson actually put this directly to Puharich during one of the latter's visits to London, although Puharich disagreed.[41] But what if Wilson was right, up to a point? What if Puharich had created the Nine – not subconsciously, but deliberately . . . ?

The puppetmaster

A major consideration is that we are entirely dependent on Puharich's own account of the first twenty years of the Nine's communications. The only record of what happened with Dr Vinod comes from him, and he is also the primary source for the Geller phase, when the Nine's words came through the hypnotised Geller and were written down later by Puharich from memory. The tape recordings either erased themselves or disappeared into thin air, after only Puharich had had a chance to listen to them. When Stuart Holroyd entered the picture in 1976 the first objective voice was heard, and this was largely based on tapes of Schlemmer's channelling sessions and what the trio chose to tell him.

Perhaps it is significant that Andrija Puharich was described by his close associate Ira Einhorn as 'the great psychic circus manager of this century'.[42] He was certainly not averse to media attention, although he kept much of his work secret. In the 1960s he played himself in an episode of *Perry Mason*, appearing as an expert witness on psychic phenomena, yet much of his career remains sketchy, and he happily compounded the mystery by introducing inconsistencies and obvious evasions into his own account of his life and work. In a real sense, he lived a double life, much of his most influential work being carried out under conditions of highest secrecy – perhaps not surprisingly, considering for whom he often worked . . .

Puharich had qualified as a doctor and neurologist at Northwestern University in 1947 under a US Army training scheme, but was then discharged from the Army on medical grounds. He set up the Round Table Foundation in Glen Cove, Maine, in 1948, and ran it until 1958, working with psychics including Eileen Garrett and Peter Hurkos, as well as first making contact with the Nine through Dr Vinod, and with Rahotep through Harry Stone. In addition Puharich was also carrying out secret research for the defence and intelligence establishments into two main areas: techniques of psychological manipulation, including the use of hallucinogenic drugs; and the military and intelligence capabilities of psychic skills. His own account records that his work with Vinod was interrupted for several months in 1953 because (despite his medical discharge) he returned to Army service.[43] According to Jack Sarfatti, a physicist on the fringes of the Puharich–Geller–Whitmore events of the mid-1970s, Puharich 'worked for Army Intelligence in the early fifties'[44] – which perhaps implies that his 'discharge' was a cover for continuing to operate in an apparently civilian capacity. It also appears that some of Puharich's medical inventions were originally developed as part of classified Army projects.[45]

In 1987, Puharich himself claimed that he had been part of a US Navy investigation called Project Penguin that researched psychic abilities back in 1948.[46] He named the head of this project as Rexford Daniels, who lived close to his home in Glen Cove in the 1950s. According to writers Peter Tompkins and Christopher Bird, Daniels – who studied the effects of electromagnetic waves on human beings – became convinced, in the 1970s, of the existence of some kind of intelligent force in the universe that operated through electromagnetic frequencies and that 'human beings can mentally interact with it'.[47]

Ira Einhorn, Puharich's close associate in the 1970s, told us recently that, although Puharich had worked for the CIA during the 1950s, he was no longer doing so twenty years later.[48] However, the evidence points very much in the other direction. Puharich's relationship with intelligence agencies almost certainly did not end in the 1950s. Uri Geller told us at a meeting in his home near Reading in England in 1998 that: 'The CIA brought Puharich in to come and get me out of Israel.'[49] Jack Sarfatti goes further, claiming: 'Puharich was Geller's case officer in America with money provided by Sir John Whitmore.'[50] And according to James Hurtak, via his Academy For Future Sciences, Puharich 'worked with the US intelligence community.'[51] By implication this was during the early 1970s when he, Hurtak, was also working with him.

We know Puharich was working with the CIA on experiments

with various techniques for inducing altered states of consciousness, which is another way of saying he worked on the potential
of mind control. We also know, at least up to a point, that Geller
worked for them – they wanted to know how he could use his
mind to influence inanimate objects and see distant locations – in
other words, to test his remote-influencing abilities. Were the
Nine somehow part of a CIA mind-control experiment?

After the Second World War, as the West moved into the Cold
War, the US military (like that of many other countries) began to
take seriously the psychological aspects of warfare, and undertook or sponsored research into this area. It covered anything
from techniques to make soldiers more efficient, through truth
drugs and methods of resisting interrogation, to the more sinister
brainwashing techniques and creation of 'Manchurian Candidate'
assassins. The military were not alone in this research.
Intelligence agencies – primarily the CIA – became heavily
involved with what it summed up as the 'search to control human
behaviour'.[52] This included exploring the possible uses of drugs,
hypnosis, electric shocks and radiation, as well as psychological,
psychiatric and sociological techniques. They were particularly
interested in investigating the effects of various chemicals and
drugs, including hallucinogens such as LSD. As Thomas Powers
wrote in his introduction to John Marks's *The Search for the
'Manchurian Candidate'*:

> It [the CIA] has spent millions of dollars on a major program
> of research to find drugs or other esoteric methods to bring
> ordinary people, willing and unwilling alike, under com-
> plete control – to act, to talk, to reveal the most precious
> secrets, even to forget on command.[53]

The first experiments were authorised by the CIA in 1950, code-
named BLUEBIRD, later renamed ARTICHOKE and then, in
1953, MKULTRA. The US Navy had a similar research program,
Project CHATTER (beginning in 1947), which pooled its
resources with the CIA projects, and the US Army had its own

version called Project OFTEN, which ran between 1968 and 1973.[54]

ARTICHOKE and MKULTRA included the investigation of narcotic plants found in Latin America and, as we have seen, Puharich had spent much of the 1950s investigating the mind-altering properties of hallucinogenic plants and fungi. And the US Army has admitted to testing LSD on nearly 7,000 service-men – 1,500 of whom were *not* volunteers – in the late 1950s.[55] It was this type of research in which Puharich was involved for defence and intelligence departments.

In the 1970s, after many questions raised about the CIA's abuses of human rights, President Gerald Ford appointed an investigative commission under Vice-President Nelson Rockefeller. The commission's references to 'behavioural con-trol research' attracted the interest of writer John Marks, who obtained 16,000 pages of previously unclassified documents relating to MKULTRA under the Freedom of Information Act, though many of the key documents had already been destroyed on the orders of the CIA's director in 1973.

Not everyone applauded Marks's revelations. In his book about the 'uses and abuses' of hypnosis, *Open to Suggestion* (1989), Robert Temple declared bluntly that he refused even to read Marks's book on the grounds that it was 'irresponsible' and 'not commensurate with national security considerations'[56] – which is manifestly untrue, as Marks had found his material using the Freedom of Information Act. Temple admits that 'the CIA has been very naughty on many occasions',[57] but this does not, in his view, excuse Marks for 'throwing mud' at them. While Temple appears to think that a mild slap on the wrist is enough for the CIA, it is worth remembering that their 'naughtiness' included mindbending experiments on US servicemen (at least 1,500 of whom were not volunteers), the inmates of jails and mental patients, which resulted in several deaths and turned many strong, healthy Americans into shambling wrecks. Very naughty.

What was Puharich's role? There is no doubt that he was very deeply committed to much of the mind control experimentation of

The Great Pyramid (top) and Sphinx (below) of the Giza plateau. Are there, as many believe, really undiscovered chambers within or beneath them, and do they contain secrets that have some relevance today?

Detail of the walls of the Valley Temple at Giza, showing the almost absurdly difficult method of fitting the great granite blocks together.

The entrance to the 'water shaft' beneat the main causeway – a current focus of interest at Giza.

Part of the Pyramid Texts from the tomb of Unas (c.2350 BCE), which reveal the richness of the religion of Heliopolis.

Right: *Osiris, god of death and resurrection, faces offerings of blue water lilies. Recent research suggests that the ancient Egyptians used these flowers to achieve shamanic enlightenment – perhaps the true source of their astonishingly advanced knowledge.*

Below: *The great god Atum (centre), the chief god of the Great Ennead – the Nine divinities of Heliopolis.*

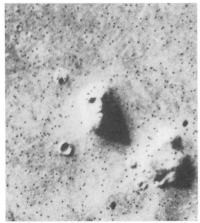

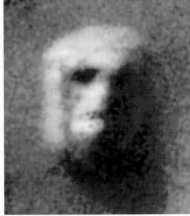

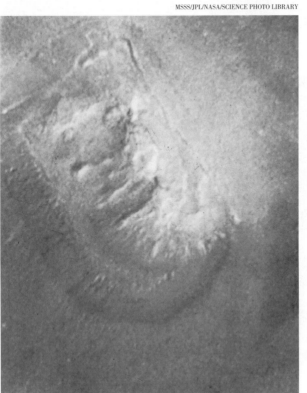

Three views of the controversial 'Face on Mars': top left: *the original 1976 Viking image;* top right: *Dr Mark J. Carlotto's enhanced version* below: *the new, less face-like, image from Mars Global Surveyor.*

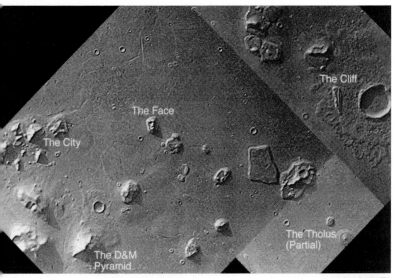

The main features of the Cydonia 'complex' on Mars.

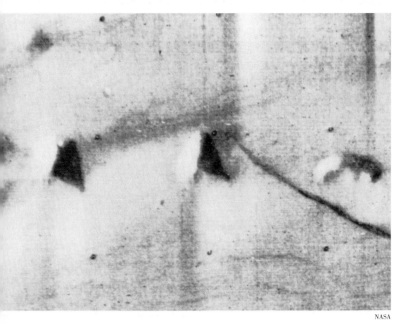

The pyramid-like features of the Elysium area of Mars, first photographed in 1971.

Under the direction of Dr Andrija Puharich (top left) several people are believed to have channelled 'Tom' – none other than the ancient Egyptian god Atum – spokesman for the Nine. These have included Phyllis V. Schlemmer (top right) and U Geller (below left). But arguably the most influential of the Nine's 'prophets' is Dr. James J. Hurtak (below right).

An early backer of Puharich's work: Vice-President Henry A. Wallace. A prominent Freemason, he was responsible for the incorporation of the mystical pyramid into the design of the dollar bill (below left).

R.A. Schwaller de Lubicz (right), 'godfather' of the New Egyptology. His extreme right-wing ideology and activities are rarely mentioned by his modern admirers. He was a great influence on, among others, Hitler's deputy Rudolf Hess.

Infamous occultist Aleister Crowley with his first wife Rose and their child (top). *It was their magical 'working' in Cairo in 1904 that appeared to open the way for, or at least inspire, later claims of contact with the ancient Egyptian gods. The Crowleys were led to the significant 'Stele of Revealing' in Cairo Museum* (below).

the military/CIA. He was certainly no mere Army doctor, whose work was confined to handing out pills and potions. In fact, even the Round Table Foundation – as Puharich himself implies in *The Sacred Mushroom* – was a front for the Army's parapsychological experiments.

When he was redrafted in February 1953 it was as a captain at the Army Chemical Center in Edgewood, Maryland, the Army's facility for research into chemical and psychological warfare and neurophysical research, where he served until April 1955, when he returned to the Round Table Foundation.[58]

Certain groups within the US Army were interested in Puharich's parapsychological work. In *The Sacred Mushroom*, he records the visit to the Round Table Foundation of an unnamed colonel, who was in charge of research for the office of the chief of psychological warfare, in August 1952.[59] He also notes that the order for his redrafting into the Army was issued the day after he briefed the Pentagon on the military uses of parapsychology in November 1952.[60] It also seems that, from Puharich's account, only some people within the military command were interested in parapsychology. Although he was encouraged by certain of his superiors – who had clearly arranged for him to be drafted back into the Army – they also expressed concern about possible 'adverse political reaction'.[61]

The Army's interest in the Round Table Foundation continued even after Puharich had left active service in April 1955. In *The Sacred Mushroom* he describes a planned visit to the Foundation by an Army general and his staff in September 1957, which was cancelled at the last minute because 'there was some compelling security reason unknown to him [the General] which made it undesirable for military officials to express an interest in our kind of research'.[62] This was an odd choice of words – not that it was politically unwise to be associated with such controversial work, but that they cancelled for a 'security reason'. Such factionalism within the military and political establishments was also a factor in the remote-viewing research of the 1970s. While it had enthusiastic advocates in the Pentagon, intelligence community and political hierarchy, others believed such things were a waste of time or, worse, that such 'dabbling in the occult' was a work of the Devil.

From Puharich's account, it appears that his role at the Army Chemical Center was simply that of an ordinary medical doctor, basically a GP for the base. This was absolutely untrue. The Army's real interest, the reason why they re-employed Puharich, was not just in the development of the military potential of ESP, but also the possibility of finding a drug that would stimulate psychic abilities. This is the task they set Puharich, although in *The Sacred Mushroom* he suggests that it was just a vague arrangement that never really went anywhere. It did launch his research into shamanism, though.

Significantly, against this background the first communications with the Nine were established through Dr Vinod and Harry Stone between 1953 and 1955. Even more remarkable, given the specific nature of the Army's interest in Puharich, the Harry Stone communications about the ancient Egyptian drug that stimulated psychic functioning also happened at this time.

The CIA's interest in hallucinogens was escalating rapidly in the early 1950s. They approached R. Gordon Wasson, who had identified the use of psychoactive mushrooms in Mexico (known locally as 'God's flesh'), to invite him to work for them and their MKULTRA project, but he refused. This did not stop them from using him: when he planned an expedition to Mexico in 1956, he was approached by a man called James Moore, who arranged funding from the Geshickter Foundation for Medical Research. Wasson later discovered that Moore was a CIA agent, and it is now established that the Geshickter Foundation was a standard 'conduit' for CIA funds. The money for Wasson's expedition actually came from MKULTRA's Subproject 58.[63]

Puharich met Wasson to discuss his research in February 1955, recording that he drew up a report on Wasson's work for the US Army.[64] Either the CIA had actually commissioned this report, or it drew their attention to Wasson in the first place. (The Army's Chemical Center at Edgewood, where Puharich was stationed, is known to have conducted joint experiments with the CIA's MKULTRA team.)[65]

Although a banker by profession, Wasson was a highly respected amateur mycologist. His article in *Life* magazine in 1957 about his own experience of the Mexican 'sacred mushroom' caused a sensation, and was largely responsible for the psychedelic craze of the next decade. As a direct result of reading this article Timothy Leary went to Mexico to find the mushrooms and had his first hallucinogenic experience.[66] The psychedelic movement can pinpoint the moment of its birth to 29 June 1955, the night that Wasson himself partook of 'God's flesh', the experience described in the *Life* article. On that very night, Wasson had arranged to conduct the remote-viewing experiment with Puharich, but as his mind was elsewhere at the time, he was not much use.[67]

Information about hallucinogens was of great interest to both the Army and the CIA, for reasons that would make *The X-Files* seem comparatively tame. The Army Chemical Center at Edgewood – where Puharich was stationed – collaborated with a special programme within the CIA's MKULTRA project that aimed to find ways 'to program new memories into the minds of an amnesiac subject'.[68] John Marks learned about this from a participant in the late 1950s, and wonders how their techniques may have 'improved' since then. Another key figure in the MKULTRA experiments was Dr Sidney Gottlieb, head of the CIA's Technical Services Division, who personally supervised experiments in conjunction with the Army Chemical Center in 1953, when Puharich was working there.[69] Gottlieb was still head of this division in 1972, when it gave Hal Puthoff of SRI the funds for his preliminary research into remote viewing.[70]

During the 1950s and 1960s, Puharich belonged to an organisation of scientists and businessmen called Essentia Research Associates in New York. It undertook research into psychic abilities on behalf of government agencies such as the Pentagon, NASA and the Atomic Energy Commission. Perhaps understandably, information about Essentia is hard to come by, but we do know that Puharich presented a paper on their behalf to the Pentagon as early as November 1952, entitled 'An Evaluation of the Possible Usefulness of Extrasensory Perception in Psychological Warfare'.[71] This is very strange, for according to the official account, the Pentagon's interest in psychic abilities only began in the early 1970s, with the remote-viewing experiments at SRI, yet Puharich and Essentia were doing similar work for them at least twenty years earlier.

Curiously Puharich's work with the Brazilian healer Arigó in the 1960s seems to have been part of an Essentia Research Associates project that was sponsored by NASA.[72] Puharich and a wealthy businessman – and former US Navy intelligence officer – named Henry Belk, were called to Brazil in 1963 to take a look at Arigó by one John Laurance, an engineer working for RCA on NASA satellite projects. He had, in fact, been part of the committee that originally established the space agency in 1958.[73]

Puharich's connections with Essentia continued until at least 1977, when they published the proceedings of a parapsychological conference in Iceland, where he is listed as their president.[74] But the 1960s present Puharich's life at its most elusive, although it is known that between 1958 and 1971 he was research director for the Intelectron Corporation, a company he founded to develop medical devices. It is known that he worked at the US Army hospital at Fort Ord, California, though what he did there is not recorded. He made several visits to Brazil to study Arigó and was also engaged in some (undefined) work for the Atomic Energy Commission in 1968, although it is known that he was working for the head of biophysics, Paul Henshaw, who led the American team that studied the effects of the Hiroshima atom bomb.[75] But although there are only tantalising fragments of information about him during this period, mentioned in passing in his own writings or in isolated references by others, it is clear that Puharich's status within official circles was very high. It has even been claimed that he was on the medical staff of the White House during this period. Only with his involvement with Geller from 1971 did his career become more high-profile in the public mind and therefore more easily charted. But even then the available tit-bits do not always give the full picture.

With its close connections to the Army's psychological warfare programme, the Round Table Foundation itself was not quite the independent paranormal research centre that Puharich implied. It also received support from some very interesting and influential people. Top of the list was Henry Wallace (1888–1965), the former Vice-President of the United States, who gave substantial grants to the Foundation through the Wallace Fund.[76]

One of America's most controversial and highly individual politicians, the Democrat Wallace was second-in-command to Roosevelt from 1940 to 1944 and was narrowly defeated by Truman for the Vice-Presidential nomination in 1944. He was forced to resign from office as Secretary of Commerce in 1946 because of his opposition to US policies regarding Russia and the atomic bomb. He coined the slogan the 'People's Century', which many believe is an accurate description of this era of democracy and uneasy egalitarianism.

A devout, fundamentalist Christian, Wallace believed that God had chosen America to be the leader of the world and that his own place in the scheme of things was hardly that of a humble footsoldier for Christ. As Dwight MacDonald wrote in his 1948 biography of Wallace: 'Just as he thinks of America as the nation destined by God to lead the world, so Wallace thinks of himself as a Messiah, an instrument through whom God will guide America onward and upward.'[77] Wallace was also deeply interested in mysticism and spiritualism and was a prominent Freemason. He wrote in 1934:

It will take a more definite recognition of the Grand Architect of the Universe before the apex stone [the cap-stone of the pyramid on the US Great Seal] is finally fitted into place and this nation in the full strength of its power is in position to assume leadership among the nations in inaugurating 'the new order of the ages'.[78]

In fact, Wallace, as Secretary of State for Agriculture in the 1930s, was responsible for the Great Seal (the Masonic symbol of the eye in the pyramid) being incorporated into the design of American dollar bills.

Wallace was a follower of the mystic Nicholas Roerich, whom he sent on special missions to Tibet and Outer Mongolia, it is said because he was convinced that some kind of evidence of the Second Coming of Jesus Christ was to be found there.[79] Perhaps not surprisingly, his political opponents, especially J. Edgar Hoover – the all powerful head of the FBI – made great capital out of leaked letters from Wallace to Roerich that began 'Dear Guru'.

In the 1930s, Wallace – along with other more or less fundamentalist politicians and wealthy people – had an idea to convert China to Christianity, and it is thought he involved Roerich in this plan as an emissary to Chinese leaders.[80] Perhaps this is the reason for Edgar Cayce's 'prophecies' – which sound so ridiculous now – about the imminent Christianisation of China. Might not Cayce have been using his influence as a 'prophet' to whip up financial support for Wallace's rather ambitious plans? And the similarities between Cayce and Wallace's resounding words about the noble part of Freemasonry in the future of America add another dimension to their shared ideals, and go some way towards explaining why Cayce's pronouncements seem to covertly promote the politician's interests.

Henry Wallace was certainly one of the key figures who lurked behind the scenes of Puharich's Round Table Foundation, as witnessed by, among others, medium Eileen Garrett. In her autobiography she recalls that Wallace visited them while experiments were being carried out around 1949 or 1950.[81] American researcher Terry L. Milner has also found provocative connections between those funding the Round Table Foundation and a joint military body called the Armed Forces Special Weapons Project, primarily concerned with atomic weapons – and that some of the medical research on the effects of radiation was 'subcontracted' to the Round Table Foundation.[82]

This is the background against which the initial contact with the Nine took place through Dr Vinod. As more is known about Puharich the more complex – and murkier – the picture becomes. His talent and expertise in certain fields appeared to know few bounds: in parapsychological research, psychological manipulation using hypnosis and drugs (both chemical and plant-derived) and neurology. Puharich had also achieved great expertise in another area directly relevant to the Nine contacts. This was the field of electronics.

As early as 1947 Puharich, according to investigative journalist Steven Levy, became interested in the study of paranormal abilities, 'specifically . . . in ways he could document them, and perhaps enhance them, by electronic means'.[83] But he had another, long-abiding interest in the use of electronic devices. Almost from the start of his career, he had been fascinated with the idea of using radio waves as a means of communicating directly with an individual, essentially by beaming thoughts straight into their brains. Soon after qualifying as a doctor, he became interested in the phenomenon by which an individual accidentally picks up radio transmissions, hearing them in their head, for example, through the fillings in their teeth. One of Puharich's close colleagues in this work was Warren S. McCulloch, the pioneer of cybernetics, whose work was funded in part by the Josiah Macy Jr Foundation, a known CIA conduit.[84]

In the late 1950s and 1960s, Puharich worked on various electrical and electronic techniques, ostensibly to enable the deaf or hearing-impaired to hear again. Stuart Holroyd wrote that Puharich had devised an electrical deaf aid that conveyed radio waves directly to the skin.[85] Several of these admirable devices were patented by Puharich, and have been successfully used in the treatment of deafness. More suggestive, however, is his invention of a miniaturised radio transmitter that could be hidden inside a tooth,[86] which explains at least the reasoning behind the rather bizarre accusation that Uri Geller had such a device implanted in a tooth to somehow help in the creation of his 'paranormal' phenomena.[87]

When Puharich's electronic work is considered as a whole, it can be seen to be geared to the same end: to find ways to make people hear voices in their heads. This would have been particularly useful if trying to create a belief system based on 'mystical' encounters with other worldly beings in the form of auditory hallucinations.

From the accounts of contact with the Nine, it is obvious that Puharich steered his 'contactees' very much in the direction that he wanted them to go. When he first hypnotised Uri Geller, who then began to speak of extraterrestrials, it was Puharich who asked whether or not they were the 'Nine Principles' spoken of by Dr Vinod twenty years before. Perhaps not surprisingly, the answer was yes.

Hypnosis is a state of extreme suggestibility, in which the subject has a desire to tell the hypnotist whatever he or she wants to hear. The dangers of asking leading questions, and of unconscious confabulation by the subjects, have been recognised for some time, so great care must be taken when, for example, the police use hypnosis to try to improve a witness's memory of something he or she saw. Several recent scandals involving the use of hypnosis to 'recover' memories of satanic ritual abuse have only too graphically demonstrated the serious consequences that can result from uncontrolled use of the technique. Similarly, when Puharich put Bobby Horne into a hypnotic trance and he began to speak the words of an extraterrestrial intelligence called Corean, Puharich suggested to him that it was really the Nine, and the 'entity' immediately agreed. In fact, one of Puharich's close colleagues during this time, Ira Einhorn – who has his own part to play in this story – confirmed Puharich's determination to turn all psychic communication into contact with the Nine, and that he was 'humanly directing' the pattern of the channelling.[88]

Many people, when in trance, spontaneously channel spirits or other entities. In fact, thousands of people today claim to channel great historical figures – such as Mahatma Gandhi – or a variety of extraterrestrial beings. Whether they are pure hokum, or dramatisations welling up from the subject's own unconscious mind, or real independent entities is, as far as this discussion is concerned, largely irrelevant. It is the content of the channelled material that is important. (That most intelligent of mediums, Eileen Garrett, never doubted the reality of her clairvoyance nor the information it gave her, but at the same time she considered it entirely possible that her spirit guide, Uvani, was simply the product of her own subconscious.[89]) Puharich seems to have shaped his subjects' communications to conform to a consistent pattern, fitting a preconceived plan. Perhaps this was a deliberate, calculating experiment to see whether the resulting material would be consistent if his subjects could be made to channel the same source.

Interestingly, another example of this phenomenon is found in other work connected with the Nine. Don Elkins and Carla Rueckert of L/L Research had (through Carla) made contact with Ra, one of the Nine, though significantly only after meeting Puharich. Don Elkins himself had earlier experimented with methods of 'fabricating' contactees.[90] He took over a hundred subjects, who had no prior knowledge of UFOs, and under hypnosis made them channel extraterrestrials, then compared the results with the words of those who claimed to be genuinely in touch with such entities. He found that the 'fabricated' messages were very similar to the 'real' ones. Elkins then leaped to the rather unscientific conclusion that this proved the reality of extraterrestrial contact, and that contactees were not 'chosen', but that anybody could do it if in the right altered and receptive state of consciousness. (Of course, it could be argued that his data proved the opposite, demonstrating that extraterrestrial channelling is a pathological phenomenon, and that it is never 'real'.) Interestingly, several of Elkins's 'fabricated' contactees subsequently claimed UFO experiences. This seems very similar to Puharich's own research.

At the very least, Puharich's use of hypnosis was unethical and dangerous, for example, implanting hypnotic suggestions in Bobby Horne's subconscious so that Phyllis Schlemmer (not a trained hypnotist) could continue to hypnotise Horne in his absence. There is no excuse for Puharich: as a medical doctor and a trained hypnotist he knew the professional code of conduct. Clearly, however, he ignored it. Perhaps he thought of his work as being too important or too essential to bother about such *petit bourgeois* considerations.

Yet another area of Puharich's expertise, his electronic inventions, raises further disquieting possibilities. The Nine were insistent that, in his channelling work, Bobby Horne should not have any metal about his person. This injunction even extended to the metal fillings in his teeth, which they told him to have removed. Before he could carry out this injunction he woke up one morning and discovered that something very strange had happened in the night. Somehow his metal fillings had disappeared, and had been replaced with compound ones.[91] It seemed like a miracle – until one recalls Puharich's expertise in fitting miniaturised radio transmitters in teeth, not to mention his abilities as a master hypnotist. Could Puharich have manipulated the Nine's communications as part of some long-term experiment? Given his connections with intelligence agencies, was this part of a CIA programme? Many of the events that either mystify commentators or convince them that there is something genuinely unexplained about the Nine are in fact open to other interpretations if the intelligence agency connection is taken into account.

In 1973, when Puharich and Whitmore were courting Lyall Watson, trying to persuade him to become more actively involved in promoting the Nine, Watson was impressed by an odd series of events. He received a letter from his parents in South Africa, acknowledging that they had received a copy of his will. But this was impossible: not only had he not been in touch with his parents for some time, but he had not even made a will! Bewildered, he contacted his lawyers in Johannesburg, who told him that the will had been drawn up according to his telephoned instructions and then posted to him at his home in Bermuda. The will had then been returned to them with his signature. Throughout this period Watson had never moved out of London. The Nine claim to have been behind this surreal, Kafkaesque scenario, presumably to impress him with their godlike powers. Watson was duly impressed. Recounting this episode, Stuart Holroyd writes: 'He [Watson] didn't see how anyone could have contrived such an elaborate hoax, or who could have done so, and he admitted that it looked like a materialisation event contrived and executed by some intelligence.'[92]

This is a rather naive conclusion. How difficult would it be for an agency such as MI5 or the CIA to contrive and execute such a plan, with the intention of impressing Watson so he would lend his support to the Nine? (And was there an implicit threat in that these mysterious events related to his last will and testament?) In fact, in our view, Watson's assessment, given by Holroyd, would be accurate if the word 'agency' is added after 'intelligence' . . .

Certainly, the Nine can be rather flamboyant. On the evening of 26 November 1977, television broadcasts in parts of southern England were interrupted by a voice claiming to be a representative of an extraterrestrial civilisation, saying that they would be landing on Earth soon in order to prevent mankind from destroying itself. Dismissed as a student prank, few have noticed that the short message included this sentence:

> We conveyed to Sir John Whitmore and to Dr Puharich that we would interfere on your radio and television communication system to relay when the civilisations are coming close to landing on your planet.[93]

Clearly this was intended to be a fulfilment of the first part of Tom's prophecy: the 'hijacking' of radio and TV broadcasts prior to the promised mass landing. If this really were a student prank, it is odd it should include a reference to Whitmore and Puharich, and such interference with television transmissions would, of course, require sophisticated equipment and technical expertise, leading some to conclude that the message really did come from extraterrestrials.[94] However, as usual, there were only two – diametrically opposed – options considered at the time: either the whole thing was genuine and extraterrestrials had really spoken to the southern English through their television sets; or it was a hoax, just done for a laugh. The idea that such a message could be easily contrived by, for example, an intelligence agency that would have the necessary technical skills has never, to our knowledge, even been considered.

The evidence clearly suggests that the business of the Nine was not an isolated series of paranormal events but an orchestrated drama, involving outside agencies (who helped in arranging apparently inexplicable scenarios such as Lyall Watson's will), with Puharich running it from the inside.

It is almost certain that the majority of the others involved in the story would not be part of this, at least consciously. Perhaps Puharich was the only person who really knew what was going on. We are sure that Phyllis Schlemmer was, and is, not aware of this side of the operation. Writer Bruce Rux says of the Puharich–Whitmore–Schlemmer set-up of the mid-1970s: "'Lab 9" shows all the hallmarks of being an intelligence fraud, one of numerous disinformation sources employed by that particular community.'[95]

If Lab Nine was an intelligence operation, or at least a front for one, as the evidence suggests very strongly, what was the motive behind it?

For love of the space brothers

One possible explanation is that the events surrounding the Nine constituted a long-term experiment into the psychology of 'contactee cults' of the kind that have become so prevalent since the Second World War, aiming to answer certain intriguing questions. For example, how easy is it to convince a group of ordinary people that they really are 'chosen' by some superhuman entity to carry an important message to the world? How can such a belief persuasively be passed on beyond the initial circle to a wider public? And what kind of people will accept the message, and who will reject it?

It is known that the security services have long taken an interest in such cults, as Jacques Vallée has frequently testified, seeking explanations for how such beliefs originate and spread, for reasons that are entirely understandable. For example, quasireligious cults and small but subversive political groups have the potential for great social unrest and worse – the Nazis started small, after all – and they are often used for criminal and anti-social purposes, such as drug trafficking or gun-running. The sinister potential of cults occasionally surfaces: Swiss and French authorities have been alert to such dangers since the mass suicides of the Order of the Solar Temple, whose beliefs included the existence of extra-terrestrials from Sirius, and the similar suicides of members of the *Star Trek*-influenced Heaven's Gate cult in 1996. A number of the earliest UFO contactee cults that emerged soon after the flying saucer craze of the late 1940s were centred on individuals who were members of American fascist organisations. For example, William Dudley Pelley, prewar supporter of Hitler, founded a fascist group called the Silver Shirts of America in 1932 and was interned for the duration of the Second World War. Fascinated with mystical and esoteric ideas, in the late 1940s Pelley claimed to be in telepathic contact with extraterrestrials, writing a book about his experiences called *Star Guests* (1950).[96]

Another reason for official interest in such belief systems is their possible use in psychological warfare. One can imagine, for example, the wealth of possibilities in introducing cult beliefs into an enemy country in order to seriously destabilise it or to ensnare and covertly influence susceptible politicians. One of the main purposes of the intelligence community is specifically to investigate the origins, structure and spread of belief systems.

Another episode illustrates the idea that US government agencies have indulged in 'cult creation' experiments. After his first contact with the Nine through Dr Vinod, Puharich's next reported contact was through his letter from Charles Laughead, after their meeting in Mexico in 1956. Two years before, Laughead had been involved in another contactee group – with some very significant results. Their alleged extraterrestrial communications were the subject of a classic academic study into cult belief by three sociologists at the University of Minnesota, later published as *When Prophecy Fails* by Leon Festiger, Henry W. Riecken and Stanley Schachter (1956).

The contact centred on a Chicago housewife called Dorothy Martin, pseudonymously identified as 'Marion Keech' in the book. It follows an only too familiar pattern. In 1953 she had begun to develop mediumistic abilities, receiving messages via automatic writing. At first, these were 'traditional' spiritualistic communications – from her dead father and other deceased people – but a year later messages began to come through from what claimed to be extraterrestrial sources, originating from several planets, but mainly from one called Clarion. She called these beings the 'Guardians'.

A group – largely consisting of other housewives, but including a few from other walks of life, including a research scientist – gathered around her to study the content of the communications. Enthusiastic members of this curious circle were Dr Charles and Lillian Laughead (who appear as Thomas and Daisy Armstrong in *When Prophecy Fails*). The Laugheads had been Protestant missionaries in Egypt before and just after the Second World War. On a postwar visit, Lillian suffered a mental breakdown and, when prayer failed to resolve her problems, the couple came to doubt their faith, beginning a quest through other religious and esoteric systems, finally becoming particularly interested in William Dudley Pelley's writings. After a meeting with seminal UFO contactee George Adamski, they became convinced of the reality and spiritual significance of UFOs. They joined the Dorothy Martin circle and Charles became its organiser and spokesman.

On 27 August 1954, Dorothy received a warning from the Guardians of a wave of imminent catastrophes, which would include the disappearance of the east coast of the United States – as well as Britain and France – under the sea on 21 December. The Laugheads took the lead in publicising these warnings, taking the story to the press.

At this stage the group of sociologists from the University of Minnesota decided to infiltrate the group in order to make a hands-on study of the behaviour of such cults and, in particular, to see at first-hand the reactions of true believers when the prophecies failed to materialise. As we know, the east coast of the United States did not find itself in a watery grave on 21 December 1954, and neither did Britain or France. The Minnesota study charted the gradual break-up of the group and its members' struggle to come to terms with the failure, and the resulting sense of loss and bereavement that such cruel disillusionment brings in its wake. Only one or two members admitted losing their faith in the Guardians, the majority coming up with a variety of more or less plausible rationalisations – or perhaps 'irrationalisations' – to explain the failure. Some said it had been a test of faith, or that the strength of their belief had actually averted the catastrophe. Quaintly, under the circumstances, the real tension in the group was caused by arguments about which of these excuses was the right one! The circle finally collapsed under the intense weight of public humiliation and ridicule. Dorothy Martin left to join a Dianetics centre in Arizona, having been a follower of Dianetics for some time, and the rest carried on with their lives. Only the Laugheads seemed to take something lasting away from the experience. According to *When Prophecy Fails*:

> In the next two weeks the Armstrongs [Laugheads] sold their home and wound up their affairs . . . and Thomas [Charles] prepared for the role he was assuming – that of itinerant proselyter, spreading the teachings of the Guardians across the land.[97]

The Laugheads began working with other channellers, one result of which was their meeting with Puharich two years later, which was to have a profound effect on his own acceptance of the reality of the Nine.

The story of the Guardians cult may seem an all too familiar tale of a group of people obsessed with a false, quasireligious belief built up around a deluded channeller. That is certainly how the team from Minnesota University treated it. Another aspect of the story suggests something else was going on – that the events were indeed being manipulated by outside forces, but by very *terrestrial* agencies.

Dorothy Martin sometimes returned to her locked home to find letters from 'Clarion' left inside, and she would receive telephone calls direct from the Guardians when the sociologists were present, which at least indicates that they were not figments of her imagination. As a climax, when the group gathered at Dorothy's house on 18 December to await the coming cataclysm three days later, she received a long call from the leader of the Guardians, a being called Sananda, after which five young men arrived at the house, the leader of whom claimed to be Sananda himself. The group went into another room with Laughead for half an hour, followed by an hour with Dorothy Martin (from which she emerged very emotional and moved). Then the five mystery callers left. Again, all this was witnessed by the researchers.[98]

These were real events, so it is difficult to reconcile them with the Minnesota team's conclusion that it was all a collective delusion, although clearly there was scope for other interpretations, such as mistaken identity, or, more probably, a hoax. Yet if the latter, it was very carefully and painstakingly organised: the letters, telephone calls and the visit all served to reinforce the group's belief in the prophecies received by automatic writing. Obviously, another group of people existed beyond the immediate circle of true believers and were orchestrating both the events and the phenomenon of escalating belief. Why?

The most likely answer is that this shadowy but all important group were conducting their own experiment, and it is likely that they were an official but secret agency investigating the behaviour of circles based around channelled extraterrestrial communications. We know that the group *was* being used as an unwitting experimental subject by the Minnesota University researchers, and it may be significant that there was a local newspaper called *The Minnesota Clarion*.

In that case, where did Dorothy Martin's original automatic scripts originate? If she and the Laugheads were part of the plot, all she had to do was sit down and make them up. Interestingly, the story almost exactly parallels that of the Nine – although of course on a much smaller scale – and the two series of events are linked by the meeting of Laughead with Puharich two years later. Was the Guardians scenario a dry run for the Nine?

There was a sequel to the story of the Guardian group. Dorothy Martin continued to receive messages from the Guardians, who told her to change her name to 'Sister Thedra' and to travel to Lake Titicaca in Peru. Once there, she established – along with the Laugheads and the seminal mystic and contactee George Hunt Williamson – the Abbey of the Seven Rays. From this base Dorothy Martin began to prophesy the coming of the 'Time of Awakening' when Atlantis would rise from the deep and a new Saviour would rescue the righteous. In 1961 she returned to the United States, where she continued to preach her message until her death in 1988.[99]

A sinister experiment?

The hypothesis that the events surrounding the Nine were deliberately orchestrated makes sense of some otherwise puzzling aspects of the story, such as the failure of the promised mass landings of 1978. Why would the Nine risk the disillusionment of their followers when not even one alien craft, let alone fleets of spaceships, landed? On the 'experimental' hypothesis, this would be the perfect benchmark by which to test the degree of belief in the circle. If, unlike Dorothy Martin's group twenty-five years before, they could accept and rationalise such a failure – and potential humiliation – then surely the experiment would be judged a *success*?

The intimate involvement of Puharich in this scenario causes alarm bells to ring. Given his background, and the way in which he clearly manipulated the development of Nine communications in the 1970s, such a scenario – despite its *X-Files* overtones – makes much sense. It is not difficult to discern the presence of some shadowy military or intelligence agency behind the events surrounding the Nine.

Consider, for example, Puharich's Geller Kids or Space Kids, whom he tested and trained during the 1970s. There were twenty of them, the youngest nine and the oldest in their late teens, culled from seven different countries and taken to what became jokingly known as Puharich's 'Turkey Farm' at Ossining in order to develop their psychic potential. As we have seen, Puharich trained them in remote viewing, but the target locations he set them were significant: they were of military or intelligence interest and included the Pentagon, the Kremlin and even the White House.[100] It seems clear that there was an official element to these experiments, as they were being carried out at exactly the same time (1975–8) that defence and intelligence agencies were studying remote viewing in adults. We can speculate that the Ossining establishment was chosen for the children's project because it was a conveniently 'civilian' location: questions would certainly have been asked if youngsters had been experimented on inside military facilities.

The Ossining programme had even more disturbing elements: Puharich experimented on the children in order to contact extraterrestrial intelligences. As with Geller and Bobby Horne, he regularly hypnotised his young subjects, apparently in the belief that their powers did indeed come from 'aliens'. As Steven Levy wrote: 'The Kids describe strange cities with science-fiction trappings and claim to be messengers from these distant civilisations.'[101]

Given Puharich's obsession with extraterrestrial influence, not to mention his indiscriminate use of the most powerful sort of hypnosis, it would be strange if the Space Kids had not come up with such descriptions. But was Puharich simply releasing memories of real events, or was he in fact implanting them? In either case, his use of hypnosis, in what were clearly uncontrolled conditions, on children as young as nine, is extremely disquieting. (Ira Einhorn, a close associate of Puharich at this time, admitted to us that he found these experiments very disturbing.[102])

In August 1978, after the Turkey Farm was burned down in the arson attack, Puharich disappeared to Mexico, blaming the fire on the CIA, claiming that they were trying to stop his experiments with the Geller Kids.[103] He later accused the CIA of making three attempts on his life, which is particularly strange because Puharich himself was, of course, known to have worked for them. Had he somehow doublecrossed them, or in some way made enemies within the agency? And if the CIA had really tried, and failed, to kill Puharich three times, it is hardly a good advertisement for their efficiency. Perhaps they were only trying to frighten him. Whatever the truth of the matter, Puharich was not the only one who suffered at the demise of the Turkey Farm. Several of the Space Kids were severely traumatised at being so brusquely abandoned, especially after living pretty much as a family in a close, 'hothouse' atmosphere for three years.[104]

The destruction of the Turkey Farm was only part of a series of setbacks that afflicted the Puharich group in the late 1970s – which even included murder – throwing an even more sinister web of intrigue around the already tainted central figures.

The Unicorn

Another key player linking the Nine to the emerging counterculture of the 1970s was Ira Einhorn, known to his circle as 'the Unicorn', the meaning of his surname in English. He was a leading light in the world that emerged from the hippie scene to embrace a multitude of interleaved 'alternative' movements, such as ecology, new energy sources, exploration of the nature and limits of consciousness and mysticism.

Ira Einhorn became a highly sought-after industrial guru, a professional networker who put key people in touch with others, acting as a catalyst for change and improvement. He had close connections with – and was financed by – many leading industrialists, including the Canadian Bronfman family and the Rockefellers, and companies such as AT&T and McDonnell

Douglas, the military aircraft manufacturer. He was also known to be in contact with leading NASA officials.[105]

A significant point in Einhorn's career was his meeting with Puharich in 1968, at a time when the latter was working for the Atomic Energy Commission. Puharich has been described as Einhorn's 'mentor' (a term often used of him), and the two men became close colleagues during the 1970s, when he was also busy with Lab Nine: Einhorn was a frequent visitor to the Turkey Farm when the Space Kids experiments were being carried out. He was Puharich's stepping stone to other ground-breaking events taking place in the fields of psychology and physics at the time. Einhorn referred to the group of scientists of which he and Puharich were part as his 'psychic mafia'.[106] Einhorn arranged for Puharich's 1962 book *Beyond Telepathy* to be reissued by Anchor Books in 1973 (contributing his own poem as a foreword), and he also edited Puharich's account of his time with Uri Geller, *Uri* (1974), which was, in fact, less a biography of the superstar metalbender than a paean of praise for the Nine.

Einhorn's most significant contribution was, in the 1970s, the establishment of a worldwide network of scientists, industrialists, writers and philosophers at the cutting edge of new developments in physics, parapsychology, psychology and other fields. This new network consisted of 350 experts from twenty countries, with Einhorn himself acting as what he called 'planetary catalyst', circulating information to all the members. This network was funded by the Bell Telephone Company (of which Arthur M. Young was a major shareholder at that time), Einhorn always living entirely on the patronage of wealthy backers and business sponsors.[107]

Einhorn's network was the subject of a study by the Diebold Corporation in 1978, with the grandiose and somewhat impenetrable title of 'The Emergence of Personal Communication Networks Among People Sharing the New Values and Their Possible Use in Sensitizing Operating Management', which compared it to the 'Invisible College' of seventeenth-century Britain, an informal group of scientists – and, perhaps significantly, esotericists – that became the Royal Society.[108]

Einhorn's reputation took a dramatic nosedive, though. He and former cheerleader Holly Maddux had been involved in a stormy relationship since they met in October 1972, moving in together two months later. In the summer of 1977 the couple went to London, where – with Puharich – they stayed at the home of a wealthy backer, Joyce Petschek. After one of their frequent fights, Holly returned to Philadelphia alone at the end of July, apparently determined, this time, to make a final break with Einhorn. In August she stayed at one of Joyce Petschek's houses, on Fire Island in New York State, where she met a wealthy businessman called Saul Lapidus (a former executive of Puharich's Intelectron Corporation). Meanwhile, Einhorn left London to visit other contacts in Europe, returning to the United States on 21 August, where he stayed for a few days at Puharich's Turkey Farm before going back to Philadelphia. At the time Holly Maddux was staying with Lapidus, but she returned to Philadelphia on 9 September after an angry phone call from Einhorn. She was never seen alive again.

Eighteen months later, after investigations by private detectives employed by Maddux's parents, the Philadelphia police searched Einhorn's apartment and found a very badly decomposed Maddux in a trunk inside a locked cupboard on the back porch. Einhorn was arrested. The autopsy revealed she had been killed by violent blows to the head.

During the investigation into Maddux's disappearance – initially by private detectives, then by the police – there is no doubt that those involved in the Puharich set-up closed ranks around Einhorn. Saul Lapidus had been concerned when Maddux failed to return from her last meeting with Einhorn, and had asked Puharich to call him and find out what had happened. Puharich was satisfied with Einhorn's reassurance that everything was fine, which was understandable at the time, but Puharich seemed to continue to believe in Einhorn's innocence, even when he was arrested. Puharich seemed to have been more concerned about recovering papers about the Geller Kids experiments he had lent Maddux shortly before she disappeared.[109] (These were later found at Lapidus's house and returned to Puharich.)

According to Steven Levy, an American investigative journalist, associates such as Joyce Petschek actually refused to co-operate with the private investigators, so it took them over a year to piece together Maddux's last movements. Not until November 1978 did they even hear about the vital witness Saul Lapidus, with whom she was staying at the time of her disappearance.

Einhorn was released on bail on 3 April 1979, paid for by Barbara Bronfman, sponsor of the Nine's work (she is listed in the acknowledgements of *The Only Planet of Choice*). He then travelled to California to visit various contacts, including the Nine's channeller Jenny O'Connor at the Esalen Institute – where he stayed for several weeks – before spending time with the Bronfmans at their palatial Montreal home.[110] As the date of the trial loomed, 13 January 1981, Einhorn fled to London with his new girlfriend Jeanne Morrison, despite his passport having been removed by the Philadelphia Police Department, and has been a fugitive ever since. He was found guilty of murder in his absence in 1983. In 1997 he was found to be living in France under the name Eugene Mallon, but the French courts refused to extradite him (as the US authorities would not give him a new trial). During these proceedings it emerged that Einhorn had been supported financially since becoming a fugitive by Barbara Bronfman (she had divorced billionaire Charles Bronfman in 1982).[111] Einhorn lived on in France, continuing to protest his innocence, claiming that he was framed as part of an intelligence plot, either by the KGB or the CIA. In September 1998 Einhorn was rearrested as the Philadelphia legislature changed the laws specifically to enable the French authorities to extradite him. At the time of writing he is still out on bail awaiting trial.

Einhorn, however, had his own connections with the intelligence community. He worked closely with Congressman Charlie Rose, a member of the House Select Committee on Intelligence. Rose was one of the most prominent supporters of the Pentagon's remote-viewing programme, and of the use of psychic skills in defence and intelligence work in general. He is quoted as saying: 'Some people think this is the work of the Devil, other people think it's the work of the Holy Spirit.'[112] According to Jack Sarfatti, Rose told him that Einhorn was involved in national security operations,[113] although Einhorn himself recently told us that if this was true, he must have been their unwitting pawn, adding that the intelligence agencies were extremely interested in his network and the various individuals and organisations it brought together.[114]

Einhorn's contribution to the spread of belief in the Nine should not be underestimated. His role as networker supreme put him in touch with a considerable number of key people worldwide who no doubt found his personal conviction impressive and inspiring.

Significantly, just three weeks before his arrest, Ira Einhorn gave a lecture in Philadelphia in which, according to Steven Levy:

He said that for years he had been primarily interested in the relation of nonphysical entities to the physical world. This led him to revelations, he explained, that had startling consequences for our civilization.[115]

Levy also said of Einhorn's strange quest:

As he delved deeper into the world of the paranormal, he became increasingly convinced that recent psychic revelations [presumably a reference to the Nine's communications] could have significant global impact. In some scenarios, these could have alarming consequences.[116]

He goes on to stress Einhorn's role in bringing about major changes through the acceptance of the unexplained:

Through his relationship with Andrija Puharich and others, in what he jokingly called a 'psychic mafia', the Unicorn assumed a key role in the task of alerting our people about the implications of this revolution . . . in Einhorn's universe, those factors included the undeniability of UFOs, the startling discoveries in quantum physics, and the inevitability of the new world order – shaken loose by the Aquarian Transformation.[117]

Such apocalyptic beliefs were shared by others on the Puharich–Einhorn scene. Lieutenant-Colonel Thomas Bearden, Einhorn's close friend and former 'war games' analyst at the Pentagon, appeared – along with Puharich – at a conference organised by Einhorn on 'Mind over Matter' at Penn State University in 1977. (Bearden wrote the obituary for Puharich in the Newsletter of PACE, the Planetary Association for Clean Energy, in 1995.) Since retiring from the Army, Bearden has dedicated himself to researching alternative energy sources. He has written:

I believe that the accelerated time schedule for the 'New World Order' – now set for the year 2000 – is as the result of the imminent advent of (1) superluminal [faster-than-light] communication . . . and (2) overunity electrical energy systems.[118]

Bearden was on the board of the Astron Corporation, a communications research and development company contracted to the Defense Department and NASA.[119] The vice-president (and president at the time of Bearden's involvement) is Dr Joseph Jahoda, who has been involved in the ARE/Schor Foundation excavations at Giza since 1978.

Science for a New Age

Einhorn's strange career puts the events surrounding the Nine in the 1970s into a much wider context, unfolding against the emergence of radical new developments in the fields of psychology, parapsychology and quantum physics. A new generation of scientists was beginning to explore subjects previously considered as smacking too much of the lunatic fringe even to be worthy of consideration. At the heart of this new wave was an impulse to understand more about the nature – and limits – of human consciousness and its relationship to the physical universe. This work encompassed research into such areas as the subconscious mind and altered states of consciousness, including the effects of hallucinogenic drugs such as LSD, exploring new discoveries in the weird realms of quantum physics, potential new sources of energy, and parapsychology. From this family of brave new ideas came such classic and influential studies as Fritjof Capra's *The Tao of Physics*, which explored the relationship between quantum physics and Eastern mysticism; David Bohm's *Wholeness and the Implicate Order*; Joseph Campbell's *The Masks of God* on the psychology of myth; Stanislav Grof's *Realms of the Human Unconscious*, on LSD research; and many others.

Much of this ground-breaking work took place in California within a closely knit network of research institutes and foundations among which was a great sharing of ideas and much overlapping membership. Among these establishments was, of course, SRI at Menlo Park, where Targ and Puthoff's pioneering work into remote viewing was conducted, at the same time that SRI were also active at Giza.

The Esalen Institute at Big Sur, which had another establishment in San Francisco, was a prime mover in this scene. Dubbed 'the California capital of the self-realization movement',[120] it was founded in 1964 by Michael Murphy and Richard Price on land formerly inhabited by the Esselen Indians, with the aim of holding seminars on psychology, religion, parapsychology, quantum physics and related subjects. In the late 1960s and early 1970s it regularly sparked controversy, not always for the intended reasons. Naked students often claimed the lion's share of local headlines, rather than the pioneering seminars of the great thinkers of the day. Also a centre for research into psychedelic drugs, it became a focus for the counterculture of the day. More surprisingly, it has been enormously influential beyond its time and place.

Ira Einhorn led seminars at Esalen, and it was there that the Nine, channelled by Jenny O'Connor, were listed as members of staff. According to Einhorn, 'she took over running Esalen through the Nine',[121] and such was the influence of the Nine that they ordered the sacking of its chief financial officer and reorganised the entire management structure.[122] In the late 1970s the Esalen Soviet Exchange programme was developed, initially to share parapsychological research, in which rising Soviet stars of academia and politics were invited to the United States. This was to have enormous, far-reaching influence on world politics, as many of the Soviets who went to Esalen in the 1980s were to become instrumental in the shake-ups that would end the Cold War and bring about the fall of communism. It is reasonable to assume that an organisation whose members made regular trips to Moscow in the days of the Cold War *must* have been made use of by US intelligence, or at least have been monitored. Almost incredibly, several Soviet officials who would later rise to high office in the Gorbachev regime attended Jenny O'Connor's Nine seminars, together with psi enthusiasts Congressman Charlie Rose and Ira Einhorn.

The Esalen Institute now runs the Gorbachev Foundation/ USA, created by the former Soviet President in 1992 to facilitate a smooth transition from the Cold War days to a better future for all the world. One of its objectives is to work with the development of the emerging political and religious paradigms. The Institute sponsored and funded visits to the United States by Boris Yeltsin before he became Russian President, and members of the Esalen Soviet Exchange programme were the go-betweens for Richard Hoagland and Soviet Mars researchers in the mid-1980s.

The story moves in one quantum leap from a tale of dubious channelling and its disciples to another level. The Nine, through their channellers and hangers-on, have a more or less direct line to some of the world's most important men, whose decisions affect millions of lives. This is an astonishing scenario.

Another 'sister' school in this movement was, if anything, more controversial than the Esalen Institute. This was est (Erhard Sensitivity Training), the organisation founded in 1971 by Werner Erhard, a former Scientologist – and used car salesman – who decided to exploit and adapt some of Scientology's concepts and techniques for his own self-improvement system. The now notorious est held seminars that attracted such celebrities as Buzz Aldrin, Yoko Ono, John Denver and the future UFO abduction researcher John Mack, but it wasn't long before est became a dirty word. Attendees were disturbed by the fascistic regime and zombielike demeanour of the members, as well as Erhard's own dictatorial control of the organisation. Media disapproval was intense, and soon est was relegated to the scrapheap of dangerous cults. Erhard himself fled from the United States after press revelations about his private life and financial affairs. He is now believed to be somewhere in Russia.

Tellingly, Erhard's real name was John Rosenberg, but it is said that he changed his name 'to replace Jewish weakness with German strength'.[123] (His father was Jewish, but had converted to Episcopal Christianity.) Erhard had close links with the Esalen Institute and gave funds to SRI's remote-viewing project.[124] More disturbingly, Jenny O'Connor had been introduced to est in 1977, by Sir John Whitmore, before she moved on to Esalen.

A further integral part of this movement was the Institute of Noetic Sciences at Palo Alto, which was founded by Apollo 14 astronaut Edgar Mitchell in March 1973, and is 'dedicated to research and education in the processes of human consciousness to help achieve a new understanding and expanded awareness among all people'.[125] ('Noetics' comes from the Greek for 'mind'.) They were heavily involved in the psi testing of the 1970s, partly funding the Geller experiments at SRI and, until the CIA came clean about their involvement in the remote-viewing experiments in the mid-1990s, it was the Institute of Noetic Sciences that claimed to have funded the initial programme.[126] At the very least, this shows that the Institute allowed itself to be used as a cover for the CIA, and perhaps even as a conduit for the funding of the agency's more controversial experiments.

Arthur M. Young's highly influential Institute for the Study of Consciousness at Berkeley, founded in 1972, also provided a forum for some of the most daring thinkers of the day. It was here that Richard Hoagland had his meeting with Paul Shay of SRI, and also where he gave his first lecture about Cydonia in 1984. Later he was to acknowledge Arthur Young's personal influence.[127] (Young, present at the Nine's debut at the Round Table Foundation in 1953, was in fact more heavily involved in the running of the Foundation than he wanted to be known, serving as Puharich's 'second-in-command' there.[128] Young also kept secret his presence at the meeting of Puharich, Hurkos and the Laugheads in Mexico in 1956, although shortly before his death in 1995 he admitted to researcher Terry Milner that he had been present.[129])

Institutions and foundations only succeed because of the individuals who breathe life into them. One of the key figures on this scene was avant-garde physicist Jack Sarfatti, the first director of the Physics/Consciousness Research Group at the Esalen Institute, which was funded by Werner Erhard and money covertly channelled through from the Pentagon.[130] His seminars were attended by Stanislas Grof, Russell Targ, Timothy Leary, physicist Saul Paul Sirag (who became director after Sarfatti), Robert Anton Wilson, Fritjof Capra and Ira Einhorn, who was Sarfatti's literary agent.

The work carried out by this interlinked network of organisations was imaginative and innovative, presenting a serious challenge to the previous arrogant certainties of the scientific world. It was undertaken in a genuine pioneering spirit, largely born of the idealism of the youth culture of the 1960s and a desire to change the world for the better. However, a dark shadow was cast over this early idyllic promise by the involvement of the Pentagon, CIA and other security and intelligence agencies, who soon realised that the breakthroughs of these idealists had great potential in their own spheres, such as remote viewing. And they did not fail to note that research into altered states of consciousness, including the use of LSD and other drugs, also had darker applications in the various techniques of mind control. So often this research was encouraged and funded – although often covertly, through other channels – by organisations such as the CIA and the Pentagon. One of the pioneers of LSD and consciousness research, John C. Lilly, worked at the Esalen Institute for several years, as well as for the CIA, but only on the condition that his research remained unclassified. This made things difficult for him professionally, because nearly all other researchers in the field were also working on classified projects, so he was unable to share data with them or vice versa.[131]

Another case of behind-the-scenes agendas in this milieu involved Dr Brendan O'Regan, research director of Edgar Mitchell's Institute of Noetic Sciences and a consultant for SRI, as well as research director for the scientist–philosopher R. Buckminster Fuller. O'Regan arranged the experiments into the strange talents of Uri Geller at Birkbeck College, London, in 1975 and was also closely involved with the Puharich–Whitmore circle surrounding the Nine. And, since O'Regan's death in 1992, Jack Sarfatti has claimed that he was also working with the CIA at this time, writing:

> I was then [1973] simply a young inexperienced 'naive idiot' in a very very sophisticated and successful covert psychological warfare operation run by the late Brendan O'Regan of the Institute of Noetic Sciences and the late Harold Chipman who was the CIA station chief responsible for all mind-control research in the Bay Area in the 70s.[132]

As with the Nine's communications – which were intimately connected with the extraordinary cutting-edge research taking place primarily in California – the shadow of the intelligence agencies looms large.

Who spins the web?

The messages of the Nine's communications are particularly intriguing in this context because they extended over such a long time, apart from any other considerations. But what would be the point of such an exhaustive experiment by the intelligence agencies?

One plausible motive, as we have seen, is the testing of the extent that such beliefs can be created and manipulated. In the hands of such a supremely skilled puppetmaster as Puharich, this would have been worth watching closely. But perhaps it was not merely an exercise in observation and always had a definite end in mind? Perhaps the belief system was being used for some purpose that had been clearly defined from the outset.

In both of these scenarios the Nine have to be a fabrication – a hoax – but this fails to account for certain key aspects of the story. For example, the Nine's communications have continued since Puharich bowed out at the end of the 1970s. Is the experiment continuing, but under the control of someone else? Or has the belief system built up such a momentum – essentially, creating a life of its own – that it has become self-perpetuating? A few who claim contact with the Nine appear to have done so independently of each other, including Carla Rueckert and James Hurtak, but, apart from David Myers (as far as we know), most of them had some contact with Puharich.

Where Puharich's work is concerned, the big question is whether he was actually fabricating extraterrestrial contact, or experimenting with various methods of inducing it. British parapsychologist Kenneth J. Batcheldor demonstrated that genuine paranormal effects can be induced in a group simply by what he called 'artefact induction', in effect, kickstarting real paranormal phenomena simply by *cheating*.[133] He discovered that, in groups researching psychokinesis, if someone deliberately tilts the table and the group as a whole believes it to have been caused paranormally, this opens the floodgates for genuinely supernatural events to happen. Significantly, not only was Puharich certainly aware of Batcheldor's findings, but Don Elkins believed that his experiments in fabricating contactees through hypnosis actually resulted in real contact.

Puharich himself undoubtedly believed absolutely in psychic

abilities. Significantly, it appears that from quite early in his career – as described in his book *The Sacred Mushroom* – he was fascinated by the ancient Egyptian religion of Heliopolis and the possibility of contacting the gods of the Great Ennead directly. On balance, it would seem that Puharich *did* believe that such communication was at least possible, although the means of reaching extraterrestrial gods were fraught with problems. The message could become scrambled by inner 'noise' or contaminated by the medium's personal hopes and fears. But it seems that Puharich believed that it was possible to open the stargate, allowing the extraterrestrial gods to enter our dimension, as demonstrated in his use of the Space Kids to explore the idea of contact. Ira Einhorn told us that Puharich was obsessed with the space gods, because he thought that the world was in a mess and that its only hope was help from outside, from higher intelligences. Einhorn himself has no doubt that the Nine are real, objective entities, but he does not believe they are who they claim to be. He often argued with Puharich about his eagerness to take orders from them; it was their major point of disagreement.[134]

Was it Puharich's own idea to try to contact the space gods, or did it come from his superiors in the intelligence community? Senior CIA (and other) operatives may well have taken the possibility of extraterrestrial contact seriously enough to explore ways of opening a stargate. Certainly, intelligence agencies around the world were aware of the potential of psychic abilities and were in possession of abundant data that suggested strongly that shamanic-style skills successfully invite contactee-type experiences.

An example of this involved a spate of weird phenomena that erupted after a series of not particularly successful experiments with Uri Geller at the Lawrence Livermore Laboratory in California – one of the leading US nuclear weapons research centres – in 1974 and 1975.[135] The Lawrence Livermore researchers were concerned that if his abilities were genuine they could potentially threaten the operation of nuclear missiles – could he somehow trigger a warhead, for example, or interfere with a missile's guidance system? The researchers wanted to establish whether psychokinesis really existed, and if so, how effective it was, and what could be done to protect against it.

A series of tests were carried out with Geller (while keeping him well away from the main research centre, just in case). According to Jim Schnabel, they convinced them that psychokinesis was not powerful or controllable enough to pose a serious risk to their nuclear arsenal. But even so, the experiments seemed to act as an 'Open Sesame' to a startling show of spin-off phenomena. On one occasion, a metallic voice appeared on an audiotape during one of the tests, apparently speaking a sequence of random words. CIA analyst Christopher 'Kit' Green – who appears under the pseudonym 'Richard Kennett' in Schnabel's book – was then working on the CIA remote-viewing project at SRI and also monitoring their experiments with Geller. He subsequently realised that the voice was actually giving the code name of a top-secret CIA project totally unconnected with the Geller experiments.

More disturbingly, over the weeks that followed the tests, the physicists began to experience strange apparitions, both at home and in the laboratory, including miniature 'flying saucers' and strange animals such as huge, ravenlike birds – 'fantastic animals from the ecstatic lore of shamans', as Jim Schnabel calls them.[136] These were also seen by members of the physicists' families. It is as if Lawrence Livermore Laboratories had suddenly become haunted: one physicist even received a telephone call from the metallic voice. Eventually these weird events stopped, as if a temporary rip in the veil between dimensions had been abruptly zipped up again. In addition, several participants in the Pentagon/CIA's remote-viewing programmes experienced paranormal events outside of office hours, and also had apparent extraterrestrial contact, especially in connection with Mars.

These events, together with Puharich's belief in the reality of extraterrestrial contact, raise the serious possibility that the CIA and other agencies were fully aware of the 'otherworldly' element attached to their psychic spying programmes, in which apparently nonhuman entities 'came through'. After all, when a top nuclear weapons facility becomes 'haunted' and its hard-headed and sceptical scientists are so harassed by the weirdness that several of them come close to a nervous breakdown, such bizarre phenomena have to be taken seriously. They would want to know more about such things – if only to eliminate them from their psi-spy research, but, given the entities' inside knowledge of top-secret code names, they would also want to know if a more controlled kind of contact could be made with such useful intelligences and if some kind of mutually beneficial dialogue could be set up. It would make sense: if the Nine really were space gods, it is not hard to imagine the advantages of having them on the side of the United States during the Cold War, for example, or as allies during any period of history.

An article by researcher Alex Constantine quotes Rod Lewis of the American Federation of Scientists on the remote viewers 'dealing with the demonic realm', explaining: 'It's a Greek word for "disembodied intelligence". Apparently it's something they take very seriously, and unfortunately they're trying to use it for military purposes.'[137]

Many of the people involved with the Nine seem predisposed towards the idea of extraterrestrial contact, often because of their own prior experiences, for example, as mediums. And one objective of the Nine experiment appears to have been to test the possibility and controllability of such contact.

It is clear that the belief in extraterrestrial contact was a major thread running through the avant-garde work of various organisations discussed above – and that it was taken very seriously by certain key figures, one of whom was Stanislav Grof, the Czechoslovakian psychiatrist who had researched the effects of LSD in Prague, before being invited to the United States to con-tinue his work in 1965. Grof worked at several clinics and medical research centres, and wrote *Realms of the Human Unconscious: Observations from LSD Research*. It was written at, and published by, the Esalen Institute in 1975.

Grof studied the whole range of experiences under the

influence of LSD, including a number of 'paranormal' effects reported by his subjects such as apparent memories of past lives, precognition, clairvoyance and mystical experiences. Significantly, they also included out-of-body experiences and what used to be known as 'travelling clairvoyance', but which is now called remote viewing. He also discovered many experiences of 'spirit guides' or other helpful and apparently superior entities, including those claiming to be extraterrestrials.[138]

This often extended beyond mere academic interest. Many of these researchers claimed personal contact themselves. For example, Jack Sarfatti says that in 1952, when he was fourteen, he received a telephone call in which a machinelike voice announced that it was a conscious computer located on a spaceship from the future. It went on to say that Sarfatti had been chosen as 'one of four hundred bright receptive minds', and that he would begin to 'link up' with the others in twenty years' time.[139]

As prophesied by the voice, Sarfatti did indeed go on to become a gifted – if maverick – theoretical physicist. He has always been fascinated by the far reaches of scientific thinking and the more exotic aspects of quantum physics, such as the nature of time (he is a co-author of a major work called *Space-Time and Beyond*), the possibilities of faster-than-light travel and communication, and the relationship of human consciousness to quantum-level physics. He was the director of the Physics/Consciousness Research Group at the Esalen Institute and is currently developing the concept of 'post-quantum physics', which, he claims, can explain phenomena such as remote viewing. In a recent email to us he said:

I have extended David Bohm's version of quantum physics to include mental phenomena. I call this 'post-quantum physics'. Post-quantum physics violates Einstein's idea that the future cannot influence the present in detectable and controllable ways . . . Post-quantum physics purports to be the unified explanation of both ordinary consciousness and extraordinary phenomena like remote-viewing used with spectacular success during the Cold War . . . I suspect that understanding the physical nature of consciousness as a post-quantum field beyond ordinary space and time will allow us to travel to the stars and beyond both materially and mentally. We shall soon make *Star Trek* real.[140]

Sarfatti's interest in matters such as the nature of time is a direct result of the bizarre telephone call back in 1952. He believes he is to some extent still guided by his extraterrestrial contact. Could it be that nonhuman intelligences really are trying to influence the human race through individuals chosen during childhood? How else could 'they' know that Sarfatti would grow up to be an eminent physicist?

On the other hand, Sarfatti's potential was also recognised by human agencies around the same time. According to his own account, around the time of the mysterious phone call he was selected for 'an afternoon school of gifted kids' tutored by one Walter Breen.[141] This extra tuition included lectures on patriotism and 'anti-communism' by visitors from the Sandia Corporation, a major player in the US nuclear weapons research programme at that time. Breen arranged for Sarfatti to have a scholarship to Cornell University when he was just seventeen, writing a profile in which he said Sarfatti would make 'revolutionary discoveries in the foundations of physics'.[142] Breen echoed the futuristic computer's assessment of Sarfatti's vocation as a cutting-edge scientist.

Twenty years later, strange things did begin to happen around Sarfatti, but only after he had entered the heady world of the research organisations we have discussed. In 1973, he went to SRI to meet Brendan O'Regan, with whom he had an intense seventeen-hour conversation, as a result of which he began to recall the full weirdness of his telephone experience of twenty-one years before for the first time. He subsequently became director of the Physics/Consciousness Research Group at Esalen (with funding from Werner Erhard and the Pentagon), spending time with a somewhat surreal assortment of gurus, psychics and catalysts, including Puharich, Whitmore, Geller and Einhorn, at the Turkey Farm at Ossining. Sarfatti was also called upon by Brendan O'Regan to organise the experiments into Geller's abilities at Birkbeck College, London in 1975, when a huge range of startling paranormal phenomena were recorded. During this time, he was given a copy of Puharich's *Uri*, and when his mother read its account of Geller and the Nine, she was reminded of the weird telephone phenomenon, except that, to Sarfatti's great surprise, she remembered not one call, but a series of them over a period of three weeks.

Given this background, it is tempting to speculate that Sarfatti was part of a sinister, *X-Files*-type experiment in 'programming' children as part of some long-term government project. Sarfatti himself acknowledges the possibility, but thinks too much remains unexplained by this scenario. Tellingly, in a question-and-answer session on the Internet in March 1998 with one Mark Thornally, when asked whether Walter Breen could have stage-managed the phone call and computer voice, Sarfatti admitted that he could, then volunteered: 'Andrija Puharich, who was in the Army at that time I think, would have been able to do it.'

Although acknowledging that Army scientists could have contrived the phone call, Sarfatti doubts that Breen or Puharich could have planned and organised the subsequent events that only began to unfold twenty years later. It is difficult to disagree. This is one of the most puzzling aspects of the whole story, also true of events surrounding the Nine. They could have been directed by intelligences from outer space or from the future – but involvement by government agencies invites suspicion. Yet again, certain elements simply cannot be explained if they were just psychological experiments by clandestine human agencies.

Other similarities between Sarfatti's experience and the events surrounding the Nine are, of course, the dates. Both first occurred in 1952, but neither bore fruit until the early 1970s. (Sarfatti had no idea the Nine went back so far until we pointed it out.)

Many people have been impressed by the paranormal phenomena associated with the Nine, which often converts them to the cause. Another example of this happened to Saul Paul Sirag, the physicist who took over the Physics/Consciousness Research Group at Esalen after Sarfatti. He visited Ossining during the Geller communications, and was later present at Jenny O'Connor's sessions at Esalen. Sirag records a hauntingly surreal story in which he asked Geller if it was possible for him to see Spectra. Geller replied that he only had to look into his eyes. He did so – and saw the Israeli's head turn into a hawk's.[143] This story has a particular resonance because another person involved with the Puharich–Geller group at that time was Ray Stanford, who claimed extraterrestrial contact since 1954, and the beings he saw were also hawk-like.[144] (In the 1950s Stanford was an associate of another controversial contactee, George Hunt Williamson, who was, in turn, a close colleague of the fascist channeller William Dudley Pelley.)

Hawks run through the Puharich story like wine through water: he himself claims to have been told by the Nine that he was the reincarnation of the hawk god Horus, and he often described how hawks regularly appeared around him and Geller during their travels in Israel and the United States, which he took as a sign of the Nine's protection. (Incidentally, the Turkey Farm was in Hawkes Avenue, Ossining.)

The idea that scientists – with their traditional contempt for all matters paranormal – believe they are in personal contact with extraterrestrial (or other nonhuman) intelligences may seem surprising and unlikely, but many of the Nine's most devoted followers are, as we have seen, physicists. In response to Sarfatti's description of his childhood telephone conversation with a computer from the future, Brendan O'Regan said he knew of 'several hundred' similar cases, and Saul Paul Sirag stated unequivocally that over 100 scientists in the United States alone believe they were in telepathic contact with extraterrestrial intelligences.[145] John C. Lilly, another pioneer in the study of altered states of consciousness and LSD research, who spent time at the Esalen

Institute in the late 1960s, reported his own experiences of contact with 'intelligences or entities higher than myself', which he believed were 'a shared organized aspect of the Universe'.[146] He speaks of these higher intelligences as 'programmers', and developed a theory that human beings are really 'biocomputers'. He wrote: 'All human beings . . . are programmed biocomputers. No one of us can escape our own nature as programmable entities. Literally, each of us may be our programs, nothing more, nothing less.'[147] Although this sounds remarkably like a mechanistic or behaviouristic concept, Lilly was also convinced of the existence of higher intelligences – the 'programmers' – who, by implication, program human biocomputers and control the development of civilisation on Earth. These ideas are strikingly similar to James Hurtak's, as expressed in *The Keys of Enoch*.

Another leading figure in this strange élite of contactee scientists was the very respected philosopher of science, R. Buckminster Fuller,[148] whose director of research was Brendan O'Regan. Although others stop short of actually claiming personal contact, some leading figures in this investigation have affirmed their own belief that such things are not only possible, but are actually taking place. Former astronaut Edgar Mitchell spoke during a radio interview in 1996 about his belief that extraterrestrials have visited Earth. And Jerry Mishlove wrote of Arthur M. Young (who died in 1995):

He actively sought out . . . the most extreme literature in the UFO field. He wanted to read accounts from contactees and from aliens of the science and cosmology of extraterrestrial civilizations. He hoped that he might be able to expand and refine his theories based on this information. I know of no one more informed than Arthur of this very exotic area.[149]

Arthur Young also lectured in San Francisco on the reality of underground alien bases in the United States,[150] yet, once again, this may seem rather inconsistent with his academic status in the eyes of those who automatically equate a belief in 'aliens' with underachieving New Age 'flakes'. On the contrary, Young – most famous as the inventor of the rotor mechanism that made the very first viable helicopter for Bell – was respected as one of the foremost thinkers of the twentieth century. And he was also present at the Nine's very first appearance, at Puharich's Round Table Foundation in 1952/1953.

Leading scientists and thinkers not merely accepted the possibility of extraterrestrial contact, but in many cases actually claimed to experience it. Virtually all of them are part of the same network of people and organisations, centred on the avant-garde research institutes of 1970s California, with the same people repeatedly surfacing in this tangled web. For example, Brendan O'Regan, research director for R. Buckminster Fuller – who himself claimed extraterrestrial contact – 'triggered' the memory of Jack Sarfatti's weird phone call and worked with Andrija Puharich and Uri Geller at the very time they were heavily committed to the Spectra/Nine contacts.

These links go far beyond mere coincidence, but seem only to confuse the picture further. Could this immensely complex scheme, extending over many years and involving hundreds, perhaps thousands of people, really have originated with extraterrestrials? Is this evidence of a clever long-term plan from nonhuman intelligences, such as the Nine? Tempting though such a scenario may appear, the fact remains that there is a large degree of involvement – and obvious orchestration – by clandestine government agencies. Although these two hypotheses seem contradictory, there is another option. Are the shadowy presences of the intelligence agencies and the nonhuman intelligences not, as they may seem, mutually exclusive, but actually an alliance?

One thing is certain: the Nine have had an influence on a huge variety of prime movers, which is no mean achievement for entities with no visible presence or means of support. But the Nine themselves were only part of an intricate tapestry made up of many equally vivid threads. Jack Sarfatti notes, in describing a conversation in 1996 with Thomas Jenkins, a former physicist

who now runs the Gorbachev Foundation/USA: 'Tom [Jenkins]
and I had an interesting conversation in which we both noted the
amazing patterns of synchronicity linking physicists interested
in consciousness, extra-terrestrial intelligence, remote-viewing
and other fringe areas with the pivotal events that ended the Cold
War.'[151] Also writing of the milieu in which the Nine were an
inseparable part, Sarfatti says: 'The fact remains . . . that a bunch
of apparently California New Age flakes into UFOs and psychic
phenomena, *including myself*, had made their way into the highest levels of the American ruling class and the Soviet Union and
today run the Gorbachev Foundation [his emphasis].'[152]

This is a troubling scenario. As Sarfatti notes, key figures in
his scene have become 'the American ruling class and the Soviet
Union['s]', who even – arguably – brought about the end of the
Cold War, perhaps the collapse of communism itself as a force to
be reckoned with. These people may have a major part in running
the world, but they also – to an unknown degree – are influenced
by the Nine.

For this reason alone the Nine should be taken seriously, even
if this requires a massive suspension of disbelief. They may be
who they claim to be – the ancient Egyptian gods – but it seems
highly unlikely. There is another possibility: the Nine may be
real, in the sense that they are not hoaxes or delusions – and not
monsters created by Dr Frankenstein-Puharich – but genuine
nonhuman intelligences trying to deceive us into thinking that
they are the Heliopolitan Ennead for reasons of their own.[153]

We have already noted the influence that the Nine have over
the New Age, but there are other arenas in which their influence
is surprisingly, not to say disturbingly, strong. As we have seen,
Richard Hoagland gave a lecture at the United Nations, organised
by a special interest group of UN employees and representatives
called the Society for Enlightenment and Transformation (SEAT),
run by employees Susan Karaban and Mohammad Ramadan. It is
heavily influenced by the Nine, as can be inferred by the identity
of previous SEAT speakers at the UN, who included James
Hurtak and Andrija Puharich. Hurtak has also written articles for

the SEAT newsletter on the Face on Mars and extraterrestrial intelligence.

Mohammad Ramadan gave a lecture at the First Scandinavian Conference on Extraterrestrial Intelligence and Human Future in Helsinki, Finland, in November 1996, in which he quoted extensively from the Nine. The theme of his lecture was the potential impact of widespread belief in extraterrestrial communication, if and when the spaceships land. He used channelled material to illustrate what the extraterrestrials themselves thought about this, although he added words of caution about their reliability and the possibility of the message being distorted by the channellers' minds. But he has a novel solution to this problem: 'I have taken special care to use the messages taken only from their highest hierarchy, that is from beings of the 5th Dimension and above, or the ultra-terrestrials as futurist Dr James Hurtak calls them.'[154]

But we only know which extraterrestrials are fifth-dimensional because they tell us. In other words, Ramadan only trusts the entities that tell him they're trustworthy. And the only *people* who appear to be qualified to sort the extraterrestrial wheat from the chaff are Phyllis Schlemmer and James Hurtak.

Some of the figures lurking further back in the shadows also reappear time and time throughout this story, such as the American multimillionaire (and former Navy intelligence officer) Henry Belk, a close associate of Puharich in the 1950s and 1960s, and one of the few who attended his funeral in 1995. Belk appears in the acknowledgements of *The Only Planet of Choice* as the person 'who started it all', although tantalisingly, how he did this is not explained. He is known to have funded James Hurtak,[155] and the two of them were also involved with another controversial research foundation with particularly high-level connections. This was the Human Potential Foundation, which was founded in 1989 by Senator Claiborne Pell, and whose president was one of Pell's aides, C.B. 'Scott' Jones, a veteran of US Navy intelligence.

According to Jim Schnabel, 'Scott Jones was in touch with a ring of psychics around the United States, who he occasionally put in touch with various intelligence officials on operational matters.'[156] One of Jones's favourite psychics was Alex Tannous, who also worked for the US Army's Project GRILL FLAME, and in 1984 was brought in by the CIA to remote view the location of a CIA station chief who had been kidnapped in Beirut. (Tannous identified the correct place and accurately revealed that the agent was dead, although this seemed highly unlikely at the time.)[157] Jones invited Tannous to remote view the Sphinx: the results of this are unknown, although it is known that Jones sent his report to ARE.[158]

The Human Potential Foundation received funding from several prominent individuals, including Laurence Rockefeller. Its employees included Dick Farley, who resigned in 1994 after three years as director of program development.

From his inside knowledge, Farley has become extremely concerned about the increasing influence of the Council of Nine over politicians and decision-makers. He writes that the Nine 'maintain a working network of physicists and psychics, intelligence operatives and powerful billionaires, who are less concerned about their "source" and its weirdness than they are about having *every* advantage and new data edge in what *they* believe is a battle for Earth itself.'[159]

Farley records a meeting of Jones, Henry Belk and James Hurtak to discuss, among other things, the funding of the Human Potential Foundation.[160] This suggests that Hurtak's – and the Nine's – philosophy is reaching the highest levels of US politics. Jones's superior, Senator Claiborne Pell, is an extremely powerful figure in Washington. He was Chairman of the Senate's influential Foreign Relations Committee and is the elder statesman whom the younger Vice-President Al Gore has come to respect. Pell and Gore worked closely together when the latter was a senator. The two share a passionate belief in the paranormal and both are great supporters of government-funded psi research. According to Farley, Pell has 'long been a friend and advocate of [Henry] Belk's'[161] and he is on the board of Edgar Mitchell's Institute of Noetic Sciences. Uri

Geller told us how he had been brought in by Pell, Anthony Lake (later President Clinton's National Security Advisor) and Gore to help 'influence' the Russian team at arms reductions talks in Geneva in 1987.[162] Pell also arranged for Geller to secretly brief government officials on his psychic information on Soviet strategy in a secure room in the Capitol. The audience included senators and Pentagon officials.[163]

There is cause for concern here. Not only do Vice-President Al Gore and Senator Claiborne Pell share the same esoteric interests, but they are also political allies. It is reasonable to assume that Gore is familiar with the Nine; if so, how much is he influenced by their teachings – or, in the worst case scenario, even their instructions? The evidence suggests that he is by no means the only top-ranking American politician to have been drawn into the Nine's sphere of influence.

The usual suspects

By now it is plain that the Nine are behind the messages of Giza and Cydonia, and that all three are now inextricably entwined in a sort of inescapable juggernaut of the 'truth'. It is impossible to have one without the other, thanks to the sterling work of the intelligence agencies, who ensure that this new belief system is constantly being topped up with new rumours and counter-rumours, so that we will never fail to be gripped by the unfolding story. But welded firmly on to a very reasonable interest in the mysteries of Mars and the secrets of ancient Egypt lies the insidious presence of the Nine and their ever-eager disciples.

Just like the New Egyptology and the Message of Cydonia, this is a scenario in which controversial 'alternative' events are intimately connected with, if not seemingly directed by, intelligence agencies. Moreover, these three strands, although each seemingly had independent origins, have gradually, but inexorably, been drawn together like three fish caught in the same tightening net. The pronouncements of the Nine have – through

Hoagland and Myers – been integrated with the Message of Cydonia, and this in turn has been firmly welded to the mystery of the Egyptian civilisation and the search for its lost secrets.

The same individuals play major parts in all three stories. The prime example is James Hurtak, the ultimate guru, who channels the Nine, was Puharich's second-in-command at Lab Nine, was the first person to make the Mars–Egypt connection public, and was – and still is – also a major player in the events at Giza.

There is also the involvement in all three stories of SRI, an organisation with intimate connections with defence and intelligence communities in the United States. SRI crops up in Giza, in the Mars story, and, through its involvement with Puharich, in the events surrounding the Nine.

Thanks to this complex, often covert, input from clever men and women, what seems to be happening under our noses is the creation of a new belief system that efficiently brings together many different elements in order to broaden its appeal as much as possible. But does this merely represent a natural progression, a syncretism of 'fringe' ideas, or are they being spun together deliberately? And who or what really sits at the centre of this gigantic web?

This is a conspiracy of enormous proportions, so successful that it is impossible to pinpoint any one person or group as the real controllers, although we have catalogued those they use. We have seen how the Nine's circle were and are supported by very wealthy people, such as Barbara Bronfman and Joyce Petschek, but it is unlikely that they are in on the secret; they are too easily identified. It makes more sense that they, too, are being used as part of an experiment, perhaps simply to see how easy it is for outlandish beliefs to persuade such people to part with their money. Of course it also has an eminently practical purpose: it makes the operation self-financing. The CIA always has its balance sheets in mind. (In the United States there is a tradition of close ties between private business and the defence and intelligence communities, which is not so apparent in other countries. Where such a special relationship exists elsewhere, it is likely to be the result of Masonic dealings.)

There are two major elements in this gigantic, complex conspiracy. One is the apparent attempt to make contact with extraterrestrial intelligences – the Nine – using whatever means are available. The other is the exploitation of these contacts in order to promote a message. Like all propaganda, this does not depend on the reality of the communications, only on the *belief* that they are real. But why bother? What is the motive behind the business of the Nine?

There are several possible agendas:

(1) A powerful cabal is trying to establish contact with extraterrestrials, either through a physical stargate or telepathic communication/possession, in other words, channelling. This would explain the involvement of official US agencies in the search for something momentous in Egypt. In this scenario, Puharich's attempts to establish contact with the Nine were based on the belief that they really are 'out there' but that mental communication is difficult and has to be 'encouraged' in likely 'trainees'.

(2) The conspirators are deliberately building up an expectancy that such contact is about to happen. In this scenario, an entirely fictitious belief system has been constructed and disseminated through various sources.

(3) Both of the above. The conspirators are trying to establish real contact, but are also engaged in a covert 'softening-up' exercise to prepare us for the imminent return of our creators, the ancient gods of Egypt.

There is a further possibility. The conspirators themselves could be being duped – by the Council of Nine. History is replete with cases of otherworldly visions and voices that may promise heaven, but who actually deliver something quite other – or, as Shakespeare put it:

> And oftentimes, to win us to our harm,
> The instruments of darkness tell us truths,
> Win us with honest trifles, to betray's
> In deepest consequence.[164]

But never before have they had so many of the world's most powerful individuals in their insubstantial grip.

6

The Secret Masters

In an email in August 1998, Jack Sarfatti told us he was amazed at our discovery that the Nine had been known of for fifty years: he thought they dated only from the 1970s. But we were to discover that even half a century fails to cover the whole story of their strange, disquieting genesis. In the same bubbling cauldron from which the Nine was to emerge, also lay the misshapen homunculi of twentieth-century totalitarianism. We found that some of the key figures intimately involved in the Nine's lengthy gestation are surprising, not to say unsettling. The story includes such figures as L. Ron Hubbard, the consistently controversial founder of the Church of Scientology, and the flamboyant magus Aleister Crowley, who may or may not have earned his tabloid soubriquet of 'The Wickedest Man in the World', but who certainly relished such notoriety.

Godfather of the New Egyptology

R.A. Schwaller de Lubicz has had extraordinary influence on the New Egyptology, on the thought and writing of John Anthony West, Graham Hancock, Robert Bauval and many others. Although, since his death in 1961, he has become a kind of 'godfather' to such writers, Schwaller de Lubicz was, in many ways, hardly a laudable role model. His ideology – and the company he kept – would hardly endear him to today's politically correct reading public, which is presumably why his bestselling admirers fail to mention them.

We noted earlier that Schwaller de Lubicz emphasised the significance of the number nine in the ancient Egyptian religion, and also that he – uniquely – translated the Egyptian *neter*, meaning 'god', as 'principle', often speaking of the 'Nine Principles'. He wrote:

> Heliopolis teaches the metaphysics of the Cosmic Opus by revealing the creative act that scissions the *Unity Nun*; it also speaks of the *birth of the Nine Principles*, the entire basis on which the sensorial world will establish itself in becoming accessible to human intelligence.[1]

He stresses that the Ennead are 'the Nine Principles':

> Pharaonic myth illustrates this through the Heliopolitan Mystery, recounting the creation of the Great Ennead (the Nine Principles) born of Nun, the primordial waters.[2]

Schwaller de Lubicz's wife Isha (this was her mystical name – originally she was just Jeanne) explained:

> The *Neters* were not what have been infantily called 'the gods', as they are not 'gods' . . . The *Neters* are the *Principles*, they are the symbols of *functions*.[3]

This is exactly how the Council of Nine first introduced themselves to Andrija Puharich through Dr Vinod back in 1952. It was not just the term 'Nine Principles' that Schwaller de Lubicz shared with the Council of Nine, but also the same mystical interpretation of the numbers one to nine and their relationship with the number ten. As he wrote in 1913: 'As number it is 10, containing and surrounded by the nine principles, the irreducible One, the eternal fecundator.'[4] And John Anthony West wrote in *Serpent in the Sky*: 'The Grand Ennead . . . is not a sequence, but the nine aspects of Tum [Atum].'[5] This perfectly reflects the words of Tom (allegedly Atum) himself in 1974: 'We are the nine principles of the Universe, yet together we are One.'[6]

This seems to be too much of a coincidence. Had the Council of Nine read Schwaller de Lubicz, or had he written those words while under their influence, way back in the early years of the twentieth century? His master work, the three-volume *Le temple de l'homme* (*The Temple of Man*) was published in 1958, six years *after* the 'Nine Principles' had introduced themselves to Puharich through Dr Vinod. However, the key *neter*/Principle interpretation also appeared in Schwaller de Lubicz's similarly named *Le temple dans l'homme* (*The Temple in Man*), published in 1949. (It would have been very obscure in terms of its influence in the United States as it was published only in French and with a very small print run in Cairo. An English-language edition did not appear until the 1970s.) Schwaller de Lubicz first published his mystical interpretation of the number nine as long ago as 1913, in a series of articles he wrote for the French Theosophical journal *Le Théosophe*, where he described the number ten as 'containing and surrounded by the nine principles; the irreducible One, the eternal fecundator'. But at that time he did not elaborate: the parallel with the Egyptian Ennead came later.

So Schwaller de Lubicz seems to have been a key figure in the genesis of the Nine well before Puharich's machinations, taking the story much further back than we had anticipated. But as we delved further into his occult philosophy and the traditions that inspired him, a very different picture emerged from the dispassionate, scholarly mystic so carefully and respectfully portrayed by John Anthony West and others. We discovered that the occult interests of Schwaller de Lubicz are generally played down. Hancock and Bauval, for example, simply refer to him as a 'mathematician'.[7] However, the truth is that first and foremost he was an esotericist, his particular interests being Hermeticism and alchemy.

We should clarify our own position on the subject of the occult. By now it should be obvious that we ourselves are by no means opposed to most manifestations of the esoteric, and deplore the popular concept that anything 'occult' is automatically superstitious and worthless at best, and downright evil at worst. In our view, some forms of 'occultism', particularly Hermeticism, represent the highest and most noble search for knowledge the world has ever known, and many of today's scientific and technological triumphs are the end result of the so-called 'black art' of alchemical research. It may be that writers do not mention Schwaller de Lubicz's occult leanings either because they do not know about them or because they have no wish to lose their audience or waste precious pages on lengthy explanations and caveats. However, Schwaller de Lubicz's occultism is not the only aspect of his life and works that is not widely acknowledged. Less mention is made of his political ideology, with good reason, for it would seriously antagonise the majority of today's readers.

Schwaller de Lubicz has been described as a 'protofascist':[8] he was a highly influential figure in the development of the mystical underpinnings of Nazism, and a particular inspiration for Rudolf Hess, Hitler's complex, occult-minded deputy. For such a highly influential figure, Schwaller de Lubicz seemed curiously disinclined to bask in the limelight: on the contrary, he appeared to be more than content to lurk in the shadows, so it is difficult to find biographical detail about him. Only since his death – and because of his ideas about ancient Egypt – has his name reached a wider public. Apart from Isha Schwaller de Lubicz's somewhat sanitised 1963 biography of her husband, which skips over lengthy portions of his life, the only source is *Al-Kemi*, written by the American artist André VandenBroeck in 1987, but even that only covers the two-year period (1959–60) that he spent with Schwaller de Lubicz as his pupil in Plan-du-Grasse in the south of France.

VandenBroeck's book largely describes his own struggle to define why he found Schwaller de Lubicz so fascinating, and why he felt compelled to move to the south of France to be close to him. This fascination was even more of a puzzle when he discovered that his hero was in fact very much 'a man of the right'[9] – the political opposite of VandenBroeck himself – and he was shocked to the core to discover that Schwaller de Lubicz was, as befitted an *eminence grise* of the Nazi party, vehemently anti-Semitic.[10] VandenBroeck had some serious soul-searching to do, for he is himself of Jewish descent. Curiously, his mentor still held a fascination for him, and he helped out by correcting more than seventy factual errors in *Le temple de l'homme*, including some fundamental mistakes in his discussion of harmonics.[11]

VandenBroeck visited Schwaller de Lubicz's house many times before he was offered the chance to become his pupil in Hermeticism and alchemy, a rare privilege. The teacher made it clear that he only made the offer once he had ascertained that VandenBroeck knew nothing whatsoever about the subjects. As he said: 'You see, I have to be careful. There are people who would like to know what I do.' Then he added by way of explanation: 'Governments.'[12] But significantly, he elaborated on this cryptic statement, saying: 'It is well-known that both the USA and the USSR are running experiments with dabblers in all kinds of occult stuff, from psychics to pseudo-alchemists and who knows what not. It has always been a good policy not to attract attention, particularly in times like ours.'[13]

Originally simply René Schwaller, the future Nazi guru and mystical Egyptologist was born in Asnières in Alsace in 1887. After serving an apprenticeship as a chemist, at the age of eighteen he moved to Paris, where he was drawn irresistibly into occult studies and became deeply involved in the Theosophical Society. In Paris he also joined an alchemical group called the Brotherhood of Heliopolis. His name has even been put forward as that of the mysterious writer – under the pseudonym 'Fulcanelli' – of *Le mystère des cathédrales* (*The Mystery of the Cathedrals*), published in 1925, one of the most influential books to come out of that time and place. This masterwork argued that the Gothic cathedrals of medieval Europe carry encoded alchemical and esoteric symbolism in their architecture and decoration. The real identity of the author has long been hotly debated: for a time it was believed to be Schwaller de Lubicz himself,[14] but although he was not Fulcanelli, he knew and inspired the man who was: Jean-Julian Champagne.[15] In fact, it was Schwaller de Lubicz who claimed to have been the first to discover the Hermetic principles encoded in the Gothic cathedrals, enabling him to recognise the same principles in the temples of Egypt later in life.

In 1918, with his wife Isha, Schwaller founded a group called Les Veilleurs (The Watchers), to (in Isha's words): 'give a new momentum with new words, with the aim of revealing to the troubled world *the knowledge (conscience) of the aim of human existence*' [her emphasis].[16] He also founded a journal called *L'Affranchi* (*The Emancipated*), later changing its title to *Le Veilleur*. Les Veilleurs began within the Theosophical Society, but later became an independent organisation, primarily because of its political ambitions. It was mostly composed of esotericists and artists, but among its members also boasted the famous astronomer Camille Flammarion, perhaps significantly one of the first proponents of the idea of life on Mars. As the leader of this group, Schwaller took the mystical name Aor, which may also have been used as a 'pseudonym' for channelled material, for André VandenBroeck wrote, without elaborating further: 'What is signed 'Aor' comes from a mystic source . . . a private source of knowledge with which Aor alone had contact, and he took its name.'[17] One of Schwaller's greatest supporters at this point in his life was a member of Les Veilleurs, a Lithuanian nobleman and poet called O.W. de Lubicz Milocz, who in 1919 adopted Schwaller into his clan, giving him the right to use the title Chevalier de Lubicz.

Reading through the articles written by Schwaller de Lubicz and others in *Le Veilleur*, one soon discerns a rather disquieting undercurrent, exemplified in their slogan '*Hiérarchie! Fraternité! Liberté!*', substituting 'hierarchy' for the French Republic's original 'equality'. The over-riding concept in Schwaller de Lubicz's ideology was that of an élite who, being more spiritually aware than their fellow man, should be allowed to govern.

Unfortunately, this was not just an organisation with a high regard for authority. The pages of *Le Veilleur* contained strong anti-Jewish sentiments: a Christmas 1919 article called 'Letter to the Jews', written by Aor himself (or even the 'private source of knowledge' mentioned by VandenBroeck, perhaps entities he channelled), urged the Jews to return to the promised land and build their own country. Superficially, this may seem fair, not to say farsighted, but the implication was very much that Jews should get out of our beloved France – or else . . . Schwaller de Lubicz was emphatically, unequivocally, racist. He wrote in *Le Veilleur* that there is 'an insurmountable partition between one race and another',[18] and elsewhere that, based on studies of ancient Egyptian corpses, apart from a few exceptions, 'there are no *blacks* properly so called [in dynastic Egypt]'.[19] (This is patently untrue – archaeological evidence conclusively proves that the ancient Egyptian people were composed of several different races, including ones racially defined as black.[20] Indeed, many see the features of the Sphinx itself as being decidedly negroid.)

At this point in his life – in the years immediately after the First World War – Schwaller de Lubicz designed a uniform for himself and his disciples, which was subsequently adopted by the SA (Stürmabteilung – Storm Section), the forerunner of the SS, who were instrumental in Hitler's rise to power.[21] Many of the members of Les Veilleurs were involved in right-wing political events that led both directly and indirectly to the rise of fascism in Europe, such as Vivien Postel du Mas, a major influence on Rudolf Hess. The deputy führer was himself a member of a French group called Tala, which was affiliated to Les Veilleurs.[22]

In 1920, Schwaller de Lubicz disbanded the organisation, instructing the membership to carry the work into their chosen profession or field of influence. Aor and Isha's own work took them to Switzerland, where they established the Scientific Station Suhalia near St Moritz in the Alps to undertake research, with

several others, into such fringe alchemical sciences as homeo-
pathy, crystallography and the therapeutic effects of plants. They
also built an observatory. In 1927 Schwaller de Lubicz and Isha
left Suhalia for Plan-du-Grasse in the south of France, moving on
three years later to Majorca. But in 1938 they made their most
significant move – to Egypt, where they remained for fifteen
years, mainly studying the Temple of Luxor. Finally, in 1952,
they returned to their home at Plan-du-Grasse, where Schwaller
de Lubicz remained until his death in 1961.

These were not random moves, nor were they occasioned by
wanderlust or economic necessity. Neither may they have been
entirely the travels of esotericists seeking out their own kind.
Schwaller de Lubicz may have been a celebrated mystic, but he
was also a political philosopher. It is notable that his departures
from both Spain and Egypt coincided with successful right-wing
takeovers, just after the Spanish Civil War had been won by
Franco, and just after a military coup d'état in Egypt in July
1952. The victors in both cases were people of whom Schwaller
de Lubicz would undoubtedly have approved – if not the world's
greatest dictators, they were certainly dictatorial – yet he moved
on once they came to power. Perhaps he had simply done his job,
or, like many others before and after him, he combined his
occultism with intelligence-gathering, maybe on behalf of some
powerful international cabal.

Like many people in this investigation, it is a mystery how
Schwaller de Lubicz acquired his money. He came from an
ordinary family and his books – most of which were written
towards the end of his life – were never bestsellers, yet he
always seems to have been affluent. He kept on his large house
in Plan-du-Grasse for the full fifteen years that he was in Egypt.
Was he paid for his part in setting the scene for various political and military coups? Was he on some kind of retainer for his
services as undercover agent for one – or more – intelligence
agencies? Both scenarios seem likely, but Schwaller de Lubicz
was so successfully secretive that we shall probably never know
for sure.

He also always concealed the influences that shaped his own philosophy, but an examination of his ideology places him firmly in the context of a specific politico-esoteric system, a movement known as Synarchy. This is 'government by secret societies', or by a group of initiates who operate from behind the scenes. It is an analogue of 'theocracy', or rule by a priesthood. Schwaller de Lubicz was a fervent Synarchist, which is why he admired ancient Egypt so much, ruled as it was by divine kings and priesthoods. One of his books was entitled *Le roi de la théocratie pharaonique* (*The King of the Pharaonic Theocracy*).

The founder of Synarchy, a Frenchman named Joseph Alexandre Saint-Yves d'Alveydre (1824–1909), explained that the term was the opposite of anarchy. Whereas anarchy is based on the principle that the state should have no control over individuals, Synarchy proposes that it should have complete control. He proposed that Synarchists achieve power by taking over the three key institutions of social control: political, religious and economic. With its own members in positions of power, the Synarchists would, in effect, secretly govern entire states. And why stop there? One of the aims of Synarchy, from its very inception, was – from the words of a Synarchist document – the creation of a 'federal European Union'.[23] Is it any coincidence that we are now moving rapidly towards such a European state? Significantly, those words were written as far back as 1946. Interestingly, several commentators discern a sudden burst of activity by Synarchists in France in 1922, soon after Schwaller de Lubicz disbanded Les Veilleurs with the instruction to carry his ideology into their particular spheres of influence.

The Synarchists were a real threat in at least the first two decades of the twentieth century, influencing the rise of fascism, which, by and large, accords very well with their aims, although they had problems with the fanatical nationalism of Nazi Germany. The Synarchist movement was especially active in France, where it had close associations with right-wing terrorist groups such as the Cagoule (composed of army officers) and its civilian counterpart, the CSAR (Comité Secret d'Action

Revolutionnaire), which was active in the 1930s. Many members of the CSAR were also members of Synarchist orders.[24]

As might be expected from a movement dedicated to governing by secret societies, Synarchy had close ties with some of the most powerful of such organisations, including the Martinist Order, of which Saint-Yves d'Alveydre was Grand Master. As the French writer Gérard Galtier states: 'The synarchic ideal influenced all the Martinists and occultists of the beginning of the century.'[25] Not unexpectedly, Synarchists were also members of French Masonic Lodges, and their ranks included former disciples of Schwaller de Lubicz, including Vivien Postel du Mas (who wrote a document called *The Synarchist Pact* – effectively its manifesto – in the 1930s[26]) and Rudolf Hess.

Synarchy is by definition a shadowy group lurking behind many uprisings and revolutions, and whose jealous gaze is automatically fixed on any stable regime or established government unless it already conforms to their ideals. Schwaller de Lubicz's serial domiciles coincided with successful changes of government in his previous country of residence: not only was he a Synarchist in word but also in deed, truly a prime mover in the events that shaped his epoch. Indeed, history may one day come to admit, albeit reluctantly, that he was one of the major political influences of the twentieth century.

There is another aspect to Synarchy. The concept of nine legendary leaders plays a large part in its philosophy. They derived this from the fusing of two legends. One was a tale brought from India and popularised by a French diplomat and travel writer, Louis Jacolliot (1837–90), which told of the Nine Unknown Men, a secret group said to have been formed by Asoka, the third-century BCE Buddhist emperor of India, to secretly rule the world.[27] The other tradition was that of the Knights Templar, founded by nine French knights shortly after the First Crusade. The Templars were believed by Saint-Yves d'Alveydre to have represented the supreme expression of Synarchy in the medieval world, because they had almost total political, religious and financial control during the two centuries of their existence yet remained at heart a secret, heretical order whose real agenda was known only to its membership.[28]

In nineteenth-century France several secret societies all claimed to be the true descendants of the medieval Knights Templar. Saint-Yves drew upon their ideals and practices for his movement, especially those of certain types of occult Freemasonry known as the Strict Templar Observance and its successor, the Rectified Scottish Rite, thus bestowing on the primarily political movement a strong undercurrent of mysticism and magical rites.[29] This proved to be a two-way traffic, for the Synarchist ideal was adopted by several occultists and their organisations, such as Papus (Gérard Encausse, 1865–1916), an enormously influential figure who was the French Grand Master of both the Ordo Templi Orientis (OTO) and the Masonic Order of Memphis-Misraïm, whose rituals, significantly, were based on the rites and ceremonies of the ancient Egyptian priesthood. Papus considered Saint-Yves to be his 'intellectual Master'.[30] As Gérard Galtier wrote: 'Without doubt, the Martinist directors such as Papus . . . had the ambition to secretly influence the course of political events, notably by the diffusion of synarchic ideals.'[31]

Papus put the Synarchist ideals into practice by working to bring together the various secret societies of his day, merging orders where possible and creating 'confederations' where representatives of the organisations could meet. The bodies he created fragmented during the First World War, but others, notably Theodore Reuss and H. Spencer Lewis, created similar groups afterwards.[32]

Undoubtedly, Saint-Yves was hugely influential on the development of Western occultism. Theo Paijmans, an authority on nineteenth-century European esotericism, pointed out to us that Saint-Yves introduced the seminal idea of Agartha, the mysterious underground realm from which highly evolved Adepts psychically direct the development of the human race.[33] This was to become a common feature of Western occultism – as in the works of Madame H.P. Blavatsky – and was the basis for a belief in Hidden Masters, or Secret Chiefs, which we will discuss shortly. Saint-Yves claimed that he had travelled astrally to Agartha, and that he was in telepathic contact with its inhabitants. He also claimed that he had derived his Synarchist ideology from them.

Saint-Yves, Synarchist supreme, held a deeply mystical view of the evolution of civilisation, believing in the existence of an advanced ancient science and technology, as well as Atlantis. Saint-Yves believed that the Great Sphinx of Giza was built before the emergence of the Egyptian civilisation by visitors from Atlantis.[34] He explained that, as the Atlanteans were red-skinned, this was the reason the Sphinx was originally painted red (as classical authors asserted, and which seems likely, judging from the small traces of red colouring that have been found on it). Saint-Yves writes that the Atlantean civilisation existed between 18,000 and 12,000 BCE – exactly the same dates given for Altea/Atlantis by James Hurtak in *The Keys of Enoch*.[35] Significantly, a central concept in Saint-Yves's mystical writings is that of the Holy Light, otherwise known as Aor,[36] the name taken by Schwaller de Lubicz.

Saint-Yves, in his idiosyncratic reconstruction of history, describes a great Celtic warrior called Ram who conquered the 'degenerate' black races in 7700 BCE. According to Saint-Yves, it was Ram, the superhero, who created the first Synarchist Empire, which extended from Europe to India.[37] Curiously, in a discussion about far distant events, Edgar Cayce said: '[This was] some . . . years before the entry of Ram into India.'[38] This uniquely Synarchist character could only have found his way – as a historical fact – into Edgar Cayce's writings via Saint-Yves, who invented Ram and all his works.

Clear links lie between the godfather of the New Egyptology – Schwaller de Lubicz – and mystical Synarchist movements that encompass a belief in Atlantis and Nine mysterious figures who seek to rule the world. The twentieth-century legacy of today's 'Nine' is even more colourful, and involves one of the most flamboyant and controversial figures of our times – the ritual magician Aleister Crowley.

Conjurations of the 'Beast'

In March 1904 the – even by then – notorious occultist Aleister
Crowley (1875–1947) and his new wife Rose paid a visit to Cairo
where they carried out a 'magickal' operation (a 'working') in
their rented apartment. The result was unexpected. The untrained
Rose, totally ignorant of magickal workings (and, if Crowley's
somewhat disloyal description is anything to go by, of much else
too), went into trance, repeating, 'They are waiting for you.'
During the next few days, she revealed that 'they' were primarily
the god Horus, who had chosen Crowley for a special task, telling
him the ritual to facilitate contact. At first Crowley was irritated
by Rose's words – after all, he was the great magus, not her – but
then he gave her a series of questions to test the authenticity of
the communicator. When he asked her which planet was traditionally associated with Horus, she answered, correctly, Mars.[39]
   A few days later, in the Cairo Museum, Rose – who had never
visited it before – confidently led her husband through the halls
to stand before one particular exhibit, a rather unremarkable
Twenty-Sixth-Dynasty painted wooden stele showing an Egyptian
priest standing before Horus in his form of Ra-Hoor-Khuit (a
variation of Ra-Horakhti, who is closely associated with the
Sphinx). This has been known ever since in the occult world as
the Stele of Revealing. Crowley was impressed by the synchronicity of the exhibit's number – 666, the number of the Great
Beast of Revelation, which also happened to be Crowley's own
proud alter ego, thanks to an overliteral interpretation of the
Bible by his religious-maniac mother. (When we saw the stele in
April 1998, we were amused to note that, although it is now
exhibit 9422, the original 1904 label, bearing the number 666 in
a beautiful but faded copperplate hand, has been laid beside it in
the display case. Could there be Crowleyite sympathisers on the
staff of the Cairo Museum?)
   This led Crowley, somewhat reluctantly, to take his wife's words
seriously. He duly carried out the magickal ritual – now known
simply as the Cairo Working – which turned out to be a pivotal

moment not only in his own bizarre career, but also in the whole history of modern occultism. As a result of this working, he came into contact with an entity called Aiwass (sometimes, for magickal reasons, spelt Aiwaz) who, over the course of three days – 8–10 April 1904 – 'dictated' to Crowley what has become his 'gospel', *The Book of the Law*. It has been said that, without this book, it is unlikely that Crowley would have achieved his present lofty status among the new *fin de siècle* occultists. As his biographer and literary executor John Symonds writes, somewhat mischievously: 'Without the Law of Thelema [which is embodied in the Book], he would just have been a minor magician like Éliphas Lévi or MacGregor Mathers.'[40]

The purpose of the Book and the task for which Crowley had been chosen was the announcement of the advent of the Aeon of Horus, a new age that succeeded the Aeon of Osiris, when patriarchal religions based on dying and rising gods, such as Christianity, held sway. That, in turn, had succeeded the much longer era of Isis, when goddess-based spirituality was predominant (and when, if many modern anthropologists are right, the whole notion of paternity was far from being understood or accepted).

Clearly, the ushering in of a new aeon – of Horus, the Child – is no minor task, perhaps especially when the wild and difficult characteristics of children are taken into consideration. Whereas the features of motherhood and fatherhood are, by and large, relatively easy to recognise, those of newborns and youngsters are more fluid and elusive. Children are spontaneous, excitable, inquisitive and consumed by the excitement of living in the here and now, but they are also volatile and contradictory, capable of emotional excess. Their spontaneity can be exhilarating, but once the moment has past one is left facing a future for which no provision has been made. If there is such a thing as the Aeon of the Child, then those of us who live in the era of its birth should realise that we are in for a very bumpy ride.

Another characteristic of children is the natural psychic ability that seems to come as part of the human 'package', only to fall away dramatically as the reality consensus – the shared, unspoken belief that the paranormal is only good for science fiction and ghost stories but has no basis in fact – begins to corrode their heightened sensitivity. As parapsychologist Dr Ernesto Spinelli has demonstrated, the younger the child the more psychic he or she is. It is as if children really do come into the world 'trailing clouds of glory', as William Wordsworth so memorably put it, retaining memories of another realm in which the power of the mind holds sway. Paranormal abilities are a double-edged sword, however. The psychic aspect of the new Age of Horus is potentially worrying, for Crowley said that *The Book of the Law* effectively opened up communications with 'discarnate intelligences' and that: 'I have opened up communication with one such intelligence; or, rather, have been selected by him to receive the first message from a new order of beings.'[41]

Crowley was a bombast, who rejoiced in notoriety and whose descriptions of his many magickal workings were suspiciously colourful. One of his favourite, quasi-Wildean, aphorisms was 'Always tell the truth, but lead so improbable a life that no one will ever believe you'. But was Crowley telling the truth about opening up communication with 'a new order of beings'? Even if he believed it himself, had it really happened?

Was the stargate opened by none other than Aleister Crowley in Cairo back in 1904?

Crowley certainly came to believe that his spirit communicator Aiwass was one of the Secret Chiefs, a group of discarnate entities who directed the Hermetic Order of the Golden Dawn – a highly respected magickal order of which he was a member, and that this contact with Aiwass bestowed authority on him over its membership. According to the leading authority on Crowley, Kenneth Grant, Aiwass was 'an occult intelligence of incalculable power'.[42]

The notion of Secret Chiefs or Hidden Masters ran throughout nineteenth-century occultism, and is generally understood to be a convenient device whereby the leaders of various orders assumed authority by alleging they had received it from a higher source to which they alone had access, including the Unknown Superiors of some of the Neo-Templar groups of the eighteenth and nineteenth centuries, the Hidden Masters of Madame Helena Petrovna Blavatsky's highly influential movement of Theosophy and Saint-Yves's Masters of Agartha. Often, as in Blavatsky's case, the Hidden Masters were said to be spiritually advanced human beings who lived in remote parts of the world, such as the mountain fastnesses of Tibet. (Interestingly, the Secret Chiefs of the Golden Dawn appeared astrally as hawks,[43] reminding us of Saul Paul Sirag and Ray Stanford's experience with Spectra.)

Despite the potential for acclaim in his contact with Aiwass and *The Book of the Law*, Crowley had a great aversion to both. He came to believe that Aiwass was merely a manifestation arising from the depths of his own subconscious mind, and said: 'I was setting my whole strength against the Secret Chiefs. I was trying to forget the whole business.'[44]

But Crowley was not allowed to forget it. Bizarre synchronicities and weird phenomena continually pushed *The Book of the Law* under his nose, together with a series of unexplained setbacks in his career. Only when he returned to promoting the Book did the obstacles melt away, so reluctantly he came to accept that he had no option but to do the Secret Chiefs' bidding.

Crowley's subsequent career centres around two magical orders, the Ordo Templi Orientis (Order of the Oriental Templars, or OTO) – now somewhat notorious for its sexual rituals – and the less well-known Argenteum Astrum, or A∴A∴ ('Silver Star'). This was the Third Order of the Hermetic Order of the Golden Dawn. Only the highest initiates were admitted, and they were believed to be in direct contact with the Secret Chiefs. The Golden Dawn itself fragmented around 1900, largely because of a power struggle between Crowley himself and the head of the Order, Samuel Liddell MacGregor Mathers (1854–1918), but the A∴A∴ survived independently under Crowley's control. The 'Silver Star' of the order's name is Sirius, which holds a central place in its magickal philosophy, because the Secret Chiefs – the discarnate entities believed to govern the order – were somehow connected with Sirius. This would have extraordinary influence in shaping the prehistory of the Nine.

The OTO also resulted in the coming together of certain influential bedfellows. Founded in 1895 by the Austrian Karl Kellner, it was taken over after his death in 1905 by Theodore Reuss, after which it expanded rapidly. Crowley joined in 1911, and Reuss began to incorporate the teachings of *The Book of the Law* into the OTO's rituals. When Reuss died in 1922, he nominated Crowley as his successor, but many German members refused to accept him as their leader, leading to a bitter schism and a decline in Germany even before its termination by the Nazis. With either extraordinary foresight or remarkable happenchance, Crowley moved to California, mecca of the weird and wonderful, and was so successful in building up the membership that, in the words of Francis King, 'for the next ten years [until Crowley's death in 1947] California was the main centre of OTO activity'.[45]

In California the OTO and the A∴A∴ underwent significant developments. As they both fell under Crowley's influence, they were closely interlinked, but the OTO always attracted more attention because of its emphasis on sex magick (Crowley always insisted on the 'k'). We believe that this was a deliberate move by him and his followers to keep the focus away from the A∴A∴, which was in fact the more important of the two orders.

The strange legacy of Aleister Crowley

In California in the years immediately after the Second World War and following Crowley's death in England in 1947, there was a new emphasis in the philosophy of the orders. It began to be associated with extraterrestrials, rather than 'traditional' occult entities such as angels, demons or spirit guides. The major figure in this development was Charles Stansfeld Jones (1886–1950), Crowley's leading disciple, whom he described as 'my magickal son'. Jones, whose magickal name was Frater Achad, was the head of the OTO Lodge in Vancouver and was also prominent in

the A∴A∴, having been initiated in 1916. According to Kenneth
Grant: '*The Book of the Law* issued from a praeterhuman
Intelligence that used Crowley as a focus for its influence.' But he
goes on: 'Aiwaz is therefore the *type* of extra-terrestrial
Intelligence such as we may expect to come into conscious contact with, as the aeon develops.'[46] And elsewhere, Grant writes in
terms strikingly reminiscent of Tom and the Nine: 'Aiwass is the
link, the corridor through which the Impulse was transmitted
from the source of extra-terrestrial consciousness.'[47]

Under the powerful influence of Charles Stansfeld Jones, the
idea of Crowley's guides being extraterrestrial rapidly took hold in
California. One of the initiates of Jones's Vancouver lodge,
Wilfred T. Smith, established an OTO lodge in Pasadena,
California in 1930. Their temple on Mount Palomar subsequently
became the site of the Mount Palomar Observatory, which was
involved in George Adamski's controversial 'classic' UFO contact
story in the 1950s.

Like Paris in the 1890s, in the postwar years California was a
veritable hotbed of occult beliefs and practices. The great melting pot of humanity drawn into it also included the rocket
scientist John (Jack) Parsons and L. Ron Hubbard, later the
founder of the Church of Scientology.

Parsons, who has a crater on the Moon named after him, was a
pioneer in developing rocket fuels. He and his wife Helen joined
the Californian OTO in 1939, and he soon rose through the ranks,
becoming head of the branch in 1944, being described by some
as Crowley's successor. In 1949 he spoke of 'crossing the Abyss' –
a term meaning entering the A∴A∴ – and described himself as
Master of the Temple (the first of the three grades of the
A∴A∴).[48] At the same time, during the Second World War, he
was working on classified military projects, developing prototype
rockets. In 1944 the Jet Propulsion Laboratory (JPL) was established in Pasadena as a development of the Guggenheim
Aeronautical Laboratory, for which he had worked during the
war, and he was one of its early members. (Ironically, JPL now
controls space probes such as those sent to Mars.) Parsons died

on 18 June 1952 in an explosion in his laboratory, although it is still a matter of debate as to whether it was an accident or suicide. It may be that dark forces had a hand in his death. As Grant says:

> Working with the formulae of Thelemic magic [based on Crowley's *The Book of the Law*], Parsons established contact with extra-terrestrial beings of the order of Aiwass. Unfortunately, he lost control of the entities he evoked and one of them, obsessing [possessing] the woman with whom he worked [Marjorie Cameron], drove him to self-destruction.[49]

Obviously, contact with nonhuman intelligences can turn very nasty. It is not enough to communicate with them. They must be controlled, or kept in their place, which has not happened with the Nine, who are virtually worshipped by their followers. Perhaps the suicide of Don Elkins – and the near-suicide of Bobby Horne – were only too similar to the fiery death of occultist Jack Parsons.

Parsons was one of those curiously common individuals who may excel in pioneering scientific work or be involved in intelligence operations, but who is, at the same time, also deeply committed to occult beliefs and practices. Crowley himself was repeatedly accused of working for various intelligence agencies, and it seems that was the case (what is less easy to ascertain is whose side he was on). Hard-headed scientist Jack Parsons was one of those who believed most passionately in an extraterrestrial element in Crowley's magick. When the flying saucer craze began in 1947, Parsons stated that the discs would, in some way, help to convert the world to Crowley's magickal religion.[50] As things turned out, he would have a hand in helping to create quite another belief system. Parsons met L. Ron Hubbard in August 1945 and introduced him to the OTO, after which the two collaborated in magickal rituals together, although Hubbard would later claim that he only joined the order as part of an infiltration exercise by the Office of Naval Intelligence.[51] Even if true, this would be very telling about the intimate association of occult groups and intelligence agencies at that time.

Hubbard had been an admirer of Crowley since coming across a copy of *The Book of the Law* in the Library of Congress as a teenager. Whatever may be claimed for his past associations by his followers now – after all, few contemporary public figures care to be known as former friends of Aleister Crowley – in a lecture in Philadelphia in 1952 Hubbard referred to the 'Great Beast' as 'my very good friend'.[52]

Although it is easy to understand the appeal of magick to someone like Hubbard, who was naturally a mystic at heart, the involvement of a rocket scientist like Parsons is harder to comprehend. Yet this is by no means a unique combination. Many of the most influential occultists of the nineteenth and twentieth centuries were fascinated by technology. One of the few to research this neglected field is Theo Paijmans, who has written about the work of John Worrell Keely, whose ideas about sonic technology have been seized upon recently as possible explanations of how the pyramids were built,[53] although it was actually Madame Blavatsky who first made the link.[54] A striking – and very relevant – example is the fact that the reading list for new members of the Argenteum Astrum included *The Fourth Dimension* by C. Howard Hinton.[55] Published in 1904, this was one of the earliest works to deal with the subject of higher dimensions and their possible visible manifestations in our three-dimensional world. This was the direct forerunner of ideas that Richard Hoagland invokes in his Message of Cydonia. Initiates of Crowley's magickal order were required to familiarise themselves with this work, because it dealt with hyperdimensionality, which even today is considered a highly abstruse and specialised field of science and mathematics.

The magickal philosophy of the Argenteum Astrum, derived from *The Book of the Law*, has many striking parallels to that of another group of alleged extraterrestrial intelligences, the Nine. The A∴A∴'s doctrines centre on Sirius, which is regarded as a source of great magical power: Aiwass was, in effect, an emissary from Sirius. In the A∴A∴'s system of magickal correspondences, the number of Sirius is nine.[56] Crowley stressed that Mars was going to be of supreme importance in the coming Aeon of Horus, because of that deity's association with Mars. Obviously, the onset of the Aeon of Horus is connected with the dawning of the Age of Aquarius. In the A∴A∴'s system the 'influence' of Aquarius is transmitted to Earth through the planet Saturn[57] and in the Ra communications through Carla Rueckert, the Council of Nine explicitly connected themselves with that planet. Perhaps more significantly, James Hurtak teaches that Saturn plays an important role in balancing the forces in our solar system and that the pyramids of Mars are directly influenced by that planet.[58] Clearly, the Nine are a more modern manifestation of Aleister Crowley's magickal system.

In the revised 1998 edition of *The Sirius Mystery*, Robert Temple explains how he came to write the book.[59] His attention was first drawn to the Dogon's mysterious knowledge of Sirius B by Arthur M. Young, his mentor when he was a student at the University of Pennsylvania in the early 1960s. In 1966, at the age of twenty-one, Temple became secretary of Young's Foundation for the Study of Consciousness, presumably also aware that Young had been one of those present at the 'first contact' of the Council of Nine in 1952.

Young first mentioned the mystery surrounding the Dogon and Sirius to Temple in 1965. Two years later, having moved to London, Temple decided to follow up the story, and wrote to Young for details, receiving the translation of Griaule and Dieterlen's *Le renard pâle* that was later stolen by the CIA, with the injunction 'Don't get me into it'[60] and an explanation about how he had first heard about it from a character called Harry Smith, who had given him the translation.

Best known as a surrealist film-maker and artist, Harry Smith (1929–1991) was also a keen experimenter with hallucinogenic drugs, although he had a huge range of diverse interests. It was his character that fascinated all who met him. Eccentric, undisciplined, non-materialistic and mystical, he was the ideal guru.

What is not widely known is that he was also a committed member of the OTO. As another member of the order, Jim Wasserman, said of him:

> His gentleness and kindness were all-encompassing – he was, in my opinion, a saint – a modern, American, New York, shamanistic saint. And I mean that quite literally. He was a true adept. One of the most advanced spiritual teachers that I have met in my life.[61]

Born in 1929 in Oregon of Theosophist parents, and with a high-ranking Freemason as a grandfather, Smith studied anthropology at the University of Washington between 1941 and 1943. He moved to California in 1945, where he took what was to be his only regular job, as an office clerk. Thereafter he devoted himself to art, film-making, musicology and esoteric studies, surviving on grants and handouts from friends and followers for the rest of his life. He also received grants from Arthur M. Young. In the early 1950s he lived among the Kiowa in Oklahoma, studying their shamanistic rituals, involving the hallucinogen peyote.

Smith became a hero of the Beat generation of the 1950s and the hippies of the 1960s. (In the last years of his life he was supported financially by the rock band The Grateful Dead.) Among his achievements was the compilation of early American folk recordings, the Folkways anthology, which became an enormous influence on artists such as Bob Dylan, who acknowledged his debt to the collection and recorded several songs from it. Smith received a Grammy award for his contribution to popular music in 1991.

Once again, this overt success with the counterculture of the 1960s was only half the story. The innocuous-sounding Harry Smith was also a member of both the American Crowleyite orders, the OTO and the A∴A∴, and profoundly involved with esoteric subjects. He was a keen student of the Hermetica, in particular the writings of the great Renaissance occult philosopher Giordano Bruno. He spent sixteen years creating a magickal system to integrate Bruno's work with the doctrines of the OTO and the Enochian magic of the Elizabethan magus, Dr John Dee. This is serious magick; modern adepts advise that Enochian workings must not be undertaken light-heartedly or by the ill prepared, as their sheer power can backfire, causing many mental and spiritual problems. (Curiously Smith's notoriously haphazard lifestyle was completely at odds with the discipline required for such 'High Magick', which is characterised by months of preparation, intense focus and physical and mental privations.) But as usual, it was his membership of the OTO that attracted the most attention. Smith was a devoted follower of Crowley, helping republish some of his works, and designing a tarot pack still used by the OTO. He claimed to be Crowley's son; although the Beast's lifestyle virtually guaranteed the existence of illegitimate offspring, it is unlikely that Smith was actually one of that exclusive band. Both men liked to weave elaborate myths about themselves and pass them off as fact.

Significantly, the man who introduced Smith to both the OTO and the A∴A∴ in 1940s California was Charles Stansfeld Jones,[62] who, as we have seen, was extraordinarily influential in the life of Jack Parsons. It is very likely that Smith and Parsons knew each other. Parsons was head of the Californian OTO at the time and, like Parsons, Smith was a Master of the Temple of the A∴A∴.

Smith studied widely in the fields of mysticism and esotericism, but always acknowledged that his beliefs remained rooted in Crowley's works.[63] Through all the vicissitudes of his remarkably eclectic career, he remained a staunch member of both the A∴A∴ and the OTO until his death in 1991. The OTO even performed a ceremony at his memorial service at St Mark's Church in New York, which must have been something of a surprise for the Christian authorities.[64]

The complex web of our investigation can now be seen to lead back to strangely few people and groups, some of whom – such as prime mover Aleister Crowley and the future founder of Scientology, L. Ron Hubbard – have been linked with intelligence agencies. And both, in their own way, have also been connected with mind control. At the heart of this web was the occult order of the A∴A∴, which nestled inconspicuously in the shadow of the more colourful OTO, yet which has had the most extraordinary effect, not just on our dramatis personae, but also through them, on many of the key events of the twentieth century.

The A∴A∴ emphasised the importance of Sirius – the order was obliquely named after it – and believed in non-human intelligences, which, in postwar California, came to be seen as extraterrestrials. These are the key themes of Robert Temple's *The Sirius Mystery*, the inspiration for which, we now know, came ultimately from a member of the A∴A∴, via someone who was involved with the Council of Nine. This cannot be a coincidence. It is also significant that, in the 1998 edition of his book, Temple has developed his original ideas to include the notion that the 'space gods' of the Dogon, the Nommo, did not return to the Sirius system after their civilising mission to Earth, but placed themselves in suspended animation in our solar system to return to check on our progress on their awakening. Temple hints that this time may not be far away, arguing that the spaceship containing the sleeping Nommo is orbiting Saturn.[65] But why did Temple choose Saturn, of all places in the solar system, as the place where his space gods are hibernating? Perhaps an answer lies in the fact that Saturn was of great importance to both Crowley and the Nine.

Voice of the Tibetan

Sitters in the Phyllis Schlemmer circle – particularly Sir John Whitmore – often asked Tom questions about the work of the Anglo-American mystic Alice A. Bailey. We know that the Nine regard her very highly because her works appear on Tom's own recommended reading list, along with the works of Madame Helena Petrovna Blavatsky.[66]

Madame Blavatsky has been described as 'the most influential single figure of the nineteenth-century occult revival'.[67] Born in Russia (née Hahn), Madame Blavatsky soon revealed her characteristic appetite for food, magic and adventure, and the stories of her early life rival those of Aleister Crowley in their rakish and not always credible glamour. She finally settled in the United States in 1873, where she became a spiritualist medium, particularly good – one suspects – at either sleight of hand or, more charitably, at creating phenomena by artefact induction. However, mere table tilting was soon left behind, for she claimed to have made psychic contact with the Hidden Masters, or Great White Brotherhood, a group of adepts who secretly guided the human race from Tibet (derived from Saint-Yves d'Alveydre's Adepts of Agartha and the forerunners of the Secret Chiefs of the Golden Dawn). In a protracted torrent of words, she dashed out life's works *Isis Unveiled* (1877) and *The Secret Doctrine* (1888), which revealed, according to her followers, an extremely erudite synthesis of Western occult traditions and Eastern mystical religions. (According to her many critics, however, the books are garbled hotch-potches.) Her doctrines blended concepts of karma with the legend of Atlantis and the idea of 'root races', of which ours, the 'Aryan', is the fifth, the immediate successor to the Atlantean. There are two more root races to come. These ideas were a profound inspiration for the Nazis, and through Karl Haushofer (who, with Rudolf Hess, helped Hitler to write *Mein Kampf*) shaped their concept of Aryan supremacy and the 'master race'.

Blavatsky founded the Theosophical Society in 1875, providing many future leading lights of the esoteric world with the basis of their ideology, including, as we have seen, Schwaller de Lubicz, whose early career as a French Theosophist influenced his later development of Les Veilleurs.

It is the work of Alice Bailey with which the Nine are most impressed. Born in Manchester in England in 1880 as Alice La Trobe-Bateman, she had a strange experience at the age of fifteen that was to shape the whole of her life. One Sunday afternoon, a man dressed in Western clothes but wearing a turban came into her home and announced that she had been chosen for some great task that lay in the future.[68] She emigrated with her first husband to the United States, they divorced, then she discovered the then relatively new Theosophical Society, which she joined in 1918. This was to prove a momentous decision on her part. She married Foster Bailey, a prominent American Theosophist, in 1919. He was to have a profound effect on the development of her ideology, not least because he was also a high-ranking Freemason.

In 1915, while reading Madame Blavatsky's work, Bailey had a revelation: suddenly she knew the identity of her mysterious visitor of twenty years before. He was none other than the Master Koot Hoomi, the personal guide of Madame Blavatsky. Here, by implication, was her task: the continuation of the work of the founder of Theosophy.

In 1919 she made psychic contact with another of the Masters, a Tibetan called Djwhal Khul (often referred to simply as 'The Tibetan' or the 'Master DK'). Through Bailey, the Tibetan dictated a series of twenty-four books of esoteric teaching, expanding Blavatsky's doctrines into a system that included beings from other worlds who guide the evolution of the human race. They do this through a group of adepts called the Hierarchy of Brothers of Light (or simply, the Hierarchy), based in the Gobi Desert. Significantly, the Hierarchy is also sometimes referred to as the 'Great Council'. Alice Bailey wrote of them in her *Initiation, Human and Solar* (1922): '[They are] the Group of spiritual beings on the inner planes of the solar system who are intelligent forces of nature, and who control the evolutionary processes.'[69] Most significant, however, is the fact that much of Bailey's teaching is identical to James Hurtak's in *The Keys of Enoch*, and also echoes the work of Edgar Cayce.

The key to Bailey's esoteric philosophy was the concept of The Seven Rays, spiritual emanations from the 'Seven Planes of the Solar System'. Interestingly, as we have seen, Dorothy Martin, the contactee from Chicago, called her mystical organisation – cofounded with the Laugheads – 'The Abbey of the Seven Rays'.

And the concept of the sacred number seven features prominently in the philosophy of Arthur M. Young, who derived his idea of seven levels of material existence from the notable Theosophist A.P. Sinnett's channelled *The Mahatma Letters*.[70]

The Tibetan's teachings centre on the coming 'New Age, the Age of Aquarius', for which the Hierarchy are preparing humanity. This process will be, he says, in three phases: the first was between 1875 and 1890, which was activated through Madame Blavatsky; the second 1919 (the Tibetan's first contact with Alice Bailey) to 1949 (her death); and the third and final phase was to begin in 1975 and last until 2025. Early in the twenty-first century a great initiate, the World Teacher, is to appear, resulting in the emergence of a new root race. This is, of course, remarkably similar to the teachings of Edgar Cayce concerning the opening of the Hall of Records at Giza, which he claimed would usher in a New Age, the return of the 'Great Initiate' and the beginnings of a new race. The words of the Hierarchy after 1975 were to be transmitted to the world through the medium of radio.

Bailey's personal mission was to 'prepare the world on a large scale for the coming of the World Teacher, and to take the necessary steps before They Themselves [the Hierarchy] come out among men, as many of them surely will towards the end of this century'.[71] The similarity with the message of the Nine is glaringly obvious, but it grows even stronger. Part of Bailey's work, as instructed by the Tibetan, was to set up a series of disciples to be known, for self-evident reasons, as the Groups of Nine, each group having specific roles such as healers, political organisers or educators of the New Age.[72] There were to be nine such groups, with a tenth – also made up of nine initiates – to coordinate their work in the now-familiar pattern of nine plus one. Unfortunately, the process of setting up the Groups of Nine was interrupted by a curiously unforeseen circumstance – the Second World War.

The emphasis on nine as the 'number of power' is, of course, significant. When the 'Nine Principles' first made contact via Dr Vinod, it was to a group of nine sitters assembled by Puharich.

(The doctor himself always tried to surround himself with groups made up of eight others, such as the 'nucleus' of followers at Lab Nine in Ossining, made up of nine people on Tom's instruction.) Sir John R. Sinclair, in a 1984 book about Alice Bailey, finds the similarities between her stress on the significance of groups of nine and Schwaller de Lubicz's Nine Principles remarkable, illustrating these similarities by quoting from that bastion of the New Egyptology, John Anthony West, in his *Serpent in the Sky*.[73]

But there are other significant connections: Bailey and Puharich's communications reveal striking similarities that go much further, well beyond the realms of coincidence. The Masters in Bailey's system, although led by a being called the Lord of the World, who comes from a higher realm, are spiritually evolved human beings who have been 'promoted' to the Hierarchy, and who have been incarnated as the great names of religion and esotericism, such as the 'Master Jesus'. The Tibetan often used just their initials: the two Masters with leading roles in preparing the world for the final phase are known as the Master R and the Master M.[74] The representatives of the Nine who spoke through Dr Vinod called themselves 'R' and 'M'.[75]

Does this suggest independent confirmation of contact with real beings through different people? Or have the more recent communications simply been deliberately shaped to fit the predictions of the Tibetan? Philip Coppens drew our attention to a lecture given by Puharich in Upland, California on 6 November 1982, in which he summarised his work and how it had developed. He admitted that his early experiments at the Round Table Foundation were inspired by reading the works of Alice Bailey[76] – and this was before his work with Dr Vinod. At the very least, this proves that Puharich was already aware of the Tibetan's teachings before his first contact with the Nine.

Another significant aspect of Bailey's work was the importance attached to Sirius. The star has a central role in Theosophical doctrines, where it is described as a kind of energy centre – likened to a cosmic equivalent of the human 'third eye' – with a powerful effect on our own solar system.[77] In Bailey's view, it similarly channels energy, from the 'cosmic centre' through our solar system to Earth. Although there are many such influences, it is Sirius that is by far the most powerful and important. In her book *Initiation, Human and Solar*, she describes a series of 'paths' taken by initiates as they develop spiritually. One of them is called the Path of Sirius, but as this is the most secret little is said openly about it. As she said:

> Very little can be communicated about this Path . . . In the mystery of this influence, and in the secret of the sun Sirius, are hidden the facts of our cosmic evolution, and incidentally, therefore, of our solar system . . .[78]

> First and foremost is the energy or force emanating from the *sun Sirius*. If it might be so expressed, the energy of thought, or mind force, in its totality, reaches the solar system from a distant cosmic centre *via* Sirius. Sirius acts as the transmitter, or the focalizing centre, whence emanate those influences which produce self-consciousness in men.[79]

The Tibetan adds that this energy does not reach Earth directly from Sirius, but is first beamed to Saturn, before passing on to us.[80] This agrees with the Council of Nine's pronouncements through Carla Rueckert and with Hurtak's teachings.

The Tibetan, communicating through Alice Bailey, also makes another major connection – with the secret teachings of Freemasonry. According to the Tibetan, Freemasonry is a terrestrial version of an initiatory school that exists on Sirius, and that the various hierarchical degrees of Freemasonry are parallels, or analogues, of the different levels of initiation that an adept must go through in order to enter 'the greater Lodge on Sirius'. The Tibetan claimed that the Masons have a very ancient connection with Sirius:

> Masonry, as originally instituted far back in the very night of time and long ante-dating the Jewish dispensation, was

organised under direct Siriun influence and modelled as far as possible on certain Siriun institutions.[81]

Such statements can, of course, be taken with more than a pinch of salt, but they may help to explain the frequent involvement of Freemasons in the events of this investigation, including those surrounding the Giza and Mars conspiracies. And Alice Bailey herself was no stranger to direct Masonic influence – her second husband, Foster Bailey, was not only a leading light of the Theosophical Society and a devotee of his wife's channelled teachings, but also a prominent Freemason. His book *The Spirit of Masonry* (1957) stated his intention 'to bring to the Craft certain inner meanings of our Order', based on the Tibetan's teachings.[82] He also lectured on the subject to his brothers (who were members of the Ancient and Accepted Scottish Rite, the dominant form of American Freemasonry) and wrote that Freemasonry was a remnant of the 'primeval religion' that had once been common to the whole world, citing the pyramids of Egypt and South America as 'witnesses' of this ancient world religion.[83] (The idea of a common wisdom tradition in the ancient world is, of course, a major feature of Graham Hancock's increasingly fervent message, with its strong suggestion that the religion of old has some significance for our immediate future. This concept also underpins the largely Masonic belief in the coming New World Order.)

This is a truly explosive mixture. On the one hand the hugely seminal channelled teachings of Alice Bailey appear to have been influenced by the Masonic beliefs of her husband, but on the other it seems that, through Foster Bailey, the American Masons themselves were influenced by Alice Bailey's teachings, at least where Sirius was concerned. The result is a hybrid, based both on tradition and 'revealed' material, each in its way, perhaps, just as open to question. Could Foster Bailey have made sure that his brother Masons espoused his wife's channelled teachings about the 'Siriun' origins of Freemasonry as their own? Could this also be the reason why Robert Temple's *The Sirius Mystery* attracted so much interest from American Freemasons? And Henry Wallace, one-time Vice-President of the United States and sponsor of Andrija Puharich, was a high-ranking – and passionately committed – Freemason and Theosophist, just like Foster Bailey himself.

Masons themselves may well claim that they knew about Sirius before Foster Bailey began to promote it. The American writer Robert Anton Wilson records that one of his many contacts from secret and esoteric societies both in the United States and Europe told him that the secret of the 33rd Degree – the highest rank in American Freemasonry – was that the Craft was in contact with intelligent beings from Sirius.[84] Wilson himself pours scorn on this, but in any case, only other 33rd degree Masons will know whether or not it is true. Sirius does feature largely in Masonic lore, though, since every lodge room is decorated with a symbol called the Blazing Star, considered by Masonic authorities to represent Sirius.[85]

The great nineteenth-century American Freemason, Albert Pike, records a Masonic legend that specifically links the number nine to a stellar tradition connected with Sirius. This tells of the 'Nine Elect', the apprentice Masons who sought to avenge the death of their Master, Hiram Abiff, tracking one of his murderers to a certain cave. The Nine Elect are symbolised by the sequential rising of nine bright stars, including those of Orion's Belt, which precedes the rising of Sirius.[86] (The Elect of Nine is the 9th degree of the Ancient and Accepted Scottish Rite.)

What at first appears to be the Tibetan's curious notion that Freemasonry is some kind of extraterrestrial institution is also found in other 'inspired' writings – this time those of H.C. Randall-Stevens, who way back in the 1920s wrote of secret chambers beneath the Sphinx and the Great Pyramid. Like Alice Bailey, he did not need to be in a trance to communicate with his guide, but simply took dictation from a voice in his head. The first of these dictation sessions happened on 9 February 1925, and they continued every night for several weeks, with little to show for it – just a page or so at a time. The communications always took place at, or around, nine o'clock in the evening. (Dr Vinod's first contact with the Nine began at 9pm precisely.)

Randall-Stevens had two discarnate communicators, Adolemy (previously incarnated as Moses) and Oneferu. Between them, they described Giza as a 'Pyramidal Masonic centre' and talked of 'Cosmic Masonry', explaining: 'The emigrants from Atlantis were people governed by the laws of Cosmic Freemasonry and those who landed in Egypt built centres of Masonic Initiation from which the country was administered.'[87]

In the 1950s Randall-Stevens established a group called the Knights Templars of Aquarius on the instructions of his guides. (It still exists, with its headquarters in the Channel Islands.) From his own words it seems that the communications finally moved on to trance mediumship, as in 1956 they were tape recorded. In *The Wisdom of the Soul* (1956) he writes:

> The authority for the teachings and statements contained within its pages belongs to the Osiran Group, an Order within the Brotherhood of Master Masons, who are working through specific Initiates now incarnate in different parts of the world.[88]

Although there are many similarities between Randall-Stevens's and Alice Bailey's received wisdom, there are differences too, and Randall-Stevens' communicators, like the Council of Nine, also make elementary mistakes. For example, they refer to the Sphinx as 'that great granite image',[89] but of course it is made entirely of limestone.

As with many of the threads in this investigation, once again we find ourselves looking towards James Hurtak. *The Keys of Enoch* draws on many ideas from the same esoteric milieu encompassing Crowley, Blavatsky, Schwaller de Lubicz and Alice Bailey. Hurtak, Blavatsky and Bailey all term the ultimate authority in the universe the Great White Brotherhood, although Hurtak has upgraded their domicile from somewhere in Tibet to somewhere in the galaxy. But, like Bailey, Hurtak refers to them as the 'Hierarchy'. And surely it is no coincidence that Hurtak's *The Keys of Enoch* gives precisely the same dates for the duration of Atlantis – 18,000–12,000 BCE – as Saint-Yves d'Alveydre, the founder of Synarchy. Whatever else *The Keys of Enoch* might be, it is notably well versed in the work of other esoteric authors, particularly those of the late nineteenth century.

A new global religion

We were amazed to discover that links between the modern phenomenon of the Council of Nine and various occult organisations and esotericists such as Synarchy, Aleister Crowley and Alice Bailey had already been brought together with a 'Council of Nine' as far back as the 1930s. Under the bizarre pseudonym of 'Inquire Within', research by Christina Stoddard, former head of a schismatic Golden Dawn order called the Stella Matutina, appeared in two books, *Light-Bearers of Darkness* (1935) and *The Trail of the Serpent* (1936). They sounded a warning about the creation of new religious belief systems by apparently independent – but in fact connected – groups. Stoddard herself, like Schwaller de Lubicz and Alice Bailey, held extreme right-wing views, but even she was disturbed by what she saw as the increasingly iron grip of Synarchy on the esoteric world.

Stoddard discussed Saint-Yves's Synarchist objectives, specifically the control of the three key pillars of society, political, religious and economic institutions. She pointed out that this seemed to be happening in the religious sphere. Unlike the days when Christianity was the only sanctioned religion in the West, there were many different belief systems, making this area harder to control. To reverse this trend, the religions must first be unified, not by trying to supplant them, but by absorbing their main elements and effectively creating a new global religion. The best way of achieving this goal would be for some authoritative and charismatic leader to take control by explaining that God or the gods have, over the course of history, revealed certain truths to different people, which manifested as apparently disparate religions. But they all emanated from the same God. All that was needed was an understanding of the fundamental principles and the higher levels of spirituality to which mankind may now aspire. Tellingly, Stoddard gave as the prime example of this Synarchist synthesis the doctrines of Alice A. Bailey.[90]

The Trail of the Serpent describes a recent rivalry between Reuben Swinburne Clymer and H. Spencer Lewis, who both claimed to be the legitimate head of American Rosicrucianism. Clymer (a 32nd degree Mason), claimed that he had been given his authority by no less a person than the social reformer Paschal Beverly Randolph (1825–75) – a friend of Abraham Lincoln – whom the European Rosicrucians had authorised to take the Order to America in 1852, many years before H. Spencer Lewis founded AMORC. The resulting dispute led to Clymer taking the matter to court, which found in his favour and accepted his registration of the title 'Rosicrucian' in 1935.

Clymer claimed that the doctrines of his society, the Fraternitas Rosae Crucis, were endorsed by a secret order that directed it from France – called the Council of Nine. He published a letter from them in 1932, which proclaimed:

This is the New Dispensation, and the work of the Spiritual and Mystical Fraternities must be re-established throughout the world, so that all peoples may be taught the Law and thereby enabled to apply it towards universal improvement as the only means of saving mankind . . . We, the Council of Nine, have selected your organization, as one of the oldest in America, to help do this work.[91]

The letter was signed by the excessively immodest 'Comte M. de St Vincent, Premier Plenipotentiary of the Council of Nine of the Confraternities of the World'. As with the Synarchist ideal, Clymer's group – as Stoddard points out – professed 'to embrace the esoteric side of all religions'.[92] Another title of the Council of

Nine, according to Clymer, was the 'Secret School',[93] which will prove to have extraordinary significance. The important point here is that the term 'Council of Nine' was in use in the 1930s, specifically linked to the same politico-esoteric milieu in France that spawned Schwaller de Lubicz.

Many of the nineteenth-century writings of Dr Paschal Beverly Randolph, Clymer's mentor, contain such precise parallels with the later Nine material and the teachings of Alice Bailey's Tibetan that they stretch coincidence far beyond breaking point. Randolph believed that throughout history a series of initiatory orders has existed which is controlled by higher spiritual beings known as the Great White Brotherhood, and Clymer claimed that the Grand Master of his order was directly accountable to them.[94] More important is the fact that Randolph used the name 'the Hierarchy' to describe these higher spiritual beings[95] – the same term used by Bailey, Hurtak, Puharich and Whitmore. And besides believing that a Council of Nine directs certain esoteric schools from France, Randolph writes of a Council of Twenty-Four[96], which also appears in Hurtak's *The Keys of Enoch*. Interestingly, Randolph believed that 'spiritual beings from other planets' often visit Earth.[97]

With distinctly synarchist overtones, Clymer described the Hierarchy as 'guardians of the world's religions'[98] (which is surely very odd, as many of them are exclusivist and teach intolerance – and worse – towards the others. One wonders what game plan these guardians really have in mind.)

Apart from his Rosicrucian Order, Clymer set up several inter-connected esoteric organisations, including the Secret Schools and a mystical brotherhood known as the Priesthood after the Order of Melchizedek. He claimed that the latter was already well established in France, and that its secrets originated in a manu-script handed down from the Paris Temple – in other words, from the Knights Templar.[99]

In his ground-breaking 1979 book, *Messengers of Deception*, Jacques Vallée describes his investigations into an occult group called the Order of Melchizedek. He first encountered them in

Paris, becoming interested in their fusion of 'traditional' esoteric ideas with a belief in extraterrestrial contact. When he returned to his adopted home in San Francisco, Vallée was surprised to find that the same group was operating right on his own doorstep in California. He soon realised that the Order of Melchizedek has many such branches throughout the world.

In April 1976 he met James Hurtak, who was appearing with Andrija Puharich on a San Francisco television programme. In conversation afterwards, Hurtak described his experience of having *The Keys of Enoch* beamed into him in 1973. He then invited Vallée 'to join a new psychic group designed to change the destinies of the world by occult means'.[100] This group was known, Hurtak explained, as the Sons of Light of the Order of Melchizedek. But Vallée was no fool, having had his suspicions honed over decades of researching UFO contactee stories. He writes:

> Where does this alleged wisdom come from? From the distant stars? I am beginning to wonder. *Could the source of the so-called 'wisdom' be right here on Earth?* Could there be human manipulators behind all this?[101]

And who is this Melchizedek? Also spelled Melchisedec, he appears in Genesis 14:18–20 as the priest-king of Salem who blessed Abraham. Later, Paul speaks of the 'Order of Melchisedec' in somewhat mysterious terms in his Epistle to the Hebrews (Chapters 5–7): it appears to have been a special order of priests distinct from the Levites, which has fired imaginations ever since. Like other Biblical characters such as Enoch, who are clearly important but about whom little information is given, the 'Order of Melchisedec' is fertile ground for speculation. As a result the name turns up, almost as a cliché, in many of the more unconventional Christian systems. It is the name of the senior priesthood of the Church of Jesus Christ of Latter Day Saints, or Mormons, to which all male members aspire after their earlier membership of the 'Aaronic' priesthood. Confusingly, however, several esoteric – and Christian fundamentalist – groups all call themselves the Order of Melchizedek. For example, there is a small Order in Applegate, California, which has existed since 1889.[102]

The Order with which Vallée associates Hurtak has a particularly interesting agenda. Their literature reveals that, to them, Melchizedek has exactly the same role as Alice Bailey's Lord of the World, that of a higher being who descended to Earth in the 'Lemurian epoch', guiding the spiritual evolution of the human race. His Order is endowed with a somewhat grandiose – if rather sinister-sounding – goal. As Hurtak writes in *The Keys of Enoch*:

> The Order of Melchizedek is in charge of the *consciousness reprogramming* that is necessary to link physical creation with the externalization of the divine hierarchy [our emphasis].[103]

The Keys of Enoch and the doctrines of Alice Bailey can be seen as *one and the same*, although Hurtak's version is careful to boast a New Age gloss. They even use the same words – the Hierarchy, Seven Rays, root races – to describe identical concepts.

What Hurtak is attempting to do matches the Synarchist interpretation of the works of Alice Bailey given by Christina Stoddard. We have already seen how *The Keys of Enoch* outlines a system that incorporates all the major religions of the Western world as well as New Age beliefs. Christianity, Judaism and even Mormonism, fashionable Eastern religions and indigenous beliefs (such as those of the Native Americans): Hurtak's theology embraces them with equal fervour. He also claims to explain the 'message' that lies behind them all.

The dark side of Sirius

The esoteric concept of the importance of Sirius also appears – this time in a markedly twisted form – in the doctrines of the

Order of the Solar Temple, whose mass deaths shocked the world in the mid-1990s. On the night of 4–5 October 1994, fifty-three members of the cult died in Switzerland and Canada, while on 15–16 December 1995, another sixteen died in France in what were probably suicide pacts, although many suspect it was coldly premeditated ritual murder. Yet this was not the end of just another minor, if mad, cult. The Order itself did not die with its faithful on those tragic nights, and neither is the Order of the Solar Temple an organisation of little consequence. Its influence stretches very high up the social ladder.

The Order of the Solar Temple was closely connected with another group, the confusingly similarly named Sovereign Order of the Solar Temple, founded at the chateau of Arginy, in the Beaujolais region of France, on 12 June 1952.[104] One individual who was instrumental in this event was the alchemist Eugène Canseliet, who was previously a member of the Brotherhood of Heliopolis with Schwaller de Lubicz.[105] The Sovereign Order soon made inroads into high society, being officially recognised by Prince Rainier III of Monaco, although its relationship with his family was much more intimate: his wife, the legendary Princess Grace, was actually a member.[106]

The exact relationship between the Sovereign Order of the Solar Temple and the more notorious Order of the Solar Temple, which was created around 1980, is hotly disputed. Was it an offshoot, a breakaway group, or the result of a merger between the Sovereign Order and some other neo-Templar society? Perhaps the truth will remain elusive because the Sovereign Order has since been keen to play down its connections with its notorious cousin. But some relationship exists, as several leaders of the Order of the Solar Temple had once been members of the Sovereign Order, and perhaps even continued to be . . . More fundamentally, the doctrines of both orders were identical.

The 'manifesto' of the Sovereign Order of the Solar Temple, entitled *Pourquoi le resurgence de l'Ordre du Temple?* (*Why the Revival of the Order of the Temple?*), published under the pseudonym 'Peronnik' in Monte Carlo in 1975, talks of the existence of a planet called Heliopolis, which orbits Sirius. The leaders of both Orders believed that they were in contact with the inhabitants of this planet. 'Peronnik' explains:

> Several times in the past interplanetary missions have left Heliopolis in the direction of our Earth. This was notably the case during the erection of the Great Pyramid, when, after an agreement was made with certain Egyptian initiates to consolidate and perfect the esoteric initiation, a mission of 25 specialists came to contribute to the construction itself.[107]

The Orders' doctrines also emphasise the importance of the secret priesthood of Melchizedek: the man himself being an emissary of Heliopolis/Sirius, who returned to his home planet when his mission was completed.[108] The Sovereign Order's book explicitly proclaims them as a *Synarchist* organisation, thereby linking them directly to the ideology of Schwaller de Lubicz.[109]

Significantly, the reason for the alleged suicide of the sixty-nine cult members was that they believed their souls would return 'home' to the Sirius system. Documents posted to the media on 5 October 1994 by the leaders of the cult include the statement: 'The Great White Lodge of Sirius has decreed the Recall of the last authentic Bearers of an Ancestral Wisdom.'[110] Although they have put their own idiosyncratic – not to say perverted – twist on the idea, it clearly derives from the works of Alice Bailey, who explicitly uses the term 'Great White Lodge' in the context of Sirius. And, of course, the Solar Temple stressed the importance of the Great Pyramid, which, they claim, will be the focus for some momentous event in the next few years.

Following the Lion Path

The concept of contact with Sirius has become somewhat fashionable in certain circles in the last few years. In 1985 a book entitled *The Lion Path* appeared on the New Age market. The author, given as one 'Musaios', claimed to outline an ancient Egyptian system of individual transformation and enlightenment, derived primarily from the Pyramid Texts. The Osiris-king's journey to the otherworld to become a 'body of light' before taking a new, Horus, form, was seen as a description of the process of transformation undergone by every soul after death, but which can also be experienced during life (an idea that we believe is truly revelatory). Now, Musaios promises us, that transformation is open to everybody.

However, disappointingly, what really emerges from *The Lion Path* is a passive process, a series of meditation exercises, described in superficial and simplistic New Age speak, to be carried out at astrologically significant times, with the objective of enabling the practitioner to 'tune in' to higher intelligences in the universe – specifically those in the Sirius system.

To follow the Lion Path, one simply has to meditate in the correct way at specific times, tuning in to astrological forces (using a completely reinvented astrology that includes two as yet undiscovered planets in our solar system, as well as Sirius A and B). The final force, the object of the Lion Path, is Sirius. When contact with Sirius is achieved, the practitioner will have achieved personal transformation, though Musaios fails to say exactly what will happen as a result. The clear implication is that some form of communication will have been established with the beings from Sirius. Musaios writes:

In the Vulcan(-Ptah) Session and interval we begin to assemble the seed-pod (in terms of consciousness-space, a starship or flying disk) for later travel to the domain of Sirius; and in the Horus Session we begin to use it. During the Vulcan Session 're-wiring' and the new circuitry for that super-shamanic journey are prepared. In the Vulcan-Sothic or 25th Session the process is completed.[111]

The passivity of the exercises is, in itself, a direct contradiction of the principles on which the Lion Path claims to be based. The journey in the Pyramid Texts is essentially an active process, in which the individual is directly responsible for the outcome. It is not a passive state in which they simply allow outside forces to direct them.

The Lion Path includes an illustration of a 'divine eye' with a hieroglyph which, the caption tells us, means 'Lord of the Nine'. This must be the Great Ennead. Why does Musaios specifically use the term 'the Nine'?

The ultimate aim of the Lion Path is, we are told, the formation of a 'liaison group' of humans with the intelligences on Sirius. As Musaios wrote in 1985:

> The future of humanity depends on its most developed and highest evolved representatives. To form as complete a liaison group of them as possible is the great opportunity . . . that is offered humanity until 1994: an emergency door to an evolutionary process that would otherwise be aborted. Thereafter the liaison group continues the process.[112]

This liaison group is to have a momentous task:

> Nothing less is in the offing than the possibility of the course of human history being changed via the group of persons who will have availed themselves of the various starting times and who will have followed through for the development called for.[113]

(The original exercises for the Lion Path were intended to culminate in April 1994; however, as that date approached a new edition of the book announced that the Path had been extended to 23 November 1998.)

The intention appears to be the creation of a group of people who have done the spiritual exercises of the Lion Path and successfully achieved contact with Sirius. Then they will rule – or at least speak for – the world.

Musaios sums up the objective of the Lion Path with this quote from the Book of the Dead: 'Now I speak with a voice and accents to which they listen and my language is that of the star Sirius.'[114] (It should be pointed out that this is Musaios' own translation of this passage. R.O. Faulkner's rendition is: 'I have spoken as a goose until the gods have heard my voice, and I have made repetition for Sothis.'[115])

Attempts to contact beings from Sirius are not, by now, unfamiliar to this investigation. Not only do the Council of Nine claim that their chosen followers on Earth are conduits for Siriun communications, but Alice Bailey also wrote of the Path of Sirius as being the highest aspiration a seeker could have. But what is Musaios's intention with his Lion Path? And who is the man behind the pseudonym?

It is not difficult to discover his true identity. 'Musaios' is none other than Dr Charles Musès, the internationally renowned mathematician and cyberneticist. We know, not just from suspicions arising from the way Musaios frequently references Musès's work, and indeed vice versa, but also – significantly – from the fact that John Anthony West reveals the identity of the two in *Serpent in the Sky* when discussing *The Lion Path*.[116]

Undoubtedly, Musès is one of the most erudite and brilliant thinkers of today. A highly respected mathematician, inventor of the complex theory of 'hypernumbers', Musès's work, in the words of his biography, 'span[s] problems on the complex interfaces between sociology, biology, psychology, philosophy, and mathematics.'[117] He has also written extensively on mythology. Musès is also famed as a neural cyberneticist: tellingly, however, in the early 1960s he worked with Warren S. McCulloch,[118] who was Andrija Puharich's mentor in his early work on electronic implants, such as tooth radios and the like. Curiously, Musès's master work, entitled *Destiny and Control in Human Systems* came out the same year that his pseudonymous *The Lion Path* was published, yet the contrast between the two is, at first, inexplicably extreme. On the one hand, his masterwork is scholarly and erudite, revealing an immense breadth of learning, and providing astonishingly astute insights, yet on the other he produces what many of his academic admirers would dismiss as quaint and – frankly – almost mindless New Age pap. What on earth was Musès up to?

Perhaps it is significant that he was also one of the pioneers of the idea of extraterrestrial visitations in mankind's early history. In the late 1950s, he undertook a study of certain Babylonian legends, reaching the same conclusions as Robert Temple in *The Sirius Mystery*: that they were actually accounts of visitations by amphibious aliens.[119] Temple never mentions Musès's work, which is curious because they were both close to the same hugely influential man: Arthur M. Young. Musès was the editor of the journal of Young's Institute for the Study of Consciousness, and also co-edited a book with Young. Temple – as we have seen – was Young's protégé, and briefly secretary of the Foundation For the Study of Consciousness.

If nothing else, the Musaios story reveals that some of the finest minds in the world are being co-opted, or volunteering themselves, into a network of people willing to contact beings from Sirius. Yet do people such as Musès – and indeed, James Hurtak – really believe that such things are possible? And can they really find no better representatives for our home planet Earth than 'flaky' New Age channellers?

The heart of the matter

Secret Chiefs, Hidden Masters, initiates and higher beings from Sirius: all may appear to swirl around each other like individual bees, but their motivations – and their secrets – lie in their membership of the same hive. We can now see that apparently unconnected cults and esoteric groups share certain key figures and beliefs – surprisingly, even suspiciously, few, in fact. These are the ingredients in a heady mix now being expertly moulded into nothing less than a new religion for the twenty-first century by those with very much their own design in mind.

We conclude that the Council of Nine's communications have definite antecedents in the occult and mystical milieu of the late nineteenth and early twentieth centuries. Some of the Council of Nine material of today is strikingly similar to its earlier manifestations, and this is obviously not coincidental. For example:

* Aleister Crowley's 'Aiwass' communications, which began in 1904, led to his creation (or perhaps reformation) of the Argenteum Astrum, his magickal order that laid great emphasis on Sirius. In postwar California, Aiwass and the 'Secret Chiefs' (nonhuman intelligences) of the A∴A∴ came to be identified as extraterrestrial rather than occult entities. Then began a tortuous, but undeniable, chain of influence: a member of the Californian A∴A∴, Harry Smith, became an acknowledged influence on Arthur M. Young – Puharich's 'second-in-command' at the Round Table Foundation in the 1950s – who directly inspired the writing of *The Sirius Mystery* by Robert Temple. This book has, in turn, been extremely influential on the New Egyptology and the belief in extraterrestrial involvement in the origins of Egyptian (and other) civilisations.

* Certain of R.A. Schwaller de Lubicz's ideas – such as the Nine Principles – turn up in the earliest communications from the Council of Nine. He was a member of the Theosophical Society and a leader of the Synarchist movement, which has close connections with societies of which Crowley was a member and which are part of esoteric traditions in which groups of nine are important. Schwaller de Lubicz has become the godfather of the New Egyptology, inspiring many of its leading researchers.

* Alice Bailey's 'Tibetan' communications are the most obvious precursor to those of the modern Council of Nine. Vinod's 1952 communications are virtually a continuation of Bailey's, just as Hurtak's *The Keys of Enoch* is essentially an update of her work. Her career also began in the Theosophical Society, and the direct influence of Sirius and its inhabitants on Earth was a key part of

the Tibetan's doctrine. Moreover, Bailey's communications also made a direct connection between Sirius and Freemasonry, an idea that was possibly already circulating among the higher ranks of American Freemasonry but which in any case would have been brought to their attention by her husband, Foster Bailey. Another prominent American Mason, who, as a student of Theosophy, was open to Bailey's ideas was Henry Wallace, who was a major backer of Puharich's Round Table Foundation. To clinch matters, Puharich is known to have studied the works of Alice Bailey shortly before beginning his research at the Round Table Foundation in the late 1940s.

* Other information channelled by famous and influential psychics such as H.C. Randall-Stevens and Edgar Cayce, while not having direct connections with the Nine – as far as we know – does show remarkable similarities with their teachings.

Underpinning the apparently disparate systems of Schwaller de Lubicz, Crowley and Bailey was an unquestioning acceptance of Madame Blavatsky's basic principles, such as the idea of 'root races'. Essentially they were Theosophist in background and fundamental belief, no matter how different their own developed systems may appear to be.

The initial contact with the Council of Nine at the Round Table Foundation in 1952–3 seems to draw the main sets of communications together into one coherent scheme. But how do we explain these connections? Basically, there are two options:

(1) The various communications in the early part of this century – through Crowley, Bailey, Cayce and Randall-Stevens – may represent some kind of genuine, non-Earthly intelligence, who are making contact through 'psychic' (telepathic) means with several different people in various guises. The variations could have been part of a deliberate plan, or have been merely the side effects of difficulties in 'coming through' different psychics. But in this scenario, the final 'coming out' of the Council

of Nine solved the problem by focusing on a group of 'accredited' and 'official' conduits (such as Phyllis Schlemmer), effectively making sense of the overall story.

(2) It is possible that communications with the Council of Nine, begun by Puharich and Arthur Young, were consciously modelled on the earlier communications, perhaps as an elaborate experiment in the creation, and manipulation, of belief systems.

Neither solution is entirely satisfactory. There certainly seems to have been an element – to say the least – of manipulation on the part of Puharich, yet he himself appears to have genuinely believed in the possibility of such communications.

Another important factor in the postwar communications is the evident involvement of official government agencies such as the Pentagon and intelligence organisations like the CIA. We have seen their hand in the Round Table Foundation in the 1950s and in the events surrounding Lab Nine, as well as extending their influence into, and shaping, the daring new thinking of the 1970s.

Since that time, the Nine's communications seem to have become more driven and purposeful, with a clearer agenda, linking their message to Cydonia and the mysteries of Egypt. And through works such as Hurtak's *The Keys of Enoch*, the Nine are now reaching a considerably wider audience. Their message may not stand up to scrutiny, but few people know about their background – or their mistakes. Their impact, as a whole, is increasingly significant.

One scenario does make sense: the phenomenon of the prewar communications emerged spontaneously. Claims of contact with non-human entities were nothing new, but what was different was: (1) improved methods of communication that made it easy to spread the word and for connections to be made (books by Blavatsky, Crowley, Bailey, Cayce and Randall-Stevens were circulating in Europe and the United States simultaneously); (2) all of these contacts carry essentially the same message of coming global change, even if it is expressed in different terms – Crowley's New Aeon of Horus, Bailey's New Age, Cayce's 'return of the Great Initiate', Randall-Stevens's Age of Aquarius. This was a new phenomenon. Whereas, for example, the rise of spiritualism in the mid-nineteenth century had popularised the idea of communication with discarnate beings, it had never been associated with any sense of impending upheaval.

It is easy to imagine that when this new trend in entity communication came to official notice, government agencies would have wanted to know what was going on. The corridors of power would have buzzed with urgent questions: Are the communications real? Will the prophesied changes actually take place? Is contact possible with nonhuman, extraterrestrial, beings, even with the old 'gods' themselves? Possibly as part of the new interest in psychological warfare and psychic abilities after the Second World War, the US government – through various outlets – seemed to focus attention specifically on the subject of communication with entities from the 1940s onwards. This might not have been official policy. All it needed was some individuals in the military and intelligence community to take the idea of contact seriously. If it was real, it could prove very useful.

It is a mistake to think that the military mind is inevitably coldly pragmatic. General Patton, for example, was a fervent believer in reincarnation, and Britain's Air Marshal Dowding was a top spiritualist who believed himself to be in touch with dead airmen. By reaching Freemasons, Alice Bailey's (or rather, the Tibetan's) ideas also had a hotline to the movers and shakers of American society. It is hard to get much nearer to the top of the tree than the Vice-President, and Vice-President Henry Wallace was steeped in esoteric and mystical ideas. But the political and military mind *is* conditioned for expediency: its over-riding concern is to use anything and everything to further its goals or cause. If they were interested in contact with aliens, it would be to answer one question only: how can we turn it to our own advantage?

So if 'they' began to treat the idea of contact with other intelligences seriously, what would be the next step? It would seem logical to carry out experiments, which is precisely what Puharich's Round Table Foundation did. In fact, there is no doubt about this: Terry Milner's research shows that the Foundation was a front for the military to carry out psychological and medical experiments in the background of the public arena. Again, Henry Wallace's involvement in funding the Foundation is significant. Puharich's parapsychological experiments at Glen Cove centred specifically on people who, like Eileen Garrett, claimed communication with some kind of entity. This explains why Puharich first took Vinod there – and for whom he was working.

There is another highly significant factor in an assessment of the role of Puharich. It appears that he was actively seeking contact or, more precisely, seeking to observe and experiment with other people who made contact. This is important because the 'prewar' channellers seemed to fall into the practice spontaneously. They never sought it. Even the great magician Crowley was taken aback by the appearance of the entity called Aiwass.

What did these experiments demonstrate? What did Puharich conclude from them? Were the communications real, or delusions?

Once a phenomenon has been identified, it is then used. The change of direction in the Nine's communications at the beginning of the 1970s, and the development of more distinct overtones in their message, occurred once they had established themselves and could start to spread their propaganda. But just what are the Council of Nine and their message being used for? Why are so many prominent leaders in so many fields keen to promote them, with greater or lesser degrees of openness, as in the case of Richard Hoagland and his Message of Cydonia?

There is, in our view, an over-riding need for caution here. Alarm bells may be heard clear and strong, for true or false, now the Nine have become the property of the intelligence agencies, it is wise to be vigilant – and perhaps even afraid.

7

Endtimes: The Warning

There is undoubtedly a widespread expectation that these are the 'endtimes', that apocalyptic events are on the horizon and that the end of the world may *really* be nigh. High-profile books and films are now implanting the idea that some major – and highly devastating – event will soon ravage the world. And even if mankind does somehow survive the coming cataclysm it will be as traumatised and hopeless refugees, desperate for strong, empowered leadership.

At the forefront of this mood of escalating doom and disaster is the unique, febrile excitement generated by the very idea of the Millennium. It is as if the year 2000 marks the pinnacle of all our hopes and fears, although the negative aspects are constantly emphasised at the expense of more positive and optimistic expectations. The Millennium, as such, only makes sense in a Christian context, supposedly marking 2000 years since the birth of Jesus, but now virtually everyone is caught up in the hysteria. With all eyes on the next few years, what a pity it would be if nothing happened, and what a temptation for certain individuals and cabals to ensure that it does . . .

For Christians the endtimes fever means the Second Coming of Jesus, as predicted in the New Testament, with the concomitant apocalyptic events described with perhaps excessive zeal in the

Book of Revelation. We are led to believe that if Jesus, believed to be the epitome of Divine Love, returns to Earth in glory then he comes to initiate the final conflict between the forces of good and evil – the battle of Armageddon.

The Christian expectation is only part of the story. For example, New Agers have been prepared for this time – the dawning of the Age of Aquarius – for years, largely because of their acceptance of the prophecies of the sixteenth-century French occultist, Michel de Notre-Dame, more familiarly known as Nostradamus. From his psychic interpretation of astrological data, he singled out the year 1999 as a particularly disastrous one for mankind if the usual New Age interpretation of his obscurely worded 'quatrains' is accepted. Critics have pointed out that virtually any prophecy can be read into his words, rather like the 'code' read recently into the words of the Hebrew Bible.[1] Yet to question Nostradamus to a New Ager is rather like criticising the Bible to a fundamentalist Christian. Even so, if the author of the Book of Revelation – believed to be St John of Patmos – may be one of the two major creators of the Millennium, Nostradamus is very much the other. On to these gnarled roots have since been grafted all the other endtimes expectations drummed up so expertly by the many characters now revealed to be integral parts of the great conspiracy to exploit Millennium fever.

Even materialists, who scorn all religious or quasimystical beliefs, are experiencing pangs of increasing uncertainty about the future. Perhaps a global economic collapse will open the door through which will burst the four Horsemen of the Apocalypse: Famine, Pestilence, War and Death. They point to the current economic upheavals in the Far East, in Russia and elsewhere and fret about the future of the worldwide money markets, nervously projecting disaster around the time of the Millennium. If nothing else, the materialists point out that, at best, the Millennium Bug will cause chaos; because of a simple (if disastrous) lack of foresight on the part of many computer-builders, the software will not recognise the year 2000.

(Ironically, thanks to the prevailing hysteria, it will be the only thing that doesn't.) It may well lead to utter financial collapse on an international scale and at worst to rioting in the streets and martial law. And of course it is the Millennium itself that will activate the Bug.

One does not have to be a rabid fundamentalist or even an overanxious businessperson to suffer from Pre-Millennium Tension. We have seen in recent years – even recent months – an acceleration of global warming and its associated disturbances in weather patterns. Earth has been battered by a series of hurricanes, earthquakes, tidal waves and tornadoes, and there is a sense that even this is just a curtain-raiser to some much larger natural cataclysm. One is left wondering whatever next? Never before has so much tension, so much vulnerability been felt by so many, and never before has such desire for action been so cynically harnessed on such a scale.

Not everyone is dreaming, though. In a world of dreamers those who rarely sleep are kings. Where there is vulnerability, there will always be those who cynically seek to exploit it, and where there are those who seek to exploit, they will cynically create the vulnerability in the first place.

We are undoubtedly approaching the twenty-first century with increasing anxiety, which is the way our puppetmasters want it. The collective mood of heightened expectancy is a breeding ground for precisely the sort of belief system whose emergence we have charted in this book.

What we call the stargate conspiracy is the fostering of a belief that extraterrestrial 'gods' created the human race and presided over its civilisation – and that those gods are about to return. This belief is being promoted in different ways to different groups of people, but the underlying themes are always the same. Once these beliefs have entered into the collective consciousness, it will be relatively easy to use them as the foundation for a new religion. The ultimate aim of every organised religion has always been social control, and this one, we fear, will be no exception.

Cosmic countdown

Many groups and individuals are currently exploiting not only Millennium fever but also twenty-first-century anxiety. But of this cynical and often downright pernicious multitude, the activities of one particular type of group present the most thought-provoking and disturbing cautionary tale. These are the relatively new 'space brother' or UFO-centred cults. It would be a mistake to underestimate either the sheer numbers involved, or, indeed, the power of their beliefs. For example, the Raelian movement, which believes that all Raelians will be given eternal life by the coming space beings, has 40,000 members, and this is a relatively minor cult.[2] Many similar groups promote essentially the same message.

Against this background we must now set our discoveries about the Egypt–Mars conspiracies and the machinations of various groups. Make no mistake: the Millennium is absolutely central to their secret agenda – although the onset of the year 2000 is likely to mark only the beginning of a process that will reach its climax in the early years of the twenty-first century. James Hurtak, for example, highlights 2003 as a particularly key year.

Throughout this investigation different subjects, which appear at first to be independent of each other, seem to come together quite naturally. Carrying us along with the apparent logic, these links may seem to be reasonable, so that we are not surprised or disturbed when a coherent picture emerges. As we have seen, its main components are:

* The belief that the ancient Egyptian monuments are the product of a mysterious civilisation of great antiquity, which may have been in contact with, or even created by, extraterrestrials. Through certain lasting 'records' – especially the Great Pyramid and the Sphinx – that civilisation left us messages about our future, specifically about some imminent event of global proportions. This is somehow tied in with the Millennium and the Age of Aquarius.

* The idea that extraterrestrial beings remembered as the 'gods' were responsible for the civilising of mankind, as in Robert Temple's *The Sirius Mystery*.

* The discovery of what appear to be anomalous features on Mars, which, if proven to be artificial, can only be the product of a civilisation that existed on that planet in the distant past. This, too, has a message for us today.

* The ongoing communications from the Council of Nine, which have been unfolding since 1952. They claim to be the Great Ennead – the Nine gods of Heliopolis. We have seen that the Council of Nine have increasing influence, not only over the New Age, but also politicians and multimillionaires.

Each of these major strands is based on a genuine mystery: the mysterious knowledge of the Dogon concerning Sirius; the evidence that the Sphinx is of far greater antiquity than is officially believed; the Viking images of Cydonia that appear to show genuinely unexplained features; and the apparently 'miraculous' phenomena surrounding the Council of Nine. These strands appear to be naturally coalescing: apparent connections have been found between the Cydonian monuments and those of Giza. The major *raison d'être* of Richard Hoagland, this element is now creeping into the works of others, notably Robert Bauval and Graham Hancock.

Into this developing picture come the Nine. They, too, place much emphasis on the Great Pyramid and Sphinx, even claiming to have built them. And, through the work of James Hurtak, the Martian monuments have been introduced into this increasingly complex web of connections. There is no doubt that Hoagland and Hurtak's work is directly driven by the Nine, but what of Hancock and Bauval's? Certainly, because it largely endorses Hoagland's work, *The Mars Mystery* is indirectly promoting the Nine – and to a much wider audience.

The over-riding message is that the gods are back. The

Message of Cydonia as promoted by Hoagland is that those monuments were designed to encode information for us today. When this is added to the ideas promoted by Hancock and Bauval that the Egyptian monuments also encode messages for our times, we can see that the two reinforce each other. And communications from the Nine are actually happening now.

The conclusion seems inescapable: the Nine gods who built not only the Pyramids and the Sphinx but also the structures on Mars are back. These are not just the creators of the ancient Egyptian civilisation, but of the entire human race.

However, this conclusion relies on the assumption that these strands began totally independently, that each of the discoveries were made in isolation, with connections between them only becoming apparent as time went on. But this is not the case. The entire picture seems to have been contrived according to a complex, long-term plan. For example, Robert Temple's *The Sirius Mystery* was inspired by Arthur M. Young, who was present at the initial contact with the Nine in 1953. Young's own inspiration came from Harry Smith, a high-ranking member of one of Aleister Crowley's magickal orders in which extraterrestrial intelligences, Sirius, Mars and ancient Egypt were the great pillars of their beliefs. The Nine's communications, particularly in the initial stages, seem to continue those of Alice A. Bailey, of which James Hurtak's *The Keys of Enoch* is essentially an update. Hurtak has been the prime mover in the Face on Mars debate and in the New Egyptology, and *The Keys of Enoch* comes from the Council of Nine.

An alien agenda

Is the picture complete, or are other elements of modern mythology about to be drawn into this complex web? There are already clues: Stuart Holroyd's 'biography' of the Nine, which was commissioned by Lab Nine, gave the subtext of this message away in the title: *Briefing for the Landing on Planet Earth*. Another, apparently unconnected book, *The Secret School* by Whitley Strieber, has as its subtitle *Preparation for Contact*. In fact, this is no coincidence: bestselling author Strieber, most widely known for the tales of personal contact with aliens told in *Communion*, *Transformation*, *Breakthrough* and *Confirmation*, brings the last major part of the scenario into play.

Only in 1987 did *Communion* first catapult the alien abduction phenomenon into public consciousness. In the few years since we have seen such an explosion – virtually an epidemic – of claimed abductions that the image of the Grey alien is now firmly embedded in our minds as, at the very least, a cultural icon. But to many people the Greys are considerably more than semi-cartoon characters: at least 35 per cent of all Americans now believe that these sinister extraterrestrials are repeatedly abducting humans on a vast scale.[3] This belief has, virtually overnight, begun to take on quasireligious overtones. Strieber, in *The Secret School*, passes on nine lessons given to him by the aliens for all mankind, specifically linking their message to the Face on Mars, which he claims to have been shown by his alien captor/tutors when he was a child, and to the New Egyptology of Hancock, Bauval and West. It is, as we will see, no accident that *The Secret School* enthusiastically, even incongruously, carries an endorsement by none other than Graham Hancock: 'Everyone concerned with the awesome mystery of what we are and what we may become should read *The Secret School*.' (Perhaps significantly, we have already identified the 'Secret School' as an alternative title of the Synarchist 'Council of Nine' of the 1930s.)

Hancock and Strieber may simply admire each other's books, and the matter may end there. But other, thought-provoking connections lie just under the surface, allowing many of the pieces of the jigsaw to fall finally into place. For example, Strieber had worked with Richard Hoagland, and funded Mark Carlotto's image enhancement work at Hoagland's request as early as 1985, two years before his first 'abduction' book, *Communion*, was published.[4]

Strieber was introduced to Richard Hoagland by a mutual

friend in the summer of 1984, but he makes some puzzling comments about the Mars research in his account in *Breakthrough* (1997). In discussing Mark Carlotto's enhancement of the Viking images, which used the advanced equipment made available to him through the intelligence division of The Analytical Science Corporation, he writes: 'The fact that the Mars face was reimaged on the best equipment known to man in 1985 and came out looking even more like a sculpture had been efficiently suppressed.'[5] It is difficult to begin to understand how the subject could be described as having been 'efficiently suppressed' given that Hoagland has been telling anyone who would listen about the Face – including the United Nations – besides lecturing and selling books and videos on the subject ever since.

The Secret School, however, reveals the subtext of Strieber's writings, and adds another piece to our complex jigsaw. This 1997 book describes the recovery, beginning in 1995, of further memories of his lifelong alien abduction experiences, specifically those long suppressed from his Texan childhood in the mid- to late 1950s. He recalls being part of the 'Secret School', a group of child abductees who were given lessons by their Grey captors. Although Strieber believes that he 'attended' this school for a number of years during his childhood, the memories recovered and lessons presented in the book were those given to him at the age of nine.

He recalls that, when first shown the image of the Face on Mars by John Gliedman, a scientist friend, he remembered seeing the image before, and later realised that the aliens had shown him that same image during his schooling.[6] (This may be nothing but the honest truth, but it is hard to see how the new images of the Face that reveal it to be nothing more than a large rocky outcrop fit into this scenario. Were the aliens playing a cruel joke on him? If so, it would not be the first nor the last time that apparent discarnate entities amused themselves by toying with human gullibility. Remember that Colin Wilson called such beings 'the crooks and conmen of the spirit world', while Uri Geller called the Nine 'a civilization of clowns'.)

Most significant is Strieber's attribution of the onset of his recall of the abduction experiences – which led directly to *Communion* – to being shown the picture of the Face by Gliedman. He writes:

> No matter how I explained it away, seeing the face was still an enormous event in my life, far larger than I could ever have imagined or even – until recently – understood. It may well have been the trigger that caused the close encounter of December 26 1985 [the pivotal event that led to *Communion*] to take place. The mystery of Mars and the secret school, it would turn out, were deeply bound together.[7]

The mortar that binds Strieber's agenda together lies in his emphasis on the importance of the number nine. As he writes:

> The nine lessons of my ninth summer were structured in three groups of three – a fact that has explained to me one meaning of the mysterious nine knocks that played such an important role in my encounter experience.[8]

(This parallels the nine knocks that woke Jack Parsons during a lengthy magickal working on 10 January 1946.[9])

Surely Strieber is virtually inviting us to make connections with the Council of Nine?

The Secret School described the nine lessons he was given from childhood in three triads, but he adds a tenth, a new lesson given to him by the 'visitors' on 12 November 1995: a vision of the future in 2036 (in which the United States has become a military dictatorship after terrorists have destroyed Washington with an atomic bomb). It is, by now, a familiar pattern: there are ten significant numbers, but the tenth is only there to complete and make sense of the other nine, and also to provide continuity to the next sequence.

The first lesson began with a dream in which he flew above the surface of Mars, looking down on a gigantic, sculpted face and pyramids. (He also records that, at the same age, suddenly, for no reason he can remember, he became intensely interested in ancient Egypt.[10])

The eighth lesson of *The Secret School* relates the great monuments of Egypt and other early civilisations to forthcoming changes in the world. As in Hancock, Bauval and Grigsby's *The Mars Mystery*, they were built to encode the memory of global catastrophes and to serve as a warning to future generations that such cataclysms might well come again. Strieber writes:

> We have also created a sort of mechanism that exists in our genes, that will come to light when the equinox is opposite to its current position and when the world is again threatened. This device is the secret school, and the time for which it was created is when Pisces moves into Aquarius.[11]

Clues suggest who really runs the Secret School. Tellingly, Strieber also introduces the work of Robert Bauval and the erosion of the Sphinx, fully accepting the argument that the geological evidence and the astronomical correlations of the Sphinx and the pyramids pinpoint the date of . . . that familiar year 10,500 BCE. Not surprisingly, he also dates the beginning of the Age of Aquarius as shortly after the year 2000. Perhaps that is why *The Secret School* is endorsed by Graham Hancock.

The point of Strieber's lessons is that they show a way out of the nightmare scenarios of the future, through the shift in consciousness that comes with being a Chosen One, this time as a repeated abductee who accepts the alleged meaning of the Martian monuments, the Sphinx and the pyramids as well as the reality of the 'visitors'. He writes, with real endtimes fervour:

> God . . . is about to enter the ordinary world, and the destiny of our souls as companions to the creator is to be enacted at last.[12]

So what is Whitley Strieber's part, consciously or unwittingly, in the conspiracy to insidiously create a new religion and prepare us for some imminent takeover by its adherents? An integral part of the new belief system is the blending and exploitation of all the most potent modern myths, and surely there are few more powerful than the alien abduction scenario. Here we see one of the most successful icons of our times – the Grey alien – brought together with the Face on Mars and the ubiquitous emphasis on the 10,500 BCE dating of the Giza monuments. This is all linked to the imminent Age of Aquarius and, one way or another, to the return of the space gods, or of a quasi-Christian god who will save us from all evil – especially from ourselves – *if* we believe in him.

The reality or otherwise of the abduction experience has been much debated, and goes beyond the scope of this book. One other little known connection should give us pause for thought. When American veteran journalist Ed Conroy set out to investigate objectively the story behind Whitley Strieber's *Communion* in the late 1980s, he explored all the possible connections, including parallels with such matters as folklore and the occult. He writes in *Report on Communion* (1989) that according to Kenneth Grant, Aleister Crowley claimed, in 1919, to have contacted an extraterrestrial being named Lam connected with the Sirius and Andromeda star systems. Conroy continues:

> Grant goes on to assert that other OTO members have subsequently contacted Lam, making use of his image as painted prior to 1945 by Crowley. If there can be any legitimacy granted to coincidences of the imagination, it is quite interesting that Crowley's painting 'Lam' depicts an egg-headed face characterized by a vestigial nose and mouth and two eyes in narrow, elongated slits. Its resemblance to the image on the cover of *Communion* is remarkable, save for the dimensions and qualities of the eyes.[13]

In the previous paragraph before this extract, Conroy had been drawing parallels between Crowley's magickal invocation of angelic beings and the cosmic scheme outlined in Hurtak's *The Keys of Enoch*.

We believe that genuine mysteries, real unanswered questions are, ironically, being obscured by the half-truths and inventions of this new 'religion'. The Giza monuments present huge problems for orthodox Egyptology. Even the case for the Martian monuments – especially the pyramids – retains some merit. We have no argument with real intellectual curiosity challenging these subjects. What concerns us is the presence of a campaign to impose a meaning on all these disparate subjects, to create synthetic answers that build all too easily into a new belief system that also appears to offer glib solutions to mankind's present problems, pointing the way to the future. Yet the message is always the same, and the inherent dangers are incalculable.

Whitley Strieber and Richard Hoagland played a considerable part in spreading the belief that there was something anomalous trailing the Hale-Bopp comet.[14] One result of this belief was the suicides of the members of the Heaven's Gate cult, who were convinced that a spaceship had come to collect their souls and take them to a better life. This was an extreme scenario, and their deaths cannot be blamed on the likes of Hoagland, Strieber or Courtney Brown, but surely the cult's madness is even more tragic because they died for nothing – to go to a nonexistent spaceship.

The Controllers

Let us identify the groups involved in this extraordinarily complex scenario:

(1) Researchers and writers who promote specific ideas that fuel this belief system – including Robert Bauval and Graham Hancock with their lost civilisations of 10,500 BCE; Robert Temple and his apparently scholarly version of the ancient astronaut theory; Richard Hoagland, who evangelises about the

alleged Mars/Giza connection; and Whitley Strieber, with his lessons from the Grey aliens.

We have shown how all of these writers use each other's ideas in support of their own, and consequently not only do they reinforce each other, but the end result is that one large, consistent picture emerges. This is despite the fact that the arguments are often built on very shaky foundations. All these individuals claim that their work begins with material facts – physical alignments of the pyramids, anomalous images on Mars, the mysterious knowledge of a west African tribe, or their own alien encounters – but often ends up extrapolating spiritual messages.

The work of these people provides the raw material for the emerging belief system, although they may not be conscious of the part they play. It is possible that their ideas are simply being used.

(2) Charismatic, almost gurulike individuals who promote spiritual messages derived from alleged personal revelation, such as channelled information. Into this category come James J. Hurtak, Andrija Puharich, Sir John Whitmore, Alice A. Bailey – and even the 'Great Beast' himself, Aleister Crowley. All of them have a specific spiritual message based on the firm expectation of imminent global transformation and a total belief in their source's omniscience. The contemporary members of this category exist in a kind of symbiotic relationship with the first group, using their work to provide the factual framework for their more emotive, mystical writings (for example, Hurtak's use of the Martian enigmas).

However, the traffic is not all one-way: we have seen that some of the work of the first group appears to have been contrived to fit the teachings of the second, and that unexpected connections exist between the two, as with Richard Hoagland (group 1) and David Percy and David Myers (group 2). Certain individuals, such as James Hurtak, float seamlessly between the two groups, being seen by the first group as respected academics and by the second as visionaries and prophets. Essentially, the second group takes the work of the first and imposes a meaning on it, although some of the members of the first are by no means averse to this.

(3) Above groups 1 and 2 lurk the shadowy agents of a covert agenda. We may have discerned, for example, time and again, the presence of the CIA behind many of the key events, but because it is a secret service, its real intent and role have to be pieced together. Sometimes the CIA appears to have used the cultish beliefs of group 2 as an experiment in the psychology of belief, but its interest seems to go beyond that to the point where it appears to be creating the belief system itself. The most striking example of this is the way CIA operative Andrija Puharich zealously promoted – or maybe even created – the Nine.

And Robert Temple claimed that the CIA had tried to interfere with his work on the Dogon by stealing essential research material, and that then, after his book was published, it continued to harass him over a fifteen-year period. But why should it do this? It makes little sense. If it intended to obstruct his research, it was singularly unsuccessful. And why, after failing to stop the publication of his book, did it continue its campaign of harassment? The book was already in the public domain, so nothing could be done to prevent people from reading it. Neither did the CIA stop the new 1998 edition, which also describes the story of its previous interest in the book.

What did the CIA achieve by all this? If it had really wanted to stop *The Sirius Mystery*, not only did it fail miserably, but it also managed to achieve the opposite. It appears that its real intention, from the very first, was not to prevent publication, but to promote it. Its actions convinced Temple himself of the importance of his research, and the 1998 edition has now convinced his readers too. Introducing this air of intrigue, by implication the significance of the 'message' today is reinforced. It must be remembered that intelligence agencies are the masters of such psychological games.

In this category we include the behind-the-scenes activities of high-level politicians such as Henry Wallace, and the often undeniable Masonic agenda that underpins so much of this, including the 'prophecies' of Edgar Cayce.

If, as we have come to believe, there is a stargate conspiracy, then who are the conspirators and what are their aims? Can we identify any one group that might be the overall puppetmasters? As will have become obvious, this is a very complex scenario and there are no simple answers.

For example, the very mention of the CIA will, to many people, immediately identify the overall culprit as either that agency or the United States government itself. However, recent history has shown that the CIA has often pursued policies and objectives about which it has happily kept its political masters in the dark. The CIA is not synonymous with the United States government. Moreover, there have been many examples of cabals within the CIA, often reaching to the very highest level, which have used the privileges and resources of that extremely powerful organisation to further their own agendas.[15] So we can conclude that the presence of individual CIA agents does not necessarily imply that they are acting in accordance with agency or governmental policy.

Similarly, individual politicians and business people may be involved in this story for their personal satisfaction. There is no way of knowing who is the player and who is the played. And in the same way, Freemasonry figures largely throughout this book, but whether or not this is the fabled Masonic conspiracy is more open to question.

Most conspiracy theorists (we are not denying that we fit the description ourselves) tend to think in terms of one identifiable group behind every plot and hidden agenda. Unfortunately for such theorists and romanticists alike, real life is not so simple. Where conspiracies exist they are likely to involve various individuals and groups who have a vested interest in a particular outcome. It may be that the stargate conspirators include CIA operatives, Freemasons, politicians and their wealthy backers, who believe they have something to gain by creating this belief system, or fear they have something to lose if it does not happen. This conspiracy is bigger than one group or set of individuals.

What is clear is the nature of the conspiracy's objective. It is to push a particular system of belief on as many levels as possible, from the general public to genuine dyed-in-the-wool New Agers. 'They' are after all of us – hearts, minds and souls.

In their own image

In 1973 the United States government commissioned a report from SRI International[16] entitled *Changing Images of Man*, edited by Willis W. Harman and O.W. Markley, which concluded that the spread of what it termed 'the new values' – spiritual and ecological awareness and self-realisation movements – is becoming virtually unstoppable. This would bring about a transformation of society (particularly in the United States) that would radically undermine 'modern industrial-state culture and institutions' and result in 'serious social disruptions, economic decline, runaway inflation, and even institutional collapse'.[17] This report anticipates a lessening of trust in authority and a reaction against a regimented, tightly controlled society. It also suggested ways of preventing this worst-case scenario by identifying existing institutions or traditions that could be used to control and contain the impetus of the new movement. Significantly, it recommended as one of the best solutions the tradition of Freemasonry. As the report states:

> Of special interest to the Western world is that Freemasonry tradition which played such a significant role in the birth of the United States of America, attested to by the symbolism of the Great Seal (on the back of the dollar bill) . . . Thus this . . . has the potentiality of reactivating the American symbols, reinterpreting the work ethic, supporting the basic concepts of a free-enterprise democratic society, and

providing new meanings for the technological-industrial thrust.[18]

Note the similarity to the pronouncements of 1940s Vice-President Henry Wallace – and, of course, the words of Edgar Cayce.

What is particularly significant is that this report was produced by SRI International at the very time that they were heavily involved with the CIA and the US Defense Department. Imagine how it must have made alarm bells ring in the corridors of power, especially as it stressed that such a transformation of society was inevitable. The only recourse for those in positions of power and authority was for them to actively hijack the belief systems that underpinned this social unrest, moving it in whatever direction gave them the greatest advantage and retaining their control over the masses.

An important component of the new belief system is the use of the symbolism of Freemasonry. The movement has traditionally claimed to have its roots in ancient Egypt and lays particular emphasis on the esoteric significance of Sirius, which decorates every Masonic Temple in the form of the 'Blazing Star'.

Wallace, Cayce and SRI's *Changing Images of Man* report each stress the importance of the role of the United States in promoting Masonic ideals, effectively creating the ideal Freemasonic state.[19] This was the over-riding motivation of many of the originators of the Declaration of Independence, such as Thomas Jefferson. (In fact, of the fifty-six signatories to the Declaration of Independence, fifty were Freemasons, as were fifty of the fifty-five members of the convention that drew up the American Constitution.) Willis W. Harman, at one time a consultant to the White House and one of the editors of the *Changing Images* report – who was also involved in SRI's experiments with Uri Geller in the early 1970s, and, as president of the Institute of Noetic Sciences, in their first remote-viewing experiments – went on to write *An Incomplete Guide to the Future* (1976). In his book he discusses the role of Freemasonry in the founding of the

United States and defines what he calls the 'American symbols' – predominantly Masonic ideals.[21] In discussing the future of America he advocates a very similar scenario to that of *Changing Images of Man*, in other words, a society based on the principles of Freemasonry. He says:

> The specific symbols associated with the nation's birth have an additional significance. It is under these symbols, principles, and goals, properly understood, *and no others* [his emphasis], that the differing viewpoints within the nation can ultimately be reconciled.[22]

Perhaps more significantly, Harman believes that the symbol of the pyramid with the floating capstone on the Great Seal 'indicates that the nation will flourish only as its leaders are guided by supraconscious intuition',[23] and he defines this as 'divine insight'.

The fact that the SRI report draws attention to the Masonic symbolism on the back of the dollar bill is particularly interesting. The seal – originally incorporated into paper money by Henry Wallace – shows an incomplete pyramid, with its detached capstone, encompassing an open eye, floating in a halo of light. Under the pyramid are inscribed the Latin words *novus ordo seclorum* – 'new order of the ages'.

To repeat Wallace's words of 1934:

> It will take a more definite recognition of the Grand Architect of the Universe before the apex stone is finally fitted into place and this nation in the full strength of its power is in position to assume leadership among the nations in inaugurating 'the new order of the ages'.

Wallace explicitly links the return of the capstone to the Great Pyramid with the spiritual and political leadership of the United States in the world. It may therefore be significant that Zahi Hawass has announced that, as part of the Millennium Night

Celebration, a new gold capstone will be put in place on the top of the Great Pyramid. Hawass himself talks of this representing the 'finishing' of the pyramid.[24] If nothing else, it will be a very potent act of symbolism to American Freemasons.

The battle of Light and Darkness

Despite the evidence of very human manipulation, are the Nine really who they claim to be, the ancient Egyptian gods? It might even appear the case, until other factors are taken into account, notably the highly contrived nature of the alleged connection between, for example, Mars and Giza. As with the case of Richard Hoagland, once one tries to extrapolate a message, the connections fall apart. We have also seen how Bauval and Hancock's essential message – that the Egyptian monuments have a direct meaning for us today – can only work by massaging the data. Moreover, the Nine themselves are particularly apt to get their facts wrong.

There are thousands of enthusiastic believers in the hypotheses that rely upon physical evidence: measuring angles of the D & M pyramid, or aligning the Great Pyramid with Sirius. They do not, as a whole, realise that they are also tacitly opening themselves up to the spiritual message of James Hurtak, which in essence also means that of Alice Bailey. This prompts a worrying thought: will the Bailey/Hurtak *The Keys of Enoch* become the Bible of the new Millennium?

Many would see that as no bad thing, believing the teachings of both Bailey and Hurtak to be revelatory, enlightened and truly good. And it is this aspect of the whole issue of the Council of Nine that is, in our view, by far the most important. For while the objective reality – or otherwise – of the Nine is a fascinating subject, surely it is far less important than an analysis of their spiritual message. After all, it is their teaching that drives their followers, and their actions, in turn, could impinge upon us all either directly or indirectly.

No matter how compassionate, eccentric or essentially harm-less the channelled material of the Nine may appear on the surface, it actually hides a most disturbing subtext. James Hurtak in *The Keys of Enoch* describes an apocalyptic scenario in which a universal battle between the forces of light and darkness will inevitably manifest on Earth. He writes of 'a galactic war and housecleaning that is being completed throughout the universe'.[25] But is not the term 'housecleaning', like 'cleansing' – really rather sinister? It would be comforting to be able to dismiss such sus-picions as paranoid, but Hurtak also defines the Last Days in rather worrying terms:

> The conclusion of a 'divine program', after which there will be an upward spiral into the new 'master program' from the Father-Spirit Initiative. The increasing of inner 'Peace' and blessings of 'Joy' that will come with the pouring of the gifts of the Holy Spirit Shekinah upon spiritual mankind who will perceive the knowledge of the Most High God and use the wisdom of the 'Sons of Light', to prepare for Government in the Name of YHWH.[26]

He makes the situation clearer in these words: 'For those not working with the Light, it will be a time of great tribulation.'[27] As with all dogmatic, pulpit-thumping statements, there is a real, hidden danger here. Who is of the Light and who is not? More to the point, who decides? One assumes that Hurtak has no doubt about his own status, and the implication remains that he has inside knowledge about where the rest of us stand. Presumably anyone who refuses to accept his or the Nine's words are children of darkness, although his writings do suggest which groups can expect to suffer the greatest tribulation in the near future.

Hurtak's 'housecleaning' is similar in some respects to the idea of the great imminent 'harvesting' of souls that was a central theme of the teachings given by Ra through his channeller Carla Rueckert.[28] This taking up of the righteous will take place in the early years of the twenty-first century – another version of the ubiquitous Christian fundamentalist 'rapture'.

The Nine often appear to be disturbingly racist, but they are too clever to parade the fact like some New Age Goebbels ranting from the rooftops. Old-style rabble-rousing by dictators drowning in seas of braid currently stands no chance of achieving influence in the democratic West. The Nine simply imply – very strongly – the identity of those who are the Enemy. For example, in *The Only Planet of Choice*, Tom does not state baldly that the black races are inferior. Indeed, he appears to be saying quite the reverse, merely stating that they are the only ones to have evolved on Earth without any 'seeding' from extraterrestrial civilisations. Then he draws attention to this 'fact' by stressing that this should not be construed as meaning that blacks are inferior[29] – an interesting example of reverse psychology. Tom is saying, in other words, that we should not run away with the idea that blacks are inferior in any way just because they are the only members of the human race who happen not to be descended from gods. Given the human race's track record in abusing racial ideas, why should such a wise being even take the *risk* of putting the idea into our heads? Why share such potentially inflammatory information at all, if it is merely of academic interest and not intended to be the basis for any action in the future?

The racism implicit in *The Only Planet of Choice* is suspiciously reminiscent of Alice Bailey's writings, or rather, the teachings of the Tibetan she channelled. Superficially, like the words of Tom in *The Only Planet of Choice*, the message of the Tibetan – whatever one may believe about its origins – seems to stress peace, goodwill and universal brotherhood. The intentions of the Hierarchy are of the highest good. But sometimes disquieting ideas sneak in under the guise of esoteric lore. For example, in *A Treatise on Cosmic Fire* (1925), the Tibetan explains that in the coming phase of development, the Hierarchy 'will not individualise animal man as in the previous round, but will stimulate the mental germ in those members of the present human family who – as H.P.B. [Madame Blavatsky] says –

though apparently men, are without the span of mind.' To this sentence the following footnote is added: 'Such are the Veddhas of Ceylon, the Bushmen of Australia, and certain of the lowest of the African races.'[30]

Madame Blavatsky, as a Victorian, might be expected to hold what are today politically incorrect views about race. She reflects the thinking of the era on the subject. Even after the abolition of slavery, people of African origin were still considered mere beasts of burden, although it was admitted that they had souls, for were they not forcibly converted to Christianity, often at gunpoint? There remains the nagging doubt that, like Blavatsky, Bailey and Schlemmer, those who claim to channel superior beings should, surely, transcend the vagaries of racial attitudes that change with the years, speaking only timeless unchanging truths. Modern adherents of the Nine, and of Bailey, defend the implicit racism by saying bluntly that this is the way it is.

Racism has no scientific, sociological or anthropological support, no matter who suggests otherwise. Racism can take many forms; we have now come to realise that patronising attitudes can be, in their own way, just as degrading and dangerous as blatant incitements to racial hatred. The argument for 'benevolent racism' – that blacks are incapable of self-government and need the fatherly guidance of whites – was often used by the apartheid regime in South Africa to justify the well-known excesses of their somewhat less than paternal rule. In any case, surely truly wise Masters would keep quiet about it simply to avoid its potential to cause havoc, in the way that the Aryan concept was used by the Nazis. (Both the Tibetan and Tom frequently withhold other information for which, they claim, we are not ready.)

Acceptance of such ideology from alleged discarnate entities is, of course, extremely dangerous, both for the recipient and for society as a whole. It is bad enough to accept such evil from raving fanatics like Adolf Hitler, but taking it from invisible beings surely borders on criminal naivety, yet adherents of the Nine are content to accept Tom's teaching on such complex and enduringly divisive issues as the Jewish failure to accept Jesus as

Messiah, abortion, homosexuality and the spiritual inferiority of Islam. The invisible, insubstantial – and for all we know non-existent – Tom's pronouncements on such subjects is taken as, quite literally, gospel.

James Hurtak does not actually call the Muslims the 'Children of Darkness' in so many words, but talks instead about the 'anti-universe', or 'the violation of the Living Light exemplified in the Kabba, the Black Cube in Mecca.'[31] He claims it represents 'the anti-power of life' and, most tellingly, 'the anti-Christos'. The nearest he gets to a bald statement is when writing that the Black Cube 'functions with Alpha Draconis [for Hurtak, one of the seats of the "fallen spiritual powers"] for the Children of Darkness'.[32] By damning the most sacred object of Islam he is, of course, also implicitly damning Muslims themselves as the 'Children of Darkness'. One of his 'Keys' dealing specifically with the sym-bolism of the Black Cube, states:

With this key we can understand how fallen universes are delivered through the galactic wars of the Sons of Light versus the Sons of Darkness.[33]

The righteous must clearly see the spiritual dialectic taking place between those who choose the Pyramid of Light as the touchstone for evolution into the higher spiral of Light as opposed to those who choose the Black Cube.[34]

Hurtak does refer to the 'higher message' of some parts of the Koran,[35] but he seems to say that only the passages that accord with the Old Testament are worthy of note. Considering that even his more New Age pronouncements only partly obscure his own version of Christian fundamentalism, this validation of whatever agrees with the Old Testament should hardly surprise us. So what is Hurtak's view of Judaism?

Hurtak uses the word 'Israel' often and is fond of mentioning the Old Testament, but it is clear that, like Tom speaking through Phyllis Schlemmer, he thinks that the Jews were a specially holy people who made a terrible mistake by rejecting Jesus as the Messiah. And, not surprisingly, he announces that followers of the Keys are the 'True Israel'.[36] Hurtak – and others – make much of a prophecy in Isaiah 19:19–20 in relation to the Great Pyramid:

> In that day shall there be an altar to the Lord in the land of Egypt, and a pillar at the border thereof to the Lord. And it shall be a sign and for a witness unto the Lord of hosts in the land of Egypt: for they shall cry unto the Lord because of the oppressors, and he shall send them a saviour, and a great one, and he shall deliver them.

As an apparent prophecy of the Second Coming, this is a favourite quotation of Christian fundamentalists and New Agers alike. The 'altar to the Lord' has – bizarrely – become identified with the Great Pyramid, sometimes linked with the imminent discovery of a hidden chamber within it (as in Hurtak's writings). Even psychic H.C. Randall-Stevens, writing of hidden chambers beneath the Sphinx in the 1920s, uses this same prophecy, adding: 'I quote this here because my occult teaching has proved to me that the Great Sphinx and Pyramids of Gizeh is [sic] partly what is referred to.'[37] And his communicators told him that the time to which this prophecy referred was now.

It is very odd that we have never seen any of these writers continue the quotation. After saying that the Egyptians will 'know the Lord' – that is, be converted to the worship of Yahweh – it goes on (verse 22): 'And the Lord shall smite Egypt: he shall smite and heal it.' But shall he smite it in the form of the self-appointed 'righteous', like Hurtak, for its Islamic devotion? And what form shall the subsequent healing take?

We recognise with a sinking heart that recent Internet postings of Graham Hancock and Robert Bauval have taken on a new, stridently messianic tone. For example, as we noted earlier, Bauval wrote on 29 July 1998:

The millennium is rushing in. There is much work to do for

all who feel part of the same quest, namely to bring about a new and much needed spiritual and intellectual change for this planet. Giza, without a doubt, has a major role to play.

And Hancock:

Poised on the edge of a millennium, at the end of a century of unparalleled wickedness and bloodshed in which greed has flourished, humanity faces a stark choice between matter and spirit – the darkness and the light.

Presented with such authority, it is tempting to take this on face value, but does that statement bear closer scrutiny? Has not humanity always faced that 'stark choice'? And isn't the 'unparalleled' nature of twentieth-century wickedness the result of, not some quantum leap of evilness, but the invention of the means to inflict suffering on an unparalleled scale – whether the atom bomb or the Blitzkrieg bombers? We have also seen a great upsurge in matters of the spirit, of the light, in the form of unparalleled social and medical advances, in welfare reform and sensitivity towards the mentally and physically sick, and understanding of the needs of cultures so cruelly oppressed in previous epochs. It has not been all bad.

In fact, the twentieth century was simply 'unparalleled'. It was one of extremes. When it was evil it was astonishingly so, but when it showed its heart, great things were achieved that outshone all the noble writings of the most luminous and self-denying saint. It was a century of action, of communication, of enormous energy, often wrong-headed and usually wrong-footed, but – at least in the West – it was a century of hard-won freedom, a great upwelling of self-expression and an unprecedented hunger for information. It may have been corrupt but it also exposed corruption; it was certainly evil but it brought down evil with unprecedented vigour; and if it was greedy, it was happier than ever before to share more of its wealth with the less fortunate. Previous centuries would have turned their backs and left them to get on with it.

So why are Graham Hancock and Robert Bauval so keen to implant in us the idea that modern man is in a uniquely fallen state? Why do they place a sweeping – and what many would feel to be an inaccurate – emphasis on the 'unparalleled evil' of the times in which we live? Are they implying that we need to be rescued from it, and that our rescuers – our saviours – are merely waiting in the wings for us to welcome them in? Hancock and Bauval appear to be preparing us for some imminent spiritual upheaval. As Bauval portentously ended his announcement of the setting up of the Magic 12: 'The World is with Child . . .'.[38] Wittingly or unwittingly, he perfectly echoes Aleister Crowley's vision of the coming Aeon of the Child.

But is their agenda the same as Hurtak's? They are certainly familiar with him and his work, including *The Keys of Enoch*, although of course this does not mean that they are disciples of his. What *is* clear is that the essential message in their books – from *The Orion Mystery* to *The Mars Mystery* – fits the same overall agenda, bringing it to a much wider, global audience and helping to pave the way for the acceptance of Hurtak/the Nine's ideology.

Apocalypse now

The new belief system wears a coat of many colours. It derives from several different groups, which it actively draws together to make a homogenous whole. It is carefully crafted, playing on humankind's kneejerk response to certain potent symbols and emotional triggers. This strange new hybrid religion is specifically designed to appeal to the fundamentalist side of several different religions – except, of course, for Islam. Although it may appear at first glance that the teachings given through the likes of Hurtak, Schlemmer and Carla Rueckert are very modern, full of technological discussion, in fact, when stripped down to their essence, they are revealed to be no different from the more extreme beliefs of old-fashioned fundamentalist Christians.

There is the same emphasis on the apocalyptic battle between good and evil, light and dark, the expectation of the imminent advent of some kind of saviour figure, and the rapture that will carry the righteous off into heaven for eternal life while the sinners are damned forever. Although it may appear odd that James Hurtak would have so much in common with Lambert Dolphin Jr, in fact, they share many attitudes and aims. And in *The Only Planet of Choice* and *The Keys of Enoch* there is a special emphasis on Israel, both place and people, which is likely to appeal to Jewish fundamentalists. As we have seen, Lambert Dolphin Jr shares many aspirations with right-wing Israelis, which led to collaboration on investigations beneath the Temple Mount.

We have also noted that Hurtak's system embraces all the major religions of the United States – even welcoming such exclusivist groups as the Mormons. This new hybrid belief system also incorporates the main esoteric developments of the last two hundred years, such as the Great White Brotherhood, Ascended Masters, root races and Atlantis, besides major twentieth-century phenomena including Grey aliens and UFOs. This élite has notable exceptions: it does not include a major religion of African-Americans or of the Arab world. Muslims are not invited.

Skilfully puppetmastering the complex process of drawing all these threads together are, in many cases, the intelligence agencies, whose interests and involvements in the development of belief systems is now firmly established. Time and time again the anti-Muslim strand of this conspiracy becomes blindingly obvious, but why would the likes of the CIA be actively encouraging it? The whole tenor of this plot is one of preparation, of sowing the seeds of a certain mindset in as many people as possible in advance of some global event.

The possibility must be seriously considered that the conspirators are preparing the ground for some kind of major occurrence, a revelatory event that will suddenly, dramatically and radically change the world forever. What form this might take is uncertain – a carefully stage-managed 'return of the gods' to Giza before a mass audience, perhaps – but what is certain is that these people have the resources and technology to present such an event.

With or without such a stupendous moment, our minds are nevertheless being prepared to accept the beliefs and dictates of a coming new world order, whether it takes the form of stage-managed theocracy or some other kind of insidious fundamentalism. As the stories of Hitler's Germany and countless other examples from history prove beyond doubt, ordinary decent folk can only too easily be persuaded to commit atrocities against their fellow man if they truly believe it is part of a grand design – in Nazi Germany's case, the triumph of the master race. Brute force is not enough to turn the masses into monsters baying for blood; this will only happen if they are won over, hearts, minds – and souls. People are more easily persuaded by invitations to join a glorious gang, whether the Nazis or the 'righteous', by an appeal to the spirit than by mere empty rhetoric, or even brute force. Why, we wonder, is the CIA so keen to help promote anti-Islamic material? Why does it want us to think like that?

What any kind of fundamentalism does quite deliberately and explicitly is create divisions in society: Them and Us, the Light and the Dark, the Righteous and the Wicked, the Nazis and the Jews, the Israelis and the Palestinians . . . There is no room for rationality, intellectual questioning, challenge to the status quo, progress. More significantly, fundamentalists are easy to control – and their leaders have absolute power.

Control of the masses is ultimately what this is about. The idea that powerful and incredibly advanced beings will come to snatch us from the brink of disaster and make the world a better place for the future is, of course, enormously attractive. It sounds too good to be true. It may give us comfort and hope – but it comes at a price. Belief in the space gods and the heightened expectancy of their benign intervention undermines our collective self-esteem. It implies that the human race was given civilisation because it was too feeble to civilise itself, and that it has needed subtle guidance from the extraterrestrials throughout history. Now that humankind has really made a thorough mess of things, its only hope of salvation is to await the return of the gods to rectify the situation.

The image it promotes of mankind is essentially negative. It is basically the same message that made Christianity such a success as a state-sanctioned religion, taking away the autonomy of the individual and halting intellectual, scientific and cultural progress for centuries. The Christian message maintained that we were all born sinners and live only by God's grace; our only hope is the promise of post-mortem bliss, provided that we surrender to the dictates of the priesthood.

The end result is a population of willing victims, brainwashed into believing they are little better than worms, at the mercy of God or space beings, without means of salvation except through them – or, of course, their human agents. The members of the tragic cult Heaven's Gate, who happily took poison, represent an extreme form of this mode of thought: life as a mere human on Earth is worth nothing compared to escape in a spaceship, even if you have to commit suicide to reach it.

The enormous potential of space gods or UFO cults should not be underestimated. As the ever-perceptive Jacques Vallée writes (the emphasis is his) in his *Messengers of Deception* (1979):

> *The group of people who will first manage to harness the fear of cosmic forces and the emotions surrounding UFO contact to a political purpose will be able to exert incredible spiritual blackmail.*[39]

Others besides Vallée have realised this. Clearly, although there is no way of knowing all the details, the conspirators are creating the perfect conditions for something to happen to effectively give them control over the masses – over us. As we have seen, this could amount to the return of the ancient gods, or – much more likely – merely empty promises and cynically manufactured expectations.

The potential for population control is disturbing enough ordinarily, but taken together with the hysteria of endtimes expectation surrounding the Millennium, a truly explosive future is, we fear, guaranteed. Again, Jacques Vallée gets to the heart of the matter. In *Revelations* (1992), he writes: 'As we reach the Millennium, the belief in the imminent arrival of extraterrestrials in our midst is a fantasy that is as powerful as any drug, as revolutionary as any delusion that marked the last millennium, as poisonous as any of the great irrational upheavals of history.'[40]

Vallée goes on to compare this belief with the ideology of the master race that drove the Nazis to commit their worst atrocities. And in *Messengers of Deception* he lists six 'social consequences' of the hold of the UFO cults. These include '*The contactee propaganda undermines the image of human beings as masters of their own destiny*' and '*Contactee philosophies often include belief in higher races and in totalitarian systems that would eliminate democracy*.'[41]

Once before, a similar millennial mood was successfully harnessed in a way that changed the world: two thousand years ago, in a backwater of the Roman Empire, one man tapped into the prevailing hysterical messianic expectation and the result was Christianity. Theology and personal belief apart, the effect of this was to create generations of happy slaves who believed they came into the world as sinners and required the Church to order every detail of their lives. From that point of view at least, Christianity has been a huge success. But now it is largely losing its grip, something new, but similar, is required.

Could the early years of the twenty-first century see the emergence of a new Jesus or a new Moses to make sense of our puny, worthless lives and hand down from above a new set of commandments? Will the prophesied 'return of the Great Initiate' become a reality, thanks to some carefully contrived stage management? This new leader or Messiah figure will be backed by a massive politico-religious movement – a New World Order of zealots – the infrastructure of which is already in place.

Significantly, Ira Einhorn, who had a unique position as an observer of the Nine during the 1970s and who has no doubts about their reality as discarnate intelligences, warns that they are dangerous. He told us:

I wouldn't give my energies to something I couldn't see. That's very dangerous. It's giving up one's freedom, and if we do that we're back in the concentration camps . . . It's a form of psychic fascism. In ET contacts, or contacts with entities, there's got to be some democracy. You can't just *believe*. You can suspend disbelief for a while in order to experience the phenomenon, but that's as far as it goes.[42]

As we have seen, more and more people do 'just believe'. But what they will become because of it remains to be seen. There are worrying signs. As Tom/Atum, spokesman for the Council of Nine, himself says:

If it [the Earth] continues in the manner which it is now, around or after the year 2000 Planet Earth will no longer be able to exist as it is now. So the civilizations are attempting to cleanse it and bring it back into balance.[43]

Time to come of age

There are two possible interpretations of our data. In the first scenario the people behind the orchestration believe that contact with some alien intelligence – the gods of the past – is possible and they are trying to establish it. Perhaps they are searching for some physical device, a stargate, while also investigating other telepathic or psychic means of communication. This search would explain the frantic but secret activity in Egypt, which may be all the more intense if they are looking for a material doorway through which they believe the Nine will imminently step. This belief would also explain the conspirators' interest in Mars and Sirius, while on the other hand ensuring that the public make the connection between Egypt and extraterrestrials as part of a 'softening-up' exercise to prepare us for contact.

This hypothesis depends on the nature of the gods themselves. Who are they, and why should we listen to them? As we have seen, they claim to be the Nine, the ancient Ennead of Heliopolis, each representing a different kind of sovereignty, ruling a distinct area of human life and emotion. Isis was the mother goddess, who also governed magic, and Geb was the Egyptian Jove, who ruled all fruits of the earth. Those gods are bringers of good things, and we might reasonably welcome them to our planet in the expectation of the end of heartache and destitution. But what if the Nine are a Trojan Horse – it may seem harmless enough, but how do we know what really lies in wait inside?

This suspicion also occurred to Jon Povill, when he was subcontracted by Gene Roddenberry to write the movie script of *The Nine* in 1975. According to Roddenberry's biographer, Joel Engle, when Povill had completed the script:

> He recognised that if the purpose of the script was to prepare Earthlings for the arrival of these entities from beyond, then he may have been unwittingly setting up the world for an invasion of evil intent; he couldn't be sure that The Nine were necessarily benevolent.[44]

The second of our two scenarios is that the arrival of the gods or 'space brothers' is entirely and deliberately manufactured. Real space gods may never land on Earth, but the expectation of their imminent arrival could well be an end in itself, with potentially the same benefits for those who seek to control us.

In this scenario the activity at Giza could be explained merely as an attempt to control the most magically potent place on Earth – when all eyes are turned on it, and when expectations of some great revelation are at their highest. What proof could the man and woman in the street ever have that the gods really are coming? We would have to take the authorities' word for it, and by the time it had dawned on us that no god had landed – and probably never would – we could already have been effectively enslaved by a very terrestrial power, under the guise of 'strong leadership' in an alleged state of emergency.

A new religion is taking shape in the name of the Great

Heliopolitan Ennead. Already, as we have seen, many obey their instructions to the letter. But in that case, the Ennead must have undergone a remarkable metamorphosis over the millennia, since it was not the custom of the Egyptian deities to give orders or commandments. One distinctive feature of the religion was that its gods did not demand to be worshipped like the later wrathful and tyrannical Yahweh. As Michael Rice points out in *Egypt's Legacy*:

> It was not the purpose of the [Egyptian] priesthoods to 'worship' the gods . . . Unlike the gods of Sumer and particularly unlike the gods of the Semitic-speaking peoples of the ancient Near East, the Egyptian powers did not require the constant reassurance that those divinities seemed always to need.[45]

Neither did the Ennead issue commandments, nor did they instigate any holy wars. The real Nine just *were*.

Had the gods of ancient Egypt ever looked at the true heart of mankind, with all our flaws, they would not have seen slaves but proud sharers in an eternal divinity – not merely, as Whitley Strieber says, the 'companions of the creator', but each of us bearing a part of godhood ourselves, carrying the divine, creative spark. Just as the Nine gods of the Ennead represent different aspects of the One, so we are all fragments of that endless energy.

While – or perhaps because – we personally have no problem with the concept of the Egyptian gods, and, in fact, have enormous respect for that ancient religion, we have no hesitation in denouncing the Council of Nine as imposters. They are not and could never be the Nine gods of the Great Ennead because, among many other reasons, they are ignorant, divisive and show none of the true characteristics of the archetypes they are supposed to represent. But even if – suspending disbelief temporarily – they really are who they claim to be there is still, surely, a case for rejecting them: if the mighty Isis herself were to utter the same kind of pernicious nonsense as do the Nine, it would be within our rights as fully mature, thinking human beings to reject not only the message, but even the great goddess herself. Whether or not this is the only planet of choice, free will is our greatest weapon against the wiles of the insidious and subtly corrupting Nine. No one needs gods like that.

And even if – in the most unlikely scenario – the Council of Nine really are the ancient Egyptian gods, then there is yet another problem. We have no way of knowing whether their imminent return was their own idea, or whether they have been summoned by the conspirators to coincide with their own private programme of events for the future. If this is the case, then the puppetmasters of the Millennium are not only creating, then exploiting, our own expectations, but they are also exploiting the gods themselves.

Exploitation of the Ennead is not to be recommended, particularly as Set, the god of destruction who killed Osiris, is one of them. A wrathful, Yahweh-like god of the desert, he was loathed and feared, although it seems that he had his own secret cult. It is telling that while the Council of Nine – if, indeed, they are the Great Ennead – should include Set, he never appears in their channelled material. Are they saving Set up for later? Has he arrived already, hidden away in the Trojan Horse that is the Nine? Is Set *here*? And if so, what role will he play in their plans? Will he be on the side of Them – or Us? There is something sinister in the Council of Nine's avoidance of this dark god, the ultimate archetype of destruction.

Andrija Puharich, in *The Sacred Mushroom*, wrote that Sirius was the star of the *god* 'Sept',[46] which we found puzzling, because the ancient Egyptians deified Sirius as the *goddess* Sothis, who was linked with Isis. In other words, Sirius should be linked with the feminine, not the male, principle. But there are two authorities who do make the connection between Sirius and a male god – the Crowleyite writer Kenneth Grant and Aleister Crowley himself (who connect the star, and Sept, with Set).[47] We find it intriguing that, to our knowledge, the only authors to do so are

Crowley(ite) and Puharich, despite the complete lack of Egyptological evidence for this belief.

This is, in our view, symptomatic of a disturbing undercurrent of the new belief system. There is a suspicious lack of any emphasis on the feminine, even where, as with the Sirius connection, goddesses should be given their due. The puppetmasters of the new religion have effectively censored the feminine. Even though the Heliopolitan Ennead includes four goddesses – Tefnut, Nut, Isis and Nepthys – Tom never, to our knowledge, even refers to them, let alone encourages due reverence to them. Yet the worship of at least one of these goddesses, Isis, was a major part of the ancient Egyptian religion. How the Nine have changed over the centuries!

As our investigation proceeded, we began to realise how insidiously *male* this conspiracy is, and how its message is implicitly anti-feminine, especially as expressed in James Hurtak's *The Keys of Enoch*. Perhaps in order to emulate the patriarchal writings of the Old Testament – and so to appeal to both fundamentalist Jews and Christians – its tone is resolutely male-centred, and if nothing else, in our opinion, it is doing the world a great disservice by continuing to propagate such a dangerous attitude. We, among many others, have come to believe that if there is any one cause of today's ills it is the legacy of 2,000 years of orchestrated repression of women and the hatred and fear of the feminine principle. If a new belief system is necessary, surely it would be better to use it to correct past errors, not to compound them by preaching yet more patriarchal dogma?

Yet, as we have seen, there are many who want our future society to be based on Freemasonry, in the belief that it bestows spiritual and sociological enlightenment on its members – that is, with very few exceptions, on men. Masonic ideas about women tend to be resolutely outdated, unenlightened and at best patronising. Once again, we are faced with the possibility of having our society re-made in the image of male dominance, thus perpetuating many of the least admirable trends of the West's history, and in fact preventing the advent of true spiritual progress, which – if

we are to take the ancient Egyptian knowledge at all seriously –
must always be based on the opposite and equal balance of male
and female principles.

We find it offensive that the ancient Egyptian religion has been
cynically exploited by the conspirators, especially because what
it taught, above all, was the necessity for *balance* – light and
dark, male and female, as exemplified in the duo of the good goddess Isis and her dark sister Nepthys, and Isis and her consort
Osiris. Although their worshippers may have had their favourites,
the gods themselves were deemed to be absolutely equal, eter-
nally maintaining the divine balance. All this has been ignored
by those who have hijacked the Heliopolitan religion, repackag-
ing it for a mass market, and irreverently using the gods as brand
names for their new gimcrack products. The names may be the
same, but *this* Isis is merely a new label obscuring the same old,
profoundly dangerous patriarchal attitudes.

We do not deny that humanity faces enormous problems, many
of its own making. But precisely because we have decisions to
make we must not abdicate personal responsibility and hand over
our autonomy, both individual and collective, to those who come
bearing messages from the space gods, but whose strings are
being pulled by the cynical puppetmasters of government cabals
and military and intelligence agencies. To hand over our own
power is, we argue, entirely to miss the point of being human.

The extraterrestrials, as claimed by the believers, take all the
credit for all the achievements of human civilisation, but blame
us for all the failures. Why else would they have to come to
rescue us (in their nuts-and-bolts spacecraft)?

Even if the Council of Nine turn out to be real, in our own view,
they – and their pernicious message – should be roundly
rejected. Even if the human race began as their inferiors we seem
to have out-evolved them, certainly where basic morality is concerned: at least in principle we now know the difference between
good and evil, and unity and division – or we should, by now.
Recent history gives us no excuse. If Earth was ever colonised by
the star people, surely now is the time to claim our independence

from them, not to welcome them, starry-eyed and ignorant, like members of some galactic cargo cult greeting the pilots of supply planes.

Perhaps there is no better time to realise that all men and women themselves are godlike heroes of almost unlimited potential. And if there is any one over-riding message for the Millennium, it is that the time for mankind to come of age is long overdue.

Epilogue:

The Real Stargate?

The Stargate Conspiracy became, for us, a profoundly unsettling detective story, a 'case' that, whether we like it or not, involves all of us as the endtimes machine swings into action. But inevitably, having exposed the intricate layers of human agenda behind the mysteries of Egypt and Mars, we ourselves may appear to be resolutely sceptical on all matters spiritual or mystical. This is not so. Fortunately, as our investigation proceeded, certain lines of research opened up a completely new angle on many of the most intractable mysteries discussed in this book, enabling us to offer an elegant, exciting – and unashamedly otherworldly – solution to those problems.

Originally we had intended to concentrate much more on the Heliopolitan religion, and had spent many months researching the Pyramid Texts and other material, but because we soon discovered the existence of the conspiracy, our early research was very largely put aside. However, when we began to delve into the work of Andrija Puharich on shamanism, it reminded us of certain elements repeated throughout the Pyramid Texts, and gradually a revolutionary possibility began to take shape in our minds. We noted that Puharich himself linked the shamanic experience, the use of psychoactive substances and the Heliopolitan religion, although he failed to develop the idea in print (no matter how far he may have taken it privately). And we were also fascinated by the implications of the fact that the CIA have spent so much time and resources on experimenting with shamanic techniques and mind-altering drugs.

The Pyramid Texts suggested to us that the afterlife journey of the king could also describe the astral flight characteristic of shamanism. Excitingly, the latest anthropological research into the phenomenon of shamanism could well provide the key to understanding the mystery of the extraordinarily advanced knowledge of the ancient Egyptians and the secrets of the Heliopolitan religion.

The breakthrough

Shamans are what used to be called medicine men and women, natural-born psychics who are nevertheless highly trained to interpret dreams, heal the sick and guide people through knowledge that comes to them during their ecstatic trances. They are found in what are generally taken to be 'primitive' tribal societies, from Siberia to the Amazonian rain forest. These adepts take shamanic 'flights' out of the body into the realms normally inaccessible to mankind and return with specific information of great practical use.

In 1995 a remarkable book was published in Switzerland entitled *Le serpent cosmique, l'ADN et les origines du savior* (*The Cosmic Serpent, DNA and the Origins of Knowledge*) by Swiss anthropologist Jeremy Narby. (It was first published in English in 1998.) It presents the results of Narby's personal study of Amazonian shamans, and reveals the remarkable scope of the information shamans glean during the ecstatic trances they induce by taking natural hallucinogenic substances, primarily one called ayahuasca. From this research, Narby developed a theory about the origins of that knowledge that – we believe – has enormous significance for an investigation of the mysteries of ancient Egypt.

In the mid-1980s Narby was studying for his doctorate among the indigenous people of the Peruvian Amazon, working on an environmental project. Like many before him, he soon became fascinated by the astounding botanical knowledge of these so-called 'primitive' people, specifically their medicinal use of certain rare plants. He was impressed by the range of plant-derived medicines used by the tribal shamans – ayahuasqueros – and by their effectiveness, especially after they cured a long-standing back problem which European doctors had proved completely incapable of treating. The more he learned, the more intrigued he became about the ways in which the Amazonian natives had developed or acquired this knowledge. The odds against them coming up with even one of these recipes by chance or even by experimentation are simply overwhelming. There are some 80,000 species of plants in the Amazonian rain forest, so to discover an effective remedy using a mixture of just two of them would theoretically require the testing of every possible combination – about 3,700,000,000. It does not end there: many of their medicines involve several plants, and even then such a calculation does not allow for experimentation with the often extremely complex procedures necessary to extract the active ingredients and produce a potent mixture.

One good example of this mysterious medicinal knowledge is ayahuasca itself, a combination of just two plants. The first comes from the leaves of a shrub and contains a hormone naturally secreted in the human brain, dimethyltryptamine, a powerful hallucinogen only discovered by Western science in 1979. If taken orally, though, it is broken down by an enzyme in the stomach and becomes totally ineffective, so the second component of ayahuasca, extracted from a creeper, contains several substances that protect the dimethyltryptamine from that specific enzyme.

In effect, ayahuasca is a designer drug, made to order. It is as if the exact requirements of the mixture were specified in advance, then the correct ingredients chosen to meet the requirements. But how? How could anyone, even sophisticated Western botanists, have found the perfect ingredients without spending decades – perhaps even centuries – on trial and error? How can the 'primitive' Amazonian natives have known the properties of these two plants? After all, the odds against them coming up with this combination by accident are truly astronomical. As Narby writes:

> So here are people without electron microscopes who choose, among some 80,000 Amazonian plant species, the leaves of a bush containing a hallucinogenic brain hormone, which they combine with a vine containing substances that inactivate an enzyme of the digestive tract, which would otherwise block the hallucinogenic effect. And they do this to modify their consciousness.
>
> It is as if they knew about the molecular properties of plants *and* the art of combining them, and when one asks them how they know these things, they say their knowledge comes directly from hallucinogenic plants.[1]

Another example given by Narby is that of curare.[2] This powerful nerve poison is another 'made-to-order' drug, whose ingredients this time come from several different plants and fit a very precise set of requirements. As Narby points out, the natives needed a substance that, when smeared on the tips of blowpipe darts, would not only kill the animal but also ensure that it would fall to the ground. Tree monkeys, for example, if shot with an unpoisoned arrow, often tighten their grip on the branches with a reflex action and so die out of reach of the hunter. The meat itself would, of course, have to be free from poison and safe to eat. It seemed like a very tall order, but curare fits all these requirements: it is a muscle relaxant (killing by arresting the respiratory muscles); it is only effective when injected into the bloodstream – hence its delivery by blowpipe; and it has no effect when taken orally:

The invention of curare is a truly astounding thing. The most common type requires a complex method of preparation in which several plants are boiled for three days, during which lethal fumes are produced. And the final result needs a specific piece of technology – the blowpipe – to deliver it. How was all this discovered in the first place?

The problem becomes even more baffling when it is realised that forty different types of curare are used across the Amazon rain forest, all with the same properties but each using slightly different ingredients as the same plants do not grow in every region. Therefore, in effect, curare was invented forty times. The Western world only learned of it in the 1940s, when it first began to be used as a muscle relaxant during surgery.

The Amazonians themselves do not claim to have invented curare, but that it was *given* to them by the spirits, through their shamans.

These are just two examples from a vast range of vegetable mixtures used by the peoples of the Amazon, the full extent of which has not yet been catalogued by modern botanists. Realising that it was nonsense to suggest that these complex recipes could have been achieved by experimentation, Narby began to ask local people and shamans how they had acquired this knowledge. They told him that the properties of plants and the recipes for combining them are given directly to the shaman by very powerful spirit entities while he is in ecstatic trance under the influence of hallucinogens such as ayahuasca. (Of course this raises a fascinating chicken-and-egg type of problem. If the shamans discovered the secret properties of ayahuasca only by ingesting it, how did they know about them in the first place?)

This realisation led Narby on to his own personal quest to research this neglected aspect of shamanism, which included taking ayahuasca himself. Many anthropologists before Narby had recorded the claim that the shaman obtains knowledge by the ingestion of hallucinogens, but none had ever taken this seriously enough to follow it up. He found that this was a shared feature of shamanism across the world, and that the tribes ascribe the origins and the techniques of their culture to knowledge gleaned by their shamans while in ecstatic trance, during which they encounter guiding entities who teach them.

Narby himself, on his first experience with ayahuasca, encountered a pair of gigantic snakes that lectured him on his insignificance as a human being and the limits of his knowledge, which turned out to be an important personal turning point. He began to question his Western preconceptions and approached his subsequent studies in a more open-minded and less scientifically arrogant way. His own book is itself an example of the way in which the shamanic experience can impart new knowledge. Narby writes that the serpents induced thoughts in his mind that he was incapable of having himself.[3]

The properties and methods of combining plants to achieve specific results are not the only things communicated through the trance state by spiritual entities in this way. The Amazonian tribes ascribe their knowledge of specific techniques, such as the art of weaving and their mastery of woodworking, to the same source. What the shamans receive while in trance is useful knowledge that often, in the case of healing, actually saves lives.

Aside from the question of the reality of such entities, the very idea of obtaining practical tips and actual information by such a method is, to our culture, absurd. There are, surely, only two ways of obtaining knowledge: it is either worked out in logical steps by experiment or trial-and-error; or it is taught by someone who, or some other culture which, has already worked it out.

This, in a nutshell, forms the problem of the origins of the knowledge of the ancient Egyptians, such as how they built the 'impossible' Great Pyramid. Techniques appeared to come out of nowhere, without any apparent process of logical or historical development. Since no archaeological evidence of stage-by-stage technological development has been found, it can be assumed that the process never occurred. This may seem crazy, but where are all the failed pyramids predating those of the Old Kingdom? The only alternative seems to be that the ancient Egyptians learned their techniques whole and fully formed from somebody else – a lost civilisation, or visiting extraterrestrials perhaps.

What if there is a third way of obtaining useful and unique information: the way of the shaman, where knowledge is somehow obtained directly from its source?

The extraordinary botanical knowledge of the Amazonian peoples forms, in fact, an exact parallel to the building expertise of the ancient Egyptians. Not only should it lie beyond the skills of their time and place, but it also stands far in advance of today's scientific knowledge.

Questions and answers

Shamanism is considered to be a phenomenon of 'primitive' societies, those who still live at roughly the level of the Stone Age while surrounded by the extreme sophistication of the modern world. It was outgrown by the 'advanced' cultures thousands of years ago. However, can we imagine that shamanic rituals could be practised as a culture moved from primitive to advanced, perhaps at an even more sophisticated level than is found in today's Amazonian rain forest? If such a phenomenon could be conceived, what would be the limits of the knowledge obtained through the shamans' curious art?

Several writers have recently noted clear signs of shamanistic influence at work in ancient Egypt. Andrew Collins, for example, has written of the shamanistic nature of the 'Elder Culture' that he believes was responsible for the great achievements of Egypt, but he has also surmised that they developed the advanced techniques that enabled them to build the pyramids and carve the Great Sphinx.[4] Could the priesthood of Heliopolis have been in essence a college of shamans, free to apply their closely guarded techniques for purposes of pure research? Could the shamanic hypothesis explain how the pyramid builders knew how to quarry, transport, shape and position immense blocks of stone, among many other baffling examples of their knowledge?

This would also account for an aspect of the ancient Egyptians' knowledge that has not been properly explored – its curiously selective nature. While they are justly famed for their mysterious expertise in pyramid building, there are certain areas that – perhaps bizarrely – appear to have been unknown arts to them. We have noted that, despite the use of colossal granite and limestone blocks and the extraordinary skill used in shaping them, the walls of the Valley Temple at Giza have been built in an oddly primitive way. And one sophisticated architectural feature completely missing in ancient Egypt was the arch. Perhaps this is because the development of the arch requires a conceptual leap, and its construction requires a theoretical knowledge of weight distribution. Maybe this is also the reason why the Egyptians do not seem to have mastered the art of bridge-building.

Recently French Egyptologist Jean Kerisel has argued persuasively that cracks in the granite slabs forming the ceiling of the King's Chamber were not, as previously thought, the result of an earthquake, but happened while the Great Pyramid was actually under construction.[5] This, he suggests, was because the builders did not understand the consequences of working with two materials – limestone and granite – of different composition, which would compress at different rates under the enormous weight of stone pressing down on them. (If Kerisel is correct, this would also cast doubt on the theory that the cavities above the King's Chamber were intended as stress-relieving chambers for the building.)

We have observed that the Amazonian shamans receive specific answers to specific questions, such as the herbal recipe for the cure for a specific illness, but rarely more or less than is needed. The same appears to be true of the Egyptians, who appear to have had information only about, for example, ways of moving huge blocks of stone. Because bridges and arches needed new concepts of building, they never asked the right questions in order to be told how to build them.

Could this be how the Dogon have such otherwise inexplicable knowledge of the Sirius system? If the Amazonian shamans can directly obtain information about the chemical properties of plants, could they not have asked their guides: 'Tell us about the brightest star in the sky. That one there'?

There are some very clear and sometimes strikingly precise parallels between the religion of ancient Egypt and the shamanic visions described by Jeremy Narby. Narby cites the experiences of anthropologist Michael Harner among the Conibo Indians of the Peruvian Amazon in the 1960s. Harner himself took the shamans' hallucinogenic drink and later he wrote:

> For several hours after drinking the brew, I found myself, although awake, in a world literally beyond my wildest dreams. I met bird-headed people, as well as dragon-like creatures who explained that they were the true gods of this world.[6]

'Bird-headed people', 'the true gods of this world': this seems to be startling confirmation of the reality of the ancient Egyptian pantheon, which, of course, included the ibis-headed Thoth and the hawk-headed Horus, besides many animal-headed gods and goddesses such as the lioness-headed Sekhmet and the jackal-headed Anubis. If modern tribal shamans, in their drug-induced ecstatic trances, have access to the dimension where such beings live, could it not be that the shamanic priests of Heliopolis also knew the secret of speaking to the gods directly in this way? Interestingly, Harner himself noted the similarity between the bird-headed people of his vision and the gods of ancient Egypt. (And it inevitably calls to mind Saul Paul Sirag and Ray Stanford's visions of the hawk-headed Spectra as described in Chapter 5.)

In his review of world shamanism, Jeremy Narby noted many common features, such as the prevalence of snakes as imparters of wisdom, even in areas where there are no snakes. Certain themes recur in all shamanic visions, one of the most central being that of a ladder joining heaven and earth, which the shaman ascends to meet the spirits of wisdom. As Narby says:

They talk of a ladder – or a vine, a rope, a spiral staircase, a twisted rope ladder – that connects heaven and earth and which they use to gain access to the world of spirits. They consider these spirits have come from the sky and to have created life on earth.[7]

This imagery is found in the ancient Egyptian Pyramid Texts. For example, in Utterance 478 – which speaks of Isis as the person-ification of the ladder – it says:

As for any spirit or any god who will help me when I ascend to the sky on the ladder of the god; my bones are assembled for me, my limbs are gathered together for me, and I leap up to the sky in the presence of the god of the Lord of the ladder.[8]

And another utterance says:

A ladder is knotted together by Re before Osiris, a ladder is knotted together by Horus before his father Osiris when he goes to his spirit, one of them being on this side and one of them being on that, while I am between them.[9]

Ascension to the Milky Way is a central theme of the Pyramid Texts; in Colombia the ayahuasca vine is known as the 'ladder to the Milky Way'.[10]

Recognising the concept of shamanism in the Pyramid Texts radically changes our understanding of the ancient Egyptians and their religion – and perhaps even the whole nature of human potential. Could it be that the central 'ascension of the king' is not the description of his afterlife journey as is always believed, but the shamanic flight to the 'otherworld' – the realm of guiding spirits – that is undertaken in life? The two are not mutually exclusive, for the shamans know that the realm they enter when entranced is the portal to the eternal world of light where the spirits of the dead are taken, so the Pyramid Texts can be read as a description of both the shamanic and afterlife journeys. Traditionally, the journeying shaman is believed to have actually died, to be resurrected when his soul returns.

Although shamans are very special people, born with a natural psychic gift, they are nevertheless required to undergo fearsome initiations by ordeal, the horrors of which impinge on both the physical and spiritual levels. A classic feature of the shamanic initiation is a hellish out-of-the-body experience in which they appear to be torn limb from limb, after which they are magically reassembled. As Stanislav Grof writes:

> The career of many shamans start by the powerful experiences of unusual states of consciousness with the sense of going into the underworld, being attacked, dismembered, and then being put back together, and ascending to the supernal realm.[11]

This is strikingly reminiscent of the story of Osiris, with whom the king in the Pyramid Texts is identified, who is cut into pieces by the evil god Set, but magically reassembled by his lover Isis in order to father the hawk god Horus, who is in turn regarded as the reincarnation of Osiris as well as his son. As we have seen in the extract from Utterance 478, Isis is identified with the legendary ladder, up which the reassembled king climbs to heaven – clearly, a classic shamanic image.

The role of Isis is particularly interesting because it portrays the feminine principle as being essential to the shamanic journey. In fact, the whole concept of female initiates has been sadly neglected, but perhaps for unexpected reasons. At a London conference in October 1996 called The Incident, Jeremy Narby was questioned on why all the shamans he had mentioned in his talk were men. He replied that specially selected women often sit with the ayahuasqueros as, fuelled with the drug, they embark on their out-of-the-body adventures. The women actually accompany them and share in their experience, and afterwards, when they have returned to normal consciousness, help them to remember what took place in those other realms. But the important point is that the women do all this *without taking ayahuasca*. Clearly, the female companions of the shamans have no need of chemical aids for their spiritual flights. Why is not known, possibly because women's roles have traditionally been of less interest to anthropologists.

The mathematician, cyberneticist and mythologist Charles Musès has written extensively on shamanism. (As with most of his non-New Age/mystical writings under the pseudonym of 'Musaios', these are particularly incisive and persuasive.) He has noted the nature of its essential significance:

> The point of shamanism is really not ecstasy, 'archaic' or otherwise, or even 'healing', but rather the development of communication with a community of higher than human beings and a modus operandi for attaining an eventual transmutation to more exalted states and paths.[12]

Musès goes on to make the explicit parallel between this, the underlying objective of shamanism, and the religion of ancient Egypt. He equates the Duat – the afterlife realm to which the king travels – of the Pyramid Texts, not with a mythical otherworld but with the Tibetan Bardo, where spirits live between incarnations and which certain special people can visit during life.[13]

The Pyramid Texts also speak of the 'deceased' being transformed into a 'body of light' (*aker*), which again may imply more than a straightforward afterlife existence. Charles Musès says: 'The acquisition of a higher body by an individual meant also, by that very token, the possibility of communicating with beings already so endowed.'[14] In other words, anyone with a higher body can communicate with anyone else who exists in the light. Shamans, during their trips to the invisible realm, can make contact with all the higher beings who live there.

In our opinion, Jeremy Narby's ground-breaking work on shamanism has important implications for some of the recent theories concerning the origins of Egyptian wisdom, particularly those of the 'ancient astronaut' school. Proponents of such hypotheses, such as Alan F. Alford, tend to treat the myths and religious writings, such as the Pyramid Texts, in an excessively literal way. When the ancients tell us of meetings with part-animal, part-man entities, who descend to Earth or to whom the priest ascends, and who impart specific information, such researchers assume these to be garbled stories of actual meetings with exotic beings from outer space, making gods of astronauts.

Shamans living in the Amazonian rain forest today regularly describe identical experiences – sometimes under the watchful gaze of anthropologists – without the least suggestion of a descending spaceship or visitors from a lost continent.

But who are the entities from whom shamans have always received their invaluable knowledge?

It is possible that we will never be able to answer that question fully. Even shamans know that some mysteries and secrets are never meant to be understood. But once again, the work of Jeremy Narby may provide certain exciting clues about what it is that shamans – from ancient Heliopolis to today – tap into when they enter their exalted states of consciousness.

Narby noted that the visions of shamans across the world shared certain key images, the most fundamental being that of twin serpents that live inside every creature. The penny finally dropped for him when he read about Michael Harner's experience in 1961. He saw winged, dragonlike creatures who explained to him that they 'had created life on the planet in order to hide within the multitudinous forms . . . I learned that the dragon-like creatures were thus inside all forms of life, including man'.[15] Harner himself wrote that 'one could say they were almost like DNA', but added that he had no idea where the vision came from – certainly not from his own mind, as at that time he knew nothing about DNA. Whatever the origin of the words, this was to be a major inspiration: Narby realised that the image of 'serpents' living inside every living thing is, in fact, an excellent description of the strands of DNA.

Shamans ascribe the source of their remarkable knowledge to these twin serpents, like the two Narby himself encountered. Could it be that the 'primitive' belief that all living things are animated by the same single principle, described in this ubiquitous serpentine imagery, is actually correct and that what it has always described is DNA? Narby cites numerous examples, from ancient myths and the shamanistic lore of 'primitive' cultures from Peru to Australia, to support his superb connection between the serpents and DNA.

The shamans insist that the 'serpents' possess consciousness and that they enter into real dialogue with them. If the shamans are, in reality, somehow communicating with DNA, the implication is that it must be intelligent: the DNA of the ayahuasca plants, for example, must 'know' its own properties, but will only impart them to the shaman in answer to specific questions. This means that the DNA has to understand the question and be able to communicate with the shaman's own DNA. Can the DNA of one individual living creature really communicate with that of another?

Narby's theory still has a long way to go. For example, it is hard to see how intelligent DNA can explain the knowledge the shamans receive about specific techniques, such as weaving or mixing curare. The important achievement is that he has shown that shamans derive usable information by mental contact with some nonhuman source. And they do appear to be in touch with the 'gods', or at least some strange beings who exist in another dimension and share their undoubted powers with them.

Another very significant aspect of Narby's research is his identification of a common feature throughout the shamanistic cultures (and ancient myths): divine twins as the bringers of wisdom, 'the theme of double beings of celestial origin and creators of life'.[16] He points out, for example, quoting from Claude Lévi-Strauss, that the Aztec word *coatl*, as in the name Quetzalcoatl, means both 'snake' and 'twin'.[17] (Quetzalcoatl can be interpreted as either 'feathered serpent' or 'magnificent twin'.) Narby believes that the 'twin serpents' so often encountered during shamanic flights and which he himself experienced

represent the two strands of the double helix of DNA. This
reminds us of the two sets of twins in the Heliopolitan religion
(Isis and Osiris, Nepthys and Set) as well as the Nommo of the
Dogon, as described in Robert Temple's *The Sirius Mystery*, who
are also made up of sets of twins and descend to earth to civilise
mankind.[18] Again, Narby's shamanic theory provides an elegant –
and, in our view, much more plausible – alternative to the ubiquitous 'ancient astronaut' explanation for these myths.

Perhaps DNA has other secrets to impart. The genetic code in
the human genome is made up of just 3 per cent of its total
DNA – the function of the rest is unknown, and is officially
termed 'junk DNA'. Narby suggests that a better term would be
'mystery DNA'.[19] How many 'miracles' and how much potential
does the other 97 per cent encompass?

'Spirits from the sky'

Narby's ideas about DNA and shamanism throw a completely
new light on hitherto intractable historical mysteries. Were the
outline drawings of animals and birds on the sands of Nazca in
Peru meant to be guides to and celebrations of the shaman's
flight? Did the Dogon discover the secrets of Sirius simply by
asking their shamans' spirit guides? Were the massive stone
blocks that make up the giant pyramids of Egypt manoeuvred into
place according to the advice of the 'gods' visited by their priests
in trance?

Significantly the flight of the shaman also enables him to visit
far distant places and later describe what he saw and heard there –
in other words, remote viewing. This aspect of shamanism particularly intrigued anthropologist Kenneth Kensinger, who tested it
among the ayahuasqueros of the Amazon and found that they were
able to 'bring back' accurate information about distant places, as
well as tell him about the death of a relative before he heard about
it himself.[20] (Andrija Puharich also studied the remote-viewing
potential of shamans, as described in Chapter 6.)

We asked Jeremy Narby if he agreed with us that his ideas could account for the extraordinary knowledge implicit in the building of the pyramids. He pointed out that the Aztecs, Incas and Maya had constructed comparable temples, and that 'the double serpent, or Quetzalcoatl, or Viracocha, or whatever figure you take depending on the culture, teaches about curing, healing and plants, but also about astronomy, building techniques, technology – arts and crafts in general.'[21]

Narby was cautious about stepping outside his field of specialism. But was there really an ancient Egyptian equivalent of ayahuasca – and if so, what was it? Synchronistically, the Channel 4 television series, *Sacred Weeds*, went far in answering this question. This four-part series, first shown in August 1998, featured the use of natural hallucinogens in sacred practices such as shamanism. The final programme attempted to rediscover what some believed to be an ancient Egyptian ritual drug, the blue waterlily.

Although now very rare, this plant was commonly used both recreationally and ritually by the ancient Egyptians. It is frequently depicted in wall paintings and papyri, and even forms the design of the pillars of the great temple at Karnak. Egyptologists believed it to have been merely decorative, but the programme set out to determine if it had a psychoactive effect, which may well have been exploited in ancient Egypt. Interestingly, the lily was specifically associated with Ra-Atum. Seeing the way the plant flowers, shooting a long stem out of the water which then bursts into an open flower, it is easy to see the symbolic association with Atum's bursting forth from the primeval waters.

As tested on two volunteers, an extract from the blue lily proved to have the suspected narcotic effect. Towards the end of the programme historian Michael Carmichael, an American living in Oxford who is a specialist in the shamanic use of psychoactive plants, discussed the possibility that, in higher doses, it could be used to induce shamanic experiences.

We contacted Carmichael, who worked with R. Gordon Wasson, one of the pioneers of research into the shamanic use of drugs (see Chapter 5). He told us that there is abundant evidence for the use of psychoactive drugs in ancient Egypt, saying, 'there are so many that I don't know where to begin'.[22] Several are mentioned in the Ebers Papyrus (c. 1500 BCE, the oldest known medical text in the world). They are known to have included opium (imported from Crete), mandrake and cannabis. The psychoactive substances used by ancient cultures, including Egypt, have been studied by several researchers. Little if anything of this has found its way into the Egyptological literature because of its characteristic extreme conservatism.[23]

Several other scientists and researchers have studied the shamanic practices of ancient Egypt and their use of psychoactive drugs. They include Benny Shanon, a cognitive psychologist and philosopher at the Hebrew University in Jerusalem.

Carmichael agreed emphatically with Narby's observations that useful information can be gained by shamans in their ecstatic states, from communion with otherwordly entities. He told us:

> These substances are used as vehicles to expedite shamanistic performance, in that the shaman is able to elevate his consciousness to a new level, whereby he can experience nature at a much more astute, acute and engaged level than is the normal case with human perception. He is then able to witness natural phenomena which other people are not able to witness in normal states of consciousness . . . That is what gives him his deeper and more profound insights into nature and the world.[24]

But what are the entities? Are they 'real', or elaborate constructs of the shaman's mind? Carmichael pointed out that this question involved the whole philosophical and metaphysical argument about the nature of reality itself, and was probably unanswerable. We suggested that one test of the reality of the shaman's experience was whether the knowledge he acquired actually worked – which, as we have seen, it most assuredly does. Carmichael agreed.

Turning to the question of the inexplicable knowledge of the ancient Egyptians, Carmichael – who is well acquainted with the ideas of the New Egyptology – told us:

> My own belief at this point in time is that the pyramids were not built by a space-faring race that came from a Martian colony. I see no evidence for that whatsoever . . . While it's unsound of modern Egyptologists to presume that plants and other substances were used by the ancient Egyptians in sacred contexts solely for their decorative or the aesthetic properties, it would be just as unsound for us to believe that they had to build the pyramids in exactly the way that *we* suppose that they would have built them. It might not have been slaves and whips, nor may it necessarily have been through some sort of acoustic levitational technology. It may have been some other way. There may be a technology between those extremes. Shamanistic experience could well have been the door, the gate, the stargate through which the ancient Egyptian architects and engineers were able to achieve that technology.

So what are the entities? Nature spirits, the gods, a dramatisation from the shaman's subconscious mind, somehow personifying information picked up by ESP or even DNA? Or could the shaman really be in contact with beings on some far-off world?

Jeremy Narby told us: 'I guess this is what your average Amazonian shaman would testify: travelling in his mind to another planet.' He referred to the paintings of an Amazonian shaman, Pablo Ameringo, who depicts the things he sees under the influence of ayahuasca, saying:

> Different plants contain different molecules, and they set off different kinds of visions. There are even different kinds of ayahuascas, some of which are a lot more organic and make you see things about nature on Earth, whereas others will make you see things more like distant worlds with cities

and so forth. In Pablo Ameringo's paintings you get a bit of both. If you look at the paintings of the distant cities – because this is one of the common themes that comes up in the ayahuasca literature, distant cities with hypersophisticated technology and so on – they're filled with pyramids, and Babel towers, and minarets.

Although such scenes and entities may well not originate from another planet, no one has all the answers. It will probably turn out to have a much more complex – and stranger – explanation than a straightforward extraterrestrial hypothesis. But it may be significant that Whitley Strieber has described similar visions of 'golden cities' and exotic otherworldly structures.[25] Similarly, the Space Kids, while in hypnotic trance induced by Puharich, also described alien cities. Does this imply that their experiences were basically shamanic? And – at least in the case of the Space Kids – was it the result of a deliberate experiment to induce shamanic experiences?

On the other hand, could the shamanic experience really be of extraterrestrial origin – or is such a question meaningless? Narby says:

The Western world that has started to rediscover all these old out-of-body experiences is glued down in a kind of 'fifties techno-vision that seems like kindergarten. When you've spent time with Amazonian shamans, they seem like university professors compared to kindergarteners. The old texts describe them as 'spirits from the sky'. I like the sound of that more than 'extraterrestrial intelligence', because the latter has all that kind of 'fifties baggage that isn't necessary. 'Spirits from the sky' sounds kind of beautiful.

Not everything in the shamanistic experience is beautiful, though. Narby warns:

Not all spirits are friendly and benevolent. One can make

parallels with biology quite simply. In other words, there are organisms that impart health, happiness and food to the human species, and there are others, like the HIV virus for instance, that break into the immune system and screw us up. It's all part of life. And death.

Even highly trained shamanistic initiates can encounter not just evil, but also trickster spirits. Perhaps this should be a warning to those amateurs who believe that they are in touch with the gods.

The evidence of shamans and mystics suggests strongly that there is a stargate and it is possible for individuals to step through it into a magical otherworld. But it is not a physical device like the rippling vortex machine of the movie. Just as Michael Harner's internal journey brought him face to face with animal-headed gods so reminiscent of the ancient Egyptian deities, so it seems each of us already possesses the means to meet the gods. Perhaps this is what the Hermeticists – the much later initiates of the old mystery schools – meant when they taught that man is a microcosm of the whole universe. It is interesting that Dale E. Graff, the man who was not only director of the US Army's remote viewing STAR GATE project, but also chose its highly evocative name, wrote:

> Stars send faint light from a cosmic distance. They may for-ever remain out of reach, but not the Stargate within. Our inner Stargate can be found by anyone who chooses to search.[26]

No teacher, priest or guru can locate the stargate for us, so our quest for it and its mysteries, if we care to look for it, may be long and hard. The problem is that many find it easier to listen to those who promise to deliver the stargate already neatly packaged and temptingly ajar, and to invite mighty ineffable beings to step through it to inspire us with awe, enliven our dull existence and make us feel special, chosen – until we realise that in coming through they have slammed shut the ultimate prison door through which there is no escape. The beings who come as gods may not exist beyond top-secret rooms inside government buildings or in the fevered imaginings of channellers. But even if they do come from distant star systems, we have a right to defend our minds against what is dangerous and corrupt.

If we are right, then this warning does not come a moment too soon. If we are wrong, then we still have time to learn to be proud of our humanity – and find the stargate for ourselves.

Update

With the greatest firework display the world has ever seen – and an unprecedented outbreak of good behaviour – Millennium night came and went, leaving only sore heads and slightly depleted bank balances in its wake. The celebrations, although memorable and hugely enjoyable, had not turned into rioting, violence and anarchy as many had predicted. No cults rose up to commit either mass homicide or suicide; Jerusalem did not erupt in fiery fanaticism of any sort, neither did American militia groups attempt to overturn the government. Even the dreaded 'Bug' failed to wipe the world's computers, destroying civilisation as we know it. No doubt to the disappointment of some, we woke on 1 January 2000 to a world that looked pretty much the same as it did the day before.

At Giza in Egypt the pyramids stood unmoved and unmarked by the coming of the year 2000, as enigmatic and imposing as ever. The Great Pyramid (now open again to the public[1]) remained without its long-lost capstone, still innocent of any replacement. Significantly, the ceremony in which the temporary gilded capstone that was to have been lowered into position by an Egyptian Army helicopter as the clock struck midnight – while Jean-Michel Jarre's music[2] welled up from the plateau and a giant eye of Horus was lasered onto the third pyramid[3] – was abandoned at the last minute. But as with everything connected with modern Egypt, there was more to this than meets the eye.

The months following the publication of this book in July 1999 saw a flurry of activity concerning Giza. Two major books on the politics and behind the scenes machinations appeared: *Giza: The Truth* by Ian Lawton and Chris Ogilvie-Herald, which examines the claims and counter-claims of the main players from an independent perspective, while the other book – *Secret Chamber* – was actually by one of the most prominent new Egyptologists, Robert Bauval. There was also the by-now famous BBC television documentary, the two-part *Horizon* programme on Atlantis, the second of which was devoted to a searing critique of Graham Hancock's theories.[4]

This centred on his – and Bauval's – 10,500 BCE theory, presenting the same arguments against it (to the stirring background music from the movie *Stargate*, for some reason) as we detailed in this book. In fact, the whole 10,500 BCE business is now reeling from an onslaught from several quarters: Lawton and Ogilvie-Herald attack the astronomical aspects of Bauval and Gilbert's Orion/Giza correlation theory,[5] as does the South African astronomer Professor Anthony Fairall.[6] (Although, as we pointed out, the original objections were actually raised by Robin J. Cook, who provided the diagrams for *The Orion Mystery*, back in 1996.) Even the author David Rohl – a qualified Egyptologist who, because of his willingness to challenge orthodoxy, is now largely seen as part of the alternative camp – fired a broadside in a page-long article in the *Daily Express*, attacking Hancock and Bauval for persisting in their claims about the magic date of 10,500 BCE despite the mounting evidence against it. However, as Rohl points out, Hancock and Bauval have vested interests in engendering excitement about imminent discoveries at Giza. He writes:

The stakes are high. The hero worship surrounding Hancock and Bauval would rapidly wane if no such evidence came to light. So far, their theories have, in part, been sustained by their ability to claim that the proof is just around the corner but that they are being thwarted by the powers-that-be.

However, he goes on to say that '. . . the portents are not good for the would-be messiahs of Egyptology. Since excitement peaked in the mid-Nineties, there has been a growing disillusionment'.[7]

Behind the Giza myth-making

We left the story with the weird kiss-and-make-up scenario in which the three major factions involved in the Giza controversy – the Alternative Egypt trio of Hancock, Bauval and John Anthony West; the seekers after Edgar Cayce's Hall of Records, namely the Schor Foundation and ARE; and the Egyptian archaeological authorities represented by Dr Zahi Hawass – had apparently reached what Bauval calls an 'entente cordiale'. There was the promise of exciting events such as the capstone ceremony and the 'message to the planet' by Bauval's 'Magic 12', and even that Gantenbrink's Chamber was to be opened on Millennium night. However, something seems to have put a serious spanner in the works. None of this was to happen.

Bauval's own version of events at Giza, *Secret Chamber: The Quest for the Hall of Records*, came out in November 1999, which – as might be expected – is well worth reading. It pours scorn on the conspiracies outlined in *The Stargate Conspiracy* – which we admit we find somewhat puzzling because *Secret Chamber* not only covers much of the same ground, but actually backs it up, reaching very similar conclusions about the way events at Giza have been manipulated by those with secret, esoteric agendas.

After making much of the entente cordiale and denying the existence of any conspiracies or covert agendas, Bauval has now returned to his original position, arguing that there *are* undercurrents and subtexts, particularly those of Zahi Hawass and the Schor Foundation/ARE. And not surprisingly – at least as far as we are concerned – the agendas he cites tally almost exactly with the ones that feature so prominently in this book.

The overall thesis of *Secret Chamber* is that ancient Egyptian legends – or perhaps memories – of the existence of a hidden repository of the wisdom of the Pyramid Age entered into Hermetic lore, and from there found their way into the beliefs of Rosicrucianism and Freemasonry. After Napoleon's expedition of 1798 effectively opened Egypt up to European exploitation, Freemasons and other esotericists – most recently some esotericist groups – were able to search for the fabled repository.

On this we are largely agreed. However, there is one major point on which we fail to see eye to eye. While presenting – in our view – a convincing case for those groups' covert manipulation of the potent symbolism of Giza, Bauval still insists that the Pyramids and Sphinx will – quite literally and in the very near future – somehow trigger a spiritual transformation of the world. He says:

> I truly believe that the Great Pyramid and the Giza necropolis as a whole have the innate energy to cause a powerful transcendental shift in thinking on a massive, even global scale provided that the right buttons are pushed at the right time. There is not much doubt that we are headed for a radical reformation in the way we perceive ourselves on this planet . . .
>
> I am convinced that the Giza necropolis has been designed for precisely such a purpose. I am convinced, too, that the time has come for that purpose to re-activate itself. I am also convinced that some sort of bizarre plan is being implemented at Giza to 'hijack' this all-powerful device in order to promote something else, something that the instruments of Giza were never intended to do.[8]

Apart from his belief in the transcendental triggering of Giza – on which we remain unconvinced – Bauval appears by a different route to have reached very similar conclusions to ours in the Egyptian chapters. For Bauval, the focus of this 'hijacking' was to be the Millennium night ceremony in which a helicopter was to lower a gilded capstone onto the top of the Great Pyramid, which – as we saw in Chapter 7 – would have been replete with very specific Masonic symbolism. Together with the eye of Horus projected onto the side of the pyramid this would have completed the symbolism of the Great Seal of the United States, allegedly ushering in a new era when American Freemasonry would become the dominant force in the world.

Significantly, Edgar Cayce also predicted the advent of such an American Masonic Golden Age. Some have associated this with another of his 'readings' describing a gold capstone on the Great Pyramid, which he linked with the discovery of the fabled Hall of Records.[9] It is not too hard to see where the mooted Millennium night ceremony had its origins.

Robert Bauval writes: 'There is little question that the events planned for the new millennium at Giza are highly charged with powerful ideologies. There is little question, too, that these ideologies . . . invoke the "Second Coming" of some Messianic figure as well as that of a Masonic "New World Order". It should be evident, therefore, that the placing of a gilded capstone on the Great Pyramid at the stroke of midnight on the eve of the new age is not merely a "millennium celebration" for Egypt, but could be the result of a carefully planned, carefully manipulated long-term strategy.'[10]

In his view, the potency of the ceremony would be increased by the fact that, as seen from Giza, Sirius would be culminating at midnight.[11]

However, this carefully laid plan failed utterly. Although there were throngs of merry-makers on the Giza plateau at midnight, the capstone ceremony did not happen, having been called off just a matter of days before the celebrations. Cinderella did not go to the ball – ironically, as things turned out, partly because of

Bauval's book. The Egyptian press had picked up the allegations of Masonic involvement, which led to an outcry that in turn put pressure on the Egyptian government to cancel the ceremony.[12] Freemasonry has been banned in Egypt since 1964 because of a perceived link between the Brotherhood and Zionism – and the very idea of a Masonic ritual taking place in the heart of Egypt is highly inflammatory, to say the least.

(The real irony is that the ceremony would never have happened anyway: at midnight the Giza plateau was shrouded in thick fog – perhaps the guardians of the ancient Egyptian mysteries were determined not to be mocked . . .)

It seems strange to us that in spite of warning the world about the hijacking of the symbolism of Giza – specifically the capstone ceremony – Bauval himself issued statements on the Internet urging the Egyptian Government to reconsider. He *wanted* the ceremony to go ahead, warning the Egyptians that 'The eyes of the world are watching'.[13]

Also according to *Secret Chamber*, at the stroke of midnight Gantenbrink's chamber was to be opened amid great fanfare and ceremony before the world's media.[14] This, too, failed to materialise, although the authorities still promise to open the chamber some time in the year 2000. We can only wait and see, although we may well have a long wait.

We note with disappointment that the much-hyped 'Message to the Planet', due to be relayed to the world by the Magic 12 – Bauval, Graham Hancock, Robert Temple and others – from in front of the Sphinx also never happened, like the 'Hermetic Journey' that was due to take place at places of power throughout 1999. Why these events, so emphatically built up in the preceding months, never materialised, is unknown. Moreover, the famous *entente cordiale* – brokered by Bauval himself – is now in tatters, thanks to the criticisms of the revelations of *Secret Chamber*.[15]

Both Bauval's book and Lawton and Ogilvie-Herald's *Giza: The Truth* (published in August 1999), add considerably to the detail of the strange goings-on at Giza. Most of their discoveries reinforce what we outlined in Chapter Two of this book.

Bauval presents evidence to show that the SRI International team led by Dr Lambert Dolphin that carried out explorations at Giza in the 1970s was specifically looking for the Hall of Records – something that has always been downplayed. Bauval also demonstrates that the links between the SRI team and the ARE were far stronger than either party has subsequently admitted.[16] Bauval has also confirmed the long-standing association between Dolphin and Dr James Hurtak, citing a 1992 letter in which the former describes Hurtak as 'my friend and colleague of many years'.[17]

New information arising from *Secret Chamber* and *Giza: The Truth* has highlighted other aspects of the many disputes connected with modern Giza. Dr Zahi Hawass has denied ARE's claims that they were responsible for his Egyptological education[18] – although it hardly matters because his continuing close ties with that organisation are not exactly secret.

In *Giza: The Truth* Lawton and Ogilvie-Herald add more detail on the dispute between film-maker Boris Said and Dr Joseph Schor, from testimony supplied by Schor himself and his long-term partner in ventures at Giza, Dr Joseph Jahoda, effectively calling some of Said's claims into question and making certain allegations about his conduct. In particular, Schor claims that Said leaked material covered by confidentiality agreements (the test footage showing Zahi Hawass in the tunnel in the Sphinx's rump) to, among others, Robert Bauval.[19]

Another point of contention concerns the cancellation of the Schor Foundation/Florida State University's licence to work at Giza in 1996. We have seen that Hancock and Bauval claim the credit for that, and according to Boris Said, Schor had withheld this information from him and continued the search for the Hall of Records using his commercial filming permit. Schor and Jahoda hotly dispute both claims – in fact, they say that they *never* received any official notification from Zahi Hawass or the Egyptian authorities cancelling the original licence.[20] In view of the acrimonious nature of the dispute between Said and Schor, the former's allegations that we quote in Chapter Two should be set against Schor's version as given in *Giza: The Truth*. If nothing else, the whole business demonstrates how difficult it is to get to the bottom of what is actually going on at Giza.

Another surprise development, in August 1999, was Dr Hawass' formal approval of a new licence for the Schor Foundation/FSU team to work at Giza – which specifically stated that permission was given for them to *search for the Hall of Records*.[21] This is the first time that such an astonishing objective has been cited on an official permit.

In *Secret Chamber*, Bauval disputes Gantenbrink's claims (also published in Lawton and Ogilvie-Herald) that he released details of Gantenbrink's discoveries to the media which we set out in Chapter 1. Gantenbrink told us that Bauval had released details of his discovery to the media against his wishes, without his permission and with the intention of using it to publicize his own theories. If anything, Gantenbrink was even more strident on this subject to Lawton and Ogilvie-Herald.[22]

However, in *Secret Chamber*, Bauval reproduces correspondence between himself and Gantenbrink showing that the latter *had* given him permission to publicise his discovery and that he was kept fully informed of Bauval's negotiations with the British press, resulting in the front-page story in the *Independent* on 16 April 1993. Matters came to a head when Gantenbrink sued the BBC for using video footage of the 'door' in a documentary 'The Great Pyramid: Gateway to the Stars' (based on the work of Bauval and Adrian Gilbert). The matter was finally settled out of court after – according to Bauval – the BBC lawyers were able to show that, as Gantenbrink and his film team did not have a permit for commercial filming in the Great Pyramid, the copyright for the footage was actually held by the Egyptian Supreme Council for Antiquities.[23]

Giza: The Truth also adds to our understanding of the various activities at Giza, because the authors managed to get into two of the chambers where secret tunnelling is supposed to be taking place, or at least the scene of some sort of clandestine toings and froings. They investigated the tunnel that is allegedly being dug in the Great Pyramid from Davison's Chamber towards whatever is behind Gantenbrink's door – but found no sign of it.[24] This is particularly important because this is the last allegation of clandestine tunnelling at Giza – and even that appears to have been discredited.

In Chapter Two we left the question of covert tunnelling open: virtually all the rumours of recent years turned out to be without foundation, including the detection of nine chambers beneath the Sphinx (promoted by Hancock and Bauval), the accessing of a chamber under the Sphinx containing records and artefacts (which bizarrely seems to have originated within Egyptian government circles), the so-called 'Hall of Osiris' in the Great Pyramid (advocated by Larry Dean Hunter) and the mystification surrounding the Water Shaft Chamber (begun by Boris Said and now taken up by James Hurtak and Zahi Hawass). However, as there were still some claims where a definite conclusion was impossible, we considered the possibility that there *was* some kind of clandestine activity going on, for which the wilder rumours served as some kind of smokescreen – particularly the claim about tunnelling off Davison's Chamber. But now that one also seems to have fallen by the wayside, it clarifies the issue. Now we know that there is unlikely to be anything new and exciting at Giza, it seems that certain groups want us to believe there is.

Lawton and Ogilvie-Herald also managed to get into the Water Shaft Chamber, deep beneath the causeway at Giza. The lowest of the three chambers – which contains a huge, but empty, granite sarcophagus, surrounded by a watery moat – is now the focus for some highly inventive myth-making. Although of considerable archaeological interest, the key point as far as the myth-makers are concerned is whether, as some claim, it is linked with hypo-thetical chambers beneath the Sphinx. Could this really be the entrance to the subterranean network of tunnels and chambers spoken of by Cayce and which also appears in the works of AMORC and H.C. Randall-Stevens?

In the north-west corner there is a sort of low passage (which actually leads in the direction of the Great Pyramid, not the Sphinx). But is it really a man-made tunnel? Certainly, Bauval describes it as a tunnel,[25] as does Zahi Hawass. On 2 March 1999 the chamber was the centrepiece of a live television broadcast (*Opening the Lost Tombs – Live*) by Fox TV in the US, in which Hawass leads the presenter down the shaft, describing it as his 'greatest adventure ever'. In the lowest chamber he draws attention to the 'tunnel' saying he had not excavated it yet, but 'you never know what the sands and tunnels of Egypt may hide'.[26] However, according to Lawton and Ogilvie-Herald, and judging by their photographs, this is simply a natural fault in the rock that narrows to a dead end after a few feet.[27]

By far the greatest and most dedicated myth-maker where this particular chamber is concerned is Dr James Hurtak. In lectures in Australia in 1999, he claimed that he was the one to have discovered it.[28] It emerges that when Boris Said and members of the Schor Foundation team explored the chamber in February 1997, Hurtak had accompanied them.[29] Perhaps this was remarkable enough, but in Hurtak's lectures the chamber has been transformed into Wonderland – virtually an underground city, the entrance to a series of massive chambers and temples surrounded by rivers that could only be crossed by skilful rafting. Indeed, Hurtak shows slides of himself in a raft, giving the illusion of heroic exploits across large distances. In fact, although the chamber is surrounded by water, altogether it is only 30 foot square . . . Not quite Indiana Jones style. Of course Hurtak links this location with the historical scheme outlined in his *The Keys of Enoch* – and is reported to claim that he has evidence that this 'underground city' was constructed by the people from Atlantis.[30]

It seems hard not to conclude that all these people are deliberately myth-making about rather unpromising discoveries, perhaps because there is nowhere left on the Giza plateau to spin such stories about.

Hurtak is the link between the Egyptian side of the stargate conspiracy and the New Age. Recently, British author and researcher Kevin McClure drew our attention to another aspect of

Hurtak's complex and multifaceted career: in the 1980s and early 90s, when he was best known as a UFO researcher, Hurtak was one of the foremost promoters of a link between the UFO phenomenon and the secrets of Nazi Germany. He claimed that the extraterrestrials that brought civilisation to the Middle East many thousands of years ago chose to re-establish contact with the human race in modern times with the Germany of the 1930s – on the grounds that it was the most scientifically advanced nation of the time. The extraterrestrials gave Nazi scientists the secret of how to construct disc-shaped flying craft: this new technology was captured by the Americans at the end of the Second World War, which is why the first wave of UFO reports in the US began in 1947.[31] Although this is an extremely unlikely scenario (one wonders why Hitler lost the war if he had access to such advanced technology) the significant point is that Hurtak finds nothing odd in the supposed fact that his advanced extraterrestrials should select Nazi Germany as their Chosen Ones.

The monster under the mask

Another major link between the Egyptian mysteries and the New Age is, of course, Edgar Cayce. Both *Secret Chamber* and *Giza: The Truth* present further evidence of the true origins of the 'Sleeping Prophet's' psychic information: Lawton and Ogilvie-Herald point out that far from being as ignorant of esoteric matters as his supporters claim Cayce was in fact well versed in Theosophical and other similar beliefs *before* he began to produce the psychic material relating to Atlantis, ancient Egypt and the Hall of Records. In particular, Cayce lectured to the Theosophical Society of Alabama in 1922, staying for several weeks with a student of such esoteric doctrines, Arthur Lammers, the following year.[32] Bauval also accepts that Cayce was well versed in Theosophical and other lore – and even traces his belief in the significance of 10,500 BCE back to the works of the poet and mystical philosopher Gerald Massey (1828–1907).[33] This makes an important connection between Cayce's psychic readings and the esoteric groups that came to influence the stargate conspiracy, revealing why Cayce's work is so significant.

Since the publication of this book we have become even more disturbed by the extreme right-wing politics that lurk under the 'love and light' of the New Age movement. We now realise that we are by no means alone in our anxiety about the potential for control of all those largely white, middle-class happy huggers, who may be genuine seekers after enlightenment and awareness. Shortly after this book came out a friend, the actress and screenwriter Christy Fearn, sent us a copy of *New Age Channelings – Who or what is being channeled?* by the Swedish-born artist and writer Monica Sjöö, which provided more pieces for this particular bit of the jigsaw. Although Sjöö unashamedly comes from an alternative, radically feminist position, she is concerned about the philosophy and politics that underpin the New Age – especially the subtext of many of the channelled messages. Sjöö, like us, discerned worrying undercurrents in the progenitors of today's New Age, primarily Madame Blavatsky and Alice A. Bailey. And like us, she sees the Council of Nine – and in particular their book, *The Only Planet of Choice* – as being insidiously sinister and dangerous[34].

Interestingly, Sjöö notes that the channelling cults, particularly the Nine, are not actually very radical. If anything, they uphold the American Dream, reinforcing white, Christian middle-class values and the concept of a ruling elite. Perhaps, she muses, such teachings emanate from intelligence agencies such as the CIA?[35] (We recall the findings of the SRI report entitled 'Changing Images of Man' – see Chapter 7.)

Monica Sjöö particularly picks up on the anti-Semitic, racist and stridently patriarchal tone of the great New Age godmothers, Blavatsky and Bailey – especially the latter. She notes that Bailey's spirit guide, the Tibetan (or 'the Master D.K.'), proclaimed on the day that the atom bomb was dropped on Nagasaki that it was ushering in a new age by releasing cosmic energy, linking the nuclear flash with the Light of the initiate. Surely even more disgusting is the Tibetan's view of the effect of using the atomic firestorm on thousands of living Japanese. As Sjöö says: 'Bailey and D.K. go on to say that the Japanese, whose nervous system is of the 4th root-race, were due to be destroyed "... and the consequent release of their imprisoned souls is a necessary happening; it is the justification of the use of the atomic bomb on the Japanese population."'[36]

Alice Bailey's teachings are still the fundamental philosophy of the New Age. Not only does 'Tom' of the Council of Nine recommend her books, but the underlying philosophy of Dr James Hurtak is quite clearly derived from them. Given their popularity among hundreds of thousands – probably millions – of New Agers, surely this is profoundly worrying.

Another disturbing influence is the American William Dudley Pelley, who we mentioned more or less in passing in Chapter 5, but have now come to realise is much more important where the genesis of the stargate conspiracy is concerned. We referred only in passing to his 1950 *Star Guests* – now a very rare book – which was probably the first collection of channelled material from extraterrestrials ever published (he claimed it was based on material he had received in the late 1920s). Recently, however, we have managed to acquire a copy for ourselves, which certainly makes interesting reading. We were staggered to find that it brings the whole story round full circle, as it focuses not just on Sirius, but actually on Sirius B . . .[37]

According to Pelley, the human race is the product of the interbreeding between apemen and advanced extraterrestrial beings that migrated to Earth from the Sirius system. Linking this with ancient Egypt, he asserts that the union of 'half-god, half-human progeny' is symbolised by the Sphinx[38] and that the hawk-headed gods represent the Sirians[39] (shades of Puharich's hawk-headed 'Spectra').

Pelley's channelled sources told him that the human race is now composed of the descendants of the Sirian/Earth interbreeding (who he calls the 'beast-progeny of the ape-mothers of long ago'[40] or the 'indigenous biologic earth-forms'[41]) and the reincarnated spirits of the original Sirian migrants. But along the way something went wrong and the descendants of the hybrids became corrupt, so the intelligences that rule the universe sent messengers – of which Jesus was one – to 'repair' the damage.[42] This is strikingly similar to Hurtak's concept of a failure in the genetic programme that needs to be repaired. In Pelley's teaching everything is building up to the Second Coming with the advent of the Age of Aquarius.[43]

All the major elements of the doctrine underlying the stargate conspiracy – elaborated in the later Council of Nine material – were present in Pelley's seminal book. This is unlikely to be a coincidence. In fact, the circle of the 'psychic contactees' of the early 1950s was much more closely knit than is now realised. Andrija Puharich was an intimate of George Hunt Williamson, who was himself a close associate of Pelley's. Therefore it is unlikely that Puharich was unaware of Pelley's book, especially as he was keenly interested in communication with non-human entities.

However, we believe that the most significant aspect of William Dudley Pelley's influence was his politics. He was an unrepentant Fascist – an admirer of Hitler and founder of the Silver Shirts of America, who was interned as a security threat during the Second World War. What are the implications of this for his alleged channelled communications? It could be that his ideology drove his unconscious mind to fabricate them, but on the other hand if they are genuine, one has to ask why these entities chose to make contact with a Fascist . . .

Increasingly, we have become aware of the darkly disturbing elements of this story – the apparently racist undercurrents in some of the teachings of the Nine. Of course, most people involved in the New Egyptology and the New Age find racism in all its forms morally repugnant, as we do. In particular, we should make clear that the Stargate Conspiracy in no way claims that the popular authors on the mysteries of ancient Egypt hold racist or Fascist views. No doubt most of those whose work and ideas are pressed into the service of the Stargate Conspiracy – such as those of Alternative Egyptology, promoters of the Face on Mars and Baileyites and Cayceites – are as repelled by these ideologies as we are. While it was never our intention to suggest that any of these individuals hold racist or Fascist views, our principal concern is that the often faceless behind-the-scenes manipulators have no compunction in seizing their ideas and twisting them to their own ends.

Although they seem to have suffered a significant set-back with the banning of the Millennium capstone ceremony, too much has been invested in their long-term plans for this to be anything more than a temporary reverse. The timetable may have been set back, but it has not been abandoned. The process of trying to win our hearts and minds is remorseless. Investing the mysterious monuments of the ancient world with roles for which they were not built and the gods with powers of which they have no need, the conspirators will continue to seduce us with fabricated excitements.

Anyone who wishes to contribute to the debate concerning the issues raised in this book can do so through the Stargate Assembly, an on-line forum on the world wide web, at www.templarlodge.com.

Notes and References

Prologue: The Nine Gods

1. Utterance 600, trans. Faulkner, *The Ancient Egyptian Pyramid Texts*, p247.
2. Except where noted, information on the history of Heliopolis is taken from Saleh, *Excavations at Heliopolis*.
3. Saleh, vol. 1, p5; Rundle Clark, p37.
4. Lehner, *The Complete Pyramids*, p142.
5. Saleh, vol. 1, p23.
6. Hurry, p11.
7. Harris, p30.
8. Lehner, *The Complete Pyramids*, p31.
9. The translation of the Pyramid Texts that is generally accepted as the standard is that of R.O. Faulkner. There are still many parts whose meaning is obscure or debatable.
10. Lehner, *The Complete Pyramids*, p32; Rundle Clark, p37.
11. The discovery of the precession of the equinoxes is ascribed to the Greek astronomer Hipparchus of Nicaea (who coined the phrase) in 127 BCE, though he overestimated the length of the precessional cycle. In *The Death of the Gods in Ancient Egypt*, Egyptologist Jane B. Sellers, following up the theories of Giorgio de Santillana

and Hertha von Dechend in *Hamlet's Mill*, argues persuasively that the ancient Egyptians were aware of the precession.

12. Luckert, p47.
13. Ibid., p45.
14. Frankfort, *Kingship and the Gods*, p153.
15. Luckert, p50.
16. Ibid., p54.
17. Lehner, *The Complete Pyramids*, p34.
18. Rundle Clark, p35.
19. 'European Probe finds Water at Titan and Orion', Associated Press report, 8 April 1998.
20. Rice, *Egypt's Making*, p38.
21. See Coppens, 'Life Exists Since the Big Bang'; Schueller, 'Stuff of Life'.

1 Egypt: New Myths For Old

1. Lehner, *The Complete Pyramids*, p106; Kingsland, vol. 1, pp3–4.
2. On the use of *pi* and *phi*, see Rice, *Egypt's Legacy*, pp24–5. On the geodetic significance of the Great Pyramid, see Kingsland, vol. 2, p42, and Livio Catullo Stecchini's appendix to Tompkins, *The Secrets of the Great Pyramid*. For an analysis of the geometry of the Giza complex as a whole, see the books by Robin J. Cook.
3. Collins, *Gods of Eden*, p25.
4. Cook, *The Horizon of Khufu*, p52.
5. Lehner, *The Complete Pyramids*, p94.
6. Ibid., p124.
7. Edwards, p102.
8. In the 1994 BBC television documentary *The Great Pyramid: Gateway to the Stars*, produced by Christopher Mann.
9. Collins, *Gods of Eden*, pp52–7.
10. See Hapgood, *Maps of the Ancient Sea Kings*.
11. Bauval and Hancock, *Keeper of Genesis*, p248.
12. See Beaudoin, p121; Guerrier, p137.
13. Marti, p92.
14. Bauval and Hancock, *Keeper of Genesis*, p100.
15. Telephone interview with Martin Barstow, Reader in Astrophysics at the University of Leicester, 28 August 1998.
16. Beaudoin, p121.

17. Lunan, p4.
18. The European Space Agency's Hipparchos project was developed in order to make detailed measurements of the movements of the stars from beyond the Earth's atmosphere. The Hipparchos satellite was launched in 1989 and completed its survey in 1993. The data gathered – the most accurate available – was published in a seventeen-volume star catalogue, and has been available on the World Wide Web since 1997.
19. Temple, *The Sirius Mystery*, p3.
20. The inundation of the Nile was (until the Aswan Dam brought it to an end in 1964) caused by the summer monsoon in Ethiopia swelling the waters of the Blue Nile (Baines and Málek, p14). Records from the nineteenth and twentieth centuries show that the waters could start to rise in Egypt as early as 15 April and as late as 23 June, and that the period between successive inundations varied between 336 and 415 days (Parker, p32). Any correlation between the heliacal rising of Sirius and the onset of the flood could therefore only ever be approximate.
21. Allen, pp118–25.
22. Sirius was sometimes depicted as a dog in Egypt, but only from the period of Greek domination following Alexander the Great's conquest in 332 BCE, as the Greeks brought with them their own association with the Dog Star. See Lurker, p114.
23. Bauval and Gilbert, p60.
24. Temple, *The Sirius Mystery*, pp11–12.
25. Ibid., p135.
26. The identification of Hermes and Thoth is so well attested that it is, frankly, incredible that Temple should have gone unchallenged on this point for so long. In fact, the identification of the two gods is an important piece of evidence that the Hermetic works have an ancient Egyptian (rather than, as long believed, Greek) background. See, for example, Fowden, pp75–6.
27. Temple, *The Sirius Mystery*, p137.
28. Ibid., pp262–5.
29. Beaudoin, p34; Marti, p10.
30. Temple, *The Sirius Mystery*, p245.
31. Budge, *An Egyptian Hieroglyphic Dictionary*. The definition of *arq ur* is in vol. 1, p131; a list of abbreviations of source texts, showing that 'Sphinx' refers to such a source, is in vol. 1, p.lxxxvii.

32. Piehl, 'Notes de lexicographie egyptienne', p8. The Egyptians' borrowing of *argyros/arq ur* can only have occurred after the seventh century BCE, when Greek trading colonies were established at the mouth of the Nile. It is likely that the word did not enter the Egyptian language until the period of Greek domination that began in 332 BCE.

33. Temple, *The Sirius Mystery*, pp40–42.

34. Ibid., p44.

35. Ibid., p7.

36. Ibid., pp7–8.

37. Ibid., p401.

38. Edwards, p140.

39. Bauval and Hancock, *Keeper of Genesis*, p160.

40. West, *Serpent in the Sky*, p232, citing the work of forensic artist Lieutenant Frank Domingo of the New York Police Department.

41. Breasted, p324.

42. West, *Serpent in the Sky*, p67; Isha Schwaller de Lubicz, p111.

43. West, *Serpent in the Sky*, p198.

44. Ibid., p14.

45. Schoch, 'Redating the Great Sphinx of Giza'.

46. Milson, p20.

47. Hancock, *Fingerprints of the Gods*, p423.

48. Schoch, 'The Great Sphinx Controversy'.

49. Quoted in Hancock, *Fingerprints of the Gods*, p419.

50. Schoch, 'The Great Sphinx Controversy'.

51. Hancock, *Fingerprints of the Gods*, p413.

52. Hoffman (pp57–9, 68–77 and 160) gives the accepted dates for rainy periods (pluvials) in Egypt's history: the Abbassia Pluvial, which lasted from about 120,000 BCE to 90,000 BCE; the Mousterian Pluvial, 50,000–30,000 BCE; and the Neolithic Subpluvial, which began between 7000 and 6000 BCE and ended in approximately 2500 BCE. Hoffman makes no mention of a wet period in the eleventh millennium BCE. This is especially significant, since Hancock uses Hoffman as his source on the ancient Egyptian climate.

53. Milson, p25.

54. Rice, *Egypt's Legacy*, p16.

55. Milson, p24.

56. Hoffman, p161.

57. Temple, *The Sirius Mystery*, pp21–2.

58. Bauval and Gilbert, p128.

59. The idea was first proposed by Egyptologist Dr Alexander Badawy and astronomer Dr Virginia Trimble in 1964 – see Bauval and Gilbert, pp103–7 and Appendix 1.

60. Bauval and Gilbert, pp179–80.

61. Ibid.

62. Lehner, *The Complete Pyramids*, pp66–7.

63. The *Daily Telegraph*, after being given the story by Bauval on 4 April 1993 – just fourteen days after Gantenbrink's discovery – ran a small article three days later. The major coverage began on 16 April, when, after further lobbying by Bauval, the *Independent* carried the story on the front page. Television news programmes covered it the same evening, and many other British and foreign newspapers the following day.

64. This and the following quotes are from an email to the authors from Rudolf Gantenbrink dated 19 August 1998.

65. For example, Churchward, *Origin and Antiquity of Freemasonry*, pp65 and 69. (Our thanks to Gareth Medway for directing us to Churchward's works.)

66. Bauval and Hancock, *Keeper of Genesis*, pp66–70.

67. Ibid., p70.

68. Cook, *The Horizon of Khufu*, p86.

69. Ibid.

70. Sunrise on the spring equinox in 10,500 BCE occurs (according to SkyGlobe's clock and calendar) at around 6.05am on 13 June. (Because our modern calendar falls out of step with the seasons when extended backwards or forwards over long periods of time, the spring equinox – currently 21–22 March – occurs progressively later in the calendar year the further back in time SkyGlobe is projected.)

It is also important to recognise that software packages such as SkyGlobe – which is primarily intended for the use of amateur astronomers looking at the night sky as it appears today – are not designed to be accurate over periods of millennia. Over such long periods, other factors – most importantly the proper motion of stars – unnecessary for everyday star-gazing come into play. Many products, SkyGlobe included, do not take these factors into account. Even those that do, unless they use the new data from the

Hipparchos satellite (see note 18 for Chapter 1 above), are liable to be inaccurate.

71. Cook, *The Horizon of Khufu*, p86.

72. Breasted, p120.

73. R.A. Schwaller de Lubicz, *Sacred Science*, pp176–7.

74. Bauval and Hancock, *Keeper of Genesis*, pp262–7.

75. Report from Dr Krupp to Michael Brass, posted on *Egyptnews*, 19 June 1998 (*Egyptnews* is an Internet private mailing list dedicated to the latest research on, and debate surrounding, the mysteries of ancient Egypt, which is edited by Chris Ogilvie-Herald, address: egyptnews@aol.com).

76. Hancock and Faiia, pp126–8.

77. See Lehner, *The Egyptian Heritage*; Roche, *Egyptian Myths and the Ra Ta Story*.

78. Robinson, *Edgar Cayce's Story of the Origin and Destiny of Man*, p79.

79. Ibid.

80. Ibid., p80.

81. Ibid., p79.

82. Ibid., p159. See also Robinson, *Is It True What They Say About Edgar Cayce?*, pp160ff.

83. Stearn, p80.

84. Carter, p86.

85. Ibid., p87.

86. Ibid., p88.

87. Stearn, p89.

88. Carter, p90.

89. Edgar Evans Cayce, p157.

90. This research will appear in Andrew Collins's forthcoming *Gateway to Atlantis*.

91. Carter, p153.

92. Lehner, *The Egyptian Heritage*, p86.

93. Bauval and Hancock, *Keeper of Genesis*, p89.

94. Ibid., p295.

95. Milson, p4.

96. Sources at ARE's Virginia Beach headquarters.

97. Sellers, p172.

98. Bauval and Hancock, *Keeper of Genesis*, p245.

99. Ibid. pp74 and 78.

100. Ibid., pp282–4 and 336–7.
101. Ibid., p282.
102. See Erman, pp373–5.
103. Saleh, p25.
104. Translations of the various Arab legends are collected in Kingsland, Vol. 2, Chapter VIII.
105. See Mackey, Chapter IX.
106. Herodotus (trans. Cary), p137.
107. Randall-Stevens, *The Teachings of Osiris*, p80.
108. Randall-Stevens, *A Voice Out of Egypt*, p174.
109. Ibid., p178.
110. Ibid., p174.
111. Lewis, *The Symbolic Prophecy of the Great Pyramid*, pp126–7 and 181–92.
112. 'An Open Letter by Robert G. Bauval', *Egyptnews*, 29 July 1998.
113. 'Comment from Graham Hancock', *Egyptnews*, 14 August 1998.
114. *Egyptnews*, 20 October 1998.
115. From Robert Bauval's lecture at the Questing Conference, London, 24 October 1998.
116. *Egyptnews*, 8 November 1998.
117. Temple, *The Sirius Mystery*, p36.

2 High Strangeness at Giza

1. Art Bell radio show, 14 January 1998.
2. Kerisel, pp37–44.
3. Hancock, 'Egypt's Mysteries: Hints of a Hidden Agenda?'.
4. Ogilvie-Herald, p5.
5. Ibid.
6. Hancock, 'Egypt's Mysteries: Hints of a Hidden Agenda?'.
7. Ibid.
8. *Hieroglyph*, no. 1, January 1997, p1.
9. Art Bell radio show, 14 January 1998.
10. Lehner, *The Complete Pyramids*, p45.
11. Tompkins, *Secrets of the Great Pyramid*, p54.
12. Ogilvie-Herald, pp4–5. Danley confirmed his original account in an email to us, dated 3 September 1998.
13. Hoagland, 'A *Secret* Tunnel being Excavated in the Great Pyramid?'.

14. Koppang, p56.
15. Kenneth and Dee Burke, p55.
16. Hawass, 'Two New Museums at Luxor and Aswan'.
17. Bayuk, 'Spotlight Interview – Dr Zahi Hawass'.
18. See report by Kate Ginn in the *Daily Mail*, 18 April 1998. This article contains several unfortunate misinterpretations of the details given to the *Mail* – see Simon Cox's statement on *Egyptnews*, 19 April 1998. We heard reports of the discovery of the three chambers from several sources in Egypt. Interestingly, it was reported on the Academy website (*http://academy.wwdc.com/archives/113.html*) in January 1998 that Dannion Brinkley claimed that he had received the same information directly from Dr Zahi Hawass himself.
19. This was the 'Robertson Panel', convened by the CIA in 1953. See Peebles, Chapter 6.
20. Tompkins, *Secrets of the Great Pyramid*, p273.
21. Hassan, p13.
22. Ibid., pp16–17.
23. Lehner, *The Complete Pyramids*, p130.
24. Dolphin, 'Geophysics and the Temple Mount'.
25. From Dolphin's resumé on his website (*http://www.best.com/~dolphin/*).
26. Dolphin, 'Geophysics and the Temple Mount'.
27. Ibid.
28. Quoted in ibid.
29. Email from Lambert Dolphin to Philip Coppens, 6 April 1998.
30. Bauval and Hancock, *Keeper of Genesis*, p91.
31. Ibid., pp91–2.
32. Email to authors from Kim Farmer of the Academy for Future Sciences, 24 September 1998.
33. Hurtak's paper, 'Subsurface Morphology and Geoarcheology revealed by Spaceborne and Airborne Radar', is available from NASA. Our thanks to Chris Ogilvie-Herald for bringing this to our attention, and to Philip Coppens for confirming the details with NASA.
34. Email from Kim Farmer of AFFS, 24 September 1998.
35. Ibid.
36. *Hieroglyph*, no. 1, January 1997, p3.
37. Email from Kim Farmer of AFFS, 24 September 1998.

38. Ibid.

39. Bauval and Hancock, *Keeper of Genesis*, p91, quoting SRI's official 1977 report.

40. Ibid., p92.

41. Bauval and Hancock, *Keeper of Genesis*, p92.

42. Zahi Hawass and Mark Lehner, 'The Passage Under the Sphinx', in Berger, Clerc and Grimal, p201.

43. Bauval and Hancock, *Keeper of Genesis*, p93.

44. From Boris Said's video *Legends of the Sphinx* (Magical Eye Productions, 1998, written and produced by Boris Said, directed by Michael Calhoun).

45. *Hieroglyph*, no. 1 (January 1997).

46. Robert G. Bauval, 'A Meeting with Dr Joseph Schor in New York', posting on Equinox 2000 website, 26 October 1998 (*http://www.projectequinox2000.com*).

47. Statement by Boris Said in his *Legends of the Sphinx* video.

48. Hawass first publicly announced the termination of the project's licence in July 1996 on a South African radio programme, saying that he had written to the Schor Foundation and Florida State University revoking their licence (*Hieroglyph*, no. 1, January 1997). However, the team somehow managed to continue their work at Giza for a further five months and even managed to return in February 1997, using Boris Said's commercial filming permit to gain access to the plateau. According to Said (*Legends of the Sphinx* video), at this stage he had not been told by Schor that the project's licence had been revoked.

49. Keller, p16.

50. Hoagland made this claim on the Art Bell radio show on 22 September 1996. See *Hieroglyph*, no. 1, p3.

51. *Legends of the Sphinx* video.

52. John Anthony West, 'ARE Conference at Virginia Beach'.

53. Lewis, *The Symbolic Prophecy of the Great Pyramid*, pp184–5.

54. Randall-Stevens, *A Voice out of Egypt*, p194.

55. See Ogilvie-Herald and Lawton for their first-hand account of the shaft and chambers.

56. The *Daily Telegraph*, 4 March 1935. Our thanks to Chris Ogilvie-Herald for supplying us with a copy of this article.

57. Questing Conference, Conway Hall, London, 24 October 1998.

58. 'Statement from John Anthony West and Graham Hancock' dated

17 May 1998, circulated widely on the Internet.

59. Robert Bauval, posting on Sphinx group website, 17 July 1998 (*http://www.m-m.org/jz/sphinx.html*).

60. Bauval and Hancock, posting on Sphinx group website, 19 July 1998.

61. *Egyptnews*, 27 September 1998.

62. *Hieroglyph*, no. 2, May 1998, p3.

63. Ibid., pp2–3.

64. Ibid., p3.

65. Robert Bauval, posting on *Egyptnews*, 13 August 1998.

66. Robert Bauval, posting on *Egyptnews*, 20 September 1998. (From the most recent reports – e.g. *Egyptnews*, 22 September 1998 – it appears that the Schor Foundation/Florida State University team has been unsuccessful.)

67. *Daily Mail*, 15 June 1998.

68. 'Official Statement re Operation Hermes Ltd', posted on *Egyptnews* on 1 August 1998. The statement was signed by Hancock, Bauval and several other authors, including Colin Wilson, Andrew Collins and Alan Alford.

69. Questing Conference, London, 25 October 1998.

70. Appleby, 'Over the Top'. Appleby does not mention Simon Cox by name, but it is clear who he is referring to. Cox's report was included in the Hancock, Bauval, et al *Egyptnews* statement of 1 August 1998.

71. Alan F. Alford, posting on Ancient Astronaut Society Research Association news group (*http://www.aas-ra.org*), 15 September 1998.

72. This sequence is shown in Boris Said's *Legends of the Sphinx* video.

73. Telephone interview with Jill Freeman, director of AMORC's Rosicrucian Museum, 12 March 1999.

74. Hunter and Hillier, 'The Hall of Osiris'. (Hillier has since dissociated himself from the theories and allegations contained in this article. Hunter stands by them.)

75. Robinson, *Edgar Cayce's Story of the Origin and Destiny of Man*, p79.

76. Georgina Bruni wrote an account of the meeting in her column in *Sightings* magazine, September 1997. Other details were given in conversations with the authors.

77. A. Robert Smith, p290.
78. Ibid., Chapters 5–8.
79. Ibid., p48.
80. Ibid., p56.
81. Ibid.
82. Ibid., p120.
83. Ibid., Appendix C.
84. Ibid., p298.
85. Ibid., p297.
86. Ibid., p132.
87. Ibid., p120.
88. Ibid., p130.
89. Ibid., Chapter 21.
90. Ibid., pp173–4.
91. Ibid., p296.
92. Collins, *Gods of Eden*, p171.
93. Bauval and Hancock, *Keeper of Genesis*, p316.
94. The following information about the history of SRI is taken from Leslie, *The Cold War and American Science*, and Lowen, *Creating the Cold War University*.
95. Leslie, p242.
96. Ibid., p251.
97. For a detailed history of the US government's research into, and use of, remote viewing, see Schnabel.
98. Budge, *An Egyptian Hieroglyphic Dictionary*, vol. 2, pp654–5.
99. Schnabel, pp175–84.
100. Targ and Puthoff, Chapter 7.
101. Schnabel, Chapter 7; Puthoff, 'CIA-Initiated Remote Viewing Program at Stanford Research Institute'.
102. Schnabel, pp142–3.
103. Morehouse, p83.
104. Ibid., p73.
105. Lambert Dolphin, in response to a query from 'Brother Blue', posted on *sci.archaeology* newsgroup, 19 July 1998.
106. Gardner, *Urantia*, p142.
107. Email from Kim Farmer, AFFS, 24 September 1998.
108. See especially Constantine, *Virtual Government* and '"Remote Viewing" at Stanford Research Institute or Illicit Mind Control Experimentation?'.

109. See Bauval and Hancock, 'Mysteries of Mars', especially the third instalment (20 August 1996), and *Hieroglyph*, no. 1, January 1997.
110. Bauval, 'The Face on Mars and the Terrestrial Connection'.
111. Temple, *The Sirius Mystery*, p.v.
112. Niklas Rasche, review of *The Mars Mystery*, *Fortean Times*, no. 113, August 1998, p55.

3 Beyond the Mars Mission

1. Holroyd, *Briefing for the Landing on Planet Earth*, p63.
2. *The Pyramids of Mars*, written by Stephen Harris, directed by Paddy Russell and produced by Philip Hinchcliffe (1975).
3. Sagan, p153.
4. See NASA, *Viking 1: Early Results*; Zubrin and Wagner, Chapter 2; Sagan, pp137–49.
5. See Zubrin and Wagner, pp31–5; Swartz, 'Mars as an Abode of Life', in McDaniel and Paxson.
6. Crowley and Hurtak, pp14–15.
7. Email to authors from Kim Farmer of the Academy for Future Sciences, 24 September 1998.
8. Bauval and Hancock, 'Mysteries of Mars', part 3.
9. Ibid.
10. Hoagland, *The Monuments of Mars*, pp98–100.
11. Ibid., p472. Hoagland's book is dedicated to Roddenberry, among others.
12. Ibid., p136.
13. Ibid., p49.
14. Ibid., pp62-64. Mark Carlotto has pointed out that Hoagland's measurement of the orientation of the Face to the Martian north-south meridian is wrong – by perhaps as much as 10 degrees – and all his subsequent calculations and deductions are therefore in error. See Carlotto, pp165–6.
15. Hoagland, *The Monuments of Mars*, pp136–43.
16. Ibid., p160.
17. Ibid., p166.
18. Schnabel, p277.
19. Hoagland, *The Monuments of Mars*, pp181–7.
20. Ibid., p335.

21. Ibid., pp323–4.
22. Ibid., p337.
23. In his lecture at the United Nations, recorded in *Hoagland's Mars Vol. II: The United Nations Briefing – The Terrestrial Connection*, BC Video Inc, 1993 (produced by David S. Percy, directed by Bill Cote).
24. Torun's work is summarised in Hoagland, *The Monuments of Mars*, Chapter XVII. Torun's own papers have not yet been published.
25. Hoagland, *The Monuments of Mars*, p373.
26. Ibid., p127.
27. Ibid., p342.
28. Hoagland's lecture is the subject of the video *Hoagland's Mars Vol. II* (see note 23, Chapter 3).
29. *Fortean Times*, no. 117, December 1998, p7.
30. From McDaniel's website (*http://www.mcdanielreport.com*), quoted in *Nexus*, vol. 5, no. 4, June/July 1998.
31. Lindemann, 'Cydonia Disappoints, But Controversy Continues'.
32. Rickard, p30.
33. Ibid.
34. DiPietro, Molenaar and Brandenburg, pp103–12.
35. The full title of McDaniel's report is *On the Failure of Executive, Congressional, and Scientific Responsibility in Investigating Possible Evidence of Artificial Structures on the Surface of Mars and in Setting Mission Priorities for NASA's Mars Exploration Program*.
36. DiPietro, Molenaar and Brandenburg, p130.
37. Email to the authors from Mark Carlotto, 4 September 1998.
38. Ibid.
39. Hoagland, *The Monuments of Mars*, p362.
40. Ibid., p289.
41. Hancock, Bauval and Grigsby, p196.
42. Crowley and Hurtak, p55; Joan Wucher King, p219.
43. Joan Wucher King, p219.
44. Ibid., pp219 and 300.
45. Hoagland, *The Monuments of Mars*, p287; Bauval, 'The Face on Mars and the Terrestrial Connection'.
46. Budge, *An Egyptian Hieroglyphic Dictionary*, vol. 1, pp493 (*her*/face) and 500 (Heru/Horus).
47. Hoagland, *The Monuments of Mars*, p361.

48. Ibid., p298.
49. The concept of Flatland was devised in 1884 by the Reverend Edwin Abbott, under the pseudonym of A. Square, in *Flatland, a romance of many dimensions*.
50. Hoagland, *The Monuments of Mars*, pp351–6.
51. Ibid., p326.
52. Whitehouse, p17. Note that Whitehouse, in error, ascribes this latitude to the Face, not the D and M Pyramid. However, a similar mistake is by Hoagland himself, who gives this as the latitude of the City (*The Monuments of Mars*, p326). These errors have no bearing on the central point, which is that the apparently precise latitudes used by Hoagland and Torun are, in fact, wrong.
53. Van Flandern, 'An Alternative Hypothesis of Cydonia's Formation', in McDaniel and Paxson.
54. Hancock, Bauval and Grigsby, p53.
55. Hoagland, *The Monuments of Mars*, p352.
56. Carlotto, p180.
57. *The Face on Mars: The Avebury Connection* video, Aulis Publishers, 1994 (produced and directed by David S. Percy).
58. Interview with David S. Percy in London, 29 August 1998.
59. *The Face on Mars: The Avebury Connection* video.
60. Hoagland, *The Monuments of Mars*, p381.
61. Our thanks to Niklas Rasche and Rob Irving for this information.
62. Rob Irving, telephone interview, 12 August 1998.
63. Hoagland, *The Monuments of Mars*, pp366–7.
64. Ibid., p351.
65. Ibid., pp194–8. Avinsky's article appeared in the August 1984 issue of *Soviet Life*.
66. Ibid., p204.
67. *Hieroglyph*, no. 1, January 1997.
68. Temple, *The Sirius Mystery*, p35.
69. Carlotto, pp88–9.
70. Gardner, *Urantia*, p142.
71. Ibid.
72. Email to authors from Kim Farmer of the Academy for Future Sciences, 24 September 1998.
73. Gardner, *Urantia*, p142.
74. Morehouse, p137.
75. Ibid., pp128–34.

76. Courtney Brown, Chapter 4.

77. On Art Bell's radio show in May 1997, Hoagland claimed that he had information that NASA were suppressing pictures of Hale-Bopp that had been taken with the Hubble telescope, and appealed to listeners to lobby the space agency for their release. In response, NASA pointed out that it had issued some 4,500 images of the comet on the Internet, including those taken by Hubble. ('NASA Bops Comet Conspiracy Theory', *Florida Today Space Online*, 13 May 1997.)

78. Brandenburg, 'Newly Discovered Mars Meteorites Suggest Long-Term Life', in McDaniel and Paxson.

79. Hancock, Bauval and Grigsby, p26.

80. Ibid., pp21–2.

4 Contact?

1. Bennett and Percy, p486.

2. Hurtak, pp.vii–viii.

3. Vallée, *Messengers of Deception*, p133.

4. Hurtak, p287.

5. Hancock, Bauval and Grigsby, pp75 and 79.

6. Bauval and Hancock, 'Mysteries of Mars', part 3.

7. *Legends of the Sphinx* video.

8. In an email on 7 August 1998 we asked Robert Bauval about the source of his published statements about Hurtak's claims concerning Mars. In his reply dated 30 August 1998, Bauval referred us to *The Keys of Enoch*.

9. Puharich, *Uri*, pp14–15.

10. Ibid., pp16–17.

11. Ibid., p10.

12. Ibid., p254.

13. Puharich and Hurkos's mission concerned the 'Acámbaro figurines', interest in which has recently revived. Deposits of over 30,000 pre-Colombian clay figurines were unearthed in the vicinity of Acámbaro in the 1930s and 1940s, including, among more conventional subjects, reproductions of extinct animals such as dinosaurs. If genuine, these would, of course, seriously challenge the standard view of evolution and history. However, a study of the objects by independent archaeologist Neil Steede, made at the

behest of BC Video Inc., found that the anomalous figures were of recent manufacture (see *Jurassic Art*, BC Video Inc., 1997).

The exact purpose of Puharich and Hurkos's visit to Acámbaro is unknown, as both men give reticent accounts of this episode. Puharich says only that the visit was made to 'help solve an archaeological problem' (*Uri*, p18). In his autobiography, Hurkos (who makes no mention of the meeting with the Laugheads) states only that the visit was made at the request of a 'man connected with the [Round Table] foundation' and that, although he discovered some 'statues' using his psychic abilities, they were not allowed to take them out of Mexico, as they had no permit (Hurkos, pp162–4).

14. Puharich, *Uri*, pp19–22.
15. Geller, p205.
16. Holroyd, *Briefing for the Landing on Planet Earth*, p49.
17. Puharich, *Uri*, pp90–6.
18. Ibid., p113.
19. Ibid., p124.
20. Ibid.
21. Ibid., p127.
22. Ibid., p144.
23. Ibid., p172.
24. Whether Geller worked for Israeli intelligence before his first visit to the United States is unclear. There are suggestions that Mossad had at least shown an interest in Geller when he first came to public attention in Israel, although Guy Lyon Playfair records that Geller was reluctant to go into details about the level of his involvement at that time (Geller and Playfair, p195). Playfair also states that SRI scientists Targ and Puthoff were briefed by Mossad about Geller in 1973 (ibid., p196). American engineer Eldon Byrd, who undertook experiments on Geller in 1975 and was questioned by CIA agents about them, told reporter John Strausbaugh in 1996 that he had been told by the CIA that they had decided not to use Geller because of his work for Mossad, which would effectively make him a double agent.
25. See Geller and Playfair, Chapter 3; Strausbaugh.
26. Schnabel, pp96–7.
27. See Strausbaugh. This *New York Press* article is reproduced on Uri Geller's website (*http://www.tcom.co.uk/hpnet/*).

28. Puharich, *Uri*, p173.
29. Geller and Playfair, pp178, 197–9.
30. Levy, pp165–7.
31. Holroyd, *Briefing for the Landing on Planet Earth*, pp50–51.
32. Ibid., pp56–7.
33. Ibid., pp58–60.
34. Steele, 'The Road to Atlantis?'.
35. Holroyd, *Briefing for the Landing on Planet Earth*, p63.
36. Ibid., p82–8.
37. Schlemmer and Bennett, p331.
38. Holroyd, *Briefing for the Landing on Planet Earth*, pp142–3.
39. Engel, pp165–6, 174–8.
40. *UFO Magazine*, vol. 9, no. 13 (1995), citing articles in *Cinescape* and *Hollywood Reporter*.
41. Holroyd, *Briefing for the Landing on Planet Earth*, pp193–207.
42. Ibid., pp278–9.
43. Sarfatti, 'In the Thick of it!'; Gardner, *Science: Good, Bad and Bogus*, pp287–8.
44. Elkins, Rueckert and McCarty, p47.
45. Ibid., p98.
46. Mark Probert was a trance medium who in the 1940s and 1950s, channelled information for an organisation called the Borderland Sciences Research Foundation in California. This was one of the first groups to combine mediumship with a belief in extraterrestrials, with Probert questioning his spirit guides on the emerging mystery of flying saucers. Probert had a number of spirit guides, including famous names such as Thomas Edison, and, while it is true that his mediumship centred on an 'inner circle' of nine guides, these were allegedly discarnate humans. Despite the assertions of 'Ra', there is no suggestion in Probert's work that his guides were themselves extraterrestrial intelligences, nor is there any similarity between the content of Probert's communications and those from the later Council of Nine.
47. Elkins, Rueckert and McCarty, p99.
48. In an interview at his London home on 29 August 1998, Percy told us that he appears under a pseudonym as one of the questioners in *The Only Planet of Choice*.
49. Holroyd, *Briefing for the Landing on Planet Earth*, p158.
50. Ibid., p159.

51. Levy, p253.
52. Bennett and Percy, pp486–7.
53. Petrie, p36.
54. Puharich, *The Sacred Mushroom*, pp31–2.
55. Hurkos, pp161–2.
56. Puharich, *The Sacred Mushroom*, p75.
57. Ibid., p128.
58. Ibid., p170.
59. Hurtak, p487.

5 Behind the Mask

1. Myers and Percy, p87.
2. Schlemmer and Bennett, p126.
3. Ibid., p169.
4. Ibid., p192.
5. Ibid., p197.
6. Ibid., Chapter 6.
7. Ibid., p156.
8. Ibid.
9. Bauval and Hancock, *Keeper of Genesis*, pp248–9; Hancock, *Fingerprints of the Gods*, pp449–50.
10. Hurtak, pp33–4.
11. Ibid., p43.
12. Ibid., p232.
13. Schlemmer and Bennett, p126.
14. Hurtak, p.viii.
15. Ibid., p85.
16. Schlemmer and Bennett, pp179–80.
17. Ibid., p173.
18. Ibid., p.v.
19. Hurtak, Introduction.
20. Vallée, *Messengers of Deception*, p136.
21. Holroyd, *Briefing for the Landing on Planet Earth*, p341.
22. Hurtak, p169.
23. Ibid., p329.
24. Ibid., p330.
25. Ibid., p566.
26. Myers and Percy, pp464–5.

27. Palden Jenkins, telephone interview, 30 July 1998.
28. Statement from James Hurtak and the Magical Eye team, in *Academy* (website bulletin), no. 118 (*http://academy.wwdc.com/archives/118.html*).
29. Schlemmer and Bennett, p148.
30. Holroyd, *Briefing for the Landing on Planet Earth*, p101.
31. Genesis 28.
32. Schonfield, p278.
33. Holroyd, *Briefing for the Landing on Planet Earth*, p159.
34. *Hoagland's Mars, Vol II: The United Nations Briefing – The Terrestrial Connection* video.
35. Myers and Percy, p233.
36. Temple, *The Sirius Mystery*, p5.
37. Holroyd, *Briefing for the Landing on Planet Earth*, Chapter 9.
38. Ibid., pp32–4.
39. Colin Wilson, *Mysteries*, pp538–48.
40. Colin Wilson's introduction to Holroyd, *Briefing for the Landing on Planet Earth*, p14.
41. Colin Wilson, *Mysteries*, p545.
42. Levy, p128.
43. Puharich, *Uri*, p16.
44. Sarfatti, 'In the Thick of It!', note 6. Jack Sarfatti's autobiographical writings can be found on his website (*http://www.hia.com/pcr/*).
45. This was stated by James Hurtak to researcher Terry L. Milner (email to authors from Terry Milner, 13 August 1998).
46. Milner, Part 4.
47. Tompkins and Bird, p266.
48. Ira Einhorn, telephone interview, 27 August 1998.
49. Interview with Uri Geller, Sonning, 10 February 1998.
50. Sarfatti, 'In the Thick of It!', note 6.
51. Email from Kim Farmer of AFFS, 24 September 1998.
52. Marks, p59.
53. Ibid., p.viii.
54. On mind-control experiments by US agencies, see Marks; Bowart.
55. Bowart, p90.
56. Temple, *Open to Suggestion*, p357.
57. Ibid.
58. Puharich, *The Sacred Mushroom*, pp8–13.
59. Ibid., p10.

60. Ibid., pp10–11.
61. Ibid., p37.
62. Ibid., p102.
63. Marks, p114.
64. Puharich, *The Sacred Mushroom*, p58.
65. Marks, p210; Rudgley, p74.
66. Marks, p117.
67. Puharich, *The Sacred Mushroom*, pp83–4; Marks, p111.
68. Marks, p210.
69. See Marks, Chapter 5. At Edgewood, Gottlieb oversaw the notorious LSD research programme that resulted in the suicide of one of the experimental subjects, Frank Olson.
70. Schnabel, p202.
71. See Puharich, *The Sacred Mushroom*, pp10–11; Fuller, bibliography.
72. Holroyd (*Briefing for the Landing on Planet Earth*, p46) was told by Puharich that he heard of Arigó 'quite by chance' while in Brazil 'on a mission connected with the US National Aeronautics and Space Administration'. However, according to John G. Fuller's book on Arigó – to which Puharich contributed an afterword – Puharich and Henry Belk made the trip to Brazil specifically to seek out the healer, who was being studied by NASA engineer John Laurance. It is therefore a reasonable conclusion that, bizarre though it may seem, the 'NASA mission' actually concerned Arigó's alleged abilities.
73. Fuller, p19.
74. Puharich, *The Iceland Papers*.
75. Ira Einhorn, telephone interview, 27 August 1998.
76. Milner, Part 3.
77. MacDonald, p116.
78. Wallace, pp78–9.
79. MacDonald, pp119–20.
80. Ibid. p120.
81. Garrett, *Many Voices*, p202.
82. Milner, Part 4.
83. Levy, p129.
84. Milner, Part 2.
85. Holroyd, *Briefing for the Landing on Planet Earth*, p16.
86. Geller and Playfair, p91.

87. Ibid.
88. Ira Einhorn, telephone interview, 27 August 1998.
89. Garrett, *Adventures in the Supernormal*, Chapter XII.
90. Elkins and Rueckert, Chapter 2.
91. Holroyd, *Briefing for the Landing on Planet Earth*, pp74-5.
92. Ibid., p115.
93. Williamson and Bailey, pp17–19.
94. Ibid., p18.
95. Rux, p323.
96. Vallée, *Messengers of Deception*, p193.
97. Festiger, Riecken and Schachter, p232.
98. Ibid., p152.
99. Jerome Clark, 'When Prophecy Failed'.
100. Levy, p166.
101. Ibid.
102. Ira Einhorn, telephone interview, 27 August 1998.
103. Levy, p218–20.
104. Ibid., p219.
105. Ibid., p5.
106. Ibid., p189.
107. Ibid., pp156–61.
108. Ibid., p160.
109. Ibid., p225.
110. Ibid., pp252–5.
111. Articles in the *Philadelphia Enquirer*, 21 and 23 June 1997, reproduced on their website (*http://www.phillynews.com*).
112. Quoted in Constantine, 'Rep. Charlie Rose, BNL and the "Occult"'.
113. Sarfatti, 'In the Thick of It!'.
114. Email from Jack Sarfatti to the authors, 31 August 1998.
115. Levy, p4.
116. Ibid., p189.
117. Ibid.
118. Quoted in a profile of Bearden on the Doc Hambone website (*http://www.io.com/~hambone/web/bearden.html*).
119. Ibid., and confirmed in telephone conversation with Thomas Bearden, 26 August 1998.
120. Levy, p128.
121. Ira Einhorn, telephone interview with the authors, 27 August 1998.

122. Gardner, *Science: Good, Bad and Bogus*, pp287–8.
123. Sarfatti, 'In the Thick of It!'.
124. Targ and Puthoff, p.vii.
125. From biographical information in Mitchell's *Psychic Exploration*.
126. In 1984, Willis Harman, president of the Institute of Noetic Sciences (and a social scientist at SRI), stated in his introduction to Targ and Harary's *The Mind Race* that the Institute had been the major funder of SRI's preliminary remote viewing experiments. However, since the declassification of documents relating to the project in July 1995 it has been known that it was, in fact, the CIA that sponsored these experiments. This suggests, at the very least, that the Institute of Noetic Sciences allowed itself to be used as a cover for the CIA's sponsorship.
127. Hoagland, *The Monuments of Mars*, p.xiii.
128. Terry Milner, email to authors, 13 August 1998.
129. Ibid.
130. Sarfatti, 'In the Thick of It!'.
131. Marks, p151.
132. Sarfatti, 'Quantum Quackery'.
133. See Picknett, pp210–11.
134. Ira Einhorn, telephone interview, 27 August 1998.
135. Schnabel, pp162–8.
136. Ibid., p166.
137. Constantine, 'Ed Dames and His Cover Stories for Mind Control Experimentation'.
138. Ibid., pp196–8.
139. Sarfatti, 'The Destiny Matrix'.
140. Jack Sarfatti, email to authors, 13 July 1998.
141. Sarfatti, 'The Destiny Matrix'.
142. Ibid.
143. Robert Anton Wilson, p256.
144. Ibid., p257.
145. Ibid., p72.
146. Lilly, *Centre of the Cyclone*, p97.
147. Lilly, *The Human Biocomputer*, p.viii.
148. Robert Anton Wilson, p71.
149. Posting on Arthur Young website (*www.arthuryoung.com*).
150. Vallée, *Revelations*, p81.
151. Sarfatti, 'In the Thick of It!'.

152. Ibid.
153. For studies of the question of the objective reality of discarnate – particularly extraterrestrial – intelligences, and other aspects of the 'entity enigma', see: Colin Wilson, *Alien Dawn*; Stuart Holroyd, *Alien Intelligence*; Hilary Evans; John A. Keel; and the works of Jacques Vallée.
154. Ramadan, 'Effects on Society of Public Disclosure of Extraterrestrial Presence'.
155. Farley, 'The Council of Nine'.
156. Schnabel, pp272–3.
157. Ibid., p273.
158. Posting by 'Brother Blue' on *sci.archaeology* newsgroup, 19 June 1998, which refers to a discussion with Jones on this subject.
159. Farley, 'The Council of Nine'.
160. Dick Farley, email to the authors, 21 August 1998.
161. Farley, 'The Council of Nine'.
162. Interview at Uri Geller's home in Sonning, 10 February 1998. The story is told in Strausbaugh's article.
163. US press reports of this event are reproduced on Uri Geller's website (*http://www.tcom.co.uk/hpnet/*).
164. *Macbeth*, Act I, Scene III.

6 The Secret Masters

1. R.A. Schwaller de Lubicz, *The Egyptian Miracle*, p87.
2. Ibid., p86.
3. Isha Schwaller de Lubicz, p111 (our translation).
4. R.A. Schwaller de Lubicz, *A Study of Numbers*, p51.
5. West, *Serpent in the Sky*, p66.
6. Schlemmer and Bennett, p6.
7. Bauval and Hancock, *Keeper of Genesis*, p15.
8. Saul Bellow, in his introduction to VandenBroeck.
9. VandenBroeck, p25.
10. Ibid., pp166–72.
11. Ibid., pp34–7.
12. Ibid., p51.
13. Ibid., p125.
14. See Courjeaud, pp63–6.
15. The subject of Fulcanelli's work and identity came up many

times during VandenBroeck's time with Schwaller de Lubicz, who said that he had worked closely with Fulcanelli and had sworn an oath not to reveal his true name. However, from Schwaller de Lubicz's allusions to details of 'Fulcanelli's' life – and in particular the description of his death in a Montmartre garret in 1932 – it is clear that he is referring to Champagne, who is, in any case, widely regarded as the best candidate for the role (see Courjeaud, pp85–103, and Johnson). VandenBroeck's description of a sketch of Fulcanelli hanging in Schwaller de Lubicz's house (p139) reveals that he bears a very close resemblance to Champagne.

16. Isha Schwaller de Lubicz, p16 (our translation).
17. VandenBroeck, p212.
18. Ibid., p203.
19. R.A. Schwaller de Lubicz, *Sacred Science*, p110.
20. Shaw and Nicholson, p239.
21. VandenBroeck, p166.
22. Ibid., pp239–47.
23. Geoffrey de Charnay, p46. (De Charnay was the pseudonym of Raoul Hassan. The choice of name reflects the perceived relationship between Synarchy and the medieval Knights Templar, as this was the name of one of the leading Templar officials executed in Paris in 1314 when the Order was suppressed.)
24. On twentieth-century Synarchy and its political activities, see de Charnay; Ulmann and Azeau; Bauchard.
25. Galtier, p307.
26. Postel du Mas's Revolutionary Synarchist Pact is reproduced in the appendix to de Charnay.
27. Pauwels and Bergier, pp34–8.

Another possible significant connection between the legend of the Nine Unknown Men and the later Council of Nine, researched by Philip Coppens, comes through the thriller writer Talbot Mundy (1879–1940). A former British colonial civil servant, Mundy (real name William Lancaster Gribbon) settled in New York in 1909 and became an American citizen. In 1923 he wrote a novel, *The Nine Unknown*, inspired by Louis Jacolliot's works, about a secret group in the East – referred to throughout as 'the Nine' – who exert a powerful influence on world affairs. Mundy was a Theosophist and a friend of the mystic Nicholas Roerich; from 1929 Mundy lived in an apartment above the Roerich Museum in New York. As discussed in Chapter 5, Roerich was the 'guru' of Henry Wallace, who funded Andrija Puharich's early work at the Round Table Foundation.

28. Weiss, Chapter 8.
29. On the Strict Templar Obervance and other neo-Templar societies, see our *The Templar Revelation*, pp130–32 and Appendix I.
30. Boisset, p5.
31. Galtier, p310 (our translation).
32. Ibid., p305.
33. Paijmans, p310.
34. Weiss, p247.
35. Ibid., p322.
36. See, for example, Saint-Yves d'Alveydre, *La théogonie des patriarches*, p55.
37. For a summary of Saint-Yves's account of Ram, see Weiss, Chapter 6.
38. Edgar Evans Cayce, p55. Cayce's followers are perplexed by this single reference to Ram in his psychic 'readings', since he gives no explanation of who Ram was.
39. Crowley, *The Confessions of Aleister Crowley*, pp413–15.
40. Ibid., p.xix.
41. Ibid., p419.
42. Grant, *Aleister Crowley and the Hidden God*, p8.
43. Crowley, *The Confessions of Aleister Crowley*, p482.
44. Ibid., p481.
45. Francis King, p29.
46. Grant, *The Magical Revival*, p210.
47. Grant, *Aleister Crowley and the Hidden God*, p17.
48. Rydeen, p49.
49. Grant, *Aleister Crowley and the Hidden God*, p72.
50. Rydeen, p25.
51. Robert Anton Wilson, p172.
52. Corydon and Hubbard, Jr, p48.
53. Collins, *Gods of Eden*, Chapter 7.
54. Paijmans, pp248–9.
55. Ibid. p251.
56. Grant, *Aleister Crowley and the Hidden God*, p115.
57. Ibid., p28.
58. Hurtak, p34.

59. Temple, *The Sirius Mystery*, pp40–44.

60. Ibid., p44.

61. Igliori, p170.

62. Ibid., p8–9.

63. Ibid., p9.

64. Ibid., p172.

65. Temple, *The Sirius Mystery*, pp33–4.

66. Holroyd, *Briefing for the Landing on Planet Earth*, p112.

67. Cavendish, p55.

68. Alice A. Bailey, *The Unfinished Autobiography of Alice A. Bailey*, p35.

69. Alice A. Bailey, *Initiation, Human and Solar*, p185.

70. Young, p.xxvi, and Appendix II.

71. Alice A. Bailey, *Initiation, Human and Solar*, p63.

72. Sinclair, pp112–19. Bailey's main work on the Groups of Nine is *Esoteric Psychology* (Volume II of *A Treatise on the Seven Rays*).

73. Sinclair, pp118–19.

74. Alice A. Bailey, *Initiation, Human and Solar*, pp57–60.

75. Puharich, *Uri*, pp14–17.

76. Puharich, 'A Way to Peace through ELF Waves'.

77. Robert Anton Wilson, p143 (quoting Dr Douglas Baker of the Theosophical Society).

78. Alice A. Bailey, *Initiation, Human and Solar*, p163.

79. Ibid., p92.

80. Ibid.

81. Alice A. Bailey, *A Treatise on the Seven Rays, Vol. V: The Rays and the Initiations*, p418.

82. Foster Bailey, p9.

83. Ibid., p32.

84. Nye, p25.

85. See, for example, Bonwick, pp89–90; Churchward, *The Arcana of Freemasonry*, p58; Pike, pp486–7.

86. Pike, pp489–99.

87. Randall-Stevens, *A Voice Out of Egypt*, p174.

88. Ibid., p13.

89. Randall-Stevens, *The Teachings of Osiris*, p43.

90. Inquire Within, *The Trail of the Serpent*, p316. Our thanks to Mark Bennett for bringing Stoddard's work to our attention.

91. Ibid., pp297–8.

92. Ibid., p297.

93. Ibid., p298.

94. Clymer, *Ancient Mystic Oriental Masonry*, p193.

95. Clymer, *Dr Paschal Beverly Randolph and the Supreme Grand Dome of the Rosicrucians in France*, p15.

96. Ibid., p14.

97. Ibid., p13.

98. Clymer, *Ancient Mystic Oriental Masonry*, p80.

99. Clymer, *Dr Paschal Beverly Randolph and the Supreme Grand Dome of the Rosicrucians in France*, p24.

100. Vallée, *Messengers of Deception*, p133.

101. Ibid., p102.

102. Ibid., p127.

103. Hurtak, p596.

104. See Peronnik, p67; Douzet.

105. Douzet, p48.

106. See Carr-Brown and Cohen.

107. Peronnik, p240 (our translation).

108. Ibid., p241.

109. For example, Article 8 of the Solar Temple's Rules and Statutes (reproduced in Peronnik) states: 'The TS [Temple Solaire] Order is placed under absolute obedience to the Synarchy of the Temple. For that purpose, Synarchy holds the fullest powers; its members are and will remain secret.'

110. See Bédat, Bouleau and Nikolas, p331.

111. Musaios, p93.

112. Ibid., p95.

113. Ibid.

114. Ibid., p97.

115. Faulkner, *The Ancient Egyptian Book of the Dead*, p144.

116. West, *The Case for Astrology*, pp56–7.

117. Musès, p219.

118. Ibid.

119. Musès and Young, p343.

7 Endtimes: The Warning

1. See Drosnin. Drosnin's claims that the letters of the Hebrew Bible contained a code giving predictions of future events, which

could be unlocked using sophisticated computer programs, received worldwide publicity in 1997. However researchers have since found that the same programs produce similar results with Hebrew versions of *War and Peace* and *Moby Dick*. Predictably, these findings have received far less publicity than Drosnin's original claims. See *Fortean Times*, no. 113, August 1998, p7.

2. BBC *Everyman* documentary, 'Contact', (produced and directed by Nikki Stockley), 1998.

3. Figure quoted in the BBC *Everyman* documentary, 'Contact'.

4. Strieber, *Breakthrough*, pp240–42.

5. Ibid., p241.

6. Strieber, *The Secret School*, pp.xviii–xix.

7. Ibid., p.xix.

8. Ibid., p.xxiii.

9. Rydeen, p18.

10. Strieber, *The Secret School*, pp3–12.

11. Ibid., p149.

12. Ibid., p226.

13. Conroy, p263.

14. When, on Art Bell's radio show on 14 November 1996, Courtney Brown announced the 'discovery' by remote viewing of the spaceship trailing Hale-Bopp, he supported it with a photograph that he claimed had been leaked to him by an anonymous astrophysicist. Strieber subsequently posted this on his website (where it was quickly exposed as a fake, being a doctored version of a picture taken by the University of Hawaii's observatory. See Keith, 'Reptoids stole my Meteorite').

    As Strieber has pointed out, his posting of the photograph did not constitute endorsement of Brown's claims. However, prior to its exposure he did encourage the public to 'meditate and try to establish a link' with the beings aboard the hypothetical spaceship. See postings on Strieber's website (*www.strieber.com*).

15. One notorious example is the 'Enterprise', a group of CIA operatives and Pentagon officials who, for over twenty years from the early 1960s to the 1980s, used their positions, access to covert channels and the protection of National Security legislation to profit from various illegal activities, primarily arms and drugs dealing and including heroin trafficking from the Far East during the Vietnam War, profiting from inflating the prices of arms sup-

plies to the Shah of Iran in the 1970s and cocaine smuggling from Central America in the early 1980s. Operations expanded as promotions gave the members access to more and more covert power – one member, Theodore Shackley, nearly became CIA director in the 1970s – until a series of scandals in the 1980s revealed the extent of their operations. Despite exposure, and the naming of the individuals concerned in the media, only one member of the Enterprise, Edwin P. Wilson, was ever prosecuted, the others being forced to resign. Wilson was sentenced to fifty-two years' maximum security imprisonment in 1982 for supplying explosives to Libya. See Cockburn; Maas.

16. The report was originally commissioned by the US Office of Education in 1968, but four years later it withdrew funding, after which the study was, apparently, financed internally by SRI. The final report was published in 1973, although it did not receive widespread circulation until 1982, when it was published by Robert Maxwell's Pergamon Press as one of the 1,000 most important works of modern times.

17. Markley and Harman, p185.

18. Ibid., pp184–5.

19. On the influence of Masonic ideals on the Constitution of the United States of America, see Baigent and Leigh, Chapter 19.

20. Harman, p108.

21. Ibid., p107–11.

22. Ibid., p111.

23. Ibid., p109.

24. From Zahi Hawass's website (*guardians.net/hawass/*).

25. Hurtak, p169.

26. Ibid., p585.

27. Ibid., p586.

28. See for example, Elkins, Rueckert and McCarty, pp92–3.

29. Schlemmer and Bennett, p126.

30. Alice A. Bailey, *A Treatise on Cosmic Fire*, p719.

31. Hurtak, p85.

32. Ibid., p86.

33. Ibid., p86.

34. Ibid., p258.

35. Hurtak, when discussing the Black Cube, adds a footnote (p86) referring to the 'higher message of Islam' and giving a reference to

the glossary. However, the glossary entry (p609) refers only to the parts of the Koran dealing with God's covenant with Israel.

36. Ibid., p263.

37. Randall-Stevens, *A Voice out of Egypt*, p167.

38. Robert Bauval, posting on *Egyptnews*, 24 September 1998.

39. Vallée, *Messengers of Deception*, p157.

40. Vallée, *Revelations*, p228.

41. Vallée, *Messengers of Deception*, p217.

42. Ira Einhorn, telephone interview, 27 August 1998.

43. Schlemmer and Bennett, p48.

44. Engel, pp175–6.

45. Rice, *Egypt's Legacy*, p58.

46. Puharich, *The Sacred Mushroom*, p31.

47. Grant, *Aleister Crowley and the Hidden God*, p225.

Epilogue: The Real Stargate?

1. Narby, p11.

2. Ibid., pp39–40.

3. Ibid., p112.

4. Collins, *From the Ashes of Angels*, Chapter 5.

5. Kerisel, pp37–44.

6. Quoted in Narby, p53.

7. Ibid., p17.

8. Faulkner, *The Ancient Egyptian Pyramid Texts*, pp165–6.

9. Ibid., p93 (Utterance 305).

10. Narby, p97.

11. Quoted in Campbell, p63.

12. Campbell and Musès, p131.

13. Ibid., p136.

14. Ibid.

15. Quoted in Narby, p55.

16. Ibid., p62.

17. Ibid.

18. The theme of twins runs through Dogon mythology and folklore. For example, the original Nommo were two sets of male and female twins. The Dogon also believe that the first human beings, their ancestors, were created in pairs of twins. See Griaule and Dieterlen, pp360–62; Marti, pp53–6.

19. Narby, p139.
20. Devereux, p124.
21. This and the following quotes from Jeremy Narby are taken from a telephone interview on 17 August 1998.
22. Michael Carmichael, telephone interview, 27 August 1998.
23. On the shamanistic use of psychoactive substances, see Rudgley; Ratsch; Devereux; Wasson and Wasson.
24. This and the following quotations are from a telephone interview with Michael Carmichael, 27 August 1998.
25. Strieber, *Transformation*, chapter 2.
26. Graff, p1.

Update

1. The Great Pyramid was finally reopened on 3 June 1999, although with a strict limit on the number of visitors allowed in each day. There is still pressure from Egyptian archaeologists, such as Dr Hawass, for visitors to be excluded altogether because of the potential for damage to the interior of the monument.

2. Jarre's work was entitled *The Twelve Dreams of the Sun*, and not, as originally reported, *Equinox 2000*.

3. In the event, presumably as a compromise, the Eye of Horus was projected onto Menkaura's Pyramid.

4. 'Atlantis Uncovered', written and produced by Jacqueline Smith, and 'Atlantis Reborn', written and produced by Chris Hale, broadcast in the UK on 29 October and 4 November 1999 respectively.

5. Lawton & Ogilvie-Herald, pp364–367.

6. Fairall, 'Orion's Belt and the Layout of the Three Pyramids at Giza'. Fairall's criticisms first appeared in the June 1999 issue of *Astronomy and Geophysics*.

7. Rohl, 'Eternal Riddle of the Sands entombed in Mystery and Academic War of Words'.

8. Bauval, *Secret Chamber*, pp.xxviii–xxix.

9. Ibid., p.xix.

10. Ibid., p.xxviii.

11. Ibid., p343.

12. See Ogilvie-Herald, 'Great Pyramid Capstone Ceremony – Cancelled!' and Bauval, 'The Golden Capstone Controversy'. The

Egyptian newspaper that took the lead in criticising the ceremony was *Al Shaab*.

13. Bauval, ibid.
14. Bauval, *Secret Chamber*, p.xviii.
15. Bauval, 'Update from Robert Bauval, 6 January 2000.'
16. Bauval, *Secret Chamber*, pp184–190.
17. Ibid., p417.
18. Ibid., p.xxi.
19. Lawton & Ogilvie-Herald, pp395–397
20. Ibid., p397
21. Bauval, *Secret Chamber*, pp303–304.
22. Lawton & Ogilvie-Herald, pp407–411.
23. Bauval, *Secret Chamber*, Chapter Eleven.
24. Lawton & Ogilvie-Herald, pp483–486.
25. Bauval, *Secret Chamber*, p300.
26. Lawton & Ogilvie-Herald, pp476–477.
27. Ibid., pp470–472.
28. For example of at the *Nexus* magazine conference in Sydney. A video of Hurtak's lecture, 'The Opening of the Time Doors in India, Asia and the Pacific', is available by mail order from *Nexus*.
29. Bauval, *Secret Chamber*, p232.
30. For example, in Paul White's account of one of Hurtak's lectures on the Library of New Age On-Line website (http://www.newage.com.au).
31. See, for example, Hurtak's contributions to the 1994 video documentary *UFO Secrets of the Third Reich*.
32. Lawton & Ogilvie-Herald, pp247–248.
33. Bauval, *Secret Chamber*, pp166–169.
34. Sjöö, pp23-26.
35. Ibid., p21.
36. Ibid., p19. Bailey's quote is from *The Externalisation of the Hierarchy*, p497.
37. Pelley, p87.
38. Ibid., p85.
39. Ibid., p86.
40. Ibid., p167.
41. Ibid., p101.
42. Ibid., p167.
43. Ibid., p166.

Bibliography

Details of the edition cited in the text are given first, followed, where applicable, by details of the first publication.

Alford, Alan F., *Gods of the New Millennium: Scientific Proof of Flesh and Blood Gods*, Eridu Books, Walsall, 1996.
The Phoenix Solution: Secrets of a Lost Civilisation, Hodder & Stoughton, London, 1998.

Allen, Richard Hinckley, *Star-Names and Their Meanings*, G.E. Stechert, London, 1899.

Alvarez, Luis W. *et al.*, 'Search for Hidden Chambers in the Pyramids', *Science*, vol. 167, February 1970.

Appleby, Nigel, *Hall of the Gods*, William Heinemann, London, 1998.
'Over the Top', special supplement to *Quest Magazine*, no. 12, October 1998.

Aubert, Raphäel and Carl-A. Keller, *Vie et mort de l'Ordre du Temple Solaire*, Editions de l'Aire, Vevey, 1994.

Baigent, Michael and Richard Leigh, *The Temple and the Lodge*, Corgi, London, 1990 (first published by Jonathan Cape, London, 1989).

Bailey, Alice A., *Discipleship in the New Age*, 2 vols., Lucis Press, New York, 1944.

The Functions of the New Group of World Servers, Lucis Publishing Co., New York, 1935.

The Externalisation of the Hierarchy, Lucis Publishing Co., London, 1957.

Initiation, Human and Solar, Lucifer Publishing Co., New York, 1922.

A Treatise on Cosmic Fire, 2 vols., Lucis Publishing Co., New York, 1925.

A Treatise on the Seven Rays, 5 vols., Lucis Publishing Co., New York, 1936–60.

The Unfinished Autobiography of Alice A. Bailey, Lucis Press, London, 1951.

Bailey, Foster, *The Spirit of Masonry*, Lucis Press, Tunbridge Wells, 1957.

Baines, John and Jaromir Málek, *Atlas of Ancient Egypt*, Phaidon Press, Oxford, 1980.

Bauchard, Philippe, *Les technocrates et le pouvoir: X-Crise, synarchie, C.G.T., Clubs*, B. Arthaud, Paris, 1966.

Bauval, Robert G., 'The Face on Mars and the Terrestrial Connection', *Quest for Knowledge Magazine*, vol. 1, no. 1, April 1997.

'The Golden Capstone Controversy: Will the Egyptians scrap the Millennium Ceremony at the Giza Pyramids?', Daily Grail website (*http://www.dailygrail.com/misc/rgb181299.html*), 19 December 1999.

Secret Chamber: The Quest for the Hall of Records, Century, London, 1999.

'Update from Robert Bauval, 6th January 2000', Daily Grail website (*http://www.dailygrail.com/misc/rgb060100.html*), 7 January 2000.

Bauval, Robert and Adrian Gilbert, *The Orion Mystery: Unlocking the Secrets of the Pyramids*, revised edition, Mandarin, London, 1995 (William Heinemann, London, 1994).

Bauval, Robert and Graham Hancock, *Keeper of Genesis: A Quest for the Hidden Legacy of Mankind*, William Heinemann, London, 1996.

'Mysteries of Mars', *Daily Mail*, 17, 19 and 20 August 1996.

Bayuk, Andrew, 'Spotlight Interview – Dr Zahi Hawass', *Guardian's Egypt On-Line* website (*http://guardians.net/egypt*), 1997.

Beaudoin, Gérard, *Les Dogons du Mali*, Armand Colin, Paris, 1984.

Bédat, Arnaud, Gilles Bouleau and Bernard Nikolas, *Les chevaliers de la mort: enquête et révélations sur l'Ordre du Temple Solaire*, TF1 Editions, Paris, 1996.

Benest, D., and J.L. Duvent, 'Is Sirius a Triple Star?', *Astronomy and Astrophysics*, no. 299, 1995.

Bennett, Mary and David S. Percy, *Dark Moon: Apollo and the Whistle Blowers*, Aulis Publishers, London, 1999.

Berger, Catherine, Gisèle Clerc and Nicolas Grimal (eds.), *Homages à Jean Leclant*, Institut Francais d'Archeologie Orientale, Paris, 1994.

Blavatsky, H.P., *Isis Unveiled: A Master-Key to the Mysteries of Ancient and Modern Science and Theology*, 2 vols., J.W. Boulton, New York, 1877.
The Secret Doctrine: The Synthesis of Science, Religion and Philosophy, 2 vols., Theosophical Publishing Co., London, 1888.

Boisset, Yves-Fred, *Les clés traditionelles et synarchiques de l'archéo-mètre*, JBG, Paris, 1977.

Bonwick, James, *Orion and Sirius*, E.A. Petherick, London, 1888.

Borderland Sciences Research Foundation, *Coming of the Guardians*, Borderland Sciences Research Foundation, Vista, 1978.

Bowart, Walter, *Operation Mind Control*, Fontana, London, 1978.

Breasted, James Henry, *Ancient Records of Egypt: Historical Documents from the Earliest Times to the Persian Conquest, Collected, Edited and Translated with Commentary*, 4 vols., University of Chicago Press, Chicago, 1906.

Brown, Courtney, *Cosmic Voyage: A Scientific Discovery of Extraterrestrials Visiting Earth*, Dutton, London, 1996.

Brunson, Margaret, *A Dictionary of Ancient Egypt*, Oxford University Press, Oxford, 1995.

Budge, E.A. Wallis, *An Egyptian Hieroglyphic Dictionary*, John Murray, London, 1920.
Egyptian Literature, Vol. I: Legends of the Gods, Kegan Paul, Trench, Trübner and Co., London, 1912.
The Gods of the Egyptians, or Studies in Egyptian Mythology, 2 vols., Methuen and Co., London, 1904.

Burke, Kenneth and Dee, 'Secret Tunnels in Egypt: An Interview with Boris Said', *Nexus*, April/May 1998.

Campbell, Joseph, *The Hero's Journey: Joseph Campbell on his Life and Work*, HarperSanFrancisco, San Francisco, 1990.

Campbell, Joseph and Charles Musès, *In All Her Names: Exploration of the Feminine in Divinity*, HarperSanFrancisco, San Francisco, 1991.

Carlotto, Mark J., *The Martian Enigmas: A Closer Look*, revised edition, North Atlantic Books, Berkeley, 1997 (first published in 1991).

Carr-Brown, David and David Cohen, 'Fall from Grace', *Sunday Times*, News Review, 21 December 1997.

Carter, Mary Ellen, *Edgar Cayce on Prophecy*, Warner Books, New York, 1968.

Cavendish, Richard (ed.), *Encyclopedia of the Unexplained: Magic, Occultism and Parapsychology*, Routledge & Kegan Paul, London, 1974.

Cayce, Edgar Evans, *Edgar Cayce on Atlantis*, Warner Books, New York, 1968.

Cayce, Hugh Lynn, *Venture Inward: Edgar Cayce's Story and the Mysteries of the Unconscious Mind*, Harper & Row, San Francisco, 1964.

Churchward, Albert, *The Arcana of Freemasonry*, George Allen & Unwin, London 1915.
Origins and Antiquity of Freemasonry, Sir Joseph Causton & Sons, London, 1898.

Clark, Jerome, 'When Prophecy Failed', *Fortean Times*, no. 117, December 1998.

Clark, R.T. Rundle, *Myth and Symbol in Ancient Egypt*, Thames & Hudson, London, 1959.

Clymer, R. Swinburne, *Ancient Mystic Oriental Masonry: Its Teachings, Rules, Laws and Present Usages which Govern the Order at the Present Day*, Philosophical Publishing Co., Allentown, 1907.
The Divine Law, the Path to Mastership: A Full Explanation of the Laws governing the Inner Development necessary to Attain the Philosophic Initiation or Mastership together with a detailed account of the Priests of Aeth or Priesthood of Melchizedek, Philosophical Publishing Co., Quakertown, 1949.
Dr Paschal Beverly Randolph and the Supreme Dome of the Rosicrucians in France, Philosophical Publishing Co., Quakertown, 1929.

Cockburn, Leslie, *Out of Control: The Story of the Reagan Administration's Secret War in Nicaragua, the Illegal Arms Pipeline, and the Contra Drug Scandal*, Bloomsbury, London, 1988.

Collins, Andrew, *From the Ashes of Angels*, Michael Joseph, London, 1996.
Gods of Eden: Egypt's Lost Legacy and the Genesis of Civilisation, Headline, London, 1998.

Conroy, Ed, *Report on Communion*, Avon Books, New York, 1989.

Constantine, Alex, 'Ed Dames and his Cover Stories for Mind Control Experimentation', Lighthouse Report website (*http://www.redshift .com/~damason/lhreport*).

'"Remote Viewing" at Stanford Research Institute or Illicit CIA Mind Control Experimentation?', Lighthouse Report website.

'Rep. Charlie Rose, BNL and the "Occult"', Lighthouse Report website.

Virtual Government: CIA Mind Control Operations in America, Feral House, Venice (Ca.), 1997.

Cook, Robin J., *The Giza Pyramids: A Study in Design*, Open Mind, London 1988.

The Horizon of Khufu, Seven Islands, London, 1996.

The Pyramids of Giza, Seven Islands, Glastonbury, 1992.

The Sacred Geometry of the Giza Plateau, Seven Islands, Glastonbury, 1991.

Coppens, Philip, 'Life Exists Since the Big Bang', *Legendary Times*, March/April 1999.

Corydon, Bent and L. Ron Hubbard, Jr, *L. Ron Hubbard: Messiah or Madman?*, Lyle Stuart Inc., Secanons, 1987.

Courjeaud, Frédéric, *Fulcanelli: Une identité révélée*, Claire Vigne, Paris, 1996.

Crowley, Aleister, *The Book of the Law*, Church of Thelema, Pasadena, 1931.

The Confessions of Aleister Crowley: An Autohagiography, Bantam Books, New York, 1971 (Jonathan Cape, London, 1969).

Crowley, Brian and James J. Hurtak, *The Face on Mars: The Evidence of a Lost Martian Civilisation*, Sun Books, South Melbourne, 1986.

de Charnay, Geoffrey, *Synarchie: Panorama de 25 années d'activité occulte, avec le réproduction intégrale du pacte synarchique*, Editions Médicis, Paris, 1946.

de Santillana, Giorgio and Hertha von Dechend, *Hamlet's Mill: An Essay on Myth and the Frame of Time*, Gambit, Boston, 1969.

Devereux, Paul, *The Long Trip: A Prehistory of Psychedelia*, Arkana, London, 1997.

Dieterlen, G., and S. de Ganay, *Le genie des eaux chez les Dogons*, Librairie Orientaliste Paul Geuthner, Paris, 1942.

DiPietro, Vincent, Gregory Molenaar and John Brandenburg, *Unusual*

Mars Surface Features, revised edition, Mars Research, Glenn Dale, 1988 (first published in 1982).

Dolphin, Lambert, 'Geophysics and the Temple Mount', posting on Dolphin's website (*http://www.best.com/~dolphin/*), 1995.

Douzet, André (edited and expanded by Philip Coppens), 'The Treasure Trove of the Knights Templar', *Nexus*, vol. 4, no. 3, April/May 1997.

Drosnin, Michael, *The Bible Code*, Orion, London, 1997.

Edwards, I.E.S., *The Pyramids of Egypt*, revised edition, Penguin Books, London, 1980 (Penguin, West Drayton, 1947).

Elkins, Don, with Carla Rueckert, *Secrets of the UFO*, L/L Research Publications, Louisville, 1977.

Elkins, Don, Carla Rueckert and James Allen McCarty, *The Ra Material: An Ancient Astronaut Speaks*, Whitford Press, Atglen, 1984.

Ellis, Ralph, *Thoth, Architect of the Universe: A Radical Reassessment of the Design and Function of the Great Henges and Pyramids*, revised edition, Edfu Books, Dorset, 1998 (first published in 1997).

Engel, Joel, *Gene Roddenberry: The Myth and the Man behind Star Trek*, Virgin, London, 1994.

Erman, Adolf, *Life in Ancient Egypt*, Macmillan & Co., London, 1894.

Evans, Hilary, *Visions, Apparitions, Alien Visitors*, Thorsons, London, 1984.

Fairall, Professor Anthony, 'Orion's Belt and the Layout of the Three Pyramids at Giza', South African Museum website (*http://www.museums.org.za/sam/planet/pyramids.htm*), December 1999.

Farley, Dick, 'The Council of Nine: A Perspective on "Briefings from Deep Space"', Brother Blue website (*http://www.brotherblue.org*), 1998.

Faulkner, R.O., *The Ancient Egyptian Book of the Dead*, revised edition, British Museum Press, London, 1985 (Limited Editions Club, New York, 1972).
The Ancient Egyptian Pyramid Texts, Oxford University Press, Oxford, 1969.

Festinger, Leon, Henry W. Riecken and Stanley Schachter, *When Prophecy Fails*, University of Minnesota Press, Minneapolis, 1956.

Fowden, Garth, *The Egyptian Hermes: A Historical Approach to the Late Pagan Mind*, Cambridge University Press, Cambridge, 1986.

Frankfort, Henri, *Kingship and the Gods: A Study in Ancient Near Eastern Religion on the Integration of Science and Nature*, University of Chicago Press, Chicago, 1948.

Fuller, John G., *Arigo: Surgeon of the Rusty Knife*, Hart-Davis, MacGibbon, London, 1974.

Galtier, Gérard, *Maçonnerie egyptienne Rose-Croix et néo-chevalrie*, Editions du Rocher, Monaco, 1994.

Gardner, Martin, *Science: Good, Bad and Bogus*, Prometheus Books, Buffalo, 1981.
Urantia: The Great Cult Mystery, Prometheus Books, Amherst, 1995.

Garrett, Eileen J., *Adventures in the Supernormal: A Personal Memoir*, Creative Age Press, New York, 1949.
Many Voices: The Autobiography of a Medium, George Allen & Unwin, London, 1969.

Geller, Uri, *My Story*, Corgi, London, 1977 (Robson Books, London, 1975).

Geller, Uri and Guy Lyon Playfair, *The Geller Effect*, Jonathan Cape, London, 1986.

Graff, Dale E., *Tracks in the Psychic Wilderness: An Exploration of Remote Viewing, ESP, Precognitive Dreaming and Synchronicity*, Element, Shaftesbury, 1998.

Grant, Kenneth, *Aleister Crowley and the Hidden God*, Frederick Muller, London, 1973.
The Magical Revival, Frederick Muller, London, 1972.

Griaule, Marcel, *Conversations with Ogôtemmeli: An Introduction to Dogon Religious Ideas*, Oxford University Press, Oxford, 1965.

Griaule, Marcel and Germaine Dieterlen, *Le renard pâle*, Institut d'Ethnologie, Paris, 1965.

Grof, Stanislav, *Realms of the Human Unconscious: Observations from LSD Research*, Viking Press, New York, 1975.

Guerrier, Eric, *Essai sur la cosmogenie des Dogon: l'arche du Nommo*, Robert Laffont, Paris, 1975.

Hancock, Graham, 'Egypt's Mysteries: Hints of a Hidden Agenda', *Nexus*, vol. 3, no. 6, October/November 1996.
Fingerprints of the Gods: A Quest for the Beginning and the End, William Heinemann, London, 1995.

Hancock, Graham, Robert Bauval and John Grigsby, *The Mars Mystery: A Tale of the End of Two Worlds*, Michael Joseph, London, 1998.

Hancock, Graham and Santha Faiia, *Heaven's Mirror: Quest for the Lost Civilisation*, Michael Joseph, London, 1998.

Hapgood, Charles, *Maps of the Ancient Sea Kings: Evidence of an Advanced Civilization in the Ice Age*, Chilton Books, Philadelphia, 1966.

Harman, Willis W., *An Incomplete Guide to the Future*, W.W. Norton and Co., New York, 1976.

Harris, Michael H., *History of Libraries in the Western World*, revised edition, Scarecrow Press, London, 1985.

Hassan, Selim, *The Great Sphinx and its Secrets: Historical Studies in the Light of Recent Excavations*, Government Press, Cairo, 1953.

Hawass, Dr Zahi, 'Two New Museums at Luxor and Aswan', *Horus*, vol. 16, no. 2, April/June 1998.

Herodotus, *The Histories*, trans. Henry Cary, Folio Society, London, 1992.

Hinton, C. Howard, *The Fourth Dimension*, Swan Sonnenschein & Co., London, 1904.

Hoagland, Richard C., *The Monuments of Mars: A City on the Edge of Forever*, revised edition, Frog Ltd., Berkeley, 1996 (first edition 1987). 'A *Secret* Tunnel being Excavated in the Great Pyramid?', Enterprise Mission website (*http://www.enterprisemission.com*), 1997.

Hoffman, Michael A., *Egypt Before the Pharaohs: The Prehistoric Foundations of Egyptian Civilization*, Routledge & Kegan Paul, London, 1980.

Holroyd, Stuart, *Alien Intelligence*, David & Charles, Newton Abbot, 1979. *Briefing for the Landing on Planet Earth*, Corgi, London, 1979 *(Prelude to the Landing on Planet Earth*, W.H. Allen, London, 1977).

Hope, Murry, *Ancient Egypt: The Sirius Connection*, Element Books, Shaftesbury, 1990.

Hunter, Larry and Amargi Hillier, 'The Hall of Osiris: The Secret Chamber Inside the Great Pyramid – 30 Years of Secrecy and Deception by the Supreme Organization of Antiquities', posting on Amargi Hellier's website (*http://www.amargiland.com*), 1998.

Hurkos, Peter, *Psychic: The Story of Peter Hurkos*, Arthur Barker, London, 1961.

Hurry, Jamieson B., *Imhotep, the Vizier and Physician of King Zoser and afterwards the Egyptian God of Medicine*, revised edition, Oxford University Press, Oxford, 1928.

Hurtak, J.J., *The Book of Knowledge: The Keys of Enoch*, Academy for Future Sciences, Los Gatos, 1977.

Igliori, Paola, *American Magus: Harry Smith – A Modern Alchemist*, Inanout Press, New York, 1996.

Inquire Within, *Light-Bearers of Darkness*, Boswell Printing and Publishing Co., London, 1930.
The Trail of the Serpent, Boswell Publishing Co., London, 1936.

Johnson, Kenneth Rayner, 'The Hidden Face of Fulcanelli', *The Unexplained*, no. 42, 1981.

Keel, John A., *Operation Trojan Horse*, Souvenir Press, London, 1971.

Keith, Rebecca, 'Reptoids Stole My Meteorite', *Fortean Times*, no. 97, April 1997.

Keller, Barbara, 'A.R.E. Conference Highlights Giza Controversies', *Atlantis Rising*, no. 13, 1997.

Kerisel, Jean, 'Pyramide de Khéops: Dernières recherches', *Revue d'Egyptologie*, no. 44, 1993.

King, Francis, *The Secret Rituals of the O.T.O.*, C.W. Daniel, London, 1973.

King, Joan Wucher, *Historical Dictionary of Egypt*, Scarecrow Press, London, 1984.

Kingsland, William, *The Great Pyramid in Fact and in Theory*, 2 vols., Rider & Co., London, 1932–5.

Koppang, Randy, 'The Great Pyramid Tunnel Mystery', *Atlantis Rising*, no. 13, 1997.

Lawton, Ian and Chris Ogilvie-Herald, *Giza; The Truth – The People, Politics and History behind the World's Most Famous Archaeological Site*, Virgin Publishing, London, 1999.

Lehner, Mark, *The Complete Pyramids*, Thames and Hudson, London, 1997.
The Egyptian Heritage, based on the Edgar Cayce Readings, ARE Press, Virginia Beach, 1974.

Leslie, Stuart W., *The Cold War and American Science: The Military-Industrial-Academic Complex at MIT and Stanford*, Columbia University Press, New York, 1993.

Levy, Steven, *The Unicorn's Secret: Murder in the Age of Aquarius*, Prentice Hall Press, New York, 1988.

Lewis, H. Spencer, *Rosicrucian Questions and Answers, with Complete History of the Rosicrucian Order*, Supreme Grand Lodge of AMORC, San Jose, 1929.

The Symbolic Prophecy of the Great Pyramid, Supreme Grand Lodge of AMORC, San Jose, 1936.

Lilly, John C., *Centre of the Cyclone: An Autobiography of Inner Space*, Paladin, London, 1973.

The Human Biocomputer: Theory and Experiments, Abacus, London, 1974.

Lindemann, Michael, 'Cydonia Disappoints, but Controversy Continues', CNI News website (*http://www.cninews.com*), 1998.

Lowen, Rebecca S., *Creating the Cold War University: The Transformation of Stanford*, University of California Press, Berkeley, 1997.

Luckert, Karl W., *Egyptian Light and Hebrew Fire: Theological and Philosophical Roots of Christendom in Evolutionary Perspective*, State University of New York Press, Albany, 1991.

Lunan, Duncan, *Man and the Stars: Contact and Communication with Other Intelligence*, Souvenir Press, London, 1974.

Lurker, Manfred, *An Illustrated Dictionary of the Gods and Symbols of Ancient Egypt*, Thames & Hudson, London, 1980.

Maas, Peter, *Manhunt*, Harrap, London, 1986.

MacDonald, Dwight, *Henry Wallace: The Man and the Myth*, Vanguard Press, New York, 1948.

Mackey, Albert Gallatin, *The History of Freemasonry: Its Legendary Origins*, Gramercy Books, New York, 1996.

Manley, Bill, *The Penguin Historical Atlas of Ancient Egypt*, Penguin, London, 1996.

Markley, O.W., and Willis W. Harman (eds.), *Changing Images of Man*, Pergamon Press, Oxford, 1982.

Markowitz, Norman D., *The Rise and Fall of the People's Century: Henry A. Wallace and American Liberalism, 1941–48*, The Free Press, New York, 1973.

Marks, John, *The Search for the 'Manchurian Candidate': The CIA and Mind Control*, W.W. Norton and Co., London, 1979.

Marti, Monsterrat Palau, *Les Dogon*, Press Universitaires de France, Paris, 1957.

McCulloch, Warren S. (ed.), *Embodiments of Mind*, MIT Press, Cambridge (Mass.), 1965.

McDaniel, Stanley V., *The McDaniel Report*, North Atlantic Books, Berkeley, 1993.

McDaniel, Stanley V. and Monica Rix Paxson (eds.), *The Case for the Face: Scientists Examine the Evidence for Alien Artifacts on Mars*, Adventures Unlimited Press, Kempton, 1998.

McMoneagle, Joe, *Mind Trek*, Hampton Roads Publishers, Norfolk, 1993.

Miller, Russell, *Bare-Face Messiah: The True Story of L. Ron Hubbard*, Michael Joseph, London, 1987.

Milner, Terry L., 'Ratting Out Puharich', posting from Jack Sarfatti's website (*http://www.hia.com/pcr/*), 1996.

Milson, Peter (ed.), *Age of the Sphinx: A Transcript of the programme transmitted 27 November 1994*, Broadcasting Support Services, London 1994.

Mitchell, Edgar D., *Psychic Exploration: A Challenge for Science*, G.P. Putnam's Sons, New York, 1974.

Morehouse, David, *Psychic Warrior: The True Story of the CIA's Paranormal Espionage*, Michael Joseph, London, 1996.

Mundy, Talbot, *The Nine Unknown*, Bobbs-Merrill Co., Indianapolis, 1923.

Musaios, *The Lion Path: You Can Take It With You – A Manual of the Short Path to Regeneration for Our Times*, revised edition, House of Horus, Sardis, 1990 (first edition 1985).

Musès, Charles, *Destiny and Control in Human Systems: Studies in the Interactive Connectedness of Time (Chronotopology)*, Kluwer-Nijhoff Publishing, Boston, 1985.

Musès, Charles and Arthur M. Young (eds.), *Consciousness and Reality*, Outerbridge and Lazard, New York, 1972.

Myers, David P. and David S. Percy, *Two-Thirds*, Aulis, London, 1993.

Narby, Jeremy, *The Cosmic Serpent, DNA and the Origins of Knowledge*, Gollancz, London, 1998 (*Le serpent cosmique, l'ADN et les origines du savoir*, Georg Editeur, Geneva, 1995).

National Aeronautics and Space Administration, *Viking 1: Early Results*, NASA, Washington, 1976.

Nye, James, 'Chromosome Damage! A Random Conversation with Robert Anton Wilson', *Fortean Times*, no. 79, February/March 1995.

Ogilvie-Herald, Chris, 'A Secret Tunnel Being Excavated in the Great Pyramid', *Quest for Knowledge Magazine*, vol. 1, no. 5, 1997.

'Great Pyramid Capping Ceremony – Cancelled!', Egyptnews (*egyptnews@aol.com*), 18 December 1999.

Ogilvie-Herald, Chris and Ian Lawton, 'The "Water Shaft" – The Facts', *Egyptnews* (*egyptnews@aol.com*), 27 November 1998.

Paijmans, Theo, *Free Energy Pioneer: John Worrell Keely*, IllumiNet Press, Lilburn, 1998.

Papus, *Anarchie, indolence et synarchie: les lois physiologiques d'organisation sociale et l'esoterisme*, Chanuel, Paris, 1894.

Parker, Richard A., *The Calendars of Ancient Egypt*, University of Chicago Press, Chicago, 1950.

Pauwels, Louis and Jacques Bergier, *The Morning of the Magicians*, Mayflower Books, 1971 (*Le matin des mages*, Editions Gallimard, Paris, 1960).

Peebles, Curtis, *Watch the Skies!: A Chronicle of the Flying Saucer Myth*, Berkley Books, New York, 1995 (Smithsonian Institution Press, Washington DC, 1994).

Pelley, William Dudley, *Star Guests*, Soulcraft Chapels, Noblesville, 1950.

Peronnik, *Pourquoi le résurgence de l'Ordre du Temple?*, Editions de la Pensée Solaire, Monte Carlo, 1975.

Petrie, W.M. Flinders, *Medum*, David Nutt, London, 1892.

Picknett, Lynn, *The Encyclopaedia of the Paranormal: A Complete Guide to the Unexplained*, Macmillan, London, 1990.

Picknett, Lynn and Clive Prince, *The Templar Revelation: Secret Guardians of the True Identity of Christ*, Bantam Press, London, 1997.

Piehl, Karl, 'Notes de lexicographie egyptienne', *Sphinx: Revue critique embrassant le domaine entire de l'Egyptologie*, vol. II, Akademmiska Bokhandein, Uppsala, 1897.

Pike, Albert, *Morals and Dogma of the Ancient and Accepted Scottish Rite of Freemasonry*, A∴M∴, Charleston, 1871.

Puharich, Andrija, *Beyond Telepathy*, Picador, London, 1975 (Doubleday & Co., Garden City, 1962).

(ed.), *The Iceland Papers: Select Papers on Experimental and Theoretical Research on the Physics of Consciousness*, Essentia Research Associates, Amherst, 1979.

The Sacred Mushroom: Key to the Door of Eternity, Doubleday, Garden City, 1974 (Doubleday and Co., Garden City, 1959).

Uri: The Original and Authorized Biography of Uri Geller, Futura, London, 1974 (W.H. Allen, London, 1974).

'A Way to Peace through ELF Waves: Excerpts from a talk by Dr Andrija Puharich at the Understanding Convention of ASTARA, Upland, CA, November 6, 1982', *The Journal of Borderland Research*, March/April 1983.

Puthoff, H.E., 'CIA-Initiated Remote Viewing Program at Stanford Research Institute', *Journal of Scientific Exploration*, vol. 10, no. 1, Spring 1996.

Ramadan, Mohammad A., 'Effects on Society of Public Disclosure of Extraterrestrial Presence', Planetary Mysteries website, 1997.

Randall-Stevens, H.C. ('El Eros'), *Atlantis to the Latter Days*, Aquarian Press, London, 1954.

The Book of Truth, or the Voice of Osiris, Knights Templar of Aquarius, London, 1956.

The Teachings of Osiris, Rider & Co., London, 1927.

A Voice out of Egypt: An Adventure in Clairaudience, Francis Mott Co., London, 1935.

The Wisdom of the Soul, Aquarian Press, London, 1956.

Rasche, Niklas, 'Desert Storm', *Fortean Times*, no. 112, July 1998.

Ratsch, Christian, *The Dictionary of Sacred and Magical Plants*, Prism, Bridport, 1992.

The Gateway to Inner Space, Prism, Bridport, 1989.

Rice, Michael, *Egypt's Legacy: The Archetypes of Western Civilisation 3000–30 BC*, Routledge, London, 1997.

Egypt's Making: The Origins of Ancient Egypt 5000–2000 BC, Routledge, London, 1990.

Rickard, Bob, 'Facing Up to Mars', *Fortean Times*, no. 112, July 1998.

Robinson, Lytle W., *Edgar Cayce's Story of the Origin and Destiny of Man*, Neville Spearman, London, 1972.

Is it True What They Say About Edgar Cayce?, Neville Spearman, Jersey, 1979.

Roche, Richard, *Egyptian Myths and the Ra Ta Story, based on the Edgar Cayce Readings*, ARE, Virginia Beach, 1975.

Rohl, David, 'Eternal Riddle of the Sands entombed in Mystery and Academic War of Words', *Daily Express*, 27 January 2000.

Rudgley, Richard, *The Alchemy of Culture: Intoxicants in Society*, British Museum Press, London, 1993.

Rux, Bruce, *Hollywood vs. the Aliens: The Motion Picture Industry's Participation in UFO Disinformation*, Frog Ltd., Berkeley, 1997.

Rydeen, Paul, *Jack Parsons and the Fall of Babalon*, Crash Collusion, Berkeley, 1995.

Sagan, Carl, *Cosmos*, Futura, London, 1983 (Macdonald and Co., London, 1981).

Saint-Yves d'Alveydre, *L'Archéomètre, clef des toutes les religions et de toute les sciences de l'antiquité*, Dorbon-Aine, Paris, 1934.
Mission des Juifs, Calmann Levy, Paris, 1884.
Mission de l'Inde en Europe, mission de l'Europe en Asie: la question du Mahatmas et sa solution, Librairie Dorbon-Aine, Paris, 1910.
La théogonie des patriarches: traduction archéometrique des Saintes Ecritures, 2 vols, J.B.G. S.A.R.L., Paris, 1977 (first published in 1910).

Salah, Adbel-Aziz, *Excavations at Heliopolis, Ancient Egyptian Ounu*, 2 vols., Cairo University, 1981–3.

Sarfatti, Jack, 'The Destiny Matrix', posting on Sarfatti's website (*http://www.hia.com/pcr/*), 1996.
'In the Thick of It!', posting on Sarfatti's website (*http://www.hia .com/pcr/*), 1996.
'Quantum Quackery', posting on Sarfatti's website (*http://www.hia .com/pcr/stenger.html*), 1996.

Saunier, Jean, *Saint-Yves d'Alveydre, ou une synarchie sans enigme*, Dervy-Livres, Paris, 1981.

Schlemmer, Phyllis V. and Mary Bennett, *The Only Planet of Choice: Essential Briefings from Deep Space*, revised edition, Gateway Books, Bath, 1996 (first edition by Phyllis V. Schlemmer and Palden Jenkins, Gateway Books, Bath, 1993).

Schnabel, Jim, *Remote Viewers: The Secret History of America's Psychic Spies*, Dell Publishing, New York, 1997.

Schoch, Robert M., 'The Great Sphinx Controversy', *Fortean Times*, no. 79, February/March 1995.
'Redating the Great Sphinx of Giza', *KMT*, vol.3, no. 2, 1992.

Schonfield, Hugh J., *The Pentecost Revolution*, Hutchinson, London, 1974.

Schueller, Gretel, 'Stuff of Life', *New Scientist*, 12 September 1998.

Schwaller de Lubicz, Isha, *'Aor': R.A. Schwaller de Lubicz, sa vie, son oeuvre*, La Colombe, Paris, 1963.

Schwaller de Lubicz, R.A., *The Egyptian Miracle: An Introduction to the Wisdom of the Temple*, Inner Traditions, Rochester, 1985. (*Le miracle egyptien*, Flammarion, Paris, 1963).

Propos sur esotérisme et symbole, La Colombe, Paris, 1960.

Sacred Science: The King of the Pharaonic Theocracy, Inner Traditions International, Vermont, 1982. (*Le roi de la théocratie phaoraonique*, Flammarion, Paris, 1961.)

A Study of Numbers: A Guide to the Constant Creation of the Universe, Inner Traditions International, Rochester, 1986. (*Etudes sur les nombres*, Librairie de l'Art Independant, Paris, 1950.)

Symbol and the Symbolic: Ancient Egypt, Science and the Evolution of Consciousness, Inner Traditions International, Rochester, 1978. (*Symbol et symbolique*, Cairo, 1949)

Le temple de l'homme: Apet du Sud à Louqsor, 3 vols., Paris, 1957.

The Temple in Man: Sacred Architecture and the Perfect Man, Inner Traditions, Rochester, 1977. (*Le temple dans l'homme*, Cairo, 1949).

Sellers, Jane B., *The Death of the Gods in Ancient Egypt: An Essay on Egyptian Religion and the Frame of Time*, Penguin, London, 1992.

Shanon, Benny, 'A Cognitive-Psychological Study of Ayahuasca', *Maps*, vol. VII, no. 3, Summer 1997.

Shaw, Ian and Paul Nicholson, *British Museum Dictionary of Ancient Egypt*, British Museum Press, London, 1995.

Sinclair, Sir John R., *The Alice Bailey Inheritance*, Turnstone Press, Wellingborough, 1984.

Sjöö, Monica, *New Age Channelings – Who or What is being Channeled?*, privately published, 1998.

Smith, A. Robert (ed.), *The Lost Memoirs of Edgar Cayce: Life as a Seer*, ARE Press, Virginia Beach, 1997.

Spence, Lewis, *Myths and Legends of Ancient Egypt*, George C. Harrap & Co., London, 1915.

Square, A, *Flatland, a Romance of Many Dimensions*, Seeley & Co., London, 1884.

Stearn, Jess, *The Sleeping Prophet: The Life and Work of Edgar Cayce*, Frederick Muller, London, 1967.

Steele, John, 'The Road to Atlantis?', *The Unexplained*, no. 30, 1982.

Strausbaugh, John, 'Uri Geller: Parlor Tricks or Psychic Spy?', *New York Press*, 27 November 1996.

Strieber, Whitley, *Breakthrough: The Next Step*, HarperCollins, New York, 1995.

Communion, A True Story: Encounters with the Unknown, Century, London, 1987.

Confirmation: The Hard Evidence of Aliens Among Us, Simon & Schuster, London, 1998.

The Secret School: Preparation for Contact, Simon & Schuster, London, 1997.

Transformation: The Breakthrough, Century, London, 1988.

Targ, Russell and Keith Harary, *The Mind Race: Understanding and Using Psychic Abilities*, New English Library, Sevenoaks, 1984.

Targ, Russell and Harold E. Puthoff, *Mind-Reach: Scientists Look at Psychic Ability*, Jonathan Cape, London, 1977.

Temple, Robert, *Open to Suggestion*, Aquarian Press, Wellingborough, 1989.

The Sirius Mystery: New Scientific Evidence of Alien Contact 5,000 Years Ago, revised edition, Century, London, 1998 (Sidgwick & Jackson, London, 1976).

Tompkins, Peter, *The Magic of Obelisks*, Harper & Row, New York, 1981.

Secrets of the Great Pyramid, Allen Lane, London, 1973.

Tompkins, Peter and Christopher Bird, *The Secret Life of Plants*, revised edition, Arkana, London, 1991 (Allen Lane, London, 1974).

Ulmann, André and Henri Azeau, *Synarchie et pouvoir*, Julliard, Paris, 1968.

Vallée, Jacques, *Confrontations: A Scientist's Search for Alien Contact*, Souvenir Press, London, 1990.

Dimensions: A Casebook of Alien Contact, Sphere, London, 1990 (Souvenir Press, London, 1988).

The Invisible College: UFOs, the Psychic Solution, Dutton, New York, 1975.

Messengers of Deception: UFO Contacts and Cults, And/Or Press, Berkeley, 1979.

Passport to Magonia: From Folklore to Flying Saucers, Neville Spearman, London, 1975.

Revelations: Alien Contact and Human Deception, Souvenir Press, London, 1992.

VandenBroeck, André, *Al-Kemi: Hermetic, Occult, Political and Private Aspects of R.A. Schwaller de Lubicz*, Lindisfarne Press, Hudson, 1987.

von Däniken, Erich, *Chariots of the Gods?: Unsolved Mysteries of the Past*, Souvenir Press, London, 1969 (*Erinnerungen an die Zukunft*, Econ-Verlag, 1968).

Wallace, Henry A., *Statesmanship and Religion*, Williams and Norgate, London, 1934.

Wasson, Valentina P. and R. Gordon Wasson, 'The Hallucinogenic Mushrooms', *The Garden Journal*, January/February 1958.

West, John Anthony, 'ARE Conference at Virginia Beach', *Egyptnews* (*egyptnews@aol.com*), 12 August 1998.

The Case for Astrology, revised edition, Viking, London, 1991 (first edition by John Anthony West and Jan Gerhard Tooder, Macdonald and Co., London, 1970).

Serpent in the Sky: The High Wisdom of Ancient Egypt, Wildwood House, London, 1979.

Whitehouse, David, 'Close-Ups Unveil the "Face on Mars"', *Astronomy Now*, June 1998.

Weiss, Jacques, *La synarchie selon d'ouevre de Saint-Yves d'Alveydre*, Robert Laffont, Paris, 1976.

Williamson, George Hunt, with A. Bailey, *Other Voices*, Abelard Productions, Wilmington, 1995.

Wilson, Colin, *Alien Dawn: An Investigation into the Contact Experience*, Virgin, London, 1998.

From Atlantis to the Sphinx, Virgin, London, 1997.

Mysteries: An Investigation into the Occult, the Paranormal and the Supernatural, Granada, London, 1979 (Hodder & Stoughton, London, 1978).

Wilson, Robert Anton, *Cosmic Trigger: The Final Secret of the Illuminati*, Abacus, London, 1977.

Young, Arthur M., *The Reflexive Universe: Evolution of Consciousness*, Robert Briggs Associates, Lake Oswego, 1976.

Zubrin, Robert with Richard Wagner, *The Case for Mars: The Plan to Settle the Red Planet and Why We Must*, Simon & Schuster, London, 1996.

Index

THE UNIVERSE AND THE TEACUP

K. C. Cole

From the tiniest particles that make up our world to the farthest reaches of the universe, maths has more to teach us about ourselves than any other discipline – and yet our minds seem ill-equipped to deal with its implications. In *The Universe and the Teacup*, award-winning science writer K. C. Cole demystifies mathematics and explores its applications to our everyday lives, showing how maths can simplify problems so we can understand and solve them. Einstein's theory of relativity would have been impossible without it, but so, as she explains during this elegant and enlightening book, would building a bridge, electing a government and finding the right place to save our money.

'Stands blissfully apart from all the recent books that have tried to analyse, exploit or quell the epidemic fear of mathematics . . . K. C. Cole has a wide, wise perspective, informed by her long experience as a science writer, her humour and her common-sense irreverence'
Dava Sobel, author of *Longitude*

'Delightful . . . she has written a science book which is aimed at the non-scientist, and which should help us all to cope with the barrage of numbers which confront us every day'
Simon Singh, author of *Fermat's Last Theorem*

'Entertaining and enlightening . . . the scope is formidable, yet K. C. Cole flits through it all with a remarkably light touch'
William Hartson, *Independent*

PROGESS AND THE INVISIBLE HAND

Richard Bronk

Encouraged by apparently endless advances in scientific understanding and the exponential wonders of economic growth, belief in progress has been a central feature of Western thought since the Enlightenment. But as the next millennium approaches, there is a deepening realisation that high GNP growth, and the accelerating social and technological changes associated with it, are no longer matched by unambiguous improvement in the human condition.

Progress and the Invisible Hand argues that if the environment is to be safeguarded and poverty minimised, there remains an overriding need for the free market to be supported by a strong framework of morality, social cohesion and rational government intervention. Richard Bronk's disquieting conclusion is that if we continue to destroy the necessary balance between social co-operation and individual pursuit of self-interest, humanity will be left at the mercy of the market – condemned to be its slave rather than its master.

'Wide-ranging and thought-provoking, of absorbing interest not only to economists and philosophers but also the man and woman in the street who is worried about the direction in which society is moving'
John Gray, author of *False Dawn*

'There is much for philosophers, economists and general readers to savour . . . Richard Bronk asks some fascinating questions about the nature of human progress'
New Statesman

Time Warner Paperback titles available by post:

☐	The Universe and The Teacup	K. C. Cole	£8.99
☐	Progress and the Invisible Hand	Richard Bronk	£8.99
☐	Journey Beyond Selene	Jeffrey Kluger	£9.99
☐	Our Stolen Future	Theodora Colborn	£8.99
☐	The Quark and The Jaguar	Murray Gell-Mann	£9.99

The prices shown above are correct at time of going to press. However, the publishers reserve the right to increase prices on covers from those previously advertised without prior notice.

TIME WARNER PAPERBACKS
P.O. Box 121, Kettering, Northants NN14 4ZQ
Tel: 01832 737525, Fax: 01832 733076
Email: aspenhouse@FSBDial.co.uk

POST AND PACKING:
Payments can be made as follows: cheque, postal order (payable to Time Warner Books) or by credit cards. Do not send cash or currency.

All U.K. Orders	**FREE OF CHARGE**
E.E.C. & Overseas	25% of order value

Name (Block Letters) _____

Address _____

_____

Post/zip code:_____

☐ Please keep me in touch with future Time Warner publications

☐ I enclose my remittance £_____

☐ I wish to pay by Visa/Access/Mastercard/Eurocard

Card Expiry Date

_____